Albert Gallatin Riddle

Recollections of War Times

Reminiscences of men and events in Washington, 1860-1865

Albert Gallatin Riddle

Recollections of War Times
Reminiscences of men and events in Washington, 1860-1865

ISBN/EAN: 9783337219215

Printed in Europe, USA, Canada, Australia, Japan

Cover: Foto ©ninafisch / pixelio.de

More available books at **www.hansebooks.com**

RECOLLECTIONS OF WAR TIMES

REMINISCENCES OF MEN AND EVENTS IN WASHINGTON

1860–1865

BY

ALBERT GALLATIN RIDDLE

FORMERLY MEMBER OF THE HOUSE OF REPRESENTATIVES FROM
THE 19TH DISTRICT, OHIO

———

G. P. PUTNAM'S SONS

NEW YORK   LONDON
27 WEST TWENTY-THIRD STREET   24 BEDFORD STREET, STRAND

The Knickerbocker Press

1895

The Knickerbocker Press, New York

PREFATORY NOTE.

THE war—its policies, incidents, and men—its struggles, sufferings, and losses—its horrors, adventures, and triumphs—has been written up, dwelt upon, discussed, and talked over, in public and private, till he is a brave or a reckless man who ventures now to challenge public attention to anything further he may have to offer on that topic. Lincoln and his advisers have been written of. The great commanders have been glorified in type ; several have written their own memoirs, while every corps, division, and many brigades and regiments, have furnished historians, and many of very considerable merit.

After all, these in a way were but the gigantic mechanics of the war. Back of all the armies, back of the great Secretaries, back of the President,—of all,—was the Congress, where really the war had first to be fought. The President and all his embattled hosts were but the executive—working out—executing the mandates of this seemingly silent, invisible, but all-creative and compelling power.

Of this, save incidentally and cursorily, nobody has spoken or written, except Hon. E. G. Spaulding,[1] of the New York delegation in the House.

The philosophy of a people's history, especially a free

---

[1] His *History of the Legal-Tender Paper Money Used during the Great Rebellion*, Buffalo, 1869.

people, is to be gathered from its legislation. Whoever would rightly estimate the war must know of the men of the 37th and 38th Congresses and their legislation—especially of the 37th, who, half blindly at the first, but certainly, grasped the conditions of the great struggle, and wielded measureless power with an unswerving, fearless, but instinctive sagacity, which left to the next Congress nothing to do but to follow, and push forward along its broad and luminous way.

The iron skeleton of the war lies imbedded in the twelfth and thirteenth volumes of the *United States Statutes at Large.*

The time has not yet come for more than a memoir of this great Congress, which should be attempted at least by some one of its members who may impart to his work something of the local color and spirit of that body.

The writer is one of the few survivors of the House, where he was not so conspicuous as to make enemies, nor yet so obscure as to be unable to make himself heard, if not felt, upon some of the greatest problems that have ever received legislative solution among men.

He has long meditated something like a memoir, which he finally submits, not without misgiving. He can hardly expect great favor from the public when he has failed to win more than his own toleration for his work.

He has spoken freely, perhaps gives too much space to his own utterances, and stands too prominently in the foreground. Speaking as he does in the first person of the things he in some way helped to accomplish, and which were wrought under his eyes, his place in the memoir for one of his personality was, perhaps, inevitable.

In saying so much he neither expects nor desires to avoid criticism.

CONTENTS.

v

CHAPTER XLII.

CHAPTER XLIII.

CHAPTER XLIV.

CHAPTER XLV.

CHAPTER XLVI.

CHAPTER XLVII.

RECOLLECTIONS OF WAR TIMES.

RECOLLECTIONS OF WAR TIMES.

CHAPTER I.

INTRODUCTORY.

1817–1860.

Something of the Author—Parentage—Carried to the Western Reserve, Ohio, 1817—Hard Fortune—Political Influence of Joshua R. Giddings —Admitted to the Bar, 1840—Called the First Free-Soil Convention in Ohio, 1848—Defended the Oberlin Slave Rescuers—Formation of the Republican Party—The Fremont Campaign. Elected to the 36th Con-

ERRATUM.

Page 26, line 27—For "4th" read "42d"

whom I was the fifth, was left to struggle on as she

RECOLLECTIONS OF WAR TIMES.

CHAPTER I.
INTRODUCTORY.

1817–1860.

Something of the Author—Parentage—Carried to the Western Reserve, Ohio, 1817—Hard Fortune—Political Influence of Joshua R. Giddings —Admitted to the Bar, 1840—Called the First Free-Soil Convention in Ohio, 1848—Defended the Oberlin Slave Rescuers—Formation of the Republican Party—The Fremont Campaign—Elected to the 37th Congress in the Cleveland District—19th Ohio—Relations with Salmon P. Chase—First Visit to the Capital—The Great Men—The Two Houses of Congress—The Peace Congress.

SOME personal details seem to me required for the better understanding of certain things herein written. The Riddles of this country came from Scotland through Ireland; the Merricks, from Wales. My parentage was a result of the union of these. In 1817, when a year old, we emigrated from Monson, Massachusetts, to the township of Newbury, in the interior of the Connecticut Reserve. That territory, larger than the parent State, was so much of Connecticut and Massachusetts pushed into the limitless forests of the west. A small group of not uncultured men and women of Massachusetts built their cabins near each other there. My father died six years later, and my mother, with eight children, of whom I was the fifth, was left to struggle on as she might. An intellectual, self-poised woman, she did not fail. My childhood and boyhood were spent in many places, from some of which I departed without formal leave-taking. One of these was the school known as the Western Reserve College, but I had a very serviceable year or two at the oldest Painesville Academy.

I was pushed prematurely forward in the Harrison campaign of 1840, in which I was heard if not felt. Admitted to the bar about September 1st, I was elected prosecutor of my county at the October election following. Four fifths of our people were Whigs. I early fell under the influence of Joshua R. Giddings and Benjamin F. Wade, and became intensely hostile to slavery. Upon the nomination of General Taylor in 1848, alone I called a revolting mass-meeting, which was speedily followed by similar conventions in the other Reserve counties, and the Free-Soil party was formed, which brought an end to Whig rule in Ohio. This movement made me a member of the Ohio Legislature for two terms. I found I was unfitted for politics and removed to the city of Cleveland. With no purpose of withdrawing from the anti-slavery war, I had much to do with the organization of the Republican party, and had gained the friendship of the late Chief-Justice Chase, whose nomination for President in 1856 I much desired. I was active in the Fremont campaign, and later was entrusted with the defence of the Oberlin slave rescuers—twenty-one in all, among whom were some of the professors of Oberlin College. Two of the defendants were convicted. I failed to secure their discharge on *habeas corpus*, before a full bench of the Supreme Court of Ohio, by three to two, but I gained my purpose by the indictment for kidnapping of the party who had captured the slave. Satisfied that both cases would result in conviction, the parties interested agreed to a *nolle* for both. The matter at stake was of National as well as of State importance.[1]

In 1860 I labored for the nomination of Mr. Chase, and was entrusted with the delicate matter of arranging some details by which the late Chief-Justice Cartter of the District of Columbia, then of Cleveland, became the head of the Ohio delegation, with the immediate charge of Mr. Chase's fortunes in the Chicago Convention. Cartter became later Chief-Justice of the District of Columbia.

In all the Reserve Congressional districts, the canvass was for the nomination. That came to me easily in the campaign of 1860. The district was then known as the Nineteenth and was composed of Cuyahoga, Lake, and Geauga Counties, with two lake ports, a U. S. District Court, and a marine hospital. The patronage of the district was important, and it was deemed essential that the member should give to it early attention.

In his famous progress as president-elect, Mr. Lincoln reached Cleveland on the 15th of February, 1861, when I first met him at a great reception, and was by him invited to accompany him to Erie. This I was unable to do, but I attended him to Painesville, Ohio, where I was engaged in a trial. I was then and there afterwards treated by him with much kindness and consideration. I then formed and ever continued to have a cordial personal regard for Mrs. Lincoln.

---

[1] When John Brown, the late of Harper's Ferry, was about to be put upon trial, he applied to his friends D. R. Tilden and D. K. Cartter, both of Cleveland, and ex-Members of Congress, to come, one or both, or send counsel for his defence. They, with others, applied to me. I was then absent. Before my return, Hiram Griswold had volunteered, and gone. I was a little reluctant to appear with him in the case, and so much time had elapsed that I finally declined the undertaking, to my lasting regret.

On the evening of the day of Brown's execution, with others, I addressed a great meeting at the old Melodion Hall in Cleveland. My little speech was reported and had a circulation and attention out of all proportion to its importance. A colleague had it read in the House of Representatives during the 37th Congress.

A word in reference to the press of Cleveland at that time may be pardoned, as the course of this press had much to do with my brief career in Congress. There were two strong republican journals and of course rivals. The *Herald*, well established in wealthy surroundings, and supported by such aristocracy as Cleveland then sheltered, was the conservative organ. It stood by my rival, Mr. Franklin T. Backus, for nomination to Congressional favors. The *Leader*, recently established and in the hands of the late Edwin Cowles, was the radical advocate. Cowles, a man of strong character and inflexible purpose, was poor, his paper shaky, and some infirmities of hearing and speech were sore obstacles in his way. He was no personal or political friend of mine, had contributed no effort, not even a paragraph, to aid my canvass, and was personally unpopular. Since the organization of the Republican party, the *Herald* had monopolized the entire patronage at its disposal. The *Leader* had never been permitted to print a notice, an advertisement, or a ballot.

The editors were also severally proprietors of these sheets, and both were candidates for the post-office. I determined, regardless of personal consequences, to secure it for Cowles, though neither applicant was at first aware of my purpose. Perhaps not more than two candidates in the district knew of my intentions in their favor. I was an utter stranger in Washington, and had no information of the ways and devices of office-seeking and office-seekers, or of the methods of distribution of executive patronage. I was so utterly innocent that I had but two governing ideas: to secure the best services to the public, and by the best and most worthy available men.

On the second night of my first journey to Washington I found myself at midnight with the slow laboring train, resting in the gorge at Harper's Ferry. We had nearly a hour there. The storms clouds had drifted away and a full moon filled the narrow valley, mantled in snow, with

its flood of perpendicular light. All the buildings of the
armory lay silent in the ghostly light, which lit up the
Maryland heights as well as the wooded Virginia cliffs.
I had a half hour's stroll about the deserted streets of
the sleeping little Virginia town. The government buildings were exactly as the famous fight had left them.

In the gray of the next dawn, we drove along the imposing front of the great Capitol, which few strangers be-
hold for the first time without being deeply impressed.
Indeed Englishmen have since told me that it is by far
the noblest Parliament House in the world.

We landed ourselves at the old National Hotel, which
appeared to be still redolent with the fumes that four
years before had been so nearly fatal to Mr. Buchanan
and his friends.

There were visits to the two Houses of Congress,
which were still in session during these last days of
Buchanan and the Democracy. The handsome, and as a
presiding officer, the inflexibly impartial Breckinridge
ruled in the Senate, and the equally handsome and more
imposing Pennington misruled and snarled up the House.
I had a few calls to make; my friends the Wades were
both in the House, with John Hutchins, Edgerton, Ashley, and others of the Ohio delegation. Then there were
the great debates in the Senate to attract me. I listened
to the pathetic lamentations of Crittenden, the reply of
Colonel Baker, the caustic comments of Hale, but I did
not hear Seward. Chase was not in this Senate, but was
elected to the next.[1]

I was presented to the great Sumner, and did my poor
best to propitiate and cultivate him. But I always had
to tell him who I was, and he always asked what I had

---

[1] Dr. Seymour of Ohio who accompanied me made me acquainted with
Roscoe Conkling, and with Mrs. Conkling, and Conkling and I became
friends, and remained such until I appeared as counsel for General Fry,
before the House Committee to which their old quarrel was referred early
in 1866.

done to entitle me to his notice, and I always had to admit I had done nothing, and, as I was not born a courtier, I was obliged to give him up. I got on better with Mr. Seward. Something had commended me to him, and I was received on trust.

Our own still wonderful Corwin was in the House, with whom I had passed a week in the last canvass. Douglas, whom I had never met, was there, as was also my Ohio house-friend and opponent, George Pugh, whom I always liked. Fessenden, Hale, Seward, and Preston King, Edward D. Baker,—over whom I was so soon to lament,—Cameron, Andrew Johnson, Collamer, and Foote, Doolittle, and other distinguished men were in the Senate,—men of whom I had only read. The Demigogs and Gogs of Slavery had all departed save Breckinridge and the Missourians. There were many famous men in the House also. Then there were the Capitol, the library, the public buildings, the city, all to be gone over ere I should sort myself round to my own place.

The scoff of that day, for which history has not yet found place, "The Peace Congress," originating with Virginia and presided over by John Tyler—the "Tyler too" of 1840—had done its work and gone. Its seven propositions were under debate in the Senate, and I heard upon them Douglas, Baker, Mason, Wade, Green, and others. Among the Ohio Commissioners were Chase, Ewing, and Groesbeck, also my competitors, F. T. Backus and Reuben Hitchcock. The work of that body consisted of seven propositions to amend the Constitution in the interests of slavery, which already had a Confederacy of seven States, a President, a Congress, an Army, and a Capital of its own.

CHAPTER II.

WASHINGTON IN 1861.

FEBRUARY–MARCH, 1861.

The Capital—Washington in 1861—Capitol Hill—Everything in Ruins—
Washington a Southern City—The New Party and Men of the North—
Mr. Lincoln's Personal Danger—His High Spirits—Meeting of Lincoln
and General Scott.

WHOEVER becomes familiar with the Washington of
to-day, with its hundreds of miles of broad, smooth-
surfaced streets, bordered with a 120,000 shade trees, its
numerous parks, with their statuary, fountains, shrubbery,
and flowers, its numerous perfected public buildings and
monuments, its picturesque order of architecture for residences, will hardly be able to realize its contrast with the
Washington of 1861.

It was then as unattractive, straggling, sodden a town,
wandering up and down the left bank of the yellow
Potomac, as the fancy can sketch. Pennsylvania Avenue,
twelve rods wide, stretched drearily over the mile between
the unfinished Capitol and the unfinished Treasury building on Fifteenth Street, West, where it turned north for a
square, and took its melancholy way to Georgetown, across
the really once very beautiful Rock Creek. Illy paved with
cobble-stones, it was the only paved street of the town.
The other streets, which were long stretches of mud or
deserts of dust and sand, with here and there clumps of

poorly built residences with long gaps between them, passing little deserts of open lands, where their lines were lost, wandered from the highlands north towards the Potomac, and from the Eastern Branch (Anacosta) to Rock Creek. Not a sewer blessed the town, nor off of Pennsylvania Avenue was there a paved gutter. Each house had an open drain from its rear, out across the sidewalk. As may be supposed, the Capital of the Republic had more mal-odors than the poet Coleridge ascribed to ancient Cologne. There was then the open canal, a branch of the Chesapeake and Ohio, from Rock Creek to Anacosta, breeding malaria, tadpoles, and mosquitoes. The Tiber of to-day, ancient " Goose Creek," stagnated from the highlands through the Botanic Gardens, and Slash Run overflowed the northwest wastes of the swampy city plat.

The President's house, the little dingy State Department, set squat on the ground now occupied by the north wing of the Treasury building, the War and Navy on Seventeenth Street, the Post-Office Department, and the Interior, were the only completed public edifices of the Capital. The Washington Monument, the Capitol, and the Treasury building were melancholy specimens of arrested development.

The walls of the two wings of the Capitol had not been perfected, and the little old jug-like dome of the old central structure still occupied its place, utterly lost in the expanse of the acres of roof that it could not dominate. The building was placed at the west margin of a tableland that sloped westward, facing the east, with the surface rising several feet in the distance of one hundred and fifty yards. This was a fenced square filled with a heavy growth of forest trees, mostly the short-lived southern maple. The west approach was up an earthern terrace, which sloped down into another timbered enclosure. North and South A Streets were then in place, and each

was built up compactly, on the sides facing the Capitol,
with low, mean structures.

· Save the enclosed east and west spaces, the western
slope of Capitol Hill was open ground. Pennsylvania
Avenue passed around the north wing of the Capitol on
its eastern way, and all that open ground was covered
with the remains of building stone, lumber, and timber,
and loaded over at every place of access with the huge
iron plates for the great Capitol dome, doomed in the
counsels of the slavery hosts, never to be set in place.
Nothing more conclusively showed the predetermined destruction of the Republic than this deliberate suspension
of the completion of the Capitol and Treasury building,
then limited to the portion represented by the Colonnade,
fronting Fifteenth Street. The Capitol was unfinished
on the inside. All during the 37th Congress the old hall
of the House was a mere lumber room, unsightly and
offensive.

So also the bridges across the Potomac were found to
be in a ruinous condition, as was everything dependent
upon the will of the retiring administration. Indeed it
had borrowed money for its current expenses, and this
loan we had to provide for.

Politically, the city—the fixed population—was intensely
Southern, as much so as Richmond or Baltimore. Very
few men of culture, and none below that grade, were Republicans at the advent of "Lincoln and his Northern
myrmidons," as they were called in 1860–61. The presence of a loyal administration and Congress, with the new,
fresh blood and inspiration of a new party, called to do
heroic deeds, and moved by the inspiration of men to face
and overcome great hostile forces, to re-establish and sustain the primal rights of men, exercised an irresistible
influence upon the population, and at once and forever
silenced the open utterance of sedition and rebellion.
There were no open assaults and no secret assassinations.

The population of the District was then about 75,000, of which the city of Washington contained 61,000 ; 15,000 of these were colored, including a fraction over 3000 slaves. The old slavery code of Maryland, and indeed all the laws in force in that State at the cession to the United States in 1800, were the law of the District. The presence of slavery is always attended with sore disabilities to the nominally free of the slave race.

Mr. Lincoln passed Baltimore in safety. Just what the danger was is a mystery. My first day at the Capital was given to Congress. On the morning of the second I called upon the President-elect at the Willard. I found him on the second floor, in the large space in front of the stairway, holding an extempore reception. He was in wonderful spirits, surrounded by twenty or thirty admiring adherents, standing at his full height, which, from his lack of breadth, always seemed exaggerated. His face was fairly radiant, his wit and humor at flood-tide. His marvellous gift of improvising illustrative stories was at its best. They followed each other with great rapidity. In the midst of the flow, the majestic form of General Scott was seen grandly rising in the open stairway, steady and unswerving, as if solemnly lifted by noiseless machinery. He was accompanied by Mr. Lincoln's travelling friend, Colonel Sumner. I had seen General Scott when along our northern border in 1834, pacifying the " Hunters' lodges " of hair-brained volunteers, for " the Patriot wars," to liberate Canada, as we called the movement. As he gained the floor it was easy to fancy that one incentive to the coveted rank of Lieutenant-General was the excuse to design, and above all to wear, the magnificent uniform in which he then shone. It was the first meeting of these remarkable men since Mr. Lincoln's election. The General advanced a stride and awaited the presentation by Colonel Sumner, who in undress uniform made it in the simplest manner. It would do the drawing-room dudes of to-day good, with whom the gentlemanly art of bowing is a lost one, to have witnessed the profound grace of the old hero's acknowledgment of the presence of the President-elect, as he swept his instep with the golden plumes of his chapeau.

Two weeks later, I was present at the White House when the General presented his officers to the President. I had seen Mr. Lincoln at an earlier hour, and was asked by him to remain. A day or two before I had witnessed the presentation of the diplomats by Mr. Seward, and was curious to compare the two bodies of men. I had not long to wait. From an upper window I observed the approach of the party to the front door, which everybody then entered as they would a hotel. Mr. Cameron, Secretary of War, the least conventional of men, and General Scott, were at the head of the two files. Without a pause, Mr. Cameron opened the door and entered. Not thus did the magnificent General call upon the Commander-in-chief of the American armies. He drew himself up and awaited the return of the Secretary of War, who ran out again to see what the trouble was. On his appearance, General Scott with his own hand rang the bell in a stately way, and on the appearance of the proper attendant, gravely entered, with his official chief. The entire party numbered fourteen or fifteen. I had never seen an equal number of such fine-appearing men in uniform. All were above the average American height and remarkably well made. Among them were Wool, Sedgwick, and Lee, grave, handsome men, a striking contrast to the foreign representatives with their small active frames clad in brocaded and embroidered coats, bowing and dancing about. Save the Englishmen, there was among the diplomatic visitors not a striking-looking man.

At the Willard House interview, Colonel Sumner, with Mr. Lincoln's aid, introduced us to General Scott, who had a very gracious way of receiving those who approached him duly presented. I saw something of him later. From the Willard I went to call on Mr. Chase at the Rugby, now the Hamilton, some distance out of the real city, as then built, at the corner of K and 14th Street, N. W.[1] From there north and west were few buildings within the city limits. Mr. Chase had, as I knew, been offered the Treasury portfolio, and was in the sorest of straits as to his duty in the premises. He had just been returned to the Senate, and the intensely radical among us were very anxious to have him remain there. Where the choice of the President for his Cabinet would fall, was the gravest of problems up to the all-revealing 4th of March. While I was very desirous that he should remain in the Senate, I was very clear it was his duty to accept the Treasury portfolio; I found that one of his objections was his utter want of knowledge as to the man selected for the State Department.

A thing much talked of at the time in the Capital was that Mr. Lincoln, on Sunday the 3d, gave a dinner to seven gentlemen, and they happened to be those whose names were sent to the Senate the next day. Yet it was said that several of them at that dinner party were not informed of their intended associates. I was enabled on the Thursday or Friday of that week to inform Mr. Chase that Mr. Seward was to be the chief of the Cabinet, which was to him a great relief. I did not, however, know the name of any of the others, except Mr. Seward, selected by the President-elect, nor did any one save Mr. Chase learn from me the source of my information, nor what it was.

---

[1] Initials indicating direction are from the Capitol.

CHAPTER III.

LINCOLN'S INAUGURATION.

MARCH 4-11, 1861.

The Inauguration—General Scott's Precautions—The Inaugural Address—
Mr. Buchanan Bears Himself Manfully—The Ball—Mt. Vernon Then
and Now—Alexandria—The Congressional Cemetery—The White
House.

MONDAY morning, March 4, 1861, opened dark and
rainy. Since mid-January, there had been publications at
Baltimore and Richmond, whisperings and mutterings in
the air, of assassination and a bloody prevention of the
inauguration of Mr. Lincoln. General Scott had summoned to his aid all the spare officers, and as many of the
regular soldiers as he could reach. The regular army
contingent was small—less than a thousand. While there
was a glittering show of militia companies in the procession, none of us had any confidence in them, if soldiers
were needed. No apprehension was felt of an open,
armed invasion, but the suspicion of intended murder was
talked over, dwelt upon, and magnified, till it took the
form of a definite fear. I knew there was deposited
about the Capitol a supply of effective navy revolvers.
The trouble always is that men, however brave, who are
raw in the use of weapons, usually become nervous when
occasions arise for their use, and with guns and pistols

13

they become as dangerous to their fellows as to any supposed enemy. Many of us were supplied with our own familiar arms, and *some of us* could have used them with discretion.

The House and the members-elect were conducted to places in the well arranged Senate Chamber at 11 A.M. The President-elect, on the arm of the President, and the members-elect of his Cabinet, entered a little past twelve. I had seen and heard Mr. Buchanan at the rival Democratic conventions at Erie, September 10, 1849, and then rather admired him, Whig as I was. He was now old, with a sad, worn, withered, white face, stouter and seemingly shorter, with his well developed head in its fixed inclination to the left shoulder. He had an air of resolve and bore himself well. My compassion went out at once to the retiring, fallen man. Everybody pressed forward, eager to see the incoming ruler. The crowd that day was largely the haters, the revilers, the scorners, of the sad and seemingly friendless and deserted old man ; they crowded and pushed him rudely by, without a word or bow, and all through the awfully trying two hours he bravely and manfully bore himself by the side of his overshadowing, unshapely successor. I was glad for his sake when he was liberated, and might go away in peace.

In the accident of places on the broad extemporized platform (which extended out over the wide steps leading up to the rotunda in front of the Capitol), I was landed within four or five feet of Mr. Lincoln when he delivered his memorable and most fortunate address. Never was there a more persuasive speaker. His quaint logic and taking, unaccustomed ways were absolutely irresistible. His vocabulary was limited, he used mainly the simple words that one learns in childhood, which are always the most serviceable, and which arrange themselves easily, delivering their burden of thought with certainty and force to the minds to which they are addressed. Perhaps there was never a more immediately effective address delivered to men than this quaint, masterly performance; an impression only deepened by after-study and reflection. It was in many respects the greatest service to his country of any single labor of Mr. Lincoln's. As a forensic effort it was as effective as that delivered at the Gettysburg—that was to be.

Uninterrupted, the whole ceremony passed with *éclat*. Abraham Lincoln was now the President, and stout old James Buchanan conducted him to, and gave him full possession of, the rather dilapidated, and then wholly unattractive Executive Mansion.

We did not see General Scott in the procession. He had a battery stationed at the intersection of Delaware Avenue and B Street, near which, with his aids and spare generals, he spent the time. The sun went down with the new power in full possession of the Capitol, its hands firmly grasping the reins of Government, and with all hearts full of the hope and confidence inspired by the President's address.

THE BALL.—A hall had been extemporized in Judiciary Square, in the rear of the City Hall. I remember we passed through a colonnade and a badly lighted corridor to the back part of the Hall, and down a stairway to a huge, unfestive-looking apartment. There we saw the short and heavily formed Douglas promenading with Mrs. Lincoln, who recognized me. They were old Springfield friends, and were accompanied by Mrs. Hamlin, attended by the gallant Colonel Baker. The ball was opened by Mrs. Lincoln. I am sure Douglas was not a dancing man. Later, when the crisis came, he frankly placed himself by Lincoln's side, and made some effectively loyal speeches. He received much deserved commendation for his course. Was it not due from him to his country? Repudiated by the South, there was no other course open for him, especially as by this means he could deal the most telling blows to his former Southern allies, whose work he had so often bravely done.

That week was for me one of idleness. The Cabinet appointees were to be confirmed ere the work for the offices could begin. I made the acquaintance of the Blairs, and found I should get on well with them. They brought out Fremont in '56, for whom I did much service. There was a pilgrimage to Mount Vernon on a dark, snowy day, in a shell of a steamer whose deck was level with the river's brim. We made an hour's call at dilapidated Alexandria, loneliest of towns. It had got itself returned to Virginia by act of Congress in 1846, and has since gained as many fifties in population as Washington has thousands. From 1870 to 1880 its gain was less than five hundred. The Potomac, from the Capital down, is not an interesting river. There is the little old stone Fort Washington, below Alexandria, and Mount Vernon three or four miles below that. Looking at Washington's resting-place as I did then, under the dark-gray wintry sky, beyond the curtain of leafless forest, on the height of the overhanging bank, it struck me as the loneliest place I had ever seen. I have seen it since its restoration, under every condition and at every season, and that impression still remains. There was not then a sign of another human habitation in the wide outlook from the height where it stands. That was the time when the mansion, long abandoned by its last owner, was at its lowest stage of dilapidation, which extended to every outbuilding, servants' quarter, stable, and office. Whoever has visited it since its restoration can form no conception of the silent reign of "the abomination of desolation" that then brooded over the home and tomb of George Washington. I never, while there, repress a rising compassion, that the Father of his country should have lived in a place so lonely and so far from the active world. It is impossible for me to realize that Washington's residence made it a centre for the American historic and social world of the time.

There was, within the city limits, one even more melancholy and depressing place than Mount Vernon, the Congressional Cemetery, on the west bank of the Anacostia, the eastern branch of the Potomac. I went there a day or two after the excursion to Mount Vernon. No resting-place ever struck me with such a shuddering sense of inappropriateness as this, with its hideous and squat little gray stone cenotaphs, set up to desecrate the final beds of extinguished senators and members of the House. I was relieved on learning that members of Congress were no longer doomed to sepulture there, nor was their sleep, wherever it might be, to be disturbed by the consciousness that would certainly haunt them, that one of these ugly little monsters of coarse Potomac freestone had been set up to defame their names and memories.

The rest of the week was devoted to delegations, attendance upon the Senate, and a large correspondence. Friday night was the President's first levee, for the wide, muddy footed world at large. I was at the White House on the Illinois day, and Mrs. Lincoln showed the throngs over the house. Friday night must have obliterated the memory of all former days and nights of tramping hordes and herds.

A visitor at the White House about the time of the exit of Mr. Buchanan would have been struck by the bare, worn and soiled aspect of that part of the house devoted to the official Executive, an aspect not unlike that presented by " the breaking up of a hard winter " about a deserted farmstead.

2

CHAPTER IV.

THE CIVIL SERVICE.

MARCH, 1861.

The Civil Service of that Day—The Cleveland Post-Office—A Once Famous
Contest—The Candidates—Senator Wade an Opponent—An Unfortunate Victory for the Victor.

THE Civil Service was, like everything else, in a bad
condition. It seemed to be the prevailing idea that public business at Washington was approaching an end, and
the officials acted accordingly. The work of all the Departments was sadly in arrears. The public offices were
apparently used chiefly as lounging-places, where men
gathered to read Democratic papers, smoke, chew tobacco, and damn Lincoln and his myrmidons. The pay-
rolls bore scores of names, the owners of which never
rendered an hour's service to the United States.

The dispensation of all the local patronage of a given
Congressional district was then the inviolable perquisite
of a member in accord with the administration, and was
used for his political purposes. I went to Washington
opposed on principle to this rule. I found however that
I must dispose of the patronage or leave it as prey to men
of the orthodox faith. With no friends to be compensated and with no enemies in any sense, I had no motive but to secure the best public service, and I acted
accordingly.

The first cases brought under my notice for a motion or appointment, pertained to the Democracy. One was that of a younger brother of the famous S. S. Cox (then of Columbus, Ohio), who was for several years a clerk in the Treasury Department. I had been in the Ohio Assembly during the attempt of the Democracy (under the lead of Samuel Medary) to revolutionize the State government in 1848-49. S. S. Cox, then a young man of genius, aspiration, and quick parts, affected, though a Democrat, a very warm admiration for some of my utterances during the three or four weeks of general dismay attending the effort of the Democracy to seize and convert the House to their own purposes. Blake, one of my colleagues then in his second Congress, a restless, aspiring man, had sought notoriety by repeated tilts against " Sunset " (Cox), who was a man of fine fancy, who had already achieved a well earned literary reputation, and whose sobriquet had come to him through a glowing description of a sunset, to which his initials aptly lent themselves. In these encounters Blake had always been worsted, and his antagonism to Cox led him to demand the removal of the younger brother. Powerless himself, I was the only possible Republican to whom the elder Cox could apply. On inquiry, I found the record of the clerk was excellent for service, modest worth, good work, and faultless demeanor. I repaired to Secretary Chase, in whose department the younger Cox served, and asked for his retention. He said if I would assume the responsibility, and place on file an official request for the retention, he would make an order to that effect. I filed the paper, and the order followed.

Henry M. Slade, one of my constituents, the younger son of the late Governor Slade of Vermont, a young man of parts, fine acquirements, manners, and social qualities, but an outspoken Democrat, came to Washington with no political prospects. I took him to Mr. Chase, who had no prejudices against Democrats, and who gladly, on my recommendation, obliged a son of Governor Slade. My action in these two cases did not commend me to my Republican colleagues, none of whom, however, cared to call me to account.

I had in my mind to secure the Cleveland post-office for Edwin Cowles. It would lie between him and George A. Benedict, between the old conservative *Herald* and the infant red-blooded *Leader*. Cowles had physical defects. His utterance was very imperfect, his voice unpleasant, and his hearing singularly defective. He died an old man, never having heard the higher strains of music, nor the notes of singing birds. His mind was strong, slow, sinewy, and narrow; his notions of right and wrong, acute. He was kind-hearted and charitable. Devoted to friends, he was more devoted to enemies. His workmen, all in his service, were steadfastly loyal and true, never leaving him in distress, and although often unpaid never willing to desert him. They believed they could depend upon final reward, and they felt assured of the kindest treatment. This I came fully to know.

Benedict was not a lovable man. He was a college graduate, and had much vigor of mind. He was, however, affected by strong passions, grudges, and prejudices; under the influence of these he became unscrupulous and vindictive. He had not succeeded at the bar, and was an indifferent writer. His rival, Cowles, at the first also scarcely attempted the pen. These were the men whose shadows were projected on the field of my brief Congressional career. Neither was personally nor politically my friend. I had associated the more frequently with Benedict, with whom I had made one or two political tours.

I had suggested to Cowles, during the winter, the idea of the Post-Office. In his needs and ambition he had thought of that, but had not approached me. I said to him that it came to me as a possibility. I knew the risk

to myself of proposing him, but the danger was not without a charm. Ere the matter had taken final shape, I was
dismayed by his appearance at the Capitol. Of all men
living, he was the greatest hindrance to his own success.
He found me at Mrs. Carter's on Capitol Hill. He was
with me on the evening after his arrival. I had an immense mail, was opening and answering each letter in
course. Among them was the following:

CLEVELAND, March 5, 1861.

DEAR SIR:
   This is pure business between us. If you will recommend me for Post-
master and stand by me, I will give you $2,000, whatever the outcome.
Respectfully,

_____1

The writer of the above was a well known and reputa-
ble business man, well connected, and of high standing in
his Church.
   Turning to my paper and pen, I handed the note across
the table to Cowles and an instant later the following:

WASHINGTON, March 8, 1861.

MR. ——— :
   Yours of the 5th received this inst. Its contents render you ineligible to
any place under this administration.

A. G. RIDDLE.

As his eye took it in, he sprang up, strode around in
front of me, and with solemnity of manner asked: " Riddle, where were you born ? " As if the favored place was
to be commemorated.
   The struggle for the Post-Office was for him a vital
matter, to be pushed by all possible means, and I had resolved that he should secure it.
   The next forenoon I filed my application for the appointment of Mr. Cowles in the Post-Office Department,
a simple request unsupported by any statement except

---

¹ This letter is still among my papers.

that the Post-Office was at my place of residence. In five minutes I impressed Mr. Blair, and the judicial mind of young Kasson,[1] with the grounds upon which I acted. They saw at the time that I intended to have my way.

I was then shown the petition for the appointment of Mr. Benedict. Among the papers was the formidable recommendation of Senator Benjamin F. Wade, for whom Montgomery Blair had, next to his father, more regard, admiration and veneration than for any other man living or dead, unless it might have been Andrew Jackson.

I also lodged with Mr. Nicolay a brief statement for Mr. Lincoln, and delivered to the President the same condensed statement made to Mr. Blair. I then betook myself to Mr. Wade's quarters—at Mrs. Hyatt's on Pennsylvania Avenue—between Sixth and Seventh Streets. Mr. Wade was out, and I busied myself as I had before, with his authority, in franking to my lady friends the many finely illustrated Congressional publications of that day. The rooms were piled around with them. I also found walled about with " Pub. Docs." a huge demijohn labelled " Monongahela "—a favorite brand with the stout old Senator. When the grim proprietor came in I had some decisive words with him.[2]

He saw the force of my position and assured me that his interference was limited to the testimonial just shown me, and the word he had spoken to the President, to which Benedict was certainly entitled from him. The *Herald* had always stood by the Senator.

---

[1] Mr. John A. began his very useful and brilliant public career as Assistant Postmaster-General, under Mr. Blair. He was a man whom I liked.

[2] He had been the tender benefactor of a large-brained, large-natured elder brother of mine, educated to the bar, whom he sent forth arrayed as the Senator had never been draped himself, and who died shortly afterward of a brain disease. I had thus the strongest personal claims on the Senator. Whoever renders me a great service thereby binds himself to me for all time.

Richard C. Parsons, a personal friend of Gov. Chase, a member of his staff, and the Speaker of the Ohio House of Representatives, desired a consul-generalship. Mr. Chase gave me a note to Mr. Seward, with whom I had an interview. I found that Paris was spoken for, and London was also promised, as were other desirable capitals. Rio was offered and accepted, and the Speaker of the Ohio House of Representatives was advised by telegraph.

I had now been nearly a month at the Capital, and had, as I felt, put my Cleveland Post-Office into the safest attainable shape, and with assurances from the President, entrusted to Mr. Nicolay, my steady friend, and with like assurances from Mr. Blair, that no adverse appointment should be made without notice and "a day in court" to me I returned home. Colonel Parsons needed an airing in the Capital. On my way home we met and unwittingly passed on our respective trains. Colonel Parsons showed himself at all the public places of the Capital then open, having on his arm the eldest Miss Chase, who was the loveliest and most fascinating young woman of my time, in Washington life. Among his achievements was an hour's speech to the Postmaster-General against my luckless nominee for the Cleveland Post-Office, and from Blair's account of it to me it was effective—as of course it would be. I never learned the details of his address to Mr. Lincoln. This course was no treason to me. He appeared in his own right as a citizen of our city, and in behalf of the majority, I have no doubt, who did not approve my course.

The case hung fire. Rumors of disaster came from the Capital. I heard that Cowles had gone there, and knew that, like the great Walt Whitman, he would "raise his yop over the roofs" of the Capital. I summoned him back and hurried myself to Washington. I found that the nomination of Benedict had been sent to the President ten days before my arrival. I drove rapidly to the White House. Mr. Lincoln sent for the papers, which bore only the name of Mr. Kasson. It was a Presidential appointment, and required Blair's " M. B." It was a tub thrown to my enemy. The papers were given to me, and I hurried to the Post-Office Department. Mr. Blair placed the magical " M. B." on my application for Cowles, under which the President wrote the conclusive "A. L." The next morning I took back to Cleveland Cowles's commission. As will appear later, the victory was as fatal to the victor as that of the famous Epirote King over the Romans, though it was the making of the *Leader*. Rome was of more value to the world than was Epirus.

All the other places in question I had for the asking.

CHAPTER V.

THE BEGINNING OF THE WAR.

APRIL, 1861.

The Fall of Sumter—The North Called to Arms—The Volunteers—
Congress to Assemble July 4th.

THE epoch-making April 14th arrived, with the fall of
Sumter, followed by the President's Proclamation of the
15th, calling for 75,000 soldiers to enforce the laws of the
United States. The men of the North heard in it the
voice of God calling the people to enforce His laws, and
they stood forth extending their hands for arms and
leaders. The President also summoned Congress to
assemble on the ensuing 4th of July. The Capital was
endangered, and four days later the unarmed soldiers of
Massachusetts were set upon by the " Plug Uglies " and
" Blood Tubs " in Baltimore, and several of them were
slain.

I had been at Washington at an informal interview,
held on the day following the inauguration, with a portion
of the loyal delegates to the Virginia State Convention.
They expressed their entire satisfaction with the President's address, and assured us that they had a majority
of that convention, that they could and would control it,
and that Virginia would reject secession. The fall of
Sumter overwhelmed them, and swept the slave-breeding

25

old commonwealth into the Confederacy. It is true that the ordinance of secession was formally submitted to the people of the State, but that was not waited for. The State at once entered the Confederacy and doomed herself to dismemberment and destruction.

It had come—the convulsion that was to destroy slavery. I hailed it as such with a profound, grave, irrepressible satisfaction. I would unhesitatingly sacrifice the Constitution that had sheltered it, the Union which had guarded it, as the one unapproachable thing in its innermost embrace, to secure its extirpation. Thank God !

There was no semblance of a militia organization in Ohio. We had a thoroughly equipped show company, the Cleveland Grays; *that* we hurried off, and we then fell to organizing our first regiments, and the voice of the driller was heard in the land. The men elected their officers! the companies elected their regimental officers. Governor Denison, who appointed the Peace Commissioners, proved himself active and efficient. The Legislature, which was still in session, passed the needed statutes. Garfield—our Garfield—and J. D. Cox, both then in the Ohio Senate, had mastered the manual of arms, and had devoted months to military studies. Cox became colonel and was made a brigadier immediately. The 7th Ohio preferred the handsome, dashing Tyler to Garfield, who waited for the 4th, and so took the Hiram and Oberlin college boys. McClellan and Rosecrans took twenty-two Ohio regiments into Western Virginia in May. Camp Taylor was formed under my windows at Cleveland, and flags, drums, and very soon buttons and feathers, with guards and bayonets, ruled. Public meetings and speeches were of daily occurrence. At Painesville two of my nephews and myself early enlisted in Capt. Geo. E. Paine's Company. He was a younger brother of the chivalrous General Halbert E. Paine of Port Hudson fame.

The Paines have furnished generals, colonels, and captains from the Revolution down. My excuse was the danger of the Capital, and I was under a pledge to be in any battle fought for its safety.[1]

---

[1] It occurred to me that my six nephews in Michigan and Indiana, all I had of military age and all unmarried, had volunteered, and I decided to induce Elmer Riddle to be withdrawn. He was the *fiancé* of a lovely girl, and, although a born leader of men, I secured his release, much against his wishes. He was more useful as a citizen at home. With good address and popular manners, he became very efficient in securing volunteers. It was known that I had coerced him from active service. There was warrior blood in the Riddles of the old clans, and the great-uncles had carried arms to Quebec, and thence, by way of Saratoga, to Yorktown. Several had served with Harrison, Scott, and Brown in the war of 1812. Of the Ohio boys, Corwin Riddle served in the brilliant West Virginia campaign, entered the 7th, always pushed into the hottest place, was severely wounded at Cedar Mountain, saw both colonels shot down at Missionary Ridge, and, in weary disgust, threw his rifle into the Cuyahoga, when he crossed it to his aunt's house in Cleveland at the end. Clarence, at the close of the three months, entered a battery, refused to abandon his guns—as many did theirs in the first disastrous day of Stone River,—and won the commendation of his officers.

Darius of Indiana found an early unknown grave in the southwest. His eldest brother, Frank, left his newly wedded bride at the church, and went gaily off after the flag and drum, and won for himself a good report. Later, Elmer went with the Western Reserve boys to aid threatened Cincinnati, and the youngest of my brothers, though exempt from service, served with Governor Brough's hundred-day men. There was still Albert Clark of Indiana, who was rejected by the surgeons at home, but who later found a place in a New Jersey regiment, and fought the war through. His aunt finally discovered him, a rugged soldier, across the Potomac, and his general permitted her to take him home with her.

CHAPTER VI.

LINCOLN'S MESSAGE TO CONGRESS.

MAY–JULY, 1861.

War Spectacles in Washington—The Army Invades Virginia—The Organization of the House—Grow Elected Speaker—The Speaker's Prompter —The Position of that Congress in the War—The President's Message —Soldiers in the Field—Confiscation—Habeas Corpus.

I TOOK quarters with Mrs. Carter. I spent my three or four days before the 4th in the camps; visited the 1st and 2d Ohio Regiments at Falls Church; dined with Colonel " Fatty " McCook and Colonel Mason ; had a time with the Grays, and renewed my assurance of being on the field with them if a demonstration should be made on the Capital.¹

There were then 25,000 armed men on our side of the Potomac. The war was taking shape. I began early to realize the trouble and cost of turning intelligent men into effective soldiers. Soldiers may fight five days in a

¹ Jim Paine, the youngest brother of General Halbert E., accompanied me on our return to Alexandria later ; we found no means of reaching the Capital that night. Alexandria had then become a mere rat-haunt, given over to them and the shabbier rebs. We found a room in a so-called hotel. The apartment had doors in opposite walls, which were without fastenings. Soon after retiring, a procession each way began to pass through. Soon weary of the performance we placed a bed against each door, and, armed with my dangerous Remingtons, we cut off all further communication on that road. They were a funny-looking lot, and the so-called master disclaimed all knowledge of them in the morning.

year. The other three hundred and sixty are used in securing men and material, training and fitting them for the exceptional days on the field, and in repairing its awful waste. I was appalled at the number of sick in the hospitals which had already been set up.

There was a grand review of all the troops (some 25,000 about Washington) on the 4th, which struck me as imposing. Pennsylvania Avenue was filled from the Treasury to the Capitol with men in flashing blue, with arms sloped, marching in companies from curb to curb. That was a show, grand and imposing. I shall never forget the swell, emotion and tears of a few days later, when from a little height I saw the head of the column wheel south towards Virginia,—regiment on regiment, with knapsacks, canteens, and blankets; infantry, artillery, and cavalry, and the long train of heavy wagons. All headed south towards Virginia, to meet the rebels in arms; the issue—the perpetuity of the great Republic. *This was war.* As the heavy, moving masses of infantry smote the hard surface of the street, the sound of their simultaneous tread struck the ear like a roll of smothered thunder. I stood for hours with my eyes brimming over from an emotion that I could not wholly control. This was war. *We* should bring on the battle. That was my wish.

At noon of the 4th, the clerk of the last House in the great Hall of Representatives called the assembled members-elect to order. Twenty-four of the thirty-five States responded. K. V. Whaley and John S. Carlile came from Virginia—west of the mountains. Missouri, Kentucky, Tennessee, and Virginia were represented in the Union and Confederate Congresses. There were many conspicuous, strong and brave men in the House. Mr. Stevens will be much spoken of later on in this narrative. At the desk with him sat Justin S. Morrill, who had given his name to a tariff. He was a financier and practical economist to whom we are indebted for the agricultural colleges. E.

B. Washburn, John A. Logan, Owen Lovejoy, John A. McClernand, Wm. A. Richardson, and Isaac N. Arnold were there—all from Illinois. Colfax, Julian, Dunn, A. G. Porter, Holman, and Voorhees of Indiana; Iowa sent Samuel R. Curtis, Vandever, and James F. Wilson; Crittenden, old Governor Wickliffe, Wm. H. Wadsworth, and the always truculent Burnett, were there from Kentucky. Later Burnett left us for the Confederate Senate—where he was then overdue.

Maine was not especially strong. Anson P. Morrill, Fessenden, and Pike were her ablest. Maryland had Crisfield, Henry May, Frank Thomas, and others. The best from Massachusetts were Judge Thomas, Dawes, Gooch, Train, and Walker. Beaman was the ablest from Michigan. Windom was in his second Congress from Minnesota, and long service and fair common-sense ultimately made him famous. From Missouri, Frank Blair was the most conspicuous.

New York had many strong men : Corning, Conkling, Fenton, Olin, Pomeroy, Sedgwick, Spaulding, and Wheeler. John A. Bingham, S. S. Cox, Horton, Cutler, Noble, Pendleton, Shellabarger, and Vallandigham made Ohio stand well. Pennsylvania was well represented. Campbell, Covode, Grow, John Hickman, Kelley, McKnight, McPherson, and Thad. Stevens would make any delegation far above mediocrity. Wm. P. Sheffield saved the fame of Rhode Island. Horace Maynard, from seceded Tennessee, sat the Congress through from the beginning. Baxter and Walton, with Morrill, gave Vermont a high position. We had eight from revolted Virginia; Carlile, Segar, and Upton for a time, and Whaley were fairly good men, although Segar proved a disappointment. Potter was from Wisconsin. Conway,[1] from Kansas, did well for a time.

---

[1] Poor fellow, he finally—years later—was off color, and I defended him for a comparatively harmless shot into Senator Pomeroy's body.

The Republicans were so overwhelmingly predominant that no caucuses were held by either party for the nomination of the House officers. Thad. Stevens nominated Grow for Speaker, and Frank Blair was also nominated. Of the 159 votes cast Grow received 71, and Blair 40. The residue—48—were scattered among the Democrats, Crittenden, Phelps, Vallandigham, Corning, Cox, and Richardson, in the order named.

Grow, a man of safe and 'steady views, moderate ability, and a tendency towards adjectives and the floor, was a fairly good presiding officer. With the aid of the phenomenal "Thad," who proved the "shadow of a great rock in a thirsty land" to Speaker Pennington of the 36th Congress, the prompter who guided him, the House worked easily.'

Grow appointed Mr. Stevens Chairman of the Ways and Means. Stevens was not an economist, and by temper not a leader, but a driver—bitter, quick as electricity, with a sarcastic, blasting wit. He most frequently answered an honest inquirer for information with a dash of vitriol in the face. Short as he stood, with his large head covered with a long-haired wig ; broad-shouldered, he usually was standing when he discharged his burning, gall-tipped shafts, which he jerked out in an unpleasant voice, and immediately limped off on his short club-footed leg. No one in my time in the House ever turned on him except Judge Thomas of Massachusetts, a remarkably able man, who was a polished and most effective speaker. I fancied he had prepared his finished philippic and had held it ready. However that might be, an apt and

---

[1] Thaddeus Morris was then about eighteen, tall, well made, and had been a page at eight or nine. He developed a marvellous aptitude for House of Representatives' parliamentary law, and was a few years later promoted to the steps of the Speaker's throne—standing on his right. He carried the imbecile Pennington through the awful 36th Congress, and continued into, if not through, Colfax's time until his early death.

early occasion, some sarcasm upon the conservative views of the Boston representative, marked his justification. He took the floor, and for twenty minutes, with flashing eye and scorching tongue, he dressed and undressed the great Pennsylvanian in well-chosen and fitting terms, telling a great deal of truth about him. It did not move Stevens in the slightest. His face was usually entirely colorless; its hue did not change a shade. When the sudden storm subsided, Mr. Stevens arose and in his usual manner proceeded with the business of the House, and never after alluded to the onset of the Boston ex-Judge. As a speaker, while his matter was always full of pith, he was at the best indifferent, he was not fluent, and his voice and tone were unpleasant and monotonous, his attitude and action ungraceful, his blows were the sudden, unexpected flashes and bolts that blasted and destroyed. His admiring friend, the great Judge Black, described him in a constitutional convention of Pennsylvania, of which they were members:

" Thad. Stevens went about the hall like a buffalo bull, tossing men great and small on his horns, this way and that, upon the slightest provocation, or without any. He was the terror of the whole body, and the members huddled and hurried out of his way. Meredith was the only man who directly faced him, answered him back blow for blow and thrust for thrust, and they soon became fast friends."

Fortunately Justin S. Morrill was Mr. Stevens's second on the Ways and Means. He was broad, pleasant, a born gentleman, and always ready to inform and advise.

The 37th Congress, enveloped by huge armies, with the lurid atmosphere darkened by the smoke of battle (the artillery of which shook the walls within which its members deliberated), was an arena in which men could not win distinction or secure the attention of the press or public. Congress had long passed the stage at which a name was made by a speech or even a full term of service. The eyes and the hearts of the whole people were then with the glittering, armed hosts, over which fame with her trumpet ever hovered.

Of the new men it may be said that Judge Thomas of Massachusetts, Shellabarger of Ohio, Arnold of Illinois, Kelley of Pennsylvania, and Wadsworth of Kentucky, all made some impression, both upon the House and upon the outside world.

The President's Message dealt at length, with force and clearness, upon the cause of the extraordinary convention of Congress, reciting the matter down to the proclamation of April 15th, and carefully delineating the course of the rebellion since that time. This was followed by a thorough discussion of the right and resulting power of the States to withdraw from the Union,—" secession, the sugar-coating of the pill Rebellion," with which the South had drugged and deluded itself. The Executive would make the war decisive and short. He asked for 400,000 more men and 600,000,000 dollars.

The message was followed by reports from the Secretaries of Treasury, Navy, and War. From the last it appeared that there were then in the field, 310,000 men, of whom 80,000 were three months' men, leaving 230,000 for permanent service.

It will be remembered that for the time being the incipient war had practically dissolved parties. Indeed Mr. Fouke, a Democrat of Illinois, early presented a series of resolutions declaratory of the present state of things, the first of which proclaimed that, in the presence of this war, party lines were to be considered as abolished, and men were to unite as patriots. Holman had already secured the adoption of a resolution, the effect of which was to exclude everything not bearing directly upon the cause of this called session. There was much in the rest of the series within the interdict of this rule, and the Chair ruled them out. So Vallandigham, by resolution, undertook to forbid the use of the army to liberate slaves, while Love-

3

joy would forbid the returning of slaves who might seek refuge in our camps, to their masters.   It was impossible to move a step in any direction without encountering this matter of slavery.

The first subject discussed in the Senate was a joint resolution, approving the intervening acts of the President, which included the suspension of the writ of *Habeas Corpus*.   This resolution underwent much speech-making, especially by the Kentucky, Missouri, and Delaware Senators, and went over as unfinished business.   Breckinridge was at his strongest against it.

Nearly all the important Acts for raising and equipping armies, raising money, etc., passed the House without the yeas and nays.   Burnett, who soon after turned up in the Confederate Congress and was turned down by us, could not secure a sufficient second for the yeas and nays on these bills.

On some of the contested bills in either House, the record of the yeas and nays, when taken, illustrates the sectional and sometimes the political ground of the opposition.

The Confiscation Act passed in the Senate by 24 to 11. The nays were Breckinridge, Bright (both expelled at the next session), Carlile of Virginia, Cowan of Pennsylvania (on constitutional grounds), Johnson of Missouri, Latham of California, Pearce of Maryland, Polk of Missouri, Powell of Kentucky, Rice of Minnesota, and Saulsbury of Delaware.   In the House it passed by 60 to 48; all the Democrats and border State men except Frank Blair of Missouri voted against it.

Senator Rice, a rich old Indian trader, was the first Senator of Minnesota.   In political geology he was to be found in the same stratum of the earth's crust with Saulsbury, Pearce, and Bayard, below the old red sandstone—and without their excuse.   The Senate bill for employment of volunteers, passed by 35 to 4, the minority being Breckinridge and Powell of Kentucky, and Johnson and Polk of Missouri.

On the resolution to sustain at all hazards the supremacy of the Union, the usual loyal majority of 34 sustained it, and Breckinridge was the solitary nay. All his associates remained silent, except Saulsbury who voted with the majority.

On the 11th of July the Senate came to a vote on the expulsion of Mason, Hunter, Clingman, Bragg, Nicholson, Sebastian, Mitchell, Hemphill, and Wigfall [1]; and after a vain attempt to modify it, by declaring their seats vacant, the resolution was adopted by 32 to 10. The nays were Bayard, Bright, Johnson of Missouri, Andrew Johnson of Tennessee (who nearly always voted with the Republicans), Latham, Nesmith, Polk, Powell and Rice of course.

We of the House indulged in the luxury of one expulsion—John B. Clark of Missouri, then in arms against the Republic. Frank Blair introduced the resolution, and stated that it was a known and undisputed public matter, that Clark held a commission in the rebel army and was with Governor Jackson in the affair at Boonville, against the United States. No one questioned the allegations, but men grew squeamish or wanted an excuse, and clamored for an investigation. The majority were in unaccommodating temper, and passed the resolution 94 to 45. Many strong Republicans voted with the minority ; while Frank Thomas of Maryland and J. J. Crittenden voted with us. Although reared in slave States, no suspicion of the perfect devotion to the Union ever attached to either of these gallant old veterans.

As early as July 13th Andrew Johnson of Tennessee presented the credentials of Mr. Carlile and Mr. Willey,

---

[1] These gentlemen held seats in the 36th Congress, and their terms extended into the 37th. When their States seceded, they withdrew from the Senate. None of them appeared in the 37th, and at the time of this action of the Senate they were all active rebels.

commissioned by a legislature elected in Virginia, west of the Blue Ridge, as the *Virginia* Legislature. This was so held by the majority, and they were admitted by 35 to 5. Mr. Powell's amendment to the army bill, that the army should not be employed to subjugate a State, or destroy slavery, was rejected by the Senate by 34 to 4.

By the Act of July 22d 500,000 volunteers were called for to serve three years—if the war required that time (although Mr. Seward had said it would end in sixty days,) and the Acts of July 29th authorized an addition to the regular army of 25,000 men. We appropriated $500,000,000 for the war.

It was thus that the 37th Congress met the extraordinary exigency thrust so unexpectedly upon it; certainly it cannot be said that it was unequal to its responsibilities, nor does history show any large body of men surprised by a great emergency, which ever met it more unitedly or with a more determined spirit.

CHAPTER VII.

THE HISTORICAL CONGRESSES.

JULY, 1861.

Comparison of the Historical Congresses—President Washington and the 1st Congress under the Constitution—Mr. Madison and the Congress of 1812—Mr. Lincoln and the 37th Congress—Men and Methods of the War—Slavery to be Preserved—Crittenden's Joint Resolution.

THE old Continental Congress was the natural product of its time, convened to give expression to its sentiment and take counsel of its exigencies. Washington and the 1st Congress under the Constitution were elected to put its new machinery in motion, adjust, superintend, and impart life and vigor, steadiness and courage, to its infant processes. Mr. Madison was elected, as was the Congress of 1812, in the midst of the then chronic irritation between the Republic and Great Britain, and with the expectation of war between the two countries. They declared and fought it. Each body, each President, knew what they were elected to do.

Mr. Lincoln, his Cabinet, and the 37th Congress were elected to do anything, everything, except what fell to them to do—fight the greatest civil war of history, one of the enormous wars of modern times, involving larger armies and a wider theatre than the Napoleonic wars. It came upon them as an utter surprise.

37

The spirit of freedom and justice that finally extirpated slavery at the South had first to make a conquest of the North, every foot of which in 1835 was pro-slavery. I remember well what it then cost, and for twenty years thereafter I openly and frankly opposed slavery. The agitation produced a convulsion that shook the whole North State by State, aroused all men, and converted many. Morally, but unconsciously, the people of both sides, with all the leaders of the North, pressed forward blindly, to the inevitable war. The great contest passed logically through all stages—moral, political, legislative, judicial—and no man of the North (and perhaps few of the South) was at first in the least aware of the tendency, until, armed, they stood confronting each other, neither believing the other intended very war. It amazes us now to recall how utterly we misunderstood each other, one and all. On the morning of February 11, 1861, the President-elect started on his memorable progress through the Northern States to the Capital. He reached Washington and found that seven States of the Republic had organized a Government—a President and Congress—with its seat at Montgomery, Alabama. Its congress had convened there February 4th, had organized, adopted a constitution on the 7th, and elected its Executive on the 8th, three days before Lincoln left his home at Springfield. Mr. Lincoln was inaugurated in due form (as we have seen), in the midst of secretly armed friends, who were greatly relieved when they saw him in possession of the Executive Mansion. Still war was not believed in, and even when the forts in Charleston harbor were reduced, the assembling of Congress was delayed till July 4th.

That body convened to find over 300,000 Union soldiers in arms. On the day of its opening 25,000 soldiers marched through Pennsylvania Avenue. At that time fully one third of the available military population of the

South was under arms, from its then eleven States, with its capital at Richmond. How much time and blood it cost us to make a conquest of that capital, and only a hundred miles away !

At that time an executive or legislative position in the Government did not indicate a man's real position towards the approaching contest ; *that* depended entirely upon the personal qualities of the individual. In such times the occasion finds men out, elects, and conducts them to their places. Mr. Lincoln was not elected to carry on a war, and, save courage, firmness, purpose, had few of a warrior's qualities ; nor had any of his Cabinet larger endowments in that direction, except Montgomery Blair. He had not only enough belligerency for the rebellion, but enough to conduct at the same time many private and personal wars. " The Blairs," said Blair to me, " when they go in for a fight, go in for a funeral." He was at feud with Stanton before the rebellion ; they were not on speaking terms. He soon reached the same stage with Chase, in which Frank Blair was his ally.

In the Senate, Wade, Chandler, Baker, and one or two more were born warriors. Thad. Stevens and a very few of the House had fighting qualities. Stanton, when he reached the War Office, developed the native qualities which find exercise in war. He and Blair agreed in two things—boundless admiration for and confidence in Wade, and a determination to extinguish the rebellion. Blair was the only man who had a just conception of real war. He was a graduate of West Point, and why he and Cameron did not have each other's places, doubtless, was because Mr. Lincoln *did not expect war.* Mr. Wade, Stevens, the President, Stanton, and the average man then supposed that war meant to march upon the enemy by the shortest route, assail, hang to him, and *lick* him in the most direct way and in the least possible time. I fear all men of that opening day, not soldiers, had the same idea, and hence the "On to Richmond!" cry. Warriors are born ; war makes soldiers, and by a slow and awfully expensive process. The Indians assemble the warriors of the tribe, fight a battle, and go home ; we were *aboriginal.* We acquired more accurate notions. We developed strength, force of character, became indom- itable, inflexible, and gained a fixed purpose to conquer.

Mr. Wade soon became the first man in the Senate. His qualities, experience, temper, even level-headedness made him so. During the entire war the American peo- ple knew little, saw little of the men in Congress, and cared only that they should create and supply the needed money, and back Mr. Lincoln and the Secretary of War.

Thad. Stevens, "Old Thad.," as the leader of the more popular House—nobody cares much for the Senate save to get into it,—was the popular congressional idol of the war. Next to him ranked Wade—"Old Benj. Wade," as he had already become. Of these two men, with Edwin M. Stanton, it may truly be said that they were the most revolutionary men on the Union side of our history since the days of the Adamses and Jefferson. They had one purpose—the extinction of the rebellion ; they used whatever at hand seemed best fitted for that ; no scruple of the written Constitution troubled either of them. The conservative notion of preserving the Constitution as, next to slavery, the thing not to be touched, always and justly provoked their derision. At the very first the rebels depended on the Constitution to ward us off from invasion, nor did they then intend to invade us.

The 36th Congress, although it organized Territories *without excluding slavery*, had the courage, under the lead of Seward, Wade, and Fessenden in the Senate, and Stevens, E. B. Washburn, Corwin, Conkling, Kelley, and others in the House, to reject the Crittenden Com- promise—an amendment to the Constitution *prohibiting the abolition of slavery:* yet this Congress did many things subservient in its desire to propitiate the South. It may well be questioned, however, whether it ever went so far in the direction of conciliation as did the 37th at the called session of July 4, 1861, as we shall see.

The North was enraged. It would put down the rebellion. It but blindly felt, and groped unseeing through quite all the first year of the war, not grasping the true cause of the secession nor the real thing to be done. The war was to teach and enforce its own lesson in its own grim way. There was not a dozen of us in both Houses to whom it was given to see from the start; much fewer, if the early action of the two Houses is an exponent of the thought of individual Senators and Representatives.

Mr. Crittenden, now seventy-five years of age, the author of the Crittenden Compromise of the 36th Congress, and who had been transferred to the House to make room for Breckinridge in the Senate, presented his scarcely less famous resolution in the House the day after the first battle of Bull Run—July 22d:

Resolved by the House of Representatives of the Congress of the United States, That the present deplorable civil war has been forced upon the country by the disunionists of the Southern States, now in arms against the constitutional Government, and in arms around the Capital; that in this national emergency Congress, banishing all feelings of mere passion or resentment, will recollect only its duty to the whole country; that this war is not waged on their part in any spirit of oppression, or for any purpose of conquest or subjugation, or purpose of overthrowing or interfering with the rights of established institutions of those States, but to defend and maintain the *supremacy* of the Constitution and to preserve the Union with all the dignity, equality, and rights of the several States unimpaired, and that as soon as these objects are accomplished the war ought to cease.

In the full House, without debate, under the previous question, this resolution was passed—117 for, to 2 against it. The two were John F. Potter of Wisconsin, and one of the younger of Ohio's new men, Mr. Riddle. Lovejoy, though in his seat, remained silent. It was passed in the

Senate, after full discussion, by 30 for, to 5 against it. All
the Northern Senators voted for it save Sumner, who spoke,
but did not vote, and Trumbull, who voted against it, on
verbal grounds, with the rebel Breckinridge, and Polk,
Johnson of Missouri, and Powell; Wade and Chandler
remained silent and voted for it; Hale did not vote.
The slaveholders voted against it because it charged the
war upon them.

The Republicans, with Stevens and all of the House,
would then so wage the war as to hurt the South the least,
and slavery not at all.

The resolution, as the unanimous declaration of Congress, so significant and so amazing, which no man of that
majority now speaks of, and which is now a curious
study, was everywhere not only accepted North, but
constituted the State platform entire of the Ohio Republicans in 1862.

Thus the 37th Congress, called to this session by
the war, whose purpose it thus defined on the nineteenth day of its existence, was in a way to become the
great inner council of war;—a huge committee of ways
and means, where should work the brain, and the control-
ling will, and whence should issue the law, the mandates,
the sinews, which together should accomplish the real
purpose to be wrought out by the war itself ; a blind, im-
pelling force in turn educating, inspiring, leading, and
governing it.   In this view the President merely executed
the expressed will of Congress.   The great armies, with
their generals, in their campaigns and battles, were the
mere mechanics of the struggle.

Never was an unsophisticated man so amazed as the
gentleman from the Cleveland district, as the vote ran on.
For many minutes I supposed that I should vote alone.
Potter's suppressed " No " but partly broke the on-sweep-
ing, swelling tide.   My own resounded through the dome.
I could not keep my seat, and went back to the lobby.

Acquaintances and strangers gathered about me in angry expostulation. " What, under the heavens, do you mean? Go back and change your vote instantly," came in various forms from a dozen.

At white heat I retorted: " In God's name, gentle-men, what do you mean? Not a man of you believes that slavery is eternal. Not one is stupid enough, *not-withstanding his vote*, to believe that it can be abolished by convention. You all believe that it is to go out, when it does go, through convulsion, fire, and blood. That convulsion is upon us. The man is a delirious ass who does not see and realize this. For me, I mean to make a conquest of it ; to beat it to extinction under the iron hoofs of our war horses. It has impudently thrust away its shield of the Constitution ; has dissolved the protect-ing Union ; has uncovered itself, and *shall die*. You! you! and you!" shaking my finger in their scowling faces, "you are like children in the dark who have fright-ened themselves with tales of child-devouring ogres. You go tip-toeing about, with scared faces, whispering low, lest you waken this sleeping monster, which will eat you all up."

There were angry replies. We did not heed the Speaker's gavel, and the door-keepers came to separate and hush us. I had put myself under ban. I heard some one saying something of "his John Brown speech," and I was not to be heard. Potter and I became friends ; but on our side of the House high looks were exchanged even into the regular session.

The war was to educate these men. Let them fight, deal strong and heavy blows on the Confederacy, for any declared purpose, and every shot and shell, every bayonet thrust, will be a blow that shall tell heavily against slav-ery. They will soon bring themselves to the desired heat of ending that.

CHAPTER VIII.

BULL RUN.

JULY, 1861.

Bull Run—General Scott's Pass—At Centreville—Roar of Battle—The Hospital—The Sherman Battery—The Panic—Scenes on the Return—Fairfax Court-House—Eaton Wounded.

AFTER the crossing to Virginia by the grand army under McDowell, rumors of an approaching battle kept the Capital in a tremor of excitement and expectation, not to say of apprehension. It was known that a large rebel force was in and about Manassas. The art of securing accurate information of an enemy's force and intention had to be learned, even by the officers of the old army. I very well remember that long after the battle there was a theory that McDowell, in utter ignorance of his enemies' force, attacked a well posted army of 90,000 with about 18,000 men, and cut his way into its centre, and that his soldiers finally retired from pure exhaustion.

A day or two before the battle was fought there was a sharp encounter between a part of Tyler's division and the enemy. Colonel Richardson of Illinois, one of the heroes of the Mexican war, was present, and on his return gave some of us a striking description of it.

I was under promise to our Grays, that if a battle was fought within reach of Washington I would join them if possible, and share their fortunes on the field. At the first, fifteen or twenty members of the House were loud in their promises to witness the expected battle, which would be fought in the neighborhood of Centreville, twenty-seven miles southwest of Washington, on the Warrington turnpike. Among them none seemed more ardent than S. S. Cox, who, with his usual felicity, gives an account of *not* being there, in his very readable *Three Decades of Federal Legislation,* at page 150. There also will be found his pass, bearing the signature of Drake DeKay, *aide-de-camp,* of Washington fame. He is my authority for those who actually went :

"Among them are Colonel Wm. A. Richardson of Illinois, a soldier of the Mexican war ; General Joshua Hogan, Isaiah Morris, also of Illinois [1] ; Albert G. Riddle of Cleveland, Ohio, an eminent lawyer and a gallant man ; John A. Gurley, a Universalist minister (whom Mr. Cox afterward roasted on the floor); and Alfred Ely of Rochester. Senators Wade and Chandler go with their gallant friends to the front. With them went Sergeant-at-Arms Brown of the Senate, and Major Eaton of Michigan, a friend of Chandler's."

For some reason Mr. Cox omits the name of our other colleague, Harrison G. Blake of Ohio.

Before going I consulted General Scott as to the propriety of our presence near the field or on it, and received from him the following, which, with his signature, still ornaments a frame in my dining-room :

"WASHINGTON, July 20, 1861.

"Pass Hon. A. G. Riddle, M. C., to our advance posts, and back. He will be treated with respect and consideration by the officers and soldiers in the service of the United States.

"WINFIELD SCOTT, Commander.

"E. D. TOWNSEND, Assistant Adjutant-General."

On the next forenoon after my return to Washington, I wrote to Mrs. Riddle a hasty, yet extended account of

---

[1] He doubtless meant J. R. Morris of Ohio. Illinois had no Morris in the House then.

my experience of the day of the battle. It is now before me, dated July 22d ; some portions of it will become my text. My party was made up of my colleagues, Blake and Morris, and Thomas Brown, a distinguished Clevelander and an especial friend of Governor Chase.

I had made arrangements to leave Washington Saturday night, to enable me to join the Grays before they should march in the morning. That plan failed. We did not get off until the next morning. We had a strong carriage, a pair of stout horses, a good driver, a hamper of lunch, and four of the largest navy revolvers—necessity for the use of which I did not anticipate. I also had my Remingtons. We reached Centreville, McDowell's headquarters, about nine. Some four miles before reaching it we met a Pennsylvania regiment of three months' men, whose time expired that day, and who were hurrying away to their homes—ere the battle began—as it seemed to me. At Centreville we found the reserve, usually called the left wing, under Miles, occupying the southern slope of the hill, with several batteries of field artillery. We were told there were 7000 of all arms. The battle, judging by the ear, began with a heavy cannonade, which became general, one piece, our thirty-pounder, making itself heard above the roar.

Then there was a cessation of artillery, followed by a fierce and seemingly long-continued rattle of small-arms. The whole country was mostly wooded, and though the infantry was not more than three miles away, and we were at a considerable elevation, the only sign to the eye, of the struggle, were clouds of rising smoke above the forest. The sound seemed to recede, and finally ceased. After a considerable interval, it opened again, became louder and of wider extent, continued for an hour, receded, and entirely subsided.

At the second lull—and we had heard no word of how the battle went—we pushed forward. Some two and a half miles farther on we came in sight of a crowd of men. We had met many, mostly soldiers, straggling back toward Centreville. By these we were told that the battle was over, and the enemy retreating. We met several with slight wounds, who had passed the hasty hands of a surgeon. We found the gathering was in front of a farmhouse on the right, occupied as an emergency hospital. There were hundreds of soldiers and many officers, who had drifted out of the ranks, and a sprinkling of civilians. Some hundred yards beyond was the margin of the wood. Passing the hospital, we left our carriage, and Blake, Morris, and I pushed on—leaving our heavier arms, hampers, etc. We went on within the wood, and found the 12th New York at rest along the highway, beyond which was the 2d Ohio.

We had passed on the way from Centreville a heavy train of army wagons at a standstill, extending from headquarters past the hospital into the woods, in a continuous procession.

Farther on we passed Sherman's battery, and the 1st Ohio, and saw Col. Schenck, who was busy repairing, or building, a bridge over the main stream. In the open, I had a view of part of our men at rest on the field. In the distance, towards Manassas, was a dense cloud of dust, said to be made by the retreating foe, a glimpse of whom, with the aid of my glass, showed them apparently withdrawing. Everybody said the battle was over, the rebels beaten, and our boys, officers and men, were awaiting orders for the approaching end of the day. It was intensely hot ; the men suffering from heat and thirst. I saw more than one soldier dip up the muddy yellow water, standing in sinks in the road, and drink it.

One thing I did not understand—going out we crossed the line of fire of one or two rebel guns. I supposed they were ours, until a solid shot killed two of a clump of soldiers, and scattered the rest. It was at an open space, near a dilapidated fence. The slain were hastily drawn under the shelter of the neighboring tree trunks, where they were stretched on their backs, with their caps laid over their faces. I aided in this, and was anxious to examine the gaping track of the shot. A part of the neck and base of the skull of one was carried away, and I lifted the head by the hair for my inspection.[1]

On the return we had again to pass the line of those rebel guns. Blake made a detour to the left, and had the shelter of the trees. I kept on, and found the place entirely deserted. Not a blue coat in sight, nor had I recently heard a gun. Very soon a shot came tearing along, cutting among the near trees, and I stopped to study the effect of a six-pound shot among the branches. " It was a pursuit of knowledge under difficulties," as in the case of the younger Mr. Weller, for directly another was heard approaching, which seemed likely to strike at about my knees. It did in height, but about four feet in front *spatting* into the side of a cradle knoll. Where or behind what the guns were stationed, I never knew. A few strides forward brought me behind a protecting angle of woods.

Going on, I saw Sherman's guns limbered up, *and headed toward Centreville.* There I found Blake, and we hurried back to our carriage. Brown was there. Morris was absent. As we were about to leave the carriage on

---

[1] The most curious thing to me was the revelation of what I then feared was the basis of my real nature. The sight of the wounded had stimulated me, and at the hospital nothing could keep me from pushing forward, two of my companions reluctantly following me. We were soon on the ground of the opening skirmish and morning fight, near that part of the broken and wide extended field where the slaying of these boys in blue had occurred. I was seized with a perfectly brutish desire to kill, shed blood, destroy. I looked about for the enemy, for a rifle, missed my navy revolver, would gladly have plunged into a fight with my Remingtons. Somewhere in the ascending line, some one of the old clan of Riddle had been an awful savage—he or an old Welsh Merrick. The feeling did not entirely subside until I escaped the signs of the struggle.

our excursion to the field, he suddenly developed a quart whiskey bottle.¹ Morris was now missing, time was lapsing,—our horses, rested and refreshed, were as impatient to be off as we were. I went through the hospital, and studied the strange and increasing crowd outside. Some hundreds of straggling soldiers, many subaltern officers, and citizens. I saw none of the other members of Congress, nor had I met any of Wade's party at that time.

Finally Morris, somewhat refreshed, returned, and we took our places in the carriage and moved slowly through the crowd toward Centreville. The soldiers were without order or officers, drifting towards Centreville. I heard it said that the soldiers in the woods had been ordered back, and I had seen the guns turned that way, and did not at all apprehend the reason for these movements. These were preparatory to a retreat.

My seat in the carriage was the right-hand front, which gave me a clear outlook southwardly and back. Moving slowly, we were opposite the hospital, when with my eyes southward—over a wide, cleared field running westward behind the woods, through which the pike ran, toward the battle-field—I was surprised at seeing a small body of cavalry turn the angle of the wood, and head toward us at full speed. Of course I supposed they were our men, or why were they there? but why were they in such a hurry? The whole army as I thought was between them and the enemy. The straggling soldiers saw them, and a dozen of them ran to the fence with their weapons in position to fire. I sprang out with my heavy navy— called to my fellows: " These are Rebs! jump out and be ready for them." I think one or two followed, and I directed the coachman to take the carriage below.

---

¹ *Five quarts to the gallon*, as Frank Blair afterwards described the pattern. Morris tendered it to us, teetotalers though we were. I noticed that as we went on the whiskey went off.

4

There was a stout Virginia fence between us and the approaching horse. They came down within fifty or sixty yards, saw that we were safe from a charge, deployed into line in open order, giving them space, presented their carbines, and fired into our crowd. I had been under the roar of field-pieces, and to me this was but the popping of a row of rifle-caps. It was by this volley that young David McCook, a private and a hospital guard, was killed. I did not think of any one being hurt by such an attack. Our boys at the fence returned the fire. The range was short, and as the Rebs whirled and dashed away, as they instantly did, two or three horses ran riderless by. All the tales of a headlong charge, through and over our throngs, are baseless tales. I apprehended a nearer approach and held my fire.

Just as the enemy turned and were fleeing, I heard the cry " The Black horse ! The Black horse ! "—the first I ever heard of the Ashbys—which were to become famous cavalry. The effect of this cry must be given in the words of my letter, as quoted by Mr. Cox in the work named.[1]

" It seemed," said Mr. Riddle, " as if the very devil of panic and coward-ice seized every mortal soldier, officer, citizen, and teamster. No officer tried to rally the soldiers or do anything except to spring and run toward Centreville. There never was anything like it for a causeless, sheer, abso-lute, absurd panic on this miserable earth before. Off they went, one and all, off down the highway, over across the fields towards the woods, any-where, everywhere, to escape. The farther they ran the more frightened they grew, and though we moved as rapidly as we could, the fugitives passed us in scores. To enable them the better to run, they threw away their blankets, knapsacks, canteens, and finally muskets, cartridge-boxes, and everything else. We called to them, tried to tell them there was no danger, called them to stop, implored them to stand. We called them cowards, denounced them in most offensive terms, put out our heavy revolvers, and threatened to shoot them, but all in vain. A cruel, crazy, mad, helpless panic possessed them, and was communicated to everybody about, in front and rear. The heat was awful, although now about six ; the men were ex-

---

[1] P. 158.

hausted, their mouths gaped, their lips cracked and blackened with the powder of the cartridges bitten off in battle, their eyes starting in frenzy,—no mortal ever saw such a mass of ghastly wretches. As we came on, borne along with the mass, unable to go ahead or pause, or draw out of it, with the street blocked with flying wagons, before and behind, thundering and crashing on, we were every moment exposed to the imminent danger of being upset, or crushed, or breaking down ; and for the first time on this strange day I felt a little sinking of the heart, and doubted whether we could avoid destruction in the immense throng about us, and nothing but the skill of our driver and the strength of our carriage and endurance of our horses saved us. Another source of peril beset us. As we passed, the poor, demented, exhausted wretches, who could not climb into the high, close baggage-wagons, made frantic efforts to get onto and into our carriage. They grasped everywhere, and got onto it, into it, over it, and implored us in every way to take them on.

" No more graphic picture has been presented of the race of this army from an imaginary pursuit. The pencil of David could not do it justice. No colors can be harmonized for such a chaos. De Quincey's *Flight of a Tartar Tribe* is far less vivacious and not more thrilling."

I quote from the manuscript letter itself :

" At first they loaded us down to a stand-still. We had to be rough with them and thrust them out and off, and Brown and I guarded the doors with pistols. One poor devil did get in, and we lugged the pitiful coward a mile or two. He wore major's straps, was hatless, and had thrown away his sword ; finally I opened the door, and he tumbled—or was tumbled out."

At the awful jam at " Cub Run," where the gorge held us for a time, I saw a poor drummer boy struggling under the horses' feet, whom I rescued with much difficulty, and placed on our carriage. So I took up an exhausted New York soldier, hatless, coatless, shoeless, and to whom, when he became a little composed and his maddening thirst relieved with water from a spring rivulet, I turned over our untouched hamper. I left him and the boy at Centreville.

There was a pause at Centreville where Miles's men still stood waiting, but they did not cut off the frightful stam-pede. Instead, I saw a herd of beeves turned into the pike and headed toward Washington,—the property of a contractor, as I learned later.

Passing Centreville, the wreckage and spoil of flight increased. Axes, picks, shovels, muskets, with cartridge-boxes, boxes of crackers, fixed ammunition, etc., were strewn all the way.

Wade's carriage had passed us at a choke-up before we reached Centreville. We passed them at that place, and they passed us again where I had gotten out to gather up some desirable new Springfield rifles. I made a collection of rifles, sword-bayonets, etc., much to the chagrin of my companions, who however submitted to my whim, as Brown called it. Senator Wilson in a sulky passed me, driving as rapidly as he could, and called to me a little peremptorily to "hurry on." I called back that "if I were as much in a hurry as you seem to be, I would." When Wade passed us the second time, I directed our coachman to keep close to his carriage; his horses were not the equals of ours, and this was easy, and all the time it is to be remembered that the fleeing throngs increased in numbers, and kept at such speed as their endurance and mode of travel permitted.

About a mile the other side (from Washington) of Fairfax Court-House, at the foot of a long down-grade, the pike on the northerly side was fenced and ran along a farm. On the other side, for a considerable distance, was a wood utterly impenetrable for men, or animals larger than cats and squirrels. The spell of changing day to night was already being wrought in the wood, and its shadow was perceptible in the open lands, when the Wade carriage drew out, and up to the fence. Immediately the old Senator, his hat well back, sprang out with his rifle (which he carried to Washington when he entered the Senate, and with which he would have enforced his compact with Cameron and Chandler). He was followed by Chandler, Brown, and Eaton, all armed, and Chandler seemingly in a dangerous mood. I sprang out with my heavy navy revolver, followed by Blake and Brown and

Morris. Morris had expended his magazine at Bull
Run, and he now prudently passed out the other side, and
continued his advance on Washington. Ranging across
the pike, " with loud cries we confronted the on-sweeping
multitude, filling the broad road, and for a half mile up
to the summit, and with our weapons we commanded an
immediate halt then and there, on pain of instant loss of
brains, which none of them would miss."

Many on horseback attempted to pass. Their horses'
bits were seized, and they yielded. McDowell's bearer
of dispatches, which he showed, was passed. So the
Commissary of the 2d Wisconsin, Colonel Peck, looking
for baggage. Alas! the 2d Wisconsin soon had to look
for its young and dashing Colonel, who left West Point
in his junior year—appointed at my request by my predecessor, Edward Wade.

" All the rest we stopped ; some presented weapons. One, a teamster,
mounted on a harnessed horse, cut from an army wagon, threatened Eaton
—who had his horse by the bit—with a small pistol. There was the report
of a revolver. Eaton was shot through the left wrist. The horse, liberated,
dashed on."

As the multitude, thus dammed up, swelled and raged,
the pressure upon us became very great. Loud cries and
threats reached us in the deepening twilight. Nothing
shows more strongly the utter demoralization of the panic-
infected crowd, than that a thousand of them should permit themselves to be held up by seven men, no one of
whom had a badge of office.

Just when we were perhaps about to be overborne,
Colonel Crane, with a part of the 2d New York, stationed
at Fairfax Court-House, hearing of the loss of the battle,
with the instincts of a soldier, turned out his men and
on the double-quick came to our rescue, and took the
tumultuous mass of fugitives off our hands.

His surgeon hastily dressed Eaton's wound (the bullet

had passed between the bones), and we were soon on our journey, wiser if less sad men. This episode of our stand, even at that stirring time, was much talked of, and had its small hour of fame.

We paused at Fairfax Court-House, and an officer, whose eye caught the sparkle of my armament, asked what I intended to do with the rifles. " Carry them on till I find an officer with brains and spirit to see them put to the use for which they were intended," I replied. I had seen so many shoulder-straps and buttons without head or stomach that day, that my curt answer may be excused. " I am Major [or Captain, I don't remember now] of the New York 2d, left in command here. I will undertake to execute your wish," he responded courteously. I at once delivered to him nine rifles, as many or more bayonets, cartridge-boxes, etc.

We had taken up Cowan of Ohio (in the Treasury Department) at the hospital, whom we exchanged for Eaton (our carriage was easier and roomier), and went on.

What a weird, uncanny ride was that, in the warm July night, under the everlasting stars, for an imaginative man, with the strange experiences of the day !

When we went out in the morning no one challenged us at the block-houses, earthworks, and rifle-pits on the Virginia side of the Potomac. This morning I showed General Scott's pass, and an orderly was despatched to name the party thus designated on through the works.

CHAPTER IX.

AFTER THE BATTLE.

JULY–AUGUST, 1861.

The Battle not a Defeat, but a Draw—Disorder in the City.

I REACHED my boarding-house about two in the morning. I had not tasted food since breakfast on the way out, and was still keyed too high for sleep or for much repose.

Upon going abroad the next morning, I found the town full of the wildest rumors and of the wildest-looking stragglers in blue blouses. Clearly the whole army had returned, and the slight discipline of a few weeks of military forms had utterly disappeared, under officers often of their own choosing.

In my *Biography of Senator Wade*, in a note (p. 292), is my deliberate estimate of the battle as between the belligerents.

"*Mr. Wade at Bull Run.* Never was a battle so really and persistently misapprehended. We ran away, and so were defeated. We were not beaten on the field. At the most it was a draw. We made the assault, and, as raw troops might, got weary, and went off the field, leaving a part of the amazed foe there. *They never pursued us an inch.* Governor Sprague went and brought back his guns (left at Cub Run) the next day. A party brought off the body of Colonel Cameron (Colonel of the 73d Pennsylvania, and brother to Secretary Cameron) the second day after the battle. No rebels but dead ones were met with."

At 10 A.M. I went to my desk in the House of Representatives, and wrote my letter to Mrs. Riddle, quoted above, with the warmth and excitement of the day before still upon me. I ran it over hastily, and added a word of caution. It was not to be published, and was to be shown only to a few of the most trusted. Mrs. Riddle gave it to her brother-in-law Bruce, to be shown to Cowles of the *Leader* and post-office. It fell into the hands of the managing editor of the *Leader*. His attention was called to the inhibition of publication. When was an editor ever guided by any considerations except those of " copy." I have it with his marks. All the most striking parts were retained. All that would explain the actual conditions, justify, or excuse, were *marked out*. I was thunderstruck on receiving the *Leader* containing it. I was enraged, appalled, by the *Herald* following with it. The journal for which I deliberately risked myself, without the expectation of reward, delivered me bound into the hands of my one malignant enemy. Benedict had persistently assailed me from the day of his failure to secure the Post-Office. To none of them would I reply or permit others to. Unrestrained by considerations of truth or justice, and limited in the use of means only by the power of his invention and that of his aids, he saw his opportunity. These panic-stricken runaways were, according to the *Herald*, the remnant of a routed, annihilated army, destroyed on the field, with the victorious foe thundering after them. We were a cowardly gang of lordly Congressmen, with our fleet, strong horses driving through and over them, overcome as they were by the heat, the toils of battle, and the rage of thirst. The cowardly major was wounded, bleeding and fainting, and thrown from my carriage into the stony road, to perish under the wheels of the fleeing army wagons—and so were the spent and exhausted soldiers. Nobody now— nobody then—in the towns and villages of the district flooded over with huge editions of the *Herald*, can appreciate its instantaneous effect. A writer in the Cincinnati *Commercial*, from Cleveland, describes it in these terms: "Mr. Riddle was esteemed the most fortunate, successful, and popular man produced in this district. In a day he became the most odious."

I was burnt and hanged in effigy in more than one enraged town. In one an effigy obstinately refused to burn and was promptly and properly weighted and cast into a mill-pond. The *Herald*, with marginal notes, was showered upon me by scores, and every mail came freighted with coarse, vulgar, and obscene letters, some with the writers' names. Most of my friends were overwhelmed, and in Cleveland made no effort to stem the tide. A few strong, indignant men, came out for battle, and wrote me indignant letters. I insert one, written evidently at a white heat, from Arthur H. Thrasher of Chardon, Geauga County, a widely known lawyer and a man of decided character.

" CHARDON, Aug. 1, 1861.

" DEAR RIDDLE:

" I am moved at this moment to write you from reading the third contemptible, malignant, and outrageous article in the Cleveland *Herald* upon you, or rather professing to be upon your letter. The last is done up in doggerel. It is so outrageous that your friends here can scarcely restrain their desire to go to Cleveland and shoot Benedict like a dog, as he is. He is a miserable, malignant dog ! I am at a loss to know what course ought to be taken with the scoundrel—whether you ought to prosecute him for libel (and this last as well as the others are unquestionably libellous), or whether we ought to call a meeting here and pass resolutions that we will no longer take his libellous sheet. We are outraged and insulted every time we open it of late. Such a scoundrel ought to be ejected from society. If he is such a miserable fool as to suppose that he is going to make any capital against you among your old friends, by his fiendish efforts to garble your letter, he is past hope even. . . .

" Yours truly,

" A. H. THRASHER."

From several Cleveland friends came appeals to remain away during vacation, and if I did come home to get off the cars at the upper (Euclid) station. It would not do to brave the city. There was a general demand that I should write an explanatory, excusatory address. With this I reluctantly complied. The yellow thing from the *Daily Leader* is before me. My reader has already had too much of these personal recollections to be offered these three columns. It amuses me now to see how I reiterated the points of the letter, now drawn with a more distinct background. A paragraph or two may be offered here, to show the temper with which, at the time, I handled this personal matter.

" HOUSE OF REPRESENTATIVES,
" WASHINGTON, Aug. 5, 1861.

" A period which demands the exercise of a patriotism so unanimous and heroic that no evil passion can find voice, save a malignity that never sleeps, is not one in which an humble individual should seek to distract the public attention to his private affairs, but the course of the Cleveland *Herald*, in the estimation of friends, requires that even now I should throw myself so far upon the public indulgence as to ask its attention to the statement I am about to submit.

" That course has its origin in no political act or sentiment of mine, nor in any private hostility on my part towards that journal nor towards any of its conductors, nor on account of any discourtesy of mine, but solely for the satisfactory reason that I preferred that another Republican journal should receive the patronage of the Cleveland Post-Office. Other than this, the *Herald* has no cause of enmity to me. It will hardly claim that I was under obligations or pledges to it of any kind. To the daily attacks of that paper during the spring I made no reply, though I was urged to do so. I was determined that the Republican party should be distracted by no quarrel of mine. And were I to consult my own inclinations, I should remain silent even now, trusting that the world would some time, in the progress of the war, discover the difference between the heroic soldier who remains on the field and him who, in advance of defeat, abandons it without cause ; and that it may not be the best incentive to heroic deeds to confound one with the other.

" I am now charged in that journal, not only with a want of spirit and firmness in danger, to which I offer no reply, but with brutal inhumanity to distressed soldiers, under circumstances that deserve the scorn and execration of the world. The proof of this obliquity, I am glad to find, exists only in the contents of a letter of my own, a letter which hastily recounts my personal observations and experiences in the neighborhood of the 'Battle of July 21st.' I shall give so much of what I saw as bears on these charges, only for the purpose of disclosing the facts with which I dealt, the circumstances under which I wrote, as also the person to whom it was addressed."

No graphic pen has ever described the scenes enacted in the Capital during the three weeks following the return of that part of the army after its flight from Centreville. In the main, those who on the field had tasted the red banquet were quiet and orderly. It was the stragglers, runners, and bummers who stole out of the ranks, the small detachments in the neighborhood of the field, and along the pike, among whom the fatal contagion of panic had spread like a death-breathing pestilence, who were the most lawless. These, in herds and flocks, wandered about the streets and lower places of resort. Washington then had a licensed bar for about every seventy-five of the fixed population, and a large number of unlicensed drinking places. Its police was slight and wholly unequal to the exigency. For the most part, the first rush of volunteers was from the intelligent, orderly class of young men. Yet all know the effect upon men of the absence of home and neighborhood influences, abandoned to themselves, and to the named and nameless allurements of a Capital such as Washington then was.

For the most part the crowds were good-natured—though not always. One day, at about 4 P.M., as I went from the Capitol up the avenue, I witnessed the following: At that time much of the space below Third Street, along the Tiber to the Capitol grounds, was vacant, and here and extending into and over the avenue, was a compact crowd of 2500 or 3000 young men, all wearing the shapeless thing of blue flannel, with the inevitable three army buttons—the dread and derision of the young handsome volunteers alike from town and country. It required very acute patriotism and the prevalence of example to make the wearers feel comfortable. In the centre of the crowd a fight was going on, not according to the eminent christian of Queensbury, and there seemed to be more than one engaged. Occasionally, several who seemed to be regulators, or assistants, took part to keep the contest balanced. I had learned that a troop of the regular cavalry had just taken possession of extemporized stables and barracks on the square opposite the Rugby, and running up to some of those on the outer edge of the crowd, I said that orders had just been sent to the 3d Cavalry to come down and charge the crowd. My manner was evidently impressive, for instantly the mass began to disintegrate and disperse. I was told that there was a bet on the principals, which I doubtless caused to be declared off.

Some lively incidents arose under the cavalry in the ensuing days before the advent of McClellan. I witnessed an episode one morning south of the avenue between Seventh and Ninth Streets. This space, with the huts and old shanties of the old market, was very unlovely, having a fringe of solitary mean wooden buildings along the canal, occupied by meaner people devoted to the meanest callings known. Some trouble had arisen at one of these ulcers. A soldier had been wronged; in revenge, a half dozen others raided the place one forenoon; a small squad of the cavalry came to the rescue; one soldier got out and fled; a cavalryman gave chase. As the horse at a rapid gait came up with the fugitive, he deviated to the left without checking his speed, the soldier bent a little, threw his right hand upon the truant's collar and neck, lifted him from the ground, and with a mighty swing laid him on his horse's withers, and bore him off. I had a new conception of what a mounted athletic man, whose trained horse worked instinctively to his will, could accomplish.

CHAPTER X.

MARYLAND'S EFFORTS TO SECEDE.

APRIL–AUGUST, 1861.

Retrospective—Maryland's Efforts to Secede—Effect on the District of Columbia—The State Saved.

IT may be forgotten what persistent and nearly success-ful efforts were made to carry Maryland out of the Union with her sister border States. I first came to understand the case during this extra session. Her slave property was estimated at $50,000,000. Through her lay the northern road to the Capital; she held the thoroughfare between the north and south, and her geographical posi-tion saved her as it did Kentucky.

Mr. A. H. Handy, the State Commissioner of Missis-sippi, visited Maryland early in December, 1860. His presence was a danger; he came to induce the State to secede. His address to brave old Governor Hicks was insidious, the Governor in reply expressing strong sym-pathy with Mississippi, and enjoining prudence as well.

A *legal* secession, according to Southern constitutional law, must originate with a State legislature, Maryland's consisting of twenty-two Senators and seventy-two dele-gates. Twelve of the twenty-two Senators petitioned the Governor to convene an extra session; this meant seces-sion. *The going out of Maryland would take the District of Columbia, the Capital becoming the seat of the Con-federate government*, with all the prestige which it would thus gain in Europe. The Confederacy, as would seem to Europe, had supplanted the United States, and succeeded to its rights and immunities. A convention was held informally in Baltimore on the 18th and 19th of February, which resolved to wait the result of the Peace Convention and action of Congress. It adjourned to March 12th—*unless meantime Virginia seceded*, in which case the convention should reassemble. Should Governor Hicks decline to call a " Sovereign " convention before March 12th, then the suspending body would recommend such a convention at once. When it did meet, the Republican administration was seated in Washington, and the inaugural was working its charm. A border State convention was discussed, and a resolution against the repossession of federal property in the seceded States—which would be acts of war by the United States and would absolve Maryland from the Union—was lost.

Governor Hicks wanted to gain time. The fall of Sumter was met by the President's proclamation. A special election of Representatives to the House must be held, and that, he argued, would give the people of Maryland a chance to declare their wishes. He had opposed a reconvention of the Legislature. The riot of April 19th produced a great excitement, and thereupon the *Senator* of the Baltimore District himself issued a call— a proclamation convening the Legislature at Baltimore, the hotbed of secession and bad blood. The stout Governor met this with a proclamation to convene the Legislature at Frederick City, in the midst of a brave and loyal population, on the 26th of April. He found he could not trust the militia, whose officers to a man were secessionists. I may not follow this intensely important contest further. Governor Hicks saved Maryland, and General Butler by a stroke of strategy captured Baltimore, garrisoned Fort McHenry and held it, and thus overawed the rebellious city.

I very well remember General Butler's first visit to Washington after this exploit. I had never seen this picturesque specimen of nature's handiwork on faces, and had then rarely seen a major-general in full dress, with golden plumes, epaulets, and spurs. He came over to see the President and Secretary of War, and walking alone up the avenue to the White House, he early encountered one of our general's videttes, who took him in charge as a general at large without a permit. Butler appreciated his arrest both as a fine bit of military police and a good joke.

McClellan's coming to the Capital was like the advent of a beneficent prince. We awoke one morning to find the streets, the city, serenely free of the wandering gangs of brass and blue. They had all disappeared in a night. In his presence order and quietude at once found themselves everywhere established. As by a potent magic, obedience, discipline, neatness, and the air military ruled the camps to which the soldiers were confined; the awkward citizen began to assume the bearing of a soldier, preparing to take his place in the finely wrought mechanism of the company, regiment, brigade, division, and army corps. Never had we a more superior organizer, with the skill to turn out the completed regiment. Had his enterprise, his dash, his élan, and his tactics in the field equalled his art as a constructor and artificer of soldiers, his genius would have approached some of the renowned commanders of history. Coming as he did to the President's aid to relieve him of the chaos of his Capital, no wonder he won his heart and confidence. Simple and modest then—he adopted no style, no full dress, plumes and bullion, no glittering staff and parade—at the first not even a shoulder strap. We saw him on the avenue, a simple soldier, without any mark or insignia—alone, hurrying on, few knowing his person. When he took the field without Rosecrans, who made his first fame in West Virginia, he seemed to disappear. He was kept all winter before Manassas by twenty-seven or thirty wooden guns, and would have stayed there the next season had not L. C. Baker and his detectives tested by inspection the rebel works, and reported the real state of things there. In fact the Confederates evacuated Manassas for their own purpose. So on to the peninsula with his 90,000 men and 100 field pieces, he began to call for more men, and made regular approaches to the brush fence, behind which lay old Magruder and his 7000 rebels.

The fate of Mr. Ely of the House from Rochester, N. Y., had a depressing effect upon some of our body. His may have been the case of a cultured man, surprised by some fault in his physical and nervous make-up. In the early part of the day on the field at Bull Run, when the Cleveland Grays skirmished in, in front of the 1st Ohio, and had some sharp encounters, they found Ely apparently ill, and my personal friend, George Hoyt, rendered him some attention at a hut. The Grays changed position, and instead of keeping with them, Ely remained, —the last seen of him by our men. When picked up he may have made known his position as a Member of Congress, and though a non-combatant, which should have exempted him from capture, he was carried as a trophy to Richmond, and detained many months. This incident created some apprehension among some of our associates, several of whom thought that Congress should legislate in a more secure place. The Capital might be captured and both Houses carried off—especially as Maryland was still regarded as shaky.

Congress adjourned August 6th. It may be said of it that no similar body of our history ever remained thirty-three days in session, and in that time enacted so many and such important statutes as did this; or ever conducted its debates with such harmony, or passed its measures with such unanimity.

CHAPTER XI.

APPOINTMENT OF OHIO BRIGADIER-GENERALS.

AUGUST–NOVEMBER, 1861.

The President's Note—Our Caucus—Contest over Morgan—Raising Soldiers
—The 41st Regiment—Ball's Bluff.

THE members from Ohio received a note from the
Executive asking us to name five or six citizens of our
State, whom we would recommend for appointment as
Brigadier-Generals. Two sessions of not more than eight
or ten of us were held about the time of our adjournment, at the first of which Senators Wade and Sherman
were present, as were Vallandigham and Cox. We had no
difficulty in agreeing on McCook, Sherman, and Schenck.
To start with I named Colonel George W. Morgan, a leading Democrat, and the distinguished colonel of an Ohio
regiment in the Mexican war, of West Point education,
and admitted military ability. He was brevetted for gal-
lantry at Cherubusco where he commanded the 15th
regulars. I was surprised that Wade should oppose him
bitterly, and that Vallandigham and Cox would not support him. These gentlemen all seemed as much surprised
that I should nominate him. My reasons were put forth:
We Republicans were charged as being the culpable
cause of the war; we had, on our—the Union—side, so far
in Congress, made it purely a national, not a Republican,

contest; justice to the Democrats, as well as sound policy, demanded that they should not be discriminated against; no man in the State had a better military reputation than Colonel Morgan. It was said he was opposed to the war and would not accept. It seemed to me he should have a chance, and I was sure he would accept gladly, and that fact would silence a great many in middle and southern Ohio, and I also thought that we Republicans should show our hands now at the beginning. We had an adjournment. At the next session Morgan was named fourth without any debate.

My return home, as was thought, presaged personal war against the *Herald*. Plans of a campaign had been formed. I declared at once that there was no place for personal war in the Republican camp, and that it should not have a thought of my mind nor a minute of my time. I would cheerfully act with Benedict in raising soldiers for the new regiments, and in strengthening the Union cause.

A message to call at the Weddell House the day after my return and take luncheon, was awaiting me from Colonel McCook, who commanded the 1st Ohio, and Captain Hampson, who led the Grays at Bull Run, both of whom and their commands I was charged with libelling. Of course I accepted and went, and the heart of the city was doubtless cheered by the sight of the three on the Weddell House balcony and on the street, as together we visited the office of the *Leader* and the reading-room of the *Herald*.

Our first work was raising the 41st Ohio. At the called meetings addressed by me men were a little surprised when they heard, in my discussion of the battle of Bull Run, no allusion made to the *Herald*. When the companies for that regiment existed in skeleton, I went to Washington and secured the appointment of William B. Hazen, U. S. A., as Colonel to command it. In his interesting

book—a history of that part of the war in which he was
personally engaged—he says a *delegation* of Cleveland
gentlemen secured his appointment. He was then personally unknown at Cleveland. George Mygatt, a
brother-in-law of my friend and competitor, Backus, was
appointed Lieutenant-Colonel of the 41st, and a delegation may have gone there for *him.* This appointment, as
I think, was also referred to me. I never had cause to
complain of Mr. Cameron. Bull Run and my sketch of
it, and our stand beyond Fairfax, strengthened me at
Washington with all parties.

Hazen was personally well known to me, and was
reared in my neighborhood. He put the boys of the 41st
under rigid rules from the start, and they complained to
me of his severity. I told them to wait till they reached
the front. They went not only well drilled, but changed
to very complete soldiers, knowing how to live and to
care for themselves. My daughter presented them with a
flag, and in time they marched away.[1] I also had an order
to raise a battery to be attached to the 41st, under the
command of young Wetmore, who, though obliged to
leave West Point—being rendered unfit for the army per-
manently by a fever-sore as was supposed,—was a very
thorough soldier.

At Shiloh the 41st did good service under Mygatt,
Hazen being in command of a brigade. Mygatt led it in
a famous charge across an old field grown up with small
shrubs and briars, every spear of which was cut away by
the fierce infantry fire. How a man lived to face the
rebels who contributed to that *mowing,* Heaven only
knows!

With these public labors and some attention to the
courts, the summer and early autumn lapsed. Meantime,

---

[1] The flag was of large dimensions, with the national colors. It had the
number of the regiment, and was placed and left on the State House at
Nashville.

McClellan had ere September, been appointed to the command of the Department at Washington. A month later came the unplanned—on our side—battle of Ball's Bluff, fought by our different and detached bodies of soldiers wandering at large, under no general, against superior numbers—four or five thousand—well commanded. Out of 1700 Union soldiers who participated in the action, 1000 were killed and captured ; and, greatest loss of all, the gallant Baker fell, shot through the brain, while leading a charge. Mention of the disaster, which filled the North with horror as with sorrow, must be further made as we go on.

On the 1st of November, General Scott retired, and McClellan was made Commander-in-chief (this captain of engineers, for years out of service) over the heads of the old generals and colonels. For a time he filled the popular heart, and reigned the hero and idol.

CHAPTER XII.

THE PRESIDENT'S MESSAGE.

DECEMBER, 1861.

Effect of the War on Congress—The Armies—The President's Message—
Mr. Seward—Commissioners to Treat with the Rebels—Bill to Abolish
Slavery in the District of Columbia.

THE broad work of the called session was continued and supplemented by the regular session. It originated and matured many great measures, some of which became a part of the permanent legislation of the country in the hands of all parties. Its members became accustomed to elevated and widely extended views, to the expenditure of enormous sums, to the creation of multitudinous armies, to the daily widening of gigantic powers and to having confidence in themselves as the legislators of the Great Republic, equal to the extraordinary demands upon them, they handled their creative and sustaining powers with firm hands. This session was also marked by the antagonism of the Democrats as a party, to the Union cause, as contended for by the Republicans. They finally became the active allies of the Confederacy, as we shall see.

The two Houses assembled December 2d. At that time the hostile armies may, in outline, be said to confront each other in numbers and positions nearly as follows : General Wool had 15,000 men at Fort Monroe. Passing up the Potomac, Hooker was in the front of Washington with 10,000; McClellan's army numbered about 160,000 in eight divisions, of which Keyes and Casey's divisions were in and about Washington. Indeed, the large outside vaults and store-rooms of the Capitol were occupied by them, and the smoke of their quarters was often troublesome in the hall of the House. Counting with these, those along the railroad to Baltimore and near that city, the total must have been near 200,000. This force was later called the Army of the Potomac. Passing up the river were Kelley's troops that later Lander led up the Shenandoah; and Rosecrans had 20,000 in West Virginia.

In Kentucky, Buell had embodied 100,000. At St. Louis and Cairo, Halleck was collecting and organizing a force. In the farther west, on the frontier, 20,000 men were assembled, with the intention of marching from Kansas to the Gulf of Mexico, through New Mexico. On the Ohio and at Cairo, under Foote, lay a fleet of gunboats.

Sherman had a force in South Carolina. Burnside was soon on his way to North Carolina; and there were several regiments for his expedition. The whole has been estimated at 450,000 or 475,000 men, an army as numerous as that with which Napoleon approached the territory of Russia in 1812.

The Confederates held the most of Virginia, Kentucky, and Missouri. Their Virginia army consisted of 30,000, at Yorktown and Norfolk, a small force on the James, and the army before Washington, which held a long fortified line. Its right rested on the Potomac below Fredericksburg, supported by batteries on the Potomac. The main body was at Centreville and Manassas. It was supposed that both were fortified, as was Manassas, and the force was estimated at 75,000. The left extended to Leesburgh, with a large force at Winchester and Martinsburgh. These entire armies, estimated by McClellan at 175,000, were commanded by General Joseph E. Johnston. In Kentucky the rebel force was about 30,000, with 20,000 in Tennessee, and smaller bodies at important points on the Mississippi. They had under arms about 350,000 men, standing on the defensive.

Sometime, fifty or a hundred years hence, when some broad-browed student of our history comes, in whose brain the awful mass of public documents and statistics, and this endless, ever-swelling tide of more or less turbid memories, notes, sketches, and autobiographies, shall re-solve itself into translucent matter, and he takes up the narrative at the Genesis of the cause of this war, then the truth of what really was will be made to appear. Mr. Lincoln's message to the two Houses, and the accompa-nying reports of his Cabinet Ministers, will be found in this clear white light to be papers of pith and moment.

Eight months and a few days had elapsed since the Proclamation summoned a little more than one half of the nation to arms, against the other half, then in arms, osten-sibly to reunite and preserve the whole; and had sum-moned the nation's Congress to assemble, consider, discuss, and resolve the new conditions. To me now, who was one of the body addressed, these papers seem to have lost none of their significance. The firmness of tone, the un-conscious confidence of these nationalists in ultimate suc-cess is inspiriting.

Mr. Lincoln told us that the Court of Claims needed a grant of ampler powers; that the huge mass of Congres-sional law needed codifying, and half a score of similar things, neglected in the lazy years of peace, ought to be dealt with *now*, with half of the republic in arms to abro-gate and annihilate the whole by force, and the demolition or capture of the very Capital where this Court of Claims must sit. How we responded to these suggestions will appear. For one, I thought these things might wait.

A curious thing appears in Postmaster-General Blair's report.   It would seem that up to that time the Department had done its best to supply the rebels with the postal service.   The number of post-offices in operation during the year was 28,586.   The number of post-offices that made no return for the last quarter was 8,535.   In Virginia alone there were 161 that continued their reports. Indeed there were early in the war *complaints from within the rebel lines of the irregularity of the United States mails*.   No circumlocution, no euphemism, will enable me to give Mr. Lincoln's "*little story*" illustrating their complaint of the interruption of their " mail facilities."

It will be remembered that on the day after the battle of Bull Run, the House, 117 to 2, dedicated slavery to everlasting safety from the war.

The first thing in the House at this December session was a joint resolution by Mr. Stevens : " *Whereas that slavery has caused the present rebellion,*" " Resolved that the President and Generals declare free all slaves escaping from rebel masters, but secure compensation to loyal owners "—a decided advance for a man mute four months before.

In the meantime grim and direct old Commodore Wilkes had taken Mason and Slidell, the Confederate envoys to England,—two sons of America that she could best spare,—from an English ship, and brought them home again.   We had not more than got into our seats in the House, when Lovejoy offered a joint resolution which declared, " That the thanks of Congress are due and are hereby tendered to Captain Wilkes for his brave, adroit, and patriotic conduct, in the arrest and detention of the traitors, James M. Mason and John Slidell," and we passed it with a shout of "yeas," heard across the Atlantic, and adding much to the complicating and compromising position the exploit placed us in.   Mr. Seward saved us.   His position was the most difficult and least appreciated of any of the three Secretaries.   He gracefully apologized to Her Majesty, and we rewarded the old South Sea explorer in true British fashion by making him an Admiral. We needed an object lesson in international law.

On motion of Mr. Blair, his colleague Reid, Member of Congress, taken in arms, was expelled this first day of the session also.

On motion of Colfax, Mason, captured as above, was to be, upon the order of the President, incarcerated until Colonel Corcoran, who had been captured at Bull Run and imprisoned, be enlarged and treated as a prisoner of war.

Mr. Eliot, of Massachusetts, offered a resolution, which, among other things, declared that the President, as commander-in-chief of the armies, or a general under him, as a war measure, could by proclamation emancipate slaves.[1]

Roscoe Conkling had a resolution adopted calling for information as to the disaster of Ball's Bluff. The House also called for the incarceration of Slidell, till the wounded and captured Col. Ward be liberated and treated as a prisoner of war. These various orders of the House and motions of members on this first day show how the atmosphere of the North was changed and charged, as well as indicating the popular opinion of that day.

On the 4th of December Mr. Saulsbury offered in the Senate—with a long *Whereas*—a joint resolution to appoint Millard Fillmore, Franklin Pierce, Roger B. Taney, Edward Everett, Geo. M. Dallas, Thomas Ewing, Horace Binney, Reverdy Johnson, John J. Crittenden, Geo. E.

---

[1] This broad and correct view was in this country first taken by J. Q. Adams, in the debate on the Oregon controversy.

Polk had declared that our right to the 54° 40' was clear and unquestioned. The party war cry of that day was "54-40 or fight." Mr. Adams showed the consequence of war with Britain. A general in the field could, as a war measure, emancipate all the slaves. By consent, Mr. Giddings followed, and drew a ghastly picture of a British general landing an army on the Southern coast, made defenceless by slavery, and proclaiming freedom to the negroes found among them. In sheer terror the administration backed down, and made cowardly haste to take 49° as the northern boundary.

Pugh, and Richard W. Thompson, commissioners, to meet a like number, to be appointed by the Confederate States, to devise a plan for the preservation of the Union (and slavery), and that meantime active hostilities should cease. (They had ceased as far as McClellan was concerned.) This was laid on the table. On the same day Mr. Sumner introduced a resolution calling for copies of Gen. Halleck's order, directing that no fugitive slave should be received within his lines and camps, and all such now present be at once thrust out, and this for the *Halleckian* reason that they would give information to their masters, *whom they had run away from.* No wonder the soldiers had dubbed the old General "Old Brains." The Senate adopted this the next day.

On that same 4th, John C. Breckinridge, then a Major-General in the Confederate Army, was expelled, the vote being 36 for and no negatives; Powell of Kentucky not voting, and Polk and Johnson of Missouri and Andrew Johnson of Tennessee not present.

The 4th was a busy day in the House. The Homestead bill was reported by Mr. Lovejoy. Mr. Hutchins offered a resolution inquiring into the use of the jail of the District as a slave pen, there being fifty-five held there then, not charged with offences. Mr. Holman offered the Crittenden joint resolution of July 22d. *The House promptly laid it on the table, 71 to 65*, and one of the "gentlemen from Ohio" asked his colleagues and fellow members what the d—— they meant? Lovejoy introduced a bill prohibiting the officers and men of the army and navy from being engaged in the capture and return of fugitive slaves.

Mr. Hutchins introduced a bill to abolish slavery in the District of Columbia, and Mr. Riddle a resolution calling for a report of the number of slaves to be liberated, and their cash value as property in the slave market of the Capital.

CHAPTER XIII.

AWAKENING OF CONGRESS.

DECEMBER, 1861.

Gloom of the Winter of 1861-62.

ALREADY the two Houses, twin giants, congenitally bound to act together, helpless when divided, all power-ful when in harmony, were beginning to awaken, and but half seeing in the twilight, were clumsily fumbling about, for the unaccustomed weapons, which they felt must be within reach somewhere. They were pulling themselves together, and rising and expanding as the light grew clearer, and assuming with heroic proportions the attitude demanded by the conflict which confronted them.

"Wilson's Creek" had mitigated Bull Run, nothing had palliated Ball's Bluff; Garfield's demolition of Hum-phrey Marshal and Mill Spring seemed but to expose the gloom.

Congress was half conscious that from it must go forth the courage, inspiration, and the men, the money support and backing that could alone secure the success of the national cause.

How awfully dark and gloomy closed the last months of the year 1861, over and around the Capital. The de-pressing aspects of the war were supplemented by the unusual storms and fogs that ruled in that latitude all the

75

last of November and the first half of December.   There
were ten days of such dense fog that one standing on the
sidewalk of the avenue, would hear the roll of the interminable procession of army wagons thundering over the
cobble stones, but get no glimpse of even the outline of
the huge canvas-covered vehicles.

Then came weeks of sun-lit days and moon- and star-
lit nights, fittest weather for a winter campaign.   Surely
McClellan would move to-morrow, and more to-morrows.
We know that we had daily dress parades, and grand re-
views, and we heard rumors of his snubbing the President.   Some of us went to his wide, well-appointed
camps and saw how the soldiers lived, and thought if we
found a family thus living, apparently in want and ex-
posure, we should carry them food, and take them to
better shelter, so new and so rude was it all to us.

That, too, was the season of presenting flags and swords
with speeches.'

A Pennsylvania regiment was to be presented with a
flag or a brigadier with a golden scabbarded dress sword,
and Senator Gowan of that State was to make a speech.
He took the Johnson slide later.   I had made his
acquaintance and been asked to join the party.   N. P.
Willis, then a correspondent of his home journal, and
living in Washington, also went with us, and others.   It
was new and interesting, all but the festival at headquarters, which lasted some hours, and which was dull to a
man who could neither eat nor drink.

That was also the winter of brigadier-generals in Washington.   A man received an appointment; he hastened
to thank the President, show his bullion and uniform, go
to Brady's or Ulke's gallery and have a lot of photographs

---

¹ A young man of our Grays had reached a deserved commission, and
Henry Slade and Will Champion, Cleveland boys, wished me to present him
with a sword.   I compromised—I paid for the sword, and they went out
and presented it in a blaze of glory and adjectives.

taken in various attitudes for his lady friends. McDougal in the Senate told of an incident near the Willard—a man shied a rock at a barking dog; it glanced and struck two brigadiers. Another which was eagerly vouched for—a newsboy, cried: "Sto-a-r! Full account of a great battle!" A non-combatant in stars eagerly clutched a paper, ran it over, and returned it with—" Here, boy, I don't see any battle!" "No and *you never will!*" was the response.

Among the first acts of Secretary Stanton was an order that freed the Capital of these *ill-starred* gentlemen in buttons. The unassigned were ordered to report to some general for duty, as might be directed.

In the loose working of the scarcely formulated military machinery, by which 700,000 or 800,000 citizens were being turned into a soldiery, and the raw article transported to the various points through and to the camps near Washington, there were constantly in and about the city thousands of these young fellows in blue, who found themselves *shucked* out of their proper places, and left without transportation or means of sustenance; in which stress they were certain to apply to a Member of Congress from their district or State. Such men were constantly sent to me, and the caring for them, getting transportation and subsistence, took all a man's time and all his change, until a provost marshal and finally a military governor for the District were appointed. Then the rapidly extemporized hospitals were filled with the sick. It was astonishing how many in camp, or garrisoning the newly constructed fortifications—earthworks—about the city became ill. The statistics of the war showing this feature of the service are almost appalling. The sick were to be visited, and furnished, among other things with franked envelopes, till I found mine were making their way to drinking places. The great sanitary associations, which became not the least striking, and next to the armies in the field, the most important volunteer adjuncts of the war, were then in embryo.

These sudden convulsions, the shaking up and attempted disruption of the political compact, this eternal drum-beat, bugle calls, and marchings of regiments, with the startling headlines of the press, the rumors of battle, blood, flight, and disaster, had a disturbing influence on the visionary and weak-minded. Many of these had calls to rush to the Capital to warn, to counsel, or to take the helm and rule. I remember several of the prophetic order, and more than one who had been commissioned to place himself at the head. Luckily no fanatic of the bravo stripe then appeared.

The form of one of the religious class, lingers with distinctness in my memory,—particularly an instance of his appearance on the street. One day at early twilight I observed a broad, tall figure, draped in a long flowing garment, head uncovered, and showing masses of long black hair, moving along the street with slow and solemn stride. Suddenly as if a message came to him, he stopped, threw back his head, and casting his deep, cavernous eyes upward, he extended his elevated hands imploringly, and in a deep, solemn voice of far-reaching power, broke forth into one of the most moving invocations that ever met my ear. The street was empty and silent, and this strange figure, bare-headed, with long girded robe, seemed a newly arrived prophet from the land of the East, who had come to invoke and warn, and such in spirit he was. God was specially implored to arouse and call his chosen to come forth sandalled and girded for a long dark pilgrimage, through a desert wilderness of blood and havoc. Three or four minutes' invocation continued, then he subsided, moved on a few yards, and broke forth again. I confess that the impression was weird and uncanny. I saw him after that and heard of him several times. Yet to me he remained the same solemn mystery as on that lonely night. He was sent to invoke—to warn.

Another of the same sort had the usual trouble of his class: to get hold—to get the reins. I had observed about the White House a rather undersized man of active habits, some thirty-five years of age, seeming to have no especial errand there, who went about watching the faces of men, and listening to what they said with lively curiosity. I had also seen him about the Capitol, moving around the hall in the morning before the House opened. Once or twice he managed to remain in until after prayer, and was then hustled out. He seemed to know no one— a harmless, moon-struck young man, country-grown, neatly clad in a home-made suit of light brown. In the morning, when I could escape the soldiers and departments—(it is amazing the things a Member of Congress is asked to do, from soliciting an office to selling a patent right), I would hurry to the House; on my desk there was always an arrear of the unanswered, but—and no matter what happened—the inevitable daily letter to the dear ones at home was despatched,—the only absolutely certain thing of the day. One morning after I had seated myself, this specially-commissioned young man came in, an unusual look of resolve on his meaningless face. Seeing me alone he approached, and casting quick glances about, hesitated a moment, and then said : "You are one of the Congress fellers, aint you?" "What makes you think so?" was my response. "Wal—you are a-sittin' in one o' the seats, 'n I 've seen you 'round talkin' and actin' like one on 'em." "Well, if you won't tell *on* me," was my hesitating answer—"No—no! I won't tell. I should n't think you 'd want to have it git out. I won't tell on ye." "Well, then, I am one o' the Congress fellers." "Wal,"—brightening—"you 're one o' the very ones to help me," he replied, earnestly and assuringly. "What is it?" I asked. "Wal, you see," (stooping near me, and in a confidential tone)—"ye see I 'm sent here to take things in hand—ye see ; an' put 'em right—ye understand?" "Well," asked I, "why don't you take right hold? It needs somebody, the Lord knows!" "Yis, but somehow I can't seem t' git hold. Can't git agoin'; an' you fellers must help me, ye see." "Well, who sent you?" "God!"—solemnly. "O-o-o! He did? Well, see here—we don't have anything to do with Him. The American Congress never has had any helpers. Beside, God don't like interlopers, you know. Are you sure He sent you?" "Oh, sure as I live!" was the firm reply. "As He used to send prophets?" "Exactly, that 's it—in the Old Testament times." "Well, don't you know that when He sent a man, He always opened the way, provided the means? His man always knew how to *get hold*. If I were you, I should go right back for instructions." This was a new idea. He stood dazed and confused. Seeing a group of the House and others, who had come in, near the clerk's desk, I took him down to them, and in a solemn way told them of his mission, and asked them to see what could be done. I saw him about for some time after that, waiting, perhaps, for instructions. He was not a solitary instance. No one, not even reporters, had time to preserve in the history of the stirring events of the time the memory of these harmless flies.

CHAPTER XIV.

THE HOLIDAYS.

DECEMBER, 1861—JANUARY, 1862.

No Adjournment of Congress—A Quorum Presumed—Return to Cleveland—Governor Morton of Indiana.

WITH sharp debates, and new bills referred, with races to the departments, and some sight-showing to visitors December 30th arrived. Congress usually took eight or ten days for the holidays. We tried to work right through, but found ourselves in the House without a quorum, in which situation our arrangement was made that no call of either House should be had, and that both should continue to sit, with the understanding that quorums be *present* on Monday, January 6th. We felt this to be leave to go. I did not resolve to depart till the eve of the 31st.

How eagerly we then hied to the railroad station in the belated next dawn! What weary delays all the way! We reached Pittsburg about 1 A.M. of Sunday, and must stay there twenty-four hours. At the Monongahela House I made the acquaintance of Governor Oliver P. Morton, who had fortunately been elected Lieutenant-Governor of Indiana, with Henry S. Lane for Governor. Fortunately again, Lane was elected to the Senate, and so young Morton, full of brain, blood, brawn, and courage,

6   81

went to the lead of the copper-headed, golden-circled Indiana. The next election gave the Democrats a majority in the Legislature ; they refused to receive a message from Morton, and were about to take the command of the militia from him, when the Republicans of the body withdrew. Morton reigned without an appropriation, and Secretary Stanton advanced funds as he needed. He recruited soldiers in Kentucky, and permitted Union men of Kentucky to raise soldiers in his own southern counties and thus preserved Kentucky, in some measure at least, for the Union cause. All this was in the next few months, as he was not sworn as Governor till January 16th. Thus two men in those times, with their eager, intense patriotism, thrown into one room at the Monongahela, were made warm friends and old *acquaintances when late next day they left on different trains for home.*[1]

Henry Slade purveyed my quarters in Washington for that winter. I boarded at Joy's, corner of the avenue and 9th Street, N. W., my rooms being across 9th Street, nearly opposite. A day or two after taking possession, a man of ordinary height and figure, plainly clad, with nothing striking in look or manner, came in, and without naming himself, expressed in a few well spoken words very warm thanks for the great service I had rendered him. He said that he had been very desirous of a position, but had had no friends of influence who could approach the President to ask for it ; I was taken aback. With a flash of memory over a wide field of recent solicitation for places, no such man who should render such thanks arose to view. It was too embarrassing to say to

---

[1] Another acquaintance to be recalled. Up to that time Herbert Spencer was little more than a name to me or to anybody else on this continent. I had seen the notices of his first book : *Conditions of Human Happiness.* A gentleman at the Monongahela House had the volume, which he loaned me, and I found time to take a very deep plunge into it. What an exquisite find !

such expressions of gratitude that I did not know the
speaker—I could not ask the name, I could not presume
to not know the man receiving such benefaction from my
hand.   He was a gentleman of culture and pleasant address, and knew to whom he thus expressed himself,
therefore *he* was not mistaken.   I properly disclaimed
any title to special thanks, saying that in such times I was
only anxious to secure the best available man to the public service, without reference to parties, or a desire to advance personal friends.   With some discursive talk of the
condition of things, he took leave.   I knew from his first
words that he was a man of mark and a decided and well
known Democrat, and one known not to sympathize with
the Administration.   The thing puzzled me till Slade
came in.
   " So *General Morgan* called ? " said he.   " The d——!
So that was Morgan ?   Then our interview is explained."
"Oh! so you did   not   know him?"   "WHY, no!
Thunder !   I had the idea of a blazing hero, and here was
a modest, quiet, bookish man, rather than the famous
leader of the charge at Cherubusco.   I knew he had been
at West Point, but——"   " Well," returned Slade, laugh-
ing, " he was as disappointed in your appearance.   He
thought the man who won Wade and Sherman, Vallandigham and Sam Cox to recommend him to Lincoln as general in this war, must not only have great persuasive
power, but have also personal height and weight and
dignity."
   On my return to duty in the House, that which in time
of peace would be called " the gay world "—society—was
beginning to show animation.   In that day more depended
on the White House and Cabinet than now.   It was the
winter of the reign of the Chevalier Wykoff in Court
circles, and of the *Gipsey-Lay* at the Canterbury Theatre.
Speaker Grow began his receptions, and the leading ladies
took or resumed their days.   I boarded with the Fentons of

New York, and we were soon on pleasant terms. Mrs. Fenton was an elegant, stately woman, who kindly gave me countenance socially, and I was surprised to find how utterly unceremonious, informal, and accessible the best society official and otherwise was.

Almost the first thing of the new year in Congress was the expulsion of the two Missouri Senators, Johnson and Polk. They went out on the same day, and each by the unanimous vote of 36 to 0. They were succeeded by John B. Henderson and Robert Wilson. Henderson was a large gain, a peer of the noblest and most heroic of that Senate. Jesse D. Bright lingered in the Senate till February 5th, and "seemed loth to depart." He escaped the first bolt, to fall by the lance of the youthful Wilkinson of Minnesota. The vote on expulsion was 32 to 14. Among the nays were Cowan, Carlile, Harris, and Ten Eyck. There was thought to be a paucity of evidence, the sole thing offered against him being a letter "To his Excellency, Jefferson Davis, *President of the Confederate States,*" strongly recommending a friend who desired to *sell an improved arm.* Jesse might have been put out on "the Common Counts"—as lawyers say.

CHAPTER XV.

THE LEHMAN AND UPTON CASES.

JANUARY, 1862.

Important Questions Involved—Can an Election be Declared Void for a Paucity of Votes?—The Effect of the War on an Election in Virginia.

THE House had to settle seats under contest, two of which attracted much attention. The first was a Pennsylvania case, *Butler vs. Lehman*, and came up in January. Lehman, a slight, nervous German, a Democrat, a lawyer, held the certificate of election, and was the sitting member. Butler was a *Tammany*-like Republican boss of Philadelphia. The whole Republican delegation were strongly interested, the House being three to one Republican. The Committee of Elections were Dawes, Campbell, and Kelley of Pennsylvania, McKean, Loomis, Baxter, Worcester, Voorhees, and Menzies, two Democrats to seven Republicans. My colleague, Worcester, who brought the case with the evidence to my notice, was a fairly good lawyer, but he was timid, and doubted himself. To me it presented a deliberate attempt, by fraud, forgery, and perjury, to steal a seat. I urged him to unite with Menzies and Voorhees in a minority report, which he consented to do if I would stand by him on the floor and take the case off his hands.

Loomis opened the case for Butler. By his statement Lehman had a seeming majority of 132. Some time

after the result was declared, an alleged error was detected, and under the Pennsylvania law a recount of the
ballots was had.   The recount showed, as contended, that
in three boxes, containing ballots from nine polling places,
172 votes cast for Butler had been counted for Lehman.
The identity of the three boxes, as was contended, had
not at the recount been questioned by Lehman.   The
testimony, it was admitted, showed much looseness in the
care of the boxes, but it was claimed that the ballots coincided with the poll books.

Mr. Worcester followed Loomis in support of his report—ineffectively, as was felt by the House, and he was
cut off by the hour rule.[1]

Mr. Riddle followed Worcester.   It was a case for a lawyer personally free to appear on the right side, and stimulated by being in opposition to his party.   Mr. Riddle's
first words advised the House that he was against the majority report, at which Crittenden, Wickliff, Menzies, and
other Democrats passed over and secured seats near him.

He confined himself to two points.   Butler's case depended on his establishing the identity of the three boxes
with those admitted to have been used at the polls, and
proof of the identity of the ballots found in them as those
cast by the electors.   The boxes were in the loose custody of loose aldermen.   Each was found with an assort-
ment of about twenty boxes, to which any man could gain
access, no one of which bore any prescribed or other mark
of identity.   The Pennsylvania law authorized a recount,
but did not prescribe any rules or care for the preservation of the ballots.   The important, all-controlling evidence, were the ballots themselves.   They fell under the
ordinary rule and their execution was first to be estab-

---

[1] Worcester, a brother of the lexicographer, was angularly made up ; a
man of culture, his faculties all seemed to act independently of each other.
The same peculiarity was noticed in his physical frame ; his hands seemed
to be doing different things, and his feet trying to walk different ways.

lished before they could be considered.   Mr. Riddle read
from the majority report, which contended that *the identity of a box was established by its contents.*

MR. DAWES.—" In each box was found a sealed certificate of the names,
together with oaths of the sworn officers who conducted the poll in a particular precinct.   What more can be required to trace it right to the precinct ? "
    MR. RIDDLE.—" Do you prove the identity of the box by its contents ?
Even if you hold these certificates proven, does that establish the validity of
every loose slip of paper found in the same box?   I am speaking of the
ballots alone."
    MR. DAWES.—" Now will the gentleman tell us what he means by proving
the execution of ballots ?"
    MR. RIDDLE.—" In effect, there are many ways of proving the execution
of a paper.   It is not necessary to prove a signature, nor yet that there be
one ; a man finds a printed paper fitted to his use and uses it—that is his
execution of it.   A voter took one of these ballots prepared for him by men
who thus became his agents, and he delivered it as his ballot into hands
qualified by law to receive it.   That is his execution, his delivery of it.
Prove this, and the gentleman proves his case.   It is direct evidence.   Failing this, Butler's advocates resort to indirect, yet legal methods.   Do not
let the House be misled.   The ballots are the potent things.   The boxes
themselves are so many soulless shells, having no significance, though a
thousand times identified.   That is but one, a remote step in proof.   The
gentleman may show where these ballots, here produced, came from.   They
do show that they were found in certain boxes, in the care of certain Aldermen.   They open them and find in them certain slips of paper, some with
the name of Butler, and others with Lehman's name on them, and *without
a shadow of proof*, these are assumed to be *the ballots* actually cast for the
gentlemen at the election, and being such ballots, and found in these three
boxes, their presence in the boxes proves that the depositories *were the
boxes*, and the identity of the boxes being thus established, they obligingly
turn about and prove that the ballots found in them were the *identical votes*
cast by the voters.   Was there ever anything so logical, conclusive, and satisfactory !   Beyond this, nothing."

This was all the proof on that point, and a few pertinent
words put this matter beyond reply.
    Turning to another equally important proposition, that
these 172 votes were erroneously counted for Lehman,
when they were cast for Butler, he proceeded, according
to the *Globe*:

"A single word further on another proposition. I understand that it is not urged here by the gentlemen who represent the majority of the committee, that there is any proof implicating in fraud the parties who made these blunders, to call them by the softest name. But they say that the whole thing is to be accounted for, and that we are bound to presume there was a series of mistakes on the part of the election judges. Well, sir, in this blundering world a good deal may be charged to the account of mere accident; but when we are asked to presume that 172 independent and distinct blunders have all happened in this one case, then I say that gentlemen are indeed challenging the credulity of the House. They say that each and every one of these ballots were miscounted through mistake ; and when you come to aggregate this amazing accumulation of mistakes, you find that they reach the round sum of 172. Committed by whom ? By a single individual ? Not at all. Committed by two, three, four, six, eight, ten, or a dozen ? No. The proof is that it implicates just exactly ninety. Ninety gentlemen have thus, by a singular and general assembly of blunders, conspired through mere accident to commit this mistake, not once, but 172 distinct times. I say, sir, that the thing is too staggering. It is not to be accounted for upon any hypotheses that control the mistakes and blunders of men.

"And more than that (and here comes the most remarkable and singular feature of the most strange chapter of human mistakes and blunders), every one of them was made on one side. Singular and startling as it may seem, every mistake was made against the contestant. I say, that such an amazing feature running through this startling chapter of accidents is too much for human credulity. It cannot be accounted for upon any such hypothesis as the majority of the Committee of Elections present. If there had been a single mistake ; if there had been a single blunder, or if there had been a series of mistakes made by a single man, or pertaining to a single ward ; if there was such uncertainty as to leave the question quivering in the balance. we might charitably suppose an accident might account for the difference. But, sir, there is no process of reasoning which will tolerate our belief in such an accumulation of overwhelming systematic blunders and accidents, all in one direction, all conspiring to produce one result, without one mistake happening the other way. The only possible hypothesis by which it can be accounted for is, that this most remarkable series of mistakes happened by design—to wit, some ingenious hand took from these three boxes 172 of the votes cast for Lehman, and replaced them with 172 ballots for Butler not cast at all." [1]

---

[1] While speaking I noticed standing near and before me in the alley leading down toward the Speaker, a small wiry man facing me, evidently greatly moved, with tears unheeded streaming down his face, his body rising and sinking at the knees with the rise and fall of my sentences and voice. It was Lehman, whom I had never before seen.

McKean and Campbell (Speaker Grow had placed two of his colleagues, Campbell and Kelley, on the committee) followed at considerable length and with much warmth for Butler, and Menzies replied for the minority. The argument by these three gentlemen of the committee was conducted with ability and fairness, Menzies being the only Democrat who spoke on the case. The House ordered the vote to be taken at one P.M. the next day.

The vote was taken by yeas and nays, and Lehman retained his seat by 77 to 67 for Butler. This decision, under the conditions of the House, has always been regarded as remarkable.

Lehman proved himself to be as true a Union man as the House held.

The case of Charles P. Upton of Virginia is in many respects the most interesting in the annals of the House, and was one of the best discussed ; the decision on it was never very satisfactory to the constitutional lawyers of the House. As has been stated, Virginia took herself into the Confederacy by an ordinance passed on April 17, 1861. By the law of the State, elections for representatives in the Congress of the United States fell on the fourth Thursday (23d) of May. Upton's district was the 7th, the Alexandria District. There were at the time no organized rebel soldiery in this district, but the utmost disorder everywhere existed, and armed men were going about, and constant dread and excitement were prevalent. The election was generally everywhere disregarded. On the day designated, a poll was opened at Ball's Cross Roads, Alexandria County, by the proper officers (though a question was raised that they were not sworn), at which ten votes by qualified electors were cast for Upton, there being some showing of a few cast at other points in the District. At the extra session of July 4th, Upton, with such credentials as he could, under the existing conditions, secure, presented himself, had his name enrolled by the clerk of the 36th Congress,[1] who, as stated, organized the House. When his name was reached, objection was made to his being sworn; the matter was discussed, laid over, called up, more debate was had, and he was sworn. It was not a case of contest, but, as was later claimed, his ultimate right was thus passed upon and settled in his favor. It will be remembered that in Western Virginia, at Wheeling, a solemnly called convention of the people, by exercise of the inherent " reserved " rights of men as citizens, undertook to provide for the anarchic state in which they were left, by repudiating secession.

Among other things, by ordinance of August 20th, they authorized elections for Congress in districts which had failed to elect on the designated day. Under a proclamation *our* Governor Pierpont of Virginia issued for the election of Representatives in our Congress, polls were opened in Alexandria, the extent of his admitted jurisdiction, at which J. Ferguson Beach, a distinguished lawyer and eminent man, was voted for. He memorialized the House, and was admitted to *contest* Upton's seat. The House gave no further attention to his claim, but on the 30th of January, 1862, the committee reported that Upton was not entitled to a seat.

Mr. Upton and his friends asked me to examine his case, and if I should conclude that he was entitled to his seat, requested that I should address the House, and take that charge of it on the floor, as a member does of a bill committed to his hands.

It was claimed against him that he was not a citizen of Virginia, and that he had received no votes at an election under the Virginia laws. The former statement made no figure in the debate or in the judgment of the House. Mr. Worcester opened the argument of the case against

---

[1] For many years it has been the usage for the clerk of the last House to organize the House of the next ensuing Congress.

him.   I give from the *Globe* his statement of the status
of the 7th District on the day of election.

" The revolutionary condition of that part of Virginia where this district
is located was brought into question both by the memorial of the contestant and the answer by the sitting member.   The committee have endeav-
ored to ascertain as far as possible the facts which could be shown to have
existed to prevent or obstruct the election in this Congressional district in
the month of May last, as alleged by the contestant.   It appears from the
current history of events that a revolutionary convention, called in the State
of Virginia in the month of February, 1861, adopted what was called an
ordinance of secession.   That ordinance, in terms, repealed the ratification of the Constitution of the United States by the State of Virginia,
and resumed to the State all the rights and powers granted by that ratification.   Immediately thereafter the State of Virginia claimed to be independent, and the secession convention passed another ordinance recognizing
the independence of the confederated States.   During the month of April
of the same year, and not long after the passage of the ordinance of secession, the State of Virginia became, by the act of its convention and its Executive, a member of the Southern Confederacy. ˉ On the 24th of April of
that year, an ordinance, was passed suspending the election of members of
Congress, which ought to have taken place on the following 23d of May.   It
was provided by the law of Virginia passed in 1853, that the election of
Congress should take place at the time I have named.   The question to be
considered by the committee was the effect of that ordinance of secession
and the subsequent ordinance of the convention upon this Congressional
district.

" It made the duty of each State under the Constitution of the United
States to pass laws fixing the time, place, and manner of holding elections
for members of Congress.   The Constitution in that respect is mandatory
upon each State.   If a State has adopted a law regulating the election of
members of Congress, that law may be repealed by the same power that has
enacted it.   The convention of Virginia claimed to exercise in what it did
the powers of Legislature.   Its acts and its ordinances were received, respected, obeyed, and had the force of laws in all that portion of Virginia
east of the Blue Ridge.   All the executive officers of the State, from the
governor down to the constable, lent their aid to enforce these ordinances.
From what the committee can understand, it appears that, at the time referred to, the law for the election of members of Congress was not only in
terms suspended by the convention, but the election officers were suspended.
There were, therefore, no officers who could execute it.

" The Committee of Elections fully admit that all of these acts of that
convention were revolutionary ; that they were usurpations ; that the
people of the eastern portion of Virginia were neither legally nor morally

bound to obey them. The very usurpation, however, implies that the party
who usurps has the control and the possession of the rights and powers which
he has usurped. The question is simply one of fact, not whether it may
have been legally right for the people of the eastern portion of Virginia to
elect a member of Congress in the month of May last, but whether it was
legally, physically possible for them to do so. But the sitting member
claims, and he must claim in order to support his case, that this elective
law of 1853 was not only in force, but that he was elected in all respects in
pursuance of that law. The Constitution of the United States prescribes
the qualifications of a person entitled to a seat as a member of this House."

The argument took the ground, that the law was to be
as strictly pursued in the case, as would be required in an
ordinary healthy time of peace and reign of law, and the
claimant must present the governor's certificate, on due
return, and all the statutory requirements must be observed. This, as was argued, nullified any election or
ballots cast.

MR. RIDDLE contended that "the record showed that the House had
the case and the facts before it at the called session and passed upon them,
and it received Mr. Upton and had him sworn. Thus he is shown by the
Globe to have met the requirements. The sitting member was sworn in
after the attention of the House had been called to his position as a claimant
and when there was no adverse claim upon the floor. The fifth section of
the article of the Constitution provides that each House shall be the judge
of the election return and qualifications of its members, and shall exercise to
that extent, of course, judicial functions, and I suppose that when they have
exercised that function in a given case, they have used it up, so far as that
case is concerned. I am not aware that any provision of the Constitution,
nor any law of Congress, nor any usage of this House permits it to undertake to reconsider or review its own decision. I have never heard of such
a thing, and the effect of the administration of the oath upon this gentleman
was to make him conclusively and *bona fide* as much a member of this House
as any gentleman who occupies a seat in it, and, in my judgment, he can
only be got rid of by the same means as by which other members can be
excluded.

" Now, sir, in some cases a man comes here with only a *prima facie* case :
he is to some extent paired off with another claimant ; the House finds upon
hasty consideration that he has a claim which entitles him to receive the
oath, and in such a case it is expressly or impliedly understood, from the
fact that there is a contestant, that the case is not conclusively settled. But
I submit to the judicial consideration of the House, that when a man comes

here and claims a seat to which there is no contestant (and especially in a case where an objection is raised, and the House considers it and votes it down, and then administers the oath to him as it is administered to others), that the function of judging the qualifications and the election of that man has been exercised ; and that there is no power by which the decision may be reconsidered, unless you can charge upon the sitting members some act of fraud. There is but one other function, so far as he is concerned, which the House can exercise if they wish to vacate his seat, and that is by a motion or resolution for his expulsion, on proper cause made,—a motion which requires a two-thirds vote.

"Subsequently, on a later day in the last session, as was said by the gentleman in his opening, the question of the eligibility of this gentleman to his seat and the regularity of his election was referred to the Committee of Elections, whether for the purpose of reconsidering his admission or of predicating a resolution for his expulsion, we are not informed by the resolution itself. The committee, not quite content with reporting on this eligibility and the regularity of his election, reported, after finding that he was eligible, that he was not entitled to a seat in this House. Now, I submit that even if a majority of the House should find that he was not entitled to his seat, that would not, for reasons already stated, vacate the seat unless the majority rose to two thirds.

"Before calling attention to the report and some of its reasonings, I wish to say a word or two in regard to some very important principles that seem to me to lie a little below the ground occupied by the committee in its report. The great primal law, so to speak, which lies at the foundation of all American politics—to wit, the right of the people to govern themselves, finds its expression in this other equally primary law, that they shall so govern by their representatives. It therefore becomes of the gravest consequence that this right of expressing their preference or declaring their choice for representatives who shall carry forward the process of government, shall be by the amplest means secured to the people. This is the thing to be accomplished. All the various laws of the United States or of the several States regulating elections, are but the means employed to insure to the people the exercise of their right of choice, and to permit them, through constitutional and legal forms, to express that choice. Every presumption of fact, every intendment of law, and every construction of law and of fact are to be in favor of giving effect to this voice of the people in a given case, and can never be used to defeat it. The purpose and object to be arrived at is, What did the people wish? For the purpose of ascertaining that, we pay little respect to broad seals ; we pry them up. We do not pay much attention to enactments ; we cleave whole volumes of them asunder, so that we may arrive at the wish of the people, as it resides in them, pure as light is said to reside in the diamond. It is a defeat of the primary, as well as of the paramount, object of these various election laws, to use them, or permit them to be used, to prevent the purpose and object of the people. Wherever, whenever, and however it can be ascertained, that under the form sand color of law, a people have expressed their wish for a Representative in a given case, that wish must have effect given to it. I believe there can be no exception whatever to this rule, and that there never was.

" Now here is a Congressional district, called the 7th District of the State of Virginia. All its multiplied and various interests are to be represented on this floor. Its territory, which is a portion of the United States, the eminent domain of a variety of interests (interests of property, interests geographical and commercial, and all other, before you reach the ultimate, greatest, and last interest—the interest of the people themselves), which are to find expression and representation on this floor, or are to be denied. One would suppose that the theory was that the right of self-government, if it is to be exercised by Representatives, would carry with it the right of universal suffrage. That is not the American rule. The Constitution has left to the State authorities the right to designate who, in a congressional district having perhaps one hundred thousand inhabitants, shall give expression to their will in the selection of a Representative. It is said here by this committee that in the 7th District of Virginia this choice is to be expressed by about six thousand or eight thousand—not one tenth, nor more than one twelfth of the inhabitants. These voters are not the only persons interested in this thing. They are but the agents of the inhabitants to express their wish in a given instance, to put them in official relations with the General Government. When they have exercised that function—the voting for a Representative in Congress —they sink back again into the great mass of the constituency. They have no interest independent of that of everybody else. They are in no sense to be considered constituents in contradistinction to all the other inhabitants of their congressional district. They are the agents on the part of the people, and the agents on the part of the General Government, to put the particular congressional district in official relations with the General Government in all its various territorial, commercial, geographical, and other interests.

" Now, sir, has any law of the Congress of the United States enforced this duty on these official agents ? Does it enjoin that they shall do it ? Does it impose on them any penalty if they fail to do it ? Does any law of the State of Virginia impose this duty on them, any disability if they disregard it ? Have the people of a given congressional district any constitutional or legal power to coerce or enforce this discharge of official duty on the part of these agents, save only the sometimes strong, sometimes weak force of public opinion? None at all. Does the law of Congress or the Constitution of the United States require that all or any specified part of these official agents shall unite to express the will of the people ? Not at all. Is there any law of the State of Virginia which requires for the election of a member of Congress the concurrent action of one half, two thirds, three fourths, or of any other number? Not at all. What is the legal and constitutional conclusion from these premises ? Why, that any number, from one to ten thousand, who shall, in accordance with, and under color of the law of the State, in proper time and manner, deposit one vote or the whole number of votes for a given candidate, are entitled to have effect given to their will. Does the Constitution or any law provide that in case of an invasion of territory, or in case of an insurrection involving the majority of the inhabitants, this right to express the will of the people in the choice of their representative shall not take effect? Not at all. There is no qualification or condition of any sort appended to this right. It is complete, wholly unqualified, and unconditional.

" This gives additional strength and support to the conclusion at which I have just arrived—to wit, that any number of electors who shall attempt, in good faith and under color and form of law, to give utterance and expression to the will of the people, and shall so utter and express it, may be sufficient to exercise that power. They are agents, trustees of a power, coupled, to be sure, with an interest, but with no interest independent of the interest of all the other inhabitants of the district. It would be intolerable to admit any other rule. It seems to me, without the least disrespect to these gentlemen, that, somehow or other, if they have not found the water here too deep for them, they have found it too turbid and chilly for them to venture over it. It would almost seem as if they contented themselves with making a few incoherent excuses for not attempting the passage. It seems as if the able and distinguished lawyers who constitute the Committee of Elections brought to the adjudication of these great questions, too narrow and too technical rules, that are perhaps safe and prudent in cases of assault and battery, or in matters of book accounts, but which utterly fail, in my judgment, to measure the everlasting questions of right and wrong, as they lie hidden beneath your Constitution, and which alone give it validity and sanction.

" The question is not whether a majority or two thirds or three quarters of the qualified voters of the district actually expressed their choice ; the question is whether *any* of the qualified voters of the district attended on behalf of the people under color of law and *did* exercise the elective franchise upon the day named in the unrepealed law of the State of Virginia. If so, I insist upon it that this House must give effect to that election.

"It is conceded that the 23d of May, 1861, was the day designated by the laws of the State of Virginia for the election of members of Congress. It is conceded that on the day of the election an election was holden at the precinct of Ball's Cross Roads. It is in proof that the State authorities did formally at that place open an election for a member of Congress.

" But I am met right here with what is considered a very grave and fatal objection. It is said, although there was a law opening this poll, and although the formalities of that law were complied with in almost all respects, so far as the opening of the polls was concerned, yet the one most important element was wanting—to wit, that the conductors of that election were not sworn to open and conduct an election for a member of Congress. Is that to be allowed to disfranchise the voter? Was that his fault? Was he presumed to even know whether they had or had not been sworn ? And if he had known it, what remedy had he ? Is it to be used to defeat him of his right of choice ? He stands there a Virginia citizen. He stands there in the face of this abominable treason. He stands there with the solid earth shaking under him, and he cannot shrink behind the privacy of the ballot. He declares with loud voice, amid the opposing elements, that he votes for Charles H. Upton, for Representative in Congress. Was he a qualified elector ? There is no question made of that. There was no oath required of him. He executed the formalities under color and pursuant of the law of the State, passed in pursuance of the Constitution of the United States, and you cannot permit the technical disqualifications of any officer of that elec- tion to rob him of his right. You cannot disfranchise his district. You cannot alienate the territory. You cannot throw out by your action, with- out the right of being heard, the thousands and thousands of inhabitants who are, under the Constitution and the laws, presumed to be loyal to the Government.

" It is idle to stand here and say to me that there was not a proper return made. A majority of this same committee reported against a sitting mem- ber and for a contestant deliberately in the face of the certificate of all the returning officers. You disregarded the forms of law. You went back to the sanctuary which was said to be the depository of the ballots. You broke it open, rummaged and counted them.

" Why ? Because you wanted the clearly expressed will of the people as they actually spoke, and not as they had been made to speak."

After reciting the evidence, Mr. Riddle proceeded :

" These were the witnesses before them, and the committee were the in- quirers. They have reported these facts, but they say that the proof does not rise to the full formality which would be required for the admissibility of testimony on the part of this plaintiff or sitting member. *They* took the affirmative. This copy of the poll-book is produced, and the officers are produced, who swear that the polls were opened. No question is made about the identity or the correctness of that poll-book. It is not said by the committee that it is not a copy of a poll-book. It is not said that those votes were not cast as represented ; but it is said, to the shame and con- fusion of the committee, I submit, in view of their solemn duties, that this plaintiff has not yet produced the full measure of proof that the votes were cast. There is not a man living who will read that report who will not come to the conclusion, unshaken by the presence of a doubt, that these votes were so cast as claimed.

" But these gentlemen, not quite content with the resolution which they have reported to us, have added a sort of drizzling after-birth. They query, even if the ten votes were given, whether the paucity of votes would not defeat the election, but do not claim that it would. They say that it was not generally known in the district that Charles H. Upton was a candidate for Congress on that occasion. Admit that it was not. In Virginia a plurality elects. Suppose that you had a thousand candidates, and that nine hundred and ninety-nine of them received ten votes each, and the thousandth received eleven, would the gentlemen stand here and contend that the man with the eleven votes was not regularly elected, even though it was not generally known that he was a candidate? To sustain the validity of the election supposed, is there any more force to be given to the votes which were cast against the man who received the eleven than there would have been if they had been withheld? Does voting against a man contribute more to his election than not voting at all?

"Mr. Speaker, I have said all that I care to say. I submit, in the first place, that by the record the sitting member is entitled to his seat,—conclusively so. I say that he is only to be excluded by a vote expelling him, which requires two thirds of the House. I say, beyond that, that the conclusion is inevitable from the facts, that he was legally and constitutionally elected. I hope, therefore, that the resolution reported by the committee will be rejected. Whether any of the qualified voters of the district attended on behalf of the people under cover of law and did exercise the elective franchise upon the day named in the unrepealed law of the State of Virginia, is the question. If so, I insist upon it that this House must give effect to that election.

"It is conceded that the 23d of May, 1861, was the day designated by the laws of the State of Virginia for the election of members of Congress. It is conceded that the State of Virginia could not and did not secede from the Union so as to have the least legal or constitutional effect upon any of the citizens of that State. It is conceded that on the day of the election an election was holden at the precinct of Ball's Cross Roads. It is in proof that the State authorities did formally at that place open an election for a member of Congress. . . ."

Mr. Sheffield, an able lawyer, succeeded him for the committee. Among other things he said :

"An election implies a free choice ; the district must submit to the Constitution and laws, either voluntarily or by force of our armies, before they can be entitled to be represented here. If we undertake to permit a representation of a part of a district, what part are we to take? Can any man who can stand upon twelve inches square of ground in the district, and who is a loyal man, and who says that he represents the district, be admitted? Or, if not twelve inches, how much ?

"You may say that it is hard upon the loyal men of a district that they should suffer in consequence of the disloyalty of certain persons in that dis-

7

trict, but it is inseparable from all human institutions and affairs that the innocent shall suffer with the guilty. The innocent child suffers with the convicted father. The innocent kinsman suffers with the guilty kinsman. Under the old common law the crimes of the individual, unless the hundred purged itself, were visited upon the hundred. The inhabitants were to maintain order within the hundred and protect the rights of the people and of the public ; and if they did not, the crime was upon the hundred. And it is not for us to say that there was not some justice in it. In what part of the district do the loyal people of the district reside ? How are we to decide that question ? How is it to be determined that there were not as loyal people in other parts of the 7th District of Virginia as those ten that met at Ball's Cross Roads ? There are as true and loyal men all through the South to-day, who are overborne in disloyal neighborhoods, as there are upon this floor or anywhere in the country. There are to-day in the State of South Carolina as true and loyal men, and men as devoted to the old Constitution and the old flag, as there are anywhere in this country. These men need our sympathy, and the same claim upon our justice, as the men who held this informal election at Ball's Cross Roads. But it is impossible in human affairs to administer exact justice. All human institutions and all human actions partake of the imperfections incident to the human character.

" Now it seems to me that the only principle which we can adopt in regard to this matter is to require that a whole district shall be subjected to the law and Constitution before it shall be entitled to be represented upon this floor. Policy dictates it as well as right principle. We must inspire the ambitious men in every district, if we can, to assist in putting down this rebellion, to assist with their friends, and thereby to make a claim upon the loyalty of their districts to entitle them to the consideration of being selected by their loyal friends to represent them in the Congress of the nation. I say, then, that policy coincides with what seems to me to be the justice of the matter."

Mr. Sedgwick made an able argument, sustaining Mr. Riddle's positions.

Charles Delano spoke at length and forcibly on the same side, as did Mr. Harrison of Ohio, one of the most accomplished of the many good lawyers of the House. I can give only his concluding sentences, most effectually delivered :

" My views of this case require me to give the gentleman from Virginia the benefit of all reasonable presumptions. Giving him the benefit of those presumptions, and as he has been admitted to a seat upon the floor, and as

I do not think the gentleman who undertakes to contest his seat by virtue of an election held several months after that at which the sitting member was elected, is entitled to make such a contest—unless the gentleman who will close this debate shall convince me that I am wrong in the premises upon which I predicate my conclusion—I shall cast my vote, not to admit the gentleman from Virginia, but that he shall retain the seat he already occupies.   Not a single Congressional district in the United States, in which there are a sufficient number of loyal voters to choose a true Union member of Congress, and who exercise that choice at the time and substantially in the manner prescribed by law, shall, by any vote of mine, go unrepresented in this House."

Mr. Loomis, of the committee, replied at length, and Mr. Dawes, the chairman, closed, replying particularly to Mr. Harrison and generally to others.   His argument, as all of his were, was clear and strong.   There will be a space for him elsewhere.   He demanded the previous question.

Mr. Bingham, chairman of the Judiciary, demanded to be heard for Upton, but Dawes refused to withdraw his demand, which was sustained by the House.

Mr. Riddle moved to strike out the word " not," so that the resolution would affirm Upton's right to his seat, and demanded the yeas and nays.   The result was fifty to strike out and seventy-three to retain—and this struck Mr. Upton out of the House.   The members voted without reference to parties, and the lawyers fairly divided.

Perhaps no case was more thoroughly discussed ; certainly none was ever more fundamentally considered.   It was thus that the majority thrust from the House a legal representative, because the United States had so flagrantly failed in its duty to protect the loyal people of his district that a general poll was impossible in it, thereby leaving an ineffaceable stigma on the brow of the Republic.

CHAPTER XVI.

THE WAR FINANCIAL MEASURES.

JANUARY–FEBRUARY, 1862.

National Banks—Father of Greenbacks—Secretary Chase—A Great
Debate in the House.

IT is remembered that we had at this time, along and within the northern borders of the rebel States, over half a million soldiers, with hundreds of thousands more being enrolled, mustered in, sent forward, or already in camps and barracks at home. To sustain these men, to pay and clothe them, and to supply the awful waste of war, was one of the sorest problems thrust upon a Congress which had been elected to deal with current affairs in time of peace. It was understood that the current army expenses alone amounted to $1,500,000 per day.

Immediately after the battle of Bull Run, the New York, Philadelphia, and Boston banks came forward and offered the Secretary of the Treasury, Mr. Chase, $150,-000,000 in gold. This was about equal to the available specie of the United States at that time, the bank circulation being a fraction over $200,000,000; and we are to recollect that the sub-Treasury of 1846 was the Government's fiscal agency. Specie alone was there received, deposited, and disbursed. One of the loan bills of July authorized a suspension of the sub-Treasury law, and the

Secretary was empowered to select and use State banks. Mr. Chase believed in hard money ; he eschewed checks and bank-notes. The result was that the $150,000,000 bank loan exhausted the specie reserves, which, being paid out at points remote from money centres and channels, could not be returned in time to keep the banks firm ; and when we arrived in Washington, after the half-holidays, it was to find all the banks suspended— sub-Treasury and all. The Ways and Means Committee of the House were Stevens, Morrill, Phelps, Corning, Horton, Spaulding, Stratton, Hooper, and Maynard ; of the Senate, were Fessenden, Simmons, Howe, Pearce, Bright, and McDougal. The House sub-Committee on Banks and Currency were Spaulding, "father of the greenbacks," Hooper, who succeeded Appleton, resigned, and Corning. The last named formulated a bill to issue $50,000,000 demand Treasury notes, in sums not less than $5, on the credit of the United States, receivable for all dues to the Government, payable nowhere, and a legal tender for all possible debts. When reported to the House the amount was increased to $100,000,000, to be paid in the twenty-years' United States six per cent. bonds, the interest upon which was to be paid in coin. Morrill, Horton, and Corning were active opponents of the bill, and Stevens came into the measure finally. Mr. Chase, who had in his report recommended *the national-bank scheme, opposed the legal-tender feature,* which was the main source of contention. Mr. Chase thought his plan of national banks would afford relief. As drawn, it had sixty sections—obviously even McClellan could hardly wait for this as a relief measure.

There was a notable gathering of bank presidents, among them a son of the great Gallatin, whom our committee met *at the Treasury Department* with Mr. Chase, but beyond a thorough discussion (not reported) nothing came of it, and we were left in the House to our own devices, and to the suggestions of the press.

Mr. Spaulding, a very able man, opened the debate on the above bill in Committee of the Whole, Jan. 21, 1862. His speech covers five or six pages of the three-column quarto *Globe*, and was clear, exhaustive, and generally satisfactory. He estimated the debt at the end of the fiscal year, July 1, 1862, at $650,000,000. If the war continued, at $1,200,000,000 by July 1, 1863. The census returns of 1860 showed a valuation of private property of $16,159,-616,068—more than double that of 1850. For my readers I give his luminous statement of the financial conditions.

Mr. SPAULDING—" Mr. Chairman, this is an important measure, and I may be indulged for a few moments in explaining its objects, the situation of our finances, and the grounds upon which we rest this measure and expect it to be adopted. In the first place I will refer to the loan bills passed at the extra session of Congress, in July, in order to show how we obtained the means to carry on the Government from that time to the present, and to show how the Secretary of the Treasury has performed his duty. These bills were passed—the first on the 17th of July, and the other on the 5th of August. They gave to the Secretary of the Treasury power to pledge the credit of the United States to the extent of $250,000,000. Reflections have been made by some gentlemen on the manner in which the Secretary of the Treasury had performed his duty in borrowing that money, and with some disposition to criticise his actions. As a general reply, I will say that the Secretary has acted in strict conformity with the law, and has borrowed money at the rates authorized by Congress.

" And, sir, I am disposed, upon this floor and elsewhere, to sustain the Secretary and all Departments of the Government when they have discharged their duties in accordance with the laws which have been passed by us.

" The Secretary of the Treasury first borrowed $100,000,000, giving Treasury notes bearing seven and three-tenths per cent. interest, and he next issued United States bonds at six per cent. interest to the extent of $50,000,000, at the equivalent of par for seven per cent. bonds, and raised about $44,650,000 ; upon such loan a discount of over $5,300,000 was sustained. They were the best terms that could be obtained, and were regarded at the time as very favorable to the Government. But if he has borrowed the money at a high rate, it was authorized by the act of July. I am disposed to sustain the Secretary in what he has done. He has acted in good faith, and he should be sustained by us all.

" I may here be permitted to say, in explanation of some of the estimates which I shall introduce presently, differing, as they do, from the estimates of the Secretary of the Treasury in his annual report, that since his annual report he has changed his own views as to what the expenses of the war will be up to July next, and what they will also be up to July, 1863, and that he substantially agrees with me now as to what these expenses will be.   In the discussion of this important measure I desire, Mr. Chairman, to present the entire plan, with a view to enlist the co-operation, not only of all Departments of the Government, but also the co-operation of all the members of the House, without regard to party distinctions.   Hearty co-operation is desirable to the success of the important financial measures that will be presented.

" Our finances deserve our most serious attention.   The ways and means of carrying on the war should enlist the grave consideration of every gentleman on this floor who desires the preservation of this Government.   We were never in greater peril than at this moment.   It will require all our best energies successfully to meet the crisis through which we are passing.   I am oppressed by the magnitude of the work before us.   But, sir, I will not, I dare not—I trust we shall not any of us—shrink from the responsibility of performing every duty devolved upon us in this great crisis of our national affairs.

" The bill before us is a war measure—a measure of *necessity*, and not of choice—presented by the Committee of Ways and Means, to meet the most pressing demands upon the Treasury, to sustain the army and navy until they can make a vigorous advance upon the traitors, and crush out the rebellion.   These are extraordinary times, and extraordinary measures must be resorted to in order to save our Government and preserve our nationality.

" This bill, in addition to the $50,000,000 of demand notes, authorized by the act of July last, authorizes the Secretary of the Treasury to issue, on the credit of the United States, $100,000,000 of Treasury notes, not bearing interest, payable to the bearer at the Treasury, or at the office of the Assistant Treasurer in the city of New York, at the pleasure of the United States, and of such denominations as he may deem expedient, not less than $5 each ; and such notes, and all other United States notes payable on demand, not bearing interest, heretofore authorized, are made receivable for all debts and demands due to the United States, and for all salaries, debts, and demands owing by the United States to individuals, corporations, and associations within the United States, and are also declared lawful money and a legal tender in payment of all debts, public and private, within the United States, making altogether $150,000,000 legal-tender demand notes.

" Provision is also made for the convenient exchange of such notes for six per cent. bonds of the United States, redeemable in twenty years.

" Further, to enable the Secretary of the Treasury to fund the Treasury notes and floating debt of the United States, he is authorized to issue, on the credit of the United States, coupon bonds or registered bonds to an amount not exceeding $500,000,000, and redeemable at the pleasure of the

Government after twenty years from date, and bearing interest at the rate of six per cent. per annum, payable semi-annually ; and the bonds thus authorized are to be of such denomination, not less than fifty dollars, as may be determined upon by the Secretary of the Treasury, or in sums of not less than $2,500, for which, if requested, the Secretary of the Treasury, if he deem it expedient, may issue similar bonds, the principal and interest of which may be expressed in the currency of any foreign country, and payable there. The Secretary is authorized to issue said bonds at their par value to any creditor or creditors of the United States who may elect to receive them in satisfaction of their demands, provided that all such claims or demands shall have been first audited and settled by the proper accounting officers of the Treasury ; and the Secretary of the Treasury may also exchange such bonds at any time for lawful money of the United States, or for any of the Treasury notes that have been or may hereafter be issued under any former act of Congress, or that may be issued under the provisions of this act.

" The bill is simple and perspicuous in its terms, and easy of execution. It is a Government measure, and the officers of Government are required to execute its provisions.

" By the time the Secretary of the Treasury can get these notes engraved, printed, and signed ready for use, all other available means at his command and in the Treasury will be exhausted. This measure is therefore presented under the highest prerogatives of Government. The army and navy now in the service must be paid. They must be supplied with food, clothing, arms, ammunition, and all other materials of war, to render them effective in maintaining the Government and putting down the rebellion. Having exhausted other means of sustaining the Government, this measure is brought forward as the best that can be devised, in the present exigency, to relieve the necessities of the Treasury, and I trust it will pass without delay.

" At the extra session in July last Congress authorized the Secretary of the Treasury to borrow $250,000,000, for which he was authorized to issue coupon bonds, or registered bonds, or Treasury notes, in such proportions of each as he might deem advisable. The bonds were to be issued for twenty years at a rate not exceeding seven per cent. interest per annum, payable half-yearly ; and the Treasury notes were to be issued in denominations of not less than $50 each, at three years, with interest at seven and three-tenths per annum, payable half-yearly, and exchangeable at any time for twenty-years' six per cent. bonds. Or, at the option of the Secretary, he was permitted to issue $50,000,000 of the above loan in Treasury notes, on demand, in denominations of not less than $5 each without interest, and made receivable in payment of salaries or other dues owing by the United States ; or, in his discretion, he was authorized to issue Treasury notes at one year, bearing interest at three and sixty-five hundredths per cent. per annum, exchangeable at any time in sums of $100 or upwards for the three-years Treasury notes bearing seven and three-tenths per cent. interest, but in aggregate not to exceed $250,000,000. A further provision, however, was made, to wit : that the Secretary of the Treasury might negotiate any part of the loan for six per cent. twenty-years' bonds *at a rate not less than the equivalent of par for bonds, bearing seven per cent. interest per annum half-yearly, payable in twenty years."*

He placed before the House the opinion of Attorney-General Bates, that under the Constitution and under the condition of war we might issue legal-tender notes, and he quoted Marshall, Webster, and Kent, all Federalists, upon the extent of national power. He then concluded :

" My own impression is, that it will be best for us to adopt, in part, all of these modes for providing the means.

" 1. Raise by taxation the current year, over and above the amount received for duties on imports, the sum of $150,000,000.

" 2. Issue $100,000,000 of demand Treasury notes in addition to the $500,000,000 authorized in July, making them a legal tender in payment of debts, and exchangeable at any time for six per cent. twenty-years' bonds, with a further issue of demand notes if Congress shall hereafter deem it necessary.

" 3. Provide for the issue of all the twenty-years' six per cent. bonds that may be necessary to fund the demand Treasury notes, and other fundable Treasury notes that may be issued (say $500,000,000 six per cent. twenty-years' coupon bonds), and pledge $30,000,000 of the annual tax to pay the interest half-yearly thereon, and pledge $25,000,000 more as a sinking fund to redeem the principal in twenty years.

" 4. This tax of $150,000,000 would afford an ample basis on which to rest the credit of the Government for this large issue of Treasury notes and bonds, and would insure the punctual payment of the interest to the capitalists who might hold them.

" 5. The demand notes put in circulation would meet the present exigencies of the Government, in the discharge of its existing liabilities to the army, navy, and contractors, and for supplies, materials, and munitions of war. These notes would find their way into all the channels of trade among the people, and as they should accumulate in the hands of capitalists they would exchange them for the six per cent. twenty-years' bonds.

" These circulating notes in the hands of the people would enable them to pay the taxes imposed, and would facilitate all business operations between farmers, mechanics, commercial business men, and banks, and be equally as good as, and in most cases better than, the present irredeemable circulation issued by the banks.

"6. The $500,000,000 six per cent, twenty-years' bonds in the hands of the Secretary of the Treasury, ready to be issued, would afford ample opportunity for funding the Treasury notes as fast as capitalists might desire to exchange Treasury notes not bearing interest for coupon bonds of the United States bearing six per cent, interest, and amply secured by a tax upon the people and all their property.

" In this way the Government will be able to get along with its immediate and pressing necessities, without being obliged to force its bonds on the market at ruinous rates of discount, the people under heavy taxation will be shielded against high rates of interest, and the capitalists will be afforded a fair compensation for the use of their money during the pending struggle of the country for national existence.

" A suspension of specie payments is greatly to be deplored, but it is not a fatal step in an exigency like the present. The British Government and the Bank of England remained under suspension from 1797 to 1821–22, a period of twenty-five years. During this time, England successfully resisted the imperial power of the Emperor Napoleon, and preserved her own imperial existence. As a measure of necessity, she made the Bank of England notes virtually a legal tender by suspending the specie restriction. During all this time the people of Great Britain advanced in wealth, population, and resources. Gold is not as valuable as the productions of the farmer and mechanic, for it is not as indispensable as are food and raiment. Our army and navy must have what is far more valuable to them than gold and silver. They must have food, clothing, and the material of war. Treasury notes issued by the Government, on the faith of the whole people, will purchase these indispensable articles, and the war can be prosecuted until we can enforce obedience to the Constitution and laws, and an honorable peace be thereby secured. This being accomplished, I will be among the first to advocate a speedy return to specie payments, and all measures that are calculated to preserve the honor and dignity of the Government in time of peace, and which I regret are not practicable in the prosecution of this war.

" I do not despair ; on the contrary, I have an abiding faith in the patriotism, firmness, and resources of the people to maintain this Government. I feel that we are in great peril ; but when the people and our rulers become sufficiently aroused to fully appreciate the magnitude and probable duration of the rebellion—a rebellion that has grown into most gigantic proportions—then shall we be able to put forth the energy and the means necessary to crush it.

" An early and successful advance of our armies is of the utmost importance ; we need such an advance to sustain the financial credit of the Government ; we need it to prevent foreign intervention ; we need it to arouse the flagging energies of the people; and, above all, we need it to vindicate the courage and invincibility of our brave soldiers, who are so anxious to be led on to victory."

Mr. Vallandigham moved a substitute, which, as a whole, preserved the important provisions of the scheme of the Spaulding bill.

Very early the legal-tender provision was made the point about which the tide of debate ran and surged in the House. This was especially the theme for Mr. Pendleton's able and exhaustive speech in reply to Mr. Spaulding, at once lawyer-like and statesman-like. He closed thus:

" Mr. Webster has painted most felicitously the disastrous results to follow from this same course of conduct :

" ' A disordered currency is one of the greatest of political evils. It undermines the virtues necessary for the support of the social system, and encourages propensities destructive of its happiness. It wars against industry, frugality, and economy ; and it fosters the evil spirits of extravagance and speculation. Of all contrivances for cheating the laboring classes of mankind, none has been more effectual than that which deluded them with paper money. Ordinary tyranny, oppression, excessive taxation, these bear lightly on the happiness of the mass of the community, compared with fraudulent currencies, and the robberies committed by depreciated paper. Our own history has recorded for our instruction enough, and more than enough, of the demoralizing tendency, the injustice, and the intolerable oppression, on the virtuous and well disposed, of a degraded paper currency, authorized by law, or in any way countenanced by Government.'— *Webster's Speeches*, vol. ii., p. 81.

" Can we not learn something from the early experience of our country? Can we not learn something from the overthrow of the revolutionary Government of France by this very over-issue of depreciated paper ? Can we not learn something from those throes which the society of England endured during the long suspension of, and at its return to, specie currency in 1822? Can we not now rise to a wisdom of statesmanship which shall control the financial necessities of the country without plunging it into that gulf from which there is, with honor and safety, no recovery?

" Sir, I beg gentlemen to permit me to read, in closing what I have to say, one more lesson of wisdom from that statesman of New England, to whom I have had occasion so often already to refer. I read it with the hope that it will be engraven on the memory of every man here, and that it will enable us to avoid the evils of which he has spoken by adhering to the course which he has wisely marked out :

" ' No nation had a better currency than the United States. There was no nation which had guarded its currency with more care, for the framers of the Constitution and those who had enacted the early statutes on the subject were *hard-money men.* They had felt and duly appreciated the evils of a paper medium ; they therefore sedulously guarded the currency of the United States from debasement.   The legal currency of the United States was gold and silver coin.   This was a subject in regard to which Congress had run into no folly.   Gold and silver currency was the law of the land at home, the law of the world abroad ; there could, in the present condition of the world, be no other currency.'

"Let gentlemen heed this lesson of wisdom.   Let them, if need be, tax the energies and wealth of the country sufficiently to restore the credit of the Government.   Let them borrow whatever money in addition may be necessary—borrow it to the full extent that may be necessary—and let us adhere rigidly, firmly, consistently, persistently, and to the end, to the principle of refusing to surrender that currency which the Constitution has given us, and in the maintenance of which this Government has never, as yet, for one moment wavered."

Mr. Vallandigham would not discuss legal-tender paper. He thus warned against inflation :

"Nor is this all, nor the worst.   An immense inflation or bloat in this wonderful paper money which our financial Midas, by his touch, is to con- vert into gold, must come next.   Cheap in material, easy to issue, worked by steam, signed by machinery, there will be no end to the legions of paper devils which shall pour forth from the loins of the Secretary.   Sir, let the army rejoice ; there will be no more 'shoddy' for there will be no more rags out of which to manufacture it.

"What must follow from all this?   First, that which never has failed in times of bloated currency—high prices, extravagant speculation, enormous sudden fortunes, immense fictitious wealth, general insanity.   These be- long to all inordinate and excessive paper issues, and even to plethoras in the circulation of gold and silver, if such plethoras could occur.   But the evil will not stop here.   Every banker, every lender, every merchant, every business man, and every seller of real or personal estate, or of anything else, compelled to receive in payment for whatever he lends or sells an irredeemable paper money, dependent for its value solely upon force, and without the smallest credit, and himself having no confidence in the Gov- ernment, and no special good-will to the borrower or buyer who forces him to take its paper, will demand a still higher price, by way of insurance, than if the currency were sound and safe, no matter how much inflated.

"And now, sir, what is to be the result of all this?   What else but the result from like causes in years past in foreign countries and in our own? It is written in the commercial convulsions and sufferings of France in 1720, and in England a century later, and of the United States in 1837. The collapse follows the inflation, and is terrible and disastrous just in pro- portion as the bubble has been magnificent.   Your legal-tender laws will avail nothing. They have been tried before ; tried in this country and abroad ; and have always failed in the end. The regent of France proclaimed them in Law's time, in 1717, and what followed ? Let Mr. Thiers answer :

" ' Violent and vexatious as the measures were to sustain the credit of the notes, they were insufficient to give them a value which they did not possess. *Dishonest debtors alone used them to pay their debts.* Coin was secretly used for daily purchases, and was concealed with care. Many accumulated it clandestinely. The greater part buried it in the earth, and the rich realizers used every artifice to transfer it to foreign countries. Another portion of our coin left France, and although the exportation of specie is not necessarily injurious, it was so at this time, since it left behind only a false paper currency and an imaginary capital.' "

Of his substitute he said :

" But, Mr. Chairman, the fundamental idea of this substitute is to support and float these $150,000,000 by a nearly equal amount of taxation and revenue, payable, of course, in these notes. The Government owes the people and the people owe the Government, each $150,000,000, and these notes are primarily to be used as a common medium of payment between them. Unquestionably so long as this relation of mutual debts and credits subsists in nearly the same proportion, these notes will float in general circulation and in payments or exchanges or other commercial and business transactions between citizen and citizen, even without the funding clause ; but this clause is essential inasmuch as the expenditures of the Government very greatly exceed the $150,000,000, and because the debt present and future is, unhappily, to last for many years to come. But these notes will have this advantage over bank paper, that they are receivable at par with gold and silver in payment of Government dues, while it is not. The refusal, therefore, of the banks to receive and circulate them will avail nothing to depreciate their value, since their credit and circulation will depend, not on bank favor, but on taxes of a nearly equal amount, which must be paid at all events, and may be paid in these same notes. They will thus be beyond the reach of bull, bear, or banker. . . .

" Sir, the whole amount of specie and bank paper actually in circulation in the United States, on the 1st of May, when this increase began, was about $400,000,000, of which amount some $300,000,000 were in the States still called loyal. Of the whole amount, the Government employed in various ways $87,000,000, leaving $313,000,000 for the ordinary commercial and business transactions of the country ; of which amount about $213,000,000 were circulated in the loyal States. Meantime in nine months, though one third of the States have seceded, the expenditures and operations of the Government have gone up in the remaining two thirds from $87,000,000 to $600,000,000. To meet this immensely increased fiscal action we have but $213,000,000 of currency, gold and silver, and bank paper, not including the $50,000,000 of demand notes now in circulation."

For himself he concluded thus :

"Finally, sir, if the Committee and the House shall proceed upon the principles of justice and sound political economy which have been hitherto observed by every wise Government, and above all by this Government from the beginning, in all maintenance of its credit and good faith, I will lend a ready and an earnest support to every measure framed in conformity with these principles, and intended and calculated to build up and to sustain the public credit and good faith. Otherwise, I cannot and I will not vote to bring down upon the wretched people of this once happy and prosperous country the triple ruin of a forced currency, enormous taxation, and a public debt never to be extinguished."

This was February 3d. Hooper, manly and sincere, followed Vallandigham with perhaps the clearest statement of the triple scheme made during this remarkable debate :

" To insure our success in this contest, great and unusual exertions have already been made. An enormous army, a powerful navy, with vast stores of artillery and ammunition, have been created. In providing for the sustenance, comfort, and equipment of this army and navy, the Government have been obliged to incur expenses far exceeding in magnitude any which have been hereto known in history. To continue them in their present state of efficiency, large additional sums must be expended ; and it now becomes the duty of Congress to devise methods by which these sums can be obtained with the least hardship to the people and the least risk to the credit of the Government. . . .

" Three measures have been considered in the committee which are, to some extent, connected together, and form a comprehensive system by which it is believed the Government will be enabled to procure the sums necessary to the successful prosecution of the war, while at the same time the burden upon the capital of the country will be light, and the public will be benefited in some important particulars.

" The first of these measures is the one now before the House by which the Secretary of the Treasury is authorized to issue United States notes, not to exceed $150,000,000 in amount (including those authorized by previous laws), of denominations not less than five dollars. They are not to bear interest, but are to be issued and received as money, convertible, at the option of the holder, into six per cent. stock of the United States, the principal and interest being payable either here or abroad ; and these notes are to be a legal tender.

" The second measure consists of a tax bill, which shall, with the tariff on imports, insure an annual revenue of at least $150,000,000.

" The third is a national banking law, which will require the deposit of United States stock as security for the bank-notes that are circulated as currency. . . .

" This tax bill will give to the bonds of the United States the character so much desired by capitalists, that of a sure interest-paying security. With such a character there would be no harm done if the principal were never paid, so far as those holding the bonds are concerned, because capitalists in the aggregate do not care for the payment of their principal ; the only value which they place upon the capital is derived from the fact that it will yield them a revenue : and if at any time the capitalist should wish to use the principal of his bond, he knows that he can always sell it to another who desires to invest as much as he desires to sell. The amount of debt of the British Government is so great that the most sanguine political economist can devise no method by which it can be extinguished ; but yet the bonds representing that very debt are of great value. Capital seeks them for investment because the interes is sure ; and the only reason that they are ever below par is, not because the payment of the principal is more or less hopeless, but because the rates of interest in the market at the time being are higher than the rate provided for in the bonds. ·

" In the natural course of trade these United States notes will continue to be transferred from one to another until they come into the hands of the banks and capitalists, who will not allow them to remain long in their possession. Money for commercial purposes can now be obtained for less than five per cent. Such portion thereof of the ' United States notes,' as are not needed for circulation, and cannot be used in regular business channels in a way to earn interest, will be returned sooner or later to the Treasury Department to be converted into bonds bearing interest at the rate of six per cent. and payable in twenty years. By this process the change is completed, and these bonds of the Government will thus be made to furnish the supplies required to carry on the war without the intervention or use by the Government of bank paper. . . .

" To fail," concluded Mr. Hooper, " would not be because the nation was so poorly endowed as to be without the means of success, but because it refused to make use of them. Such a result, if it were possible, would not weaken the truth of the great principles for which we are contending, but would simply demonstrate that we, of this generation, were faithless in guarding those principles ; faithless to ourselves ; faithless to our country ; faithless to good government throughout the world ; and, since such infidelity is a violation of unquestionable duty, faithless to God."

Mr. Morrill of Vermont said :

" Mr. Chairman, engaged as I have been upon other matters of at least equal importance, I have not had the time to prepare any elaborate speech ;

but the subject of issuing $150,000,000 of paper currency and making it a legal tender by the Government at a single bound—the precursor, as I fear, of a prolific brood of promises, no one of which is to be redeemed in the constitutional standard of the country—could not but arrest my attention, and, having strong convictions of the impolicy of the measure, I should feel that I utterly failed to discharge my duty if I did not attempt to find a stronger prop for our country to lean upon than this bill—a measure not blessed by one sound precedent, and damned by all.   .   .   .

"Let no one suppose that I imagine the country to be ruined, however calamitous I might regard the passage of this bill—whether one particular measure is adopted or rejected. This Government is, thank God! too strongly entrenched in the hearts of the people not to be able to withstand more than one disaster, or more than one blunder. But it is a time when it might be pardonable morality almost to say that 'a blunder is worse than a crime.'

"We are urged by the gentleman from New York to pass this bill as 'a war measure'—'a measure of necessity'; and to enforce this idea he gives you the figures of our probable requirements if the war should be prolonged until July 1, 1863. Sir, I have no expectation of being required to support a war for that length of time. The ice that now chokes up the Mississippi is not more sure to melt and disappear with the approaching vernal season, than the rebellious armies upon its banks when our western army shall break from its moorings, and, rushing with the current to the Gulf, baptize as it goes in blood the people to a fresher allegiance. At the same time the men of the East will only ask for an opportunity to cross bayonets with the chivalry—to leave epithets and try what virtue there is in steel! That hour is approaching, and I have no fear of the result.

" 'Fly swiftly round, ye wheels of time!'

"We can close this war by the 30th day of July next as well as in thirty years. Let us second General McClellan for 'a short and sharp' conflict. By so doing we shall economize both blood and Treasury notes.

"At the last session of Congress we unwisely, as I thought, raised the pay of our army from $10 to $13 per month, as though our men could be only induced to espouse the cause of their country at the highest wages, with board and clothes in addition; but having done this, shall we avoid the contract by tendering ninety cents or less on the dollar? This is not the true way. No—

" 'At your dessert bright pewter comes too late,
    When your *first* course was all served up in plate.'

"If it must be so, I would rather say, with soldier-like frankness: 'Officers and men! the work is heavy; you have prolonged it somewhat beyond our calculations, and the monthly drain upon the Treasury is very large. We shall therefore put your pay at the old mark, but we will not whittle it down by giving you anything worth less than a hundred cents on the dollar.' "

Roscoe Conkling followed :

" Gentlemen have longed for victories to reinvigorate the languishing energies of finance. Victory would no doubt exert a potent influence ; but, sir, the Treasury will control and decide the war, not the war the Treasury. Indeed the question of money and credit is all there is before us ; it is practically the only unsettled question of the war. Armies and navies may perish, and a public credit well preserved can replace them ; but if the public credit perishes, the army and navy only increase the disaster and deepen the dishonor.

" We have patriotism and courage and fighting enough to crush the rebellion through the Union, and then to sweep from this continent every occupant of it but ourselves, and sponge off their ships from our waters. We have in the field the first army in history, the first means to conquer with. It is said that in 1811 Napoleon had 1,100,000 men, and other instances are mentioned of exceeding numbers ; but nowhere short of fabulous narrations can be found an army so numerous and, at the same time, so powerful in material, so complete in arms and equipments. Nowhere can be found an army so well paid ; nowhere a great army so well fed and cared for ; no nation has ever attempted to maintain an army at anything like the same expense. The Secretary of War says that 718,512 men have taken the field ; 77,000 of them were three-months' men, 640,637 are enlisted for the war. We have eighty-three regiments of cavalry ; eight more than France. Every one of this multitude of soldiers is entitled to at least thirteen dollars a month, besides subsistence and bounties. Sir, there is nothing like it in all history. No nation ever attempted it, or approached it ; never for any length of time. I find, in a very able report recently made to the American Geographical and Statistical Society, an instructive statement on this subject, which I ask my colleague to read."

Mr. F. A. Conkling read as follows :

" Upon an average our army, on a peace footing, has cost us $1,000 annually per man, rank and file. In the war in which we are now engaged we present the extraordinary spectacle of an army, hardly ever before equalled in numbers, hired at the rate of wages paid to able-bodied men in the various peaceful avocations from which they were drawn. To the men in the ranks, $13 per month are paid, with their food and clothing. The soldier in the French army receives only about fifty-six cents a month ; the pay of our soldiers being twenty times greater. The estimate in the French budget for 1860, was 345,908,744 francs, or $64,687,500, for an army on a

8

war footing of 762,765 men ; and, in addition, a reserve militia, on a peace footing, of 415,746 men.   We all know that the maintenance of such an army has created serious embarrassment in the finances of the Empire. They have, if we may credit foreign journals, completely changed the policy of the Emperor.   It costs this country twelve times as much to maintain a soldier in the field as it does the French Government.   Our forces now under arms are, consequently, equivalent to 7,500,000 for that country. It costs us two and a half times as much to maintain a soldier as it does the English Government.   We hire our money at twice the rate of interest. Our expenditures per man, measured by the standard of interest paid, are on a scale more than four times greater than for that country.   England can expend $1,200,000,000 a year without creating a greater burden in the shape of a public debt than $600,000,000 would be for the United States."

As to the notes to be issued :

"The whole scheme presupposes that the notes to be emitted will be lepers in the commercial world from the hour they are brought into it ; that they will be shunned and condemned by the laws of trade and value.   If this is not to be their fate, what is the sense, as was said in the Federal Constitutional Convention, in attempting to legislate their value up?"

These extracts from their speeches will hardly do justice to these very able men.   Pendleton, Vallandigham, and others had quoted from Hamilton, Marshall, Webster, and other great names.   Bingham, having the floor, said :

"I am here to-day to assert the rightful authority of the American people as a nationality, a sovereignty under and by virtue of their Constitution. In saying that the people of this Republic are one people, a sovereignty, I do not feel that I shall be confronted by any of the great names of the illustrious dead who have suddenly found favor with gentlemen upon the other side of the House.   Living, there was no epithet in our language too severe in its condemnation or too much uncharitable in its import for the fit denunciation by certain parties of the alleged political heresies of the illustrious man, Alexander Hamilton, and that other illustrious man, Daniel Webster, who for strength of intellect stood alone among the living ; and now dead, in his honored grave, sleeps alone ' by the sounding sea.'   I am not myself of that class of admirers who prosecute men while living, and heap tons of granite and pour empty adulation upon their ashes when dead. I prefer to respect them and their authority while they stand among the living men of to-day.   These great names have been invoked in this debate. For what purpose ?   For the purpose of denationalizing the American people ; for the purpose of stripping the American people of the attributes of sovereignty ; for the purpose of laying, as I have said before, at the feet and at the mercy of brokers and hawkers on 'Change the power of the people over their monetary interests in this hour of national exigency."

Bingham was one of our most effective speakers, and was usually put forward as the Republican champion. His whole speech was very forcible. He usually stirred up his opponents, and was subjected to interruptions, and rather liked them. His temper was good, his retorts and replies always happy and effective. He supported the bill in its entirety.

Sheffield, of Rhode Island, made a set speech *against* the bill.

Mr. Crisfield, of Maryland, a slaveholder, one of the ablest and best lawyers in the House, an amiable and lovable man, began by an over-modest depreciation of himself. I must make room for his manly appreciation of the President :

"Sir, I did not contribute to bring this Administration into power. I had known the President in former years, and personally I liked him. I knew him to be honest, and I believed him to be brave, and I hoped that he was patriotic. As my knowledge of him has increased, this belief and this hope have grown and are still growing. I had no affinities with the principles upon which he was presented to the American people. From the peculiar and distinctive features of the platform of his party I differed, and still differ. I lamented his election, not so much on his own account as of the disturbance I knew it would occasion. But, sir, he is here. He has been elected President of the United States. I recognize him as legally invested with all the constitutional powers of that high dignity ; and it is as well a constitutional obligation as a dictate of patriotism to give his Administration, in this hour of evil, a fair, impartial, active, and energetic support. Many things have been done under this Administration which I do not approve ; some things, I think, are positively wrong. Yet I do recognize in his public conduct an honest effort to maintain this Union of the States with unabridged privileges, and restore the Constitution to its ancient and rightful supremacy. I desire to support him in this great work. I believe it is the duty of all good citizens to sustain him. I shall, therefore, give his Administration, in all of its efforts in this great work, a fair, candid, honest, and unreserved support. Especially do I desire to support him in his financial policy. I desire to support him in that, because that of all others is the most important to national safety. If that fails, all else must fail. If you fail to obtain the requisite means, your army is disbanded, the Union is destroyed, the Constitution overturned, the country ruined, and our national life will be entirely destroyed. Hence, sir, I am disposed to view with the utmost candor, with favorable predisposition, every measure of finance presented for my acceptance, having for its purpose the national safety, and the restoration of the Constitution to its just authority."

He opposed the bill in a very able constitutional argument.

Mr. Pike of Maine, one of the strong clear men, made an able speech for the measure, as did Mr. Alley of Massachusetts.

An effort was then made to close debate—which failed. Wright of Pennsylvania opposed the bill. Mr. Horton, of the Committee of Ways and Means, made a forcible speech against it also.

Mr. Kellogg spoke for it. Judge Thomas made a short strong speech against it.

Mr. Edwards was for it.

Mr. RIDDLE (on a motion to strike out the legal-tender feature)—"Almost as soon as men began to traffic they began to observe in it certain usages. These grew with the barter and exchange of commodities until they became customs, enlarged themselves to rules of general observance and application, and finally constituted what we call the laws of trade or commerce. This code, the pure offspring of commerce, owes little to municipal law, though it often in a way dictates municipal statutes. Although it is of vast international obligation, it in no way depends upon treaties, yet in its universal dominion it has compelled the negotiation of more international compacts and arrangements than all other causes combined.

"The laws of trade may be said to be universal in their dominion, irrepealable in their nature, and sovereign in their jurisdiction.

"At first the sovereign, caring for his own wants and nothing for those of his subjects, levied his revenues in the simplest and most direct way possible—he took what he wanted. Experience ultimately demonstrated even to kings that the purposes of revenue could best be subserved by some attention to the rules of commerce. And the suggestion was cultivated and improved until the Government fiscal machinery, adjusted by a thousand years of heeded experience, was placed by the great streams and channels of commerce, and propelled by their currents without a serious detriment to trade, and with great advantage to the sovereign's revenues.

" It is obvious that the more perfect the harmony between the governmental financial machinery and these courses and currents of trade, the more prosperous and flourishing must be the condition of a given nation. It should be the purpose of the sovereign to withdraw the smallest needed amount from these streams, retain it the shortest time, and return it in an unimpaired condition. From these briefly stated premises two or three conclusions inevitably arise :

" The laws of commerce were not enacted by Congress.

" They cannot be repealed or controlled by our legislation, and any attempt to disregard them must end in disaster.

" A scheme of national finance, to be successful, must be so adjusted that its workings will harmonize and not conflict with these laws.

" A scheme that should exhaust the circulating medium that fills the channels of trade would fail.

" So, too, if those streams are inadequate to the wants of commerce and the Government, means to augment them must be found ; while that plan, based upon principles at utter war with the fundamental principles of commerce, must, upon a gigantic scale like ours, result in the destruction of both.

" The primal fundamental demands of commerce, and without which it is impossible, is an adequate supply of money—actual money ; not that which some king or Congress calls money, but that which is coined pursuant to the usages of trade, and that cannot be debased below its standard ; money and its equivalents, made its equivalents by real money's actual presence. It was early discovered that certain metals had the highest intrinsic value, below which they would, under no circumstance, ever fall, however that value might vary. This gave them a still higher exchangeable value. Nations, under the demands of commerce, seized upon these metals and stamped upon them the national estimate of their worth, made up of their intrinsic and exchangeable value, and thus coined money—as nature coins her works, with the image of truth on the outside.

" It is a singular fact that the various national standards thus made up, as applied to a given piece of these metals of known weight and fineness, are nearly identical. Below this standard real money never falls. It is the sovereign quality of money in commercial estimation, that the holders of personal service and commodities will always readily exchange them for money. Hence the holder of money can always command them, and his power to do so is limited only by the quantity of his money. If his money is limitless, his power to command services and commodities is limitless. He might buy up the political and physical dominions of the globe, purchase of kings their crowns, and make virtue triumphant by paying a premium for good deeds.

" Whoever throws into the channels of trade, in the place of money, anything less valuable than it and its equivalents, to that extent, at least, disarranges and demoralizes the whole vast and complex national and individual interests dependent upon their healthy action.

" Can money be made of paper?   Clearly not by calling it money, though all the people and their rulers should conspire under any form of solemnity to call it so, nor yet by attempting to make it perform the functions of money. Paper has no appreciable intrinsic value ; and its exchangeable value is of the lowest possible grade.   The only high degree of value it can ever attain is that which may be imparted to it by that which is written or printed upon it. Stamp on it by the national impress that it is money, and try it by a commercial test.   The holder of it would not necessarily have the power to command a moment's service or the most trifling commodity.   Say that it has the quality of discharging private liability, and yet the holder of brain and bone and muscle might not be induced to make the least exchange for it.   But it is possible that they would to a certain extent.   Give the holder of this money a limitless supply and send him into the market, and we know there is a limit beyond which he cannot get in his purchases, arising wholly from the quality of the article with which he would buy.   In the course of his transactions he would soon find that he is obliged to exchange more paper for less commodities, and this would go on until the extreme limit was reached, at which all the paper that he has parted with, as well as all he still holds, is worth less than the paper ere it was made money.

" Who now will arise and say that money can be made of paper ?

" Let the national hand inject a mass of this miscalled stuff into the channels of commerce, and what result but one can ensue ?

" As a nation we now require and must have a limitless supply of service and commodities.   Our market can furnish them.   The holders are not only friendly and favorable, but anxious to make the exchange.   Indeed, the very purpose we wish to accomplish is identical with their most cherished interests ; or, rather, upon its accomplishment depend all the values of their interests, and our need now is a supply of a commodity with which to effect the exchange.

" Money we have not, and hence cannot create its equivalents.

" In this exigency, it would be easy to issue the proposed $100,000,000 and make it by law a legal tender, or money.   Indeed, no choice seems left us but to dare the experiment in some form.   Under the wisest provisions and restrictions I look for loss, if not disaster, and I only hope we may escape the worst consequences that have hitherto attended all similar schemes ; and I trust we may, if we can still profit by the maxim that permits even fools to learn by experience.   It is apparent that the whole quantity of the circulating medium must be materially increased, for obviously that which was only equal to the demands of commerce and the ordinary wants of the Government is wholly inadequate to the same demands and the extraordinary wants of the Government.

" The Constitution furnishes ample warrant for an issue of Treasury notes ;

but it cannot be found in the loose way in which many able gentlemen derive it. They seem to regard the Constitution as a reservoir originally containing limitless power, all of which still remains, unless withdrawn by a special prohibition. In fact, it was to commence with an empty receptacle, and never contained anything except what was placed in it directly. As to this matter, even if it can be shown that the framers of that instrument did not intend to place the power to issue these notes in the Constitution, and that they supposed by refusing to deposit it there, it would not therein exist, still, with others, I find in that instrument powers and duties that clearly carry with them this power as an incident ; but I do not find it, nor any other power, merely because the Constitution does not prohibit it.

" Even if the Constitution had prohibited the Congress, as it does the States, from issuing ' bills of credit,' we still might issue Treasury notes, because they are not ' bills of credit ' ; nor are the notes issued by the State banks. Bills of credit were well understood by the framers of the Constitution, and have no essential element in common with notes such as we may issue. I may not now point out the distinctions and differences that clearly mark the two.

" The quality to be exclusively relied upon to insure the circulation of a paper medium, is the never-questioning confidence of a community in the ability and intention of its issuers to pay it. The paper, then, should bear on its face the highest proof of this ability and intention ; and no mark or characteristic that would raise a doubt or lead to inquiry should mar it. When paper, whether issued by individuals, corporations, or nations, is once issued, it is subject to precisely the same laws, and under the same circumstances will reach and produce similar results. In those respects no difference can exist. The name ' national currency ' may delude. The only possible difference that can exist between paper issued by a nation and that issued by an individual is, a nation can write better evidence of its ability and intention to pay upon its obligations, than can an individual. No other difference does or can exist. The making these notes receivable mutually between the Government and its creditors and debtors, and also a legal tender, does not and cannot fall within the evidences of the nation's ability and inclination to pay them ; nor can those characteristics in any way add to the stability of this currency, or provoke a confidence in the people to receive them.

" They are only facilities by which a most dangerous and unhealthy circulation will be stimulated and secured. I am prepared to make these notes receivable for the public dues, which does make them a qualified legal tender I admit, and gives to those who contend for the main proposition a serious advantage in the argument ; but beyond that I will not go. The power to make these notes a legal tender is a constitutional vagabond, and finds a lurking-place nowhere in our system. The proposition that because the States only were prohibited this power, and therefore we may exercise it, needs no further refutation.

"The grounds on which my distinguished colleague (Mr. Bingham) rests this power are most extraordinary. He says that the Constitution has conferred no power upon Congress at all in reference to the subject of legal tender—says nothing at all about it,—and therefore we have the power to make paper a legal tender, and money generally. Why, sir, according to him, a man might, with a tin cup of prescribed pattern, dip up a pint of water from the nearest puddle and make that a legal tender, if the Congress should so will. This is beyond the reach of argument. Not only is there no warrant for this power, but its exercise violates the whole spirit of the Constitution. Under that we may in one way impair contracts—that is, we may discharge men from the obligation of a contract by a bankrupt law ; but that we can only do by express grant of power.

" What would be the effect of making those notes a legal tender ? A man who had borrowed five hundred dollars in gold, on thirty days, could discharge himself from the obligation of his contract by the delivery of five hundred nominal dollars in this paper, which might be worth ' utter nothing.' We, by our law, give the power to do this. I cannot consent to it.

" It is ineffectual to quote to me instances where, as gentlemen say, Congress has, in another way, done something like this. It is a villainy not to be repeated.

" Still, if my colleague is right in this law, men need not take these notes unless they wish to, for all they would have to do would be to make a special bargain for gold and silver in their dealings. If so, what value is there in this proposed provision of your law, which men can so cheaply nullify.

" This quality of legal tender cannot add to the stability of this currency, nor will it induce confidence, but the reverse of both. It comes in ' a questionable shape,' bold, confessing, and shameless ; and if a man takes it at all, it is not because he wants it, but either because he must have it, or because he trusts to its characteristic to get rid of it again. Indeed, one of the arguments urged for the incorporation of this provision into this bill is, that the creditors of the Government who must take these notes must have the power to get rid of them again, as a matter of justice to them ; otherwise they might perish on their hands. The death ought to occur one remove from them. In the name of all commercial sagacity, how long do you expect to keep afloat a currency that thus has to cut its way into market —be shot into men, so to speak? How long will it be before the holders of services and commodities will refuse to exchange for it ? And when that time comes, even creditors will prefer to trust a debtor still further to taking it, and it comes to an end with almost everything and everybody who depended upon it. To this feature I cannot consent. I will vote to expunge it ; and if that fails, I will choose between the bill and its defeat."

After various briefer speeches, Mr. Stevens arose to conclude the long debate.

Mr. STEVENS.—"Mr. Chairman, this bill is a measure of necessity, not of choice. No one would willingly issue paper currency not redeemable on demand, and make it a legal tender. It is never desirable to depart from that circulating medium which, by the common consent of civilized nations, forms the standard of value. But it is not a fearful measure ; and when rendered necessary by exigencies, it ought to produce no alarm.

"The first inquiry then is, is this measure necessary ? *The late Administration left a debt of about $100,000,000.* It bequeathed to us also an ex-pensive and formidable rebellion. This compelled Congress, at its extra session, to authorize a loan of $250,000,000 ; $100,000,000 of these were taken at seven and three-tenths per cent., and $50,000,000 of six per cent. bonds, at a discount of over $5,000,000 ; $50,000,000 undisposed of. Be-fore the banks had been paid much of the last loan they broke down under it, and suspended specie payments. They have continued to pay that loan, not in coin, but in demand notes of the Government—that has kept them at par. But the last of that loan was paid yesterday ; and on the same day the banks refused to receive them. They must now sink to depreciated currency. The remaining $50,000,000 the Secretary of the Treasury has. been unable to negotiate. A small portion of it, say $10,000,000, has been issued at seven and three-tenths in payment of debts.

"All this has been used; and there is now a floating debt, audited and unaudited, of at least $180,000,000. The Secretary intended to use the balance of the authorized loan by paying it out to creditors in notes of seven and three-tenths ; that becoming known they immediately sank four per cent., and if he had preserved it, it is believed they would have run down to ten per cent. discount. But even if these could be used (about $40,000,000) there would remain due about $90,000,000, the payment of which is urgently demanded. The daily expenses of the Government are now about $2,000,000. To carry us on until the next meeting of Congress, would take $600,000,000 more, making, before legislation could be had at next session, about $700,000,000 to be provided for. We have already appropriated $350,000,000, making our entire debt $1,050,000,000.

"The grave question is, how can this large amount be raised ? The Sec-retary of the Treasury has used his best efforts to negotiate a loan of but $50,000,000, and has failed. Several modes of relief have been suggested ; the most obvious is to borrow on Government bonds, bearing an interest of six per cent. That it is known can only be effected by putting the bonds. into the market to the highest bidder. If but a small sum were wanted it might probably be had at a small discount. But if sufficient to meet our wants up to next December, or $700,000,000, were forced into the market, as it is wanted, I have no doubt they would sell as low as sixty per cent., as. in the last English war ; and even then it would be found impossible to find payment in coin. A large part of it must be accepted in the depreciated notes of non-specie-paying banks, for I suppose no one expects the resump-tion of specie payments until the war shall be ended. But as this Congress.

must provide for appropriations to the end of the fiscal year 1863, seven months more must be added to these expenses. That would require \$420,-000,000 added to these \$700,000,000 before estimated, and the aggregate would be \$1,100,000,000. This discount on the sum at forty per cent. would be \$440,000,000. At the minimum discount that any reasonable man could fix, say twenty-five per cent., it would be \$275,000,000. It would, therefore, require at least bonds to the amount of \$1,500,000,000 to produce sufficient currency to make \$1,100,000,000 and carry us to the end of the next fiscal year. This sum is too frightful to be tolerated.

" Certain bankers have suggested that the immediate wants of the Government might be supplied by pledging seven and three-tenths per cent. bonds with a liberal margin, payable in one year to the banks, who would advance a portion in gold and the rest in currency. The effect would be that Government would pay out to its creditors the depreciated notes of non-specie-paying banks. And as there is no probability that the pledges would be redeemed when due, they would be thrown into the market and sold for whatever the banks might choose to pay for them. The folly of this scheme needs no illustration.

" Another is to strike out the legal-tender clause, and make them receivable for all taxes and public dues ; but it is not proposed to make any provision for redeeming them in coin on demand. I do not believe that such notes would circulate anywhere except at a ruinous discount. No notes not redeemable on demand, and not made a *legal tender*, have ever been kept at par. Even those who could use them for taxes and duties would discredit them, that they might get them low. If soldiers, mechanics, contractors, and farmers were compelled to take them from the Government, they must submit to a heavy shave before they could use them. The knowledge that they were provided for by taxation, and would surely be paid twenty years hence, would not sustain them."

He discussed the substitutes, the motion to strike out the legal-tender provision, answered questions from everybody,—and then short speeches from several followed.

Mr. SHELLABARGER.—" Mr. Chairman, I rise to oppose the pending amendment (striking out the legal-tender provision). I did desire to submit to the committee some views touching this measure when we were in general debate, but omitted to do so in deference to the more matured views which other members of the committee desired to submit. I propose to occupy the few moments I have, in making some statements in relation to the charges of bad faith and injustice which have been so persistently, earnestly, and, doubtlessly, sincerely made by the opponents of the bill.

" Now, sir, I think it must be plain, beyond all cavil, that if these notes proposed to be issued under this bill are made of the value impressed upon them by law, so that they will be to the citizen the true and real representatives of that amount of the intrinsic wealth of the country which is stamped by law upon them as their nominal value, then there can be no practical injury, injustice, or bad faith in the law which makes them pay a debt precisely equal to the real value or wealth of the country, which that note, so made a tender, represents. It is, of course, not my purpose now either to discuss or state these views by which others see in this measure—as distinguished from those they advocate—only disaster, in the shape of 'destruction of all standards of value'; in the 'inflation of the business and the prices of the country'; in disordering the 'operations of trade and commerce'; and in the ultimate 'bankruptcy' of the Government of the people. I have no doubt this cry is made sincerely by many, and perhaps is believed by all who make it. I do not discuss the sources and reasonableness of this cry of alarm, but only wish to present a parallel to it, and say that this cry is, to my mind, as unreasonable as that other to which I allude. I find that parallel in the history of the growth of the debt of England; and in the light of that history, I declare that this cry of 'bankruptcy' and national disaster and ruin is utterly unreasonable, and just now most pernicious."

The suspension of the Bank of England was discussed further by Mr. Shellabarger.

Campbell and Morrill spoke again, Hickman interjected a short forcible speech—these under the five minutes' rule, which often produces the best debating in the House. So also Conkling, Lovejoy, and Hooper spoke, and the war of words went on. Finally the House came to a vote. The motion to strike out the legal tender was lost by a decided majority. The latest substitute was negatived by fifty-five for to ninety-five against, and the House, brought to a vote on the bill, passed it, ninety-three for, to fifty-nine against it, as follows:

YEAS.—Aldrich, Alley, Arnold, Ashley, Babbitt, Goldsmith F. Baily, Joseph Baily, Baker, Beaman, Bingham, Francis P. Blair, Jacob B. Blair, Samuel S. Blair, Blake, Buffington, Burnham, Campbell, Chamberlin, Clarke, Colfax, Cutler, Davis, Delano, Delaplaine, Duell, Dunn, Edgerton, Edwards, Ely, Fenton, Fessenden, Fisher, Franchot, Frank, Gooch, Granger, Gurly, Haight, Hale, Hanchett, Harrison, Hickman, Hooper, Hutchins, Julian, Kelley, Francis W. Kellogg, William Kellogg, Killinger, Lansing, Leary, Loomis, McKean, McKnight, McPherson,

Marston, Maynard, Mitchell, Moorhead, Anson P. Morrill, Nugen, Olin, Patton, Timothy G. Phelps, Pike, Price, Alexander H. Rice, John N. Rice, Riddle, James S. Rollins, Sargent, Shanks, Shellabarger, Sherman, Sloane, Spaulding, John B. Steele, Stevens, Trimble, Trowbridge, Upton, Van Horn, Van Valkenburgh, Van Wyck, Verree, Wall, Wallace, Charles W. Walton, Whaley, Albert S. White, Wilson, Windom, and Worcester—93.

NAYS.—Ancona, Baxter, Biddle, George H. Browne, Cobb, Frederick A. Conkling, Roscoe Conkling, Conway, Corning, Cox, Cravens, Crisfield, Diven, Dunlap, Eliot, English, Goodwin, Grider, Harding, Holman, Horton, Johnson, Knapp, Law, Lazear, Lovejoy, Mallory, May, Menzies, Justin S. Morrill, Morris, Nixon, Noble, Norton, Odell, Pendleton, Perry, Pomeroy, Potter, Richardson, Robinson, Edward H. Rollins, Sedgwick, Sheffield, Shiel, William G. Steele, Stratton, Benjamin F. Thomas, Francis Thomas, Train, Vallandigham, Voorhees, Wadsworth, E. P. Walton, Ward, Webster, Chilton A. White, Wickliffe, and Wright—59.

In the Senate the motion to strike out the legal-tender clause was lost, eleven for, to twenty-two against :

YEAS.—Anthony, Bayard, Collamer, Cowan, Fessenden, Foot, Foster, Kennedy, King, Latham, and Willey—11.

NAYS.—Chandler, Clark, Davis, Dixon, Doolittle, Harlan, Harris, Henderson, Howard, Howe, Lane of Indiana, McDougall, Morrill, Pomeroy, Rice, Sherman, Sumner, Ten Eyck, Wade, Wilkinson, Wilson of Massachusetts, and Wilson of Missouri—22.

On the passage of the bill, the vote was :

YEAS.—Anthony, Chandler, Clark, Davis, Dixon, Doolittle, Fessenden, Foot, Foster, Grimes, Hale, Harlan, Harris, Henderson, Howard, Howe, Lane of Indiana, Latham, McDougall, Morrill, Pomeroy, Rice, Sherman, Sumner, Ten Eyck, Trumbull, Wade, Wilkinson, Wilson of Massachusetts, and Wilson of Missouri—30.

NAYS.—Collamer, Cowan, Kennedy, King, Pearce, Powell, and Saulsbury—7.

Thus the bill was passed.

Some amendments of the Senate were arranged, but these votes fairly show the judgment of the Houses. The act was approved February 25, 1862. The principal things anthorized were the issue of $150,000,000, including the $50,000,000 by the act of July 17th—receivable for all dues, except duties on imports (which would remain payable in coin), and a legal-tender for all debts—to be reissued. The issue of $500,000,000 5-20 bonds, interest payable semi-annually, in coin, which might be sold for lawful money, including Treasury notes, to be held exempt from State taxation. The holders of the legal-tender notes could exchange for the bonds in sums of $100. There was also a suspension of the sub-Treasury law.

Coin received on duties was devoted to the payment of interest on the bonds.

This $150,000,000 was soon exhausted, and Secretary Chase, on the 7th of June following, asked for $150,-000,000 more ; $35,000,000 to be in sums less than five dollars. This passed the House June 11th, seventy-six for, to forty-seven against, and in the Senate July 2d, twenty-two for, to thirteen against. Sherman and other strong Republicans were with the nays. We also created the fractional currency—at first using the postal-stamp design. We had used the ordinary post-office stamps themselves for change. There were $30,000,000 of this fractional currency.[1]

---

[1] Legal-tender in the Supreme Court.

Lane Co. vs. The State of Oregon. The Supreme Court decided that legal-tender Treasury notes were not a legal-tender in payment of taxes levied by that State. 7 Wall, 71.

So in a case where by contract payment was to be made in gold. *Brownson vs. Rohdes, id.,* 259.

The court, by Chief-Justice Chase, held that a contract payable in dollars,

I may here state briefly our further financial legislation. At our third session we passed an act, approved March 3, 1863, for a loan of $900,000,000. A provision of this act prohibited, at the discretion of the Secretary of the Treasury, the funding of legal-tenders in the six per cent. bonds, and he cut such funding off. The act provided a five per cent. 10-40 bond, which the Secretary failed to float, and gold advanced ultimately to 285, or rather greenbacks, the representatives of the nation's credit and financial honor, sank to thirty-five cents of the promised dollar. When Mr. Chase left the Treasury Department, June 30, 1864, there was $1,000,000,000 of our paper afloat or sunk, which became a complex mass of greenbacks, interest-bearing notes, certificates of indebtedness, fractional currency, the currency of the new national banks, beside the bills of the suspended State banks. There are those who regard Mr. Chase's prohibition of funding demand Treasury notes into the six per cents. as the greatest mistake of the war.

The National Bank Bill passed the Senate February 12, 1863—twenty-three for, to twenty-one against,—and came to us; we passed it seventy-eight to sixty-four. The scheme made the United States bonds a basis ("atmospheric basis," as Mr. Morrill called it) of banking. This

---

made before the legal-tender acts, could not be satisfied by legal-tender notes. *Hepburn vs. Griswold*, 8 Wall, 604.

The court consisted of eight Justices ; *five*, Chase, Nelson, Greer, Clifford, and Field, made the decision, Changes in the court were made, which had reached the full number—nine, namely, Chase, Nelson, Clifford, Swayne, Miller, Davis, Field, Strong, and Bradley. This court heard full argument on all the points involved, in *Knox vs. Lee* and *Barber vs. Davis*, December term, 1870. Strong delivered the opinion of the court, five to four, holding that debts contracted before the passage of the Legal-Tender Act of February 25, 1862, were payable in legal-tender notes—thus overruling *Hepburn vs. Griswold*.

Elaborate contra opinions were delivered by the Chief Justice, Justices Clifford and Field. 12 Wall, 457.

The Chief Justice spoke bitterly, to the writer, of this result and said the President (Grant) had on this question *packed* the Court.

made a demand for bonds, and the banks could issue $300,000,000 in notes for circulation.

Returning to the second—or *first regular* session. The Internal Revenue Act was passed July 1, 1862. This laid duties on various products, liquors, incomes, trades, and occupations, and created the whole system of internal revenue, with its collectors and officers. The proceeds were really enormous.

These three—Treasury Notes, National Banks, and Internal Revenue—completed the circle of war financial measures. There was also a rebel land-tax,' and an increase of import duties.

The national bank scheme was designed by Mr. Chase as a relief war measure; it was not so regarded generally. Yet it will be seen that it was in a way the keystone of the system of credit upon which the war was fought. To give something of stability to the greenbacks, which knew no redeemer, they were made convertible into coupon gold-bearing bonds, until this was arrested by the Secretary of the Treasury. To float these again, a system of national banking was devised, resting wholly upon these very bonds, so that with the call of the greenback holders for bonds for a time and the huge demand for them created by the National Currency Act, to bank upon, a steady demand for their thousands of millions could always be depended upon, while the only vitalizing spirit that could animate the whole ever-growing porous bulk was the small driblet of gold filtered into it from the customs.

---

¹ Under this land-tax title was sought to be acquired to Arlington, converted to a national cemetery. The tax was not paid, and the estate owned by the Custises—the home of Robert E. Lee—was sold under the tax law. The sale was set aside by the United States Circuit Court, and that decision confirmed by the Supreme Court, when Congress appropriated the sum of $150,000, for which the Custis heirs conveyed the estate to the United States. —22d U. S. Stats., p. 584. also, Lee 23. U. S. 16 Otto's Rep. 196.

The author predicted this result when consulted, and urged action under the Confiscation Act.

Is there anything more dreary and uninteresting than the *Congressional Globe?* We are now weary of it, though we have heard none of the heavy guns of the Senate. There will be chances for them. I will only name some of the further more important war measures of this the first regular session, which I had left, in order to trace through the financial legislation to the end, as a more perspicuous way of dealing with the heavy and complex labors of this Congress.

We passed several acts to increase the navy; large appropriations were also made for gunboats on the western rivers, the first amount being $1,000,000. In another act we authorized the construction of twenty steam ironclad gunboats for which $10,000,000 were to be paid.

A bill for the relief of the widows of the men killed by the destruction of the frigates *Congress* and *Cumberland*, sunk by the *Merrimac*, was passed, and a new general pension code was formulated. The important act to suppress insurrection, punish treason, and confiscate the property of traitors, gave Congress much trouble in connection with the treason provisions. It was not easy to adjust these to the discriminating views of the President, who was as wise as he was discriminating.

There was also the very important captured-and-abandoned property law, under which was realized much value from cotton, tobacco, rice, resin, and other property.

We gave thanks to General Lyon; to Commodore Foote, and to the army and navy generally; to Commodore Foote again; to Commodore Goldsborough; to officers of gunboats, to Lieutenant Worden, Farragut, and General Grant. "Who is Grant? Where does he live?" was eagerly asked—this after the capture of Forts Henry and Donelson. We thanked everybody—even Halleck,—though I never knew what for. Finally we thanked McClellan.

CHAPTER XVII.

SLAVERY AGAIN.

Denationalizing Slavery—A Radical Speech.

WE had much to say and do about slavery that winter —work of a very healthy and vigorous character. Slavery became a constant target of assault, and, curiously enough, no man ventured a word in its defence or excuse. The attempt was to save it on other grounds than its merits. A great many speeches were made against it in Committee of the Whole in the House, upon the state of the Union, in which the whole subject of the war—cause, conduct, and everything connected with it, was talked over in a very direct way. The Senate was fully as industrious, and talked more. The list of the bills and joint resolutions in the two Houses, having to do with the subject, in the session with which I am dealing, was enormous.

A bill was reported to the House by Lovejoy, which proposed to make freedom national and slavery sectional, and to place slavery everywhere within the jurisdiction of the Government of the United States, in all the territories, forts, navy-yards, ships, camps, and armies. Mr. Cox, Mr. Wickliffe, and others of his faith, promptly assailed this bill. It was discussed at great length in the House, and still more largely in the Senate. It passed the House eighty-five to fifty, as follows:

YEAS.—Aldrich, Alley, Arnold, Ashley, Babbitt, Baker, Baxter, Beaman, Bingham, Francis P. Blair, Samuel S. Blair, Blake, Buffinton, Campbell, Chamberlain, Clark, Colfax, Frederick A. Conkling, Roscoe Conkling, Cutler, Davis, Delano, Diven, Duell, Dunn, Edgerton, Edwards, Eliot, Ely, Fenton, Fessenden, Franchot, Frank, Gooch, Granger, Hale, Harrison, Hickman, Hooper, Horton, Hutchins, Julian, Kelley, William Kellogg, Lansing, Loomis, Lovejoy, McKnight, McPherson, Mitchell, Moorhead, Anson P. Morrill, Justin S. Morrill, Olin, Pike, Porter, Potter, Alexander H. Rice, John H. Rice, Riddle, Edward H. Rollins, Sargent, Sedgwick, Shanks, Sheffield, Shellabarger, Stevens, Stratton, Benjamin F. Thomas, Train, Trimble, Trowbridge, Van Horn, Verree, Wall, Wallace, Charles W. Walton, E. P. Walton, Washburne, Wheeler, Albert S. White, Wilson, Windom, and Worcester—85.

NAYS.—Allen, Ancona, Joseph Baily, Biddle, Jacob B. Blair, George H. Browne, William G. Brown, Calvert, Casy, Clements, Cobb, Cox, Cravens, Crisfield, Crittenden, Dunlap, English, Girder, Haight, Hall, Harding, Holman, Johnson, Kerrigan, Knapp, Law, Lazear, Leary, Lehman, Mallory, Maynard, Menzies, Morris, Noell, Odell, Perry, John S. Phelps, Richardson, Robinson, Segar, John B. Steele, William G. Steele, Francis Thomas, Vibbard, Voorhees, Wadsworth, Ward, Webster, Wickliffe, and Woodruff—50.

In the Senate, on the final passage, the vote was:

YEAS.—Anthony, Browning, Chandler, Clark, Collamer, Cowan, Dixon, Fessenden, Foot, Foster, Grimes, Hale, Harlan, Harris, Howard, Howe, King, Lane of Indiana, Pomeroy, Rice, Simmons, Sumner, Ten Eyck, Trumbull, Wade, Wilkinson, Wilmot, and Wilson of Massachusetts —28.

NAYS.—Carlisle, Davis, Kennedy, Latham, McDougall, Nesmith, Powell, Saulsbury, Stark, and Wright—10.

By arrangement in the general debate in Committee of the Whole, Mr. Riddle secured the floor, for which he had long struggled, on January 27th.

He began with a statement of the problem then up for its final solution—the disposition of the African race in the Republic—or rather the fortune of the Republic itself —they were mutually dependent.

" I do not like this question ; I never did. I wish it were not here, nor anywhere ; but it is upon us, and we may not avoid it. It is in and about everything ; mixed with everything ; or, rather, it has itself become everything. We need not now stop to complain of it, nor blame anybody for it. We may be indignant that it so blocks up the way of the nation, and prevents the development of our own race. We may say the negro is not worth all this clamor, nor any part of it. That does not get rid of him. And you are to remember that he did not bring himself and this war here. Negroes never emigrate. He was stolen and planted here against his wish : and out of the ground which has been cursed with his alien feet has sprung this infernal question. A million of armed soldiers are debating it. It is the argument of every red field of conflict. Every morning a million of bayonets come pricking through the cloud of night to cross and clash over it. It must be solved and settled. It must be talked about ; all that everybody knows of it, or thinks about it, had better straightway be said—said as well as men can say it ; with good intent and for good purpose. Let us see it in all the lights in which it can be exhibited, and find, if may be, a way out of it. Jurists and judges declare in substance that slavery is the direct fruit of war itself. It is perpetual war waged by the master and his allies against the slave who has few allies. Being war, it must maintain itself by the constant exercise of the active principles of war—aggression and conquest. It conquers earth on which to plant itself, and sky to shelter it. It decomposes and reconstructs the very atmosphere, so as to impart life and vigor to its lungs, and makes conquest of the sentiment about it to procure immunity and toleration, if not support."

This thought is pursued until it is shown that the allies of the master have formed the slave States—and of them formed a union of all the States, and that union is made the ally of the slave master in this war.

" I know it has been argued, and urged, and believed, too, that the free States were in no way responsible for the existence of slavery in the slave States. The Constitution of the United States, and the slave code said to be enacted pursuant to its provisions, and all the various acts of the several

States imposing disabilities upon this race, are an infamous refutation of this claim, and furnish the exact measure of that responsibility.

" The aggressions of slavery continued until, in the nation as in the State, it had debauched the public morals, enchained the church, and overcome the national conscience. I need not pursue this farther. Ultimately, when the people arose to limit further conquests and overthrew it in a political contest, this slavery, in obedience to the law of its life, and pursuant to the conclusions of its own logic, appealed to its old weapon, the war club of its heathen founder.

" Sir, the election of Mr. Lincoln had little to do with this war, it would unavoidably have taken place had Mr. Douglas been elected. The course of events had conducted the struggle to this stage, and the ample and thorough preparation of the slaveholders, which they could not afford to lose, proves that they had predetermined the time of hostilities. The canker, long gnawing within, had eaten its way to the surface.

" This rebel war makes us the inevitable allies of the slave in his war against the master ; and every slaveholder is in some sense, involuntarily it may be, the ally of the rebels ; and it is a most wonderful indication that the limits of the infected region exactly coincide with the boundary lines of the slave States."

THE SLAVE AS A SUBJECT OF THE UNITED STATES OWES IT ALLEGIANCE, AND IS ENTITLED TO ITS PROTECTION.

We must permit the speaker to sustain this proposition in his own way.

" Is the slave wholly enveloped, submerged, and lost in the power and control of the master, or is there outside of the master, and above him, still another and greater power to which the slave sustains relations independent of his master ? Did it ever occur to you, gentlemen, that the slave had such relations to a power higher than the master, through which claims upon him might be asserted at utter variance with the master's claims ? I know that without question or argument it has been conceded that no such relations exist. I am bound by no such concession ; and I am to establish the contrary, and maintain it if I may.

" In our fundamental laws slaves are known only as persons—recognized as part of the great mass of persons. Does that instrument erase from them the universal quality of subjects, or stamp upon them one inconsistent with that character ? They are ' persons owing service,' which is a recognition of an obligation imposed on them by another power ; but they themselves are subordinate to the power created by the Constitution, within which they are brought by apt words of description, and this new power may impose on them obligations inconsistent with the old. They are ' persons owing service,' just as are minors and apprentices, and, in the same sense, are subjects.

So far as this Constitution has created legislative sovereignty at all, it has conferred it on the two Houses of Congress. It makes them sovereign over all persons with no exception whatever. The relation then between this Legislature and your slaves, is that of sovereign and subjects ; and I demand to know what power there is on earth that can come between this sovereign and these subjects. Do they owe you service? They owe us allegiance. Are they your slaves? They are our subjects. We are the lord paramount with the highest title. States alone are prohibited from discharging slaves from the debt of service they are said to owe. The debt of service was not created by contract nor can it be construed to come between us and our subjects. It would dethrone the sovereign.

" This reasoning is not subtile and refined, depending on technical and artificial rules, but rests on broad, well-known principles. Our right to legislate upon the person of the slave, rests upon the broad ground of a great sovereign dealing with his subject—in opposition to a private despot lording over a cringing serf. It is no reply to this to say that slavery is older than the Constitution, and was established by sovereigns not within the control of that Constitution ; because these sovereigns, who, as between themselves and their subjects, called these persons slaves, when, for our purposes, they came to surrender the mass of their subjects to our sovereignty, put in these slaves, not as slaves, but as persons ; so that while to them (the former sovereigns) they remain slaves, they are to us subjects, and by the consent of their masters. If a State can by disabilities withdraw one class of persons within its borders from our jurisdiction, it may another, and all others, which is absurd. I am not here contending for power on our part to abolish slavery, or any other relation or institution established by the States. I am only contending for the right of the sovereign paramount to control the persons of all his subjects alike, in the presence of which right all the privileges and disabilities imparted by inferior power are abrogated, of course. And I here assert that this right extends to all persons not aliens, the subjects of foreign Powers."

SLAVES MAY BY FIAT OF CONGRESS BECOME SOLDIERS.

" Not only on general principles does this power result to us from the relation of sovereign and subject, but the Constitution, in specific terms, confers a power for a given purpose, under which we can legislate upon ' persons owing service ' in a manner wholly inconsistent with the supposed rights of the master or parent.

" The eighth section of the first article authorizes us ' to raise and support armies,' and ' to provide for organizing, arming, and disciplining the militia," etc. This power of raising armies, and of organizing the militia, necessarily involves the power to designate what persons shall constitute the army or militia. We cannot legislate upon States ; and they might fail to furnish us with the requisite material ; we do legislate in all cases upon persons, and may upon all persons. Suppose that we declare that all male citizens owning unencumbered estates of the value of $50,000, shall constitute the militia ; what power could stand between them and this burden ? Or, suppose that we enact that all male persons having a visible admixture of African blood shall compose this militia ; who could interpose between us and them ? "

MR. WICKLIFFE.—I would like to make an inquiry of the gentleman. Does he contend that the Federal Government has a right to enlist slaves in the Army of the United States?

MR. RIDDLE.—I contend that it has a right to enlist "*persons* held to service." If you call them slaves, they are still our subjects.

MR. WICKLIFFE.—The gentleman knows what I mean.

MR. RIDDLE.—Certainly.

MR. WICKLIFFE.—Do I understand the gentleman as saying that the Government of the United States has a a right to enlist slaves, or persons held in service, in the army.

MR. RIDDLE.—I contend that the Government of the United States may enlist persons owing service who are our subjects.

MR. WICKLIFFE.—Then I do not wonder at the gentleman's letter to his constituents.[1]

MR. RIDDLE.—I am dealing with things in an elementary way, and quoting the language of the Constitution. If persons owing service under that Constitution are slaves, I answer unhesitatingly in the affirmative. I am here and everywhere to sustain the doctrine as best I can.

" If we were to say legislatively ' that all native male persons between the ages of eighteen and forty years shall constitute the national militia to be enrolled, organized, and disciplined as hereinafter is provided,' these questions might arise under it. A citizen of Pennsylvania might say to you : ' That person whom you propose to carry away to your camp of instruction, is my apprentice. These are the indentures, in full conformity with the laws of this Commonwealth, which give me a full right to his services and the full control of his person for a period not yet expired, and impose upon me heavy obligations for his personal well-being, which I cannot discharge if he is taken from me.' And yet you would march him away. A citizen of

---

[1] Poor old Roman. This was too much ; I had gained his heart in the Lehman case. He now gave me up.

Massachusetts tells you : 'That, gentlemen, is my minor son of lawful wed-lock. The laws of this State confirm to me his person and services until he is of the full age of twenty-one years ; you cannot come between me and him.' But you oblige the minor son to fall in at the drum-beat. 'That,' says the lordly Virginian, 'is my boy, born of a slave mother on my planta-tion ; he is my slave, my property, my chattel, don't touch him.' You have taken from the Pennsylvanian his apprentice, and from the Massachusetts father his minor son. Dare any man stand here and declare that the right of the master to his slave is more sacred than the right of the father to his son ? You may take one of these slaves, you may take all of them, to the exclusion of everybody else, for your militia, and by this means find a solu-tion of this problem if you choose. This is a power without doubt or un-certainty, pertaining to us all alike in peace and in war, the existence of which cannot be gainsaid. I thus find in the relation of the slaves to the Government ample power under the Constitution to deal effectually with their *Status*."

Mr. Riddle then discussed the power to deal with slavery as derived from the state of war, a power which necessarily belonged to Congress, where was deposited all legislative power. In another part of this extended speech, he said :

"Sir, this thing of slavery was always a religious and moral outlaw, a confessed and convicted felon with a halter about its neck, invoking execu-tion at the hands of an outraged universe. Its only defence was an alleged constitutional barrier behind which it was trenched. That barrier it has itself broken down, and it stands exposed in its hideousness to the assaults of the human race ; and who dares to say that it should not be crushed. I believe that, in the economy of God's government, the time is fully come for its extirpation—that the forces now moving the profound depths of our political compact will themselves, ere they are spent, work its demolition. To that consummation I will gladly contribute ; and I would now by a wise forecast, so far as may be, direct these agencies, so that in their beneficent mission they may work the least amount of incidental harm. Resist them we cannot ; aid them I will. Do not misunderstand or misapply this remark. This doctrine is not the teaching or practice of my party. The sentiment is my own ; and I here declare that I will now and at all times seize any op-portunity to strike slavery on its own account. I will lift my hand and ask God for strength to make that blow effectual.

"Sir, this is an eminently practical and importunate matter ; you may postpone this debate, but the question not at all. We deliberate, as no Congress under the Constitution ever before deliberated, under the very muzzles of the enemy's guns, prepared to thunder their inexorable logic upon this debated matter, leaving no doubt of their views or policy."

Some pointed things were said of the President and his policy of the war ; of him personally he spoke with tender and lofty respect :

"I profoundly respect and esteem him; I can comprehend the nature of his fearfully trying position and its surroundings ; but I am a representative of the people, the humblest of whom has a personal stake in his country equal to that of the first citizen, and I am to utter frankly the best conclusions of my judgment.   This terrible juncture requires not only all the strength of all the people, but demands the suggestions of their whole mind and thought, freely uttered.

"I regret, greatly regret, that, when we first met, the Executive could not have indicated to us and the country a decided policy. It may have been wiser to leave events to hammer it out, but ultimately they will demonstrate to him that the true course lies along this opening path which we must pursue, rugged and thorny though it be. Sir, our people expected this of him, and were disappointed.   They are in advance of the President ; in advance of us.   Their intuitions outrun our argumentation, and they are at home long ere we reach our tardy and halting conclusions.   The movement of the radical forces now in motion has produced a radical movement of the races of men not amenable to the laws of ordinary superficial political agitation ; it runs below.   When the President issued his proclamation for 75,000 men to enforce his laws, the people heard in it a proclamation of Omnipotence to enforce his laws.   They felt as if the divine hand were stretched down among them, and their hearts thrilled under the touch of the finger of God !   They looked to the President for a leader ; they almost expected to see him tower up till he caught a ray of inspiration, and became their prophet.   They see he is no prophet, and fear that he is no leader.   He coldly and timidly seats himself on the narrowest letter of the Constitution, and hesitatingly applies its feeblest and shortest instrumentalities to events bearing upon slavery, wholly out of its scope.   These rebels have gone out of and away from the Constitution, and if you would deal with them you must go out after them.

"Will not gentlemen comprehend this ?   The Constitution is predicated on the idea that all the States will remain in the orbits it defines, and when they break away from these orbits it furnishes no remedy.   Under it you may arrest, indict, and try ; but these rebels have wrenched up and carried off this whole legal machinery, and it is cowardly to stand shivering over mere constitutional names when its armies are gone.   Up and after these traitors with any and all means.   Like Milton's angels, when they encountered the masked batteries of the seceded devils, tear up the mountains, lift the islands by their tree-tops, and overwhelm them !   I revere and venerate the Constitution, but I love my country a million times more.   The one was formed and may be dissolved by the breath of men.   The other is the creation and growth of God ; and rather than that mere constitutional names should stand

in the way of the nation's salvation, better a thousand times solemnly roll
the Constitution up and lay it reverently away. These, too, are not the
sentiments of my party."

He ridiculed some features of the policy developed by
Congress; which had authorized the capture of rebel
property *used in battle*. A general in the field had been
disarmed by it; and the Secretary of War rendered
powerless. This was not the President's fault; he but
assented to it, to avoid discord.

He turned upon Mr. Wadsworth of Kentucky, who
had threatened the Republicans with the secession of the
residue of the border States. Complaint was made of
the suffering of the loyal in those States, by prosecuting
the war in them against the rebel armies, which, holding
so much of them, made a wide area of war and misrule.
The great trouble was the loss of slave property. That
was the one dominating grief.

He demanded :

" Shall the whole country perish because its salvation would bring peculiar
hardships, not to their lives or persons, but to their property alone, which
may be compensated for? In the name of all that is fearful in this exigency, what is it you demand for them, and at what a fearful hazard ? Does
not all this mean that at all events *slavery* is to be the one thing not to
suffer? Is it not weighing it naked and alone against the nation, and in a
doubtful balance? What fearful and terrible apprehensions this suggests !
And if the time ever arrives in the councils of the Executive to make the
hesitating choice, where will the patriots of the border States be found ?

'' ' Gentle Shepherd, tell us where.'

" Sir, the gentleman from Kentucky [Mr. Wadsworth] more than answers
this inquiry, and tells us where. They will strike, doubtingly and languidly,
with us, until we differ about the mode of carrying on the war, and then
against us. Be it so. Is this the measure and standard of a Kentuckian's
love of country? Were all these florid professions but painted bubbles,
filled with tainted breath ? What does he mean' Kentucky would remain
true to the Constitution and in the Union ; but then, in a given event, the
rebellion would 'grow to such proportions as to include *fifteen States*.' Let
it grow if it will. The gentleman may then lern, if he is curious, whether
we can endure the 'smell of gunpowder.' I represent the gentleman as I
understood him. Are these the descendants c the Kentuckians of 1812 ; of

that gallant host which came plunging through the woods to our far-off invaded border ; which raised the seige of Fort Meigs, and aided us to pursue and capture a British army on British soil? Do not say we are ungrateful for this, or that we would injure Kentuckians. Already thirty-five thousand bayonets have gone sparkling over the dividing river from Ohio to prove that we cannot forget ; to prove that we so detest Kentucky that we thrust our brave and beautiful ones between her and her foes, and give her a chance to rally her own sons. What do gentlemen mean by these charges on this floor ? Who is Garfield, and whence come his forty-second regiment? Who is McCook and his ninth ? Where got they their bayonets? And whence came Kinney, who planted his guns within sixty yards of murderous musketry? And the gallant Standart, and the fragile, girlish boy Wetmore, with his lion heart and Parrott guns? All save McCook and his ninth are from my own fanatic region. Standart and his heroes are from my own city, and Wetmore took his men from a single neighborhood of my district—all identical in sentiment, yet they asked no questions, they made no conditions, and they never will. The blood runs as red and hot and generous on the breezy shores of Lake Erie as in a more southern clime. If more men are needed, there are thousands ready to go—take all. The last heart shall beat and break under the war-hoof, without question or condition. No wavering or hesitation weakens an arm or checks the devotion of my people.

The speech of sixteen pages was delivered at the darkest hour of that dark winter, and an effort has been here made to reduce it to the portions which deal with the most pressing demands of that day then drawing to a crisis. It closed thus :

" To nations, as to individuals, is given but a single life ; and its hopes and opportunities are measured by the span of its to-day. Who can say when our to-day shall close? Even now its hours seem to decline and languish. The sands of its minutes are crushed to impalpable dust by the fearful burdens rolled upon them—burdens that we must carry, or under which we must perish.' [1]

---

[1] The moment a man finishes and is thought not to have failed, a page approaches, and, amid congratulations, presents a prospectus to publish. It was said at the time that this one was so liberally subscribed for that the edition would be one of the largest of the session. I remember that Mr. McKee Dunn (later General Dunn), and one or two more, came to me later and said : " Now, after the glamour and passion of your speaking have passed, I dare not send the speech into my district ; I will give you my list of names, and you may send it under your frank and have my copies." His constituents got the speech, and I received many pleasant letters from them.

CHAPTER XVIII.

THE PRESIDENT'S ORDER CONCERNING FUGITIVE SLAVES.

FEBRUARY, 1862.

A Dinner-Table Scene—Emancipation in the Senate.

SOMETIME in February an outside matter caused a good deal of feeling—feeling largely directed against the President. It was inevitable, in the disturbed condition of things in Virginia, that a great many slaves should escape and seek refuge in the District, where, as they possibly understood, we were threatening to *free* all the slaves. The black race had a way of their own of diffusing information, by which our Generals sometimes profited. General Butler early invented a convenient name for these diffusers of news ; he styled the slave "a contraband of war," and these comers from beyond rebel lines were all "reliable contrabands." Of course slave property in Maryland became unsettled and fugacious, and we had already interdicted the use of the District prisons for the confinement of runaway slaves. There came at this time from eastern Maryland six or seven slaves belonging to a constituent of Mr. Crisfield. The President was applied to in the matter, and he directed his marshal, Ward H. Lammon, to arrest and deliver the slaves to their owner. It was openly and ostentatiously done with proclamation and circumstance.

At this time we were living at Mrs. Irving's, on 4½ street. She was an ideal landlady and usually had a good class of people in her house. On this day of the returned bondmen, I was late at dinner, and reached the dining-room after the soup. There was a group of us at the lower end of the table, where Senator Pearce sat, in a high chair, like a boy on a bible, facing the handsome and still young landlady. On his left sat Dr. Welling, editor of the *Intelligencer*, and next to him was Calvert, of the old Maryland family, and I think one of the Kentucky members of Congress sat by him. On his right were Webster and Crisfield of Maryland, and my seat was next to Crisfield. Above us were ladies, gentlemen, and one or two children.

The *thing* had been pre-arranged in my group for my benefit, as I found later. I was not talkative nor hungry, and was dallying with my soup, noticing that my friends were in unusual good spirits. I should say that every day these men would discuss slavery with me, and I, like "Eve, was nothing loth," and had spoken as freely as at home or in the House. I had no more than gained my seat when Crisfield began:

"I really am coming to have not only a very great confidence in President Lincoln, but a great deal of admiration for him personally, and these have been much increased by his conduct to-day and by what I saw done pursuant to his order.'

I knew this was intended for me, but took no notice of it; it was likely to fail, when Webster, then nearly a Republican, turned and asked: "To what particular thing do you refer as happening to-day, Mr. Crisfield?"

"The return of ———'s slaves. I was present when the President issued the order to the marshal, and I saw the marshal when he delivered them up. It was very impressive."

This was quite too much. (He spoke as addressing me.)

"Mr. Crisfield," I said, "I understand you stand high as a most exemplary member of the Presbyterian Church —that you are quite a Christian example."

"I am an humble follower of that faith. I pretend to no special excellence."

"You must have experienced a special religious exaltation of soul, on witnessing this return of these poor men to their hereditary whipping-post and auction-block, *though the time will be short,*" I replied.

"I don't know," he answered, a little confused, "that I felt any special religious experience."

The conversation had attracted general attention. I felt at least two pairs of large black eyes flashing down upon me.

Mr. Pearce imperiously broke in: "The fugitive-slave law places every man at the command of the marshal, to aid in the actual seizure and delivery of slaves. What would you do, Mr. Riddle, what could you say, if you were called upon under the law by a marshal to take and deliver up these slaves?"

"Mr. Pearce," turning upon him, "you have no business to ask me that question *here.* But you have, and I will put an end to this catechism. Much as I have esteemed and respected you, before I would in any way aid in returning a slave to you, I would shoot you dead where you sit," with the emphasis of my extended arm shaking a finger in his face. I heard a dropping of knives and forks, and there were several seconds of frozen silence. The old senator was a duelist, and had a grown son ; his face became ghastly at the defiance—a moment, then it broke into a *crackled* smile, like a shattered earthen vase. "Mr. Riddle," he said, "we have all respected and admired you as a man of courage and spirit. Your spirit is a little more than the occasion requires, perhaps, but you have answered as a gentleman should. *It is not the business of a gentleman to handle slaves.*"

" Mr. Pearce," I replied, " I have no apology for my warmth; and I have only to say that at the north we have no property *that a gentleman may not handle.*"

Some months later when the old cavalier passed away, Crisfield and others asked me to speak of him in the House, and I did.

We in the House attempted to instruct the Judiciary Committee to report a bill for the repeal of the Fugitive Slave Act, but failed. The resolution was laid on the table by a vote of sixty-six to fifty-one. We did pass, by a vote of seventy-seven to forty-three, a resolution to report a bill requiring a trial by jury to establish the fugitive's status.

YEAS.—Aldrich, Alley, Arnold, Ashley, Babbitt, Baker, Baxter, Beaman, Bingham, Francis P. Blair, Blake, Buffinton, Burnham, Chamberlin, Colfax, Frederick A. Conkling, Davis, Dawes, Delano, Diven, Edgerton, Edwards, Eliot, Ely, Franchot, Gooch, Goodwin, Granger, Gurley, Haight, Hale, Hanchett, Hutchins, Julian, Kelley, Francis W. Kellogg, William Kellogg, Lansing, Loomis, Lovejoy, Low, McKnight, McPherson, Mitchell, Anson P. Morrill, Justin S. Morrill, Nixon, Timothy G. Phelps, Pike, Pomeroy, Porter, Potter, Alexander H. Rice, John H. Rice, Riddle, Edward H. Rollins, Sargent, Shanks, Sheffield, Shellabarger, Sloan, Spaulding, Stevens, Stratton, Benjamin F. Thomas, Train, Trimble, Trowbridge, Van Valkenburgh, Verree, Wall, Wallace, Washburne, Albert S. White, Wilson, Windom, and Worcester—77.

NAYS.—William J. Allen, Ancona, Baily, Biddle, Jacob B. Blair, William G. Brown, Calvert, Casey, Clements, Cobb, Corning, Crittenden, Fouke, Grider, Harding, Holman, Johnson, Knapp, Maynard, Menzies, Noble, Noel, Norton, Pendleton, John S. Phelps, Richardson, Robinson, James S. Rollins, Segar, Shiel, Smith, John B. Steele, William G. Steele, Francis Thomas, Vallandigham, Vibbard, Voorhees, Wadsworth, Webster, Chilton A. White, Wickliffe, Wood, and Wright—43.

The House governs the United States, and this vote was significant. As stated, my colleague Hutchins intro-. duced a bill for the abolition of slavery in the District of Columbia. A bill for that purpose was about the same time also introduced in the Senate by Senator Wilson. The main features of the bills were to free all persons of African descent, held to labor in the District; owners, if loyal, to be compensated in sums not exceeding $300 for each slave, on proof of their loyalty and of the value of their slaves. Commissioners, to be appointed by the President, were to hear applicants on sworn petitions, and award compensation. A million was appropriated. The bills were very fully discussed in both Houses. Mr. McDougall, an exceptionally able Senator, spoke in part as follows:

" Mr. President, I regard this measure, as I have regarded all measures bearing upon the same subject introduced into this Senate, as inopportune at this time. In saying that I regard them as inopportune, I intend to express no opinion as to their several merits. There are many measures that I would vote against at this session of Congress on the ground that this was not the time to present or consider them. This I regard as one of those inopportune measures, not necessarily, however, as governing my conduct in the same direction.

" Again, sir, I think that during this session of Congress there have been hurried upon the Senate imperfect, unmatured measures, measures under-taking to administer vast interests, which in any other council of Govern-ment where laws were to be established would have commanded the gravest and most deliberate consideration and complete and exact legislation. A great deal of immature legislation has been presented for our action, and of those measures, this bill, as it is presented to the Senate, is a specimen.

" As for the power of Congress to abolish slavery in the District of Co-lumbia, I think there cannot, at this time, be any question. That the power belongs to this Congress, to the Government here, I think is unquestionable as a question of power. Slavery is a creature of positive law ; and when the law whereby the master has the right of manumission, the right of power over the subject slaves is repealed, slavery ceases. That is unquestionably the law. We have the general administration of the laws of the District. We have the right, that is, the legal right, to abolish slavery in the District at any time we please. This cannot be matter of argument. I have no scruples or trouble on that subject.

" But, sir, as I have had occasion to say frequently in the Senate, I have thought it wise that all these disturbing questions should be postponed to some time after we have conquered our imminent difficulties. When we have disposed of the enemies of the Republic arrayed against us in the field, in the effort to accomplish which we want all the united opinion we can bring to bear about and in support of the Government; when with that united opinion we have hurled down treason and re-established the power of the Government through the Union, then would be the time to take up and consider these matters of local legislation which have been thrust on us with such great haste.

" Now, so far as slavery in the District of Columbia is concerned, it is a positive evil. I know it. We all know it. We have neither free labor nor slave labor in the District. We have neither the benefit of one system nor the other. We are hybrid in our relation to service of any kind, or the employment of labor here. This is an evil that ought to be corrected. While this is my opinion, it is also my opinion that this is not the time to correct it. Whenever the proper time had, in my judgment, come for the abolition of slavery in the District, I would have been found its earnest advocate. I would have avoided it now ; but as it is brought forward, I will meet it to-day. I am for meeting it, however, as wisely as I can. I am not for inconsiderate measures calculating none of the contingencies that belong to such important legislation.

" This bill, as it is now presented, is a simple declaration of the immediate right of all persons held to service and labor in the District to be manumitted. In the first place, apart from its operation on the individual rights of owners, and saying nothing of that, one patent fact is, that according to the latest statistical information we have, there are sixteen hundred persons held to service in the District under fifteen and over fifty years of age— persons who, either from youth or old age, are unfit and unable to maintain themselves. How does this measure, said to be a beneficent measure, provide for them ? By the law now in force the old and young have a legal right to protection and support from the persons who hold them. There are sixteen hundred of them who will be immediately set free by this bill, and all the relations between master and servant immediately dissolved. Did not the gentlemen who projected this bill consider that the moment they pass this law, they must provide—if not in this bill—for establishing places and providing clothing, subsistence, and the entire support of about sixteen hundred persons in this District, on account of their youth or old age, independent of those who may be, from disease or other causes, unable to sustain themselves. Are we prepared to build an establishment here larger than our Treasury building, larger and more extensive than our Treasury and our Post-Office buildings, as quarters for the young, old, and indigent, besides assuming the burden of their clothing, subsistence, and management ? "

Mr. Sumner said:

" Mr. President, with unspeakable delight I hail this measure and the prospect of its speedy adoption. It is the first installment of that great debt which we all owe to an enslaved race, and will be recognized in history as one of the victories of humanity. At home throughout our own country, it will be welcomed with gratitude ; while abroad it will quicken the hopes of all who love freedom. Liberal institutions will gain everywhere by the abolition of slavery at the national capital. Nobody can read that slaves were once sold in the markets of Rome, beneath the eyes of the sovereign Pontiff, without confessing the scandal to religion, even in a barbarous age ; and nobody can hear that slaves are now sold in the markets of Washington, beneath the eyes of the President, without confessing the scandal to liberal institutions. For the sake of our good name, if not for the sake of justice, let the scandal disappear.

" In early discussions of this question there were many topics introduced which now command little attention. It was part of the tactics of slavery to claim absolute immunity. Indeed, without such immunity it had small chance of continued existence. Such a wrong, so utterly outrageous, could find safety only where it was protected from inquiry. Therefore slave-masters always insisted that the petitions against its existence at the National Capital were not to be received ; that it was unconstitutional to touch it even here within the exclusive jurisdiction of Congress ; and that if it were touched, it should be only under the auspices of the neighboring States of Virginia and Maryland. On these points elaborate arguments were constructed ; but it is useless to consider them now. Whatever may be the opinions of individual Senators, the judgment of the country is fixed. The right of petition, first vindicated by the matchless perseverance of John Quincy Adams, is now beyond question, and the constitutional power of Congress is hardly less free from doubt. It is enough to say on this point, that if Congress cannot abolish slavery here, then there is no power to abolish it here, and this wrong will endure always, immortal as the Capital itself.

" But as the moment of justice approaches we are called to meet a different objection, inspired by generous sentiments. It is argued that since there can be no such thing as property in man, especially within the exclusive jurisdiction of Congress, therefore all now held as slaves at the national capital are justly entitled to freedom, without price or compensation of any kind to masters ; or, at least, that any money paid should be distributed according to an account stated between masters and slaves. Of course, if this question were determined according to divine justice, so far as we may be permitted to look in that direction, it is obvious that nothing can be due to the masters, and that any money paid belongs rather to the slaves, who for generations have been despoiled of their rights and possession. But if we undertake to audit this fearful account, pray what sum shall be allowed for the prolonged torments of the lash ? What treasure shall be voted to the slave for wife ravished from his side, for children stolen, for knowledge shut out, and for all the fruits of labor wrested from him and his fathers ?

10

No such account can be stated. It is impossible. If you once begin the inquiry, all must go to the slave. It only remains for Congress, anxious to secure this great boon, and unwilling to embarrass or jeopard it, to act practically according to its finite powers, in the light of existing usages, and even existing prejudices, under which these odious relations have assumed the form of law; nor must we hesitate at any forbearance or sacrifice, provided freedom can be established without delay.

" Testimony and eloquence have both been accumulated against slavery; but on this occasion I shall confine myself precisely to the argument for the ransom of slaves at the national capital; although such is slavery that it is impossible to consider it in any single aspect without confronting its whole many-sided wickedness, while the broad, diversified field of remedies is naturally open to review. But at some other time the great question of emancipation in the States may be more fitly considered, together with those other questions in which the Senator from Wisconsin [Mr. Doolittle] has allowed himself to take sides so earnestly, whether there is an essential incompatibility between the two races, so that they cannot live together except as master and slave, and whether the freedman shall be encouraged to exile himself to other lands or to continue his labor here at home. It is surely enough for the present to consider slavery at the national capital; and here we are met by two inquiries so frankly addressed to the Senate by the clear-headed Senator from Kansas [Mr. Pomeroy] : *First, Has slavery any constitutional existence at the national capital? and, secondly, Shall money be paid to secure its abolition?* The answer to these two inquiries will make our duty clear. If slavery has no constitutional existence here, then more than ever is Congress bound to interfere, even with money; for the scandal must be peremptorily stopped, without any postponement or any consultation of the people on a point which is not within their power.

" It may be said that, whether slavery be constitutional or not, nevertheless it exists, and therefore this inquiry is superfluous. True it exists, as a *monstrous fact ;* but it is none the less important to consider its origin, that we may understand how, assuming the form of law, it was able to shelter itself beneath the protecting shield of the Constitution. And when we shall see clearly that it is without any such just protection, that the law which declares it is baseless, and that in all its pretensions it is essentially brutal and unnatural, we shall have less consideration for the slave tyranny, which, in satisfied pride, has thus far—not without compunction at different moments—ruled the national capital, reducing all things here—public opinion, social life, and even the administration of justice—to its own degraded standard, so as to fulfil the curious words of an English poet :

" ' It serves, yet reigns as King ;
It lives, yet 's death ; it pleases full of paine.
Monster ! ah ! who, who can their being faigne ?
Thou shapelesse shape, live death, paine pleasing, servile reign.'

" It is true there can be no such thing as property in man ; and here I begin to answer the questions propounded by the Senator from Kentucky [Mr. Davis].

.   .   .   .

" To all who insist that Congress may sustain slavery in the national Capital, I put the question, where in the Constitution is the power found ? If you cannot show where, do not assert the power. So hideous an effrontery must be authorized in unmistakable words. But where are the words ? In what article, clause, or line ? They cannot be found. Do not insult human nature by pretending that its most cherished rights can be sacrificed without solemn authority. Remember that every presumption and every leaning must be in favor of freedom and against slavery. Do not forget that no nice interpretation, no strained construction, no fancied deduction, can suffice to sanction the enslavement of our fellow-men. And do not degrade the Constitution by foisting into its blameless text the idea of property in man. It is not there ; and if you think you see it there, it is simply because you make the Constitution a reflection of yourself. . . ."

Mr. Sumner spoke on full preparation and with his usual felicity. He closed thus :

" Let this bill pass, and the first practical triumph of freedom, for which good men have longed, dying without the sight, for which a whole generation has petitioned, and for which orators and statesmen have pleaded, will at last be accomplished. Slavery will be banished from the national capital. This metropolis, which bears a venerated name, will be purified ; its evil spirit will be cast out ; its shame will be removed ; its society will be refined ; its courts will be made better ; its revolting ordinances will be swept away ; and even its loyalty will be secured. If not moved by justice to the slave, then be willing to act for your own good and in self-defence. If you hesitate to pass this bill for the blacks, then pass it for the whites. Nothing is clearer than that the degradation of slavery affects the master as much as the slave ; while recent events testify, that wherever slavery exists, there treason lurks, if it does not flaunt. From the beginning of this rebellion slavery has been constantly manifest in the conduct of the masters, and even here in the national capital, it has been the traitorous power which has encouraged and strengthened the enemy. This power must be suppressed at every cost, and if its suppression here endangers slavery elsewhere, there will be a new motive for determined action.

"Amidst all present solicitudes, the future cannot be doubtful. At the national capital slavery will give way to freedom ; but the good work will not stop here. It must proceed. What God and nature decree, rebellion cannot arrest. And as the whole wide-spread tyranny begins to tumble, then, above the din of battle, sounding from the sea and echoing along the land, above even the exaltations of victory on well-fought fields, will ascend voices of gladness and benediction, swelling from generous hearts wherever civilization bears sway, to commemorate a sacred triumph, whose trophies, instead of tattered banners, will be ransomed slaves."

Mr. Davis (of Kentucky) spoke as follows:

" Mr. President, I have had some experience in legislation, and I have always made it a principle to guide my course, that where a measure was objectionable to me and I intended to vote against it, still I would vote for every proposition of amendment which, in my judgment, would improve it and make it less objectionable. It was in conformity to that principle that I voted for the amendment proposed by the Senator from Wisconsin [Mr. Doolittle] to the amendment I had the honor of offering to the Senate, and then voted for the amendment as amended ; but at the same time it was my purpose to vote against the bill on the question of its final passage, because, even as amended, I thought the bill was subject to much more of objection than approval. I do not consider that there is anything wrong in that mode of legislation. A measure may be likely to pass a deliberative assembly, and a man may be opposed to the whole principle of it and to its general provisions, yet if, in his judgment, there be amendments offered which will improve the bill, he may fairly and honorably vote for those amendments, and then vote against the bill. I make this explanation for the purpose of showing my true position in relation to the matter.

" Mr. President, I am opposed to this bill, and I shall proceed to give some reasons upon which I base my opposition to it. The reason and the judgment of men constitute a very curious subject of study. We conceive a project beforehand. We have a favorite purpose or end to subserve, and, instead of honestly and in good faith hunting for truth and for principle and testing the validity and the propriety of our project or our ends by truth and principle, we endeavor to wrest truth and principle, and do violence to both by bringing them to the support of our theories and our acts. I am as much subject to this error as any other gentleman. It is a very common one, so much so as to be almost universal. But, sir, I shall endeavor to ascertain the true principles and the facts of the case that apply to the proposition now under consideration, and by that standard I shall endeavor to try and to test the proposition itself which is involved in the bill. . . .

" The Senator from Kansas [Mr. Pomeroy] took the position that there was no law in the District of Columbia that sanctioned or recognized the existence of slavery. I think that that is a very erroneous position. What law is there that declares that any particular thing shall be the subject of property ? What law is there in any of the States of the Union that declares that land, or horses, or any other description of property which is recognized by usage, shall be property ? There is none. You will find in the bodies of the different States various acts that recognize property in particular things by name. So it is in relation to land ; so it is in relation to horses ; and so it is in relation to slaves and many other subjects. The origin of the law by which property was established in these various subjects grew out of the usages, practice, and uniform custom of the civilized world. There is the origin and sanction of property in every subject of property, and that sanction exists in relation to slaves as undeniably as it does in relation to lands, horses, or any other subject, and I shall proceed to prove it.

" The Constitution itself recognizes this property in providing that Congress may pass laws to reclaim fugitive slaves, or persons who are fugitives to whose service other persons have the right. The Government of the United States and the States themselves have in many cases recognized property in slaves. I will mention a single instance. In the war of 1812 the British forces invaded this District and portions of Maryland and Virginia, and they deported from the country a large number of slaves. By the terms of the Treaty of Ghent our Government assumed that those slaves were to be paid for by the English Government. The English Government controverted the proposition ; and the question, together with the amount to be paid, was submitted to the arbitration of the Emperor of Russia, and the Emperor of Russia awarded in favor of the United States for those deported slaves about $1,250,000, or something like that amount."

Mr. Davis had been a man of much eminence in Kentucky, and in Congress, where he served as long as he would accept a nomination. He was an old time Whig, and, as such, was elected to succeed Breckinridge. He was a great speech-maker, but hardly met the needs of the time and added little to his reputation.

Mr. Browning came to the Senate with a national reputation as an advocate and lawyer, and at once took rank with the ablest debaters of that body.

Mr. Browning, as follows :

" I do not doubt at all, Mr. President, the constitutional power to pass this bill. It is a question that has on some former occasions been before Congress for its consideration, perhaps not unfrequently at times, from the organization of Government until the present day. I have taken some pains to look back into the records of congressional proceedings, and I find that on every occasion when this proposition has been made it has been very earnestly resisted by some portion of the representatives of the slave States ; but I have not found in any one instance that opposition has been made to it on the ground of a want of constitutional power to pass the measure, but upon grounds of expediency alone. I have never myself doubted the existence of the power in Congress under the Constitution to pass this or any other legislative measure affecting the District of Columbia. The grant of power is as broad and ample as it is possible for our language to make it. Therefore, we have no difficulty at all on the score of the power of Congress to adopt the measure.

"I do not think, Mr. President, that our friends who differ from us in their views upon this bill have any cause of complaint that we choose to exercise a power which we may constitutionally exercise. They may differ from us upon the ground of expediency ; but in reference to a matter of expediency, each one must form his own judgment for himself ; and it certainly ought to constitute no ground of complaint on the part of anybody that we differ from him in our views as to the time when the measure is expedient, and the manner of executing the measure. . . .

I have no intention of going into any lengthy discussion of the question. There have been two or three different suggestions made connected with this bill, all of which are, perhaps, entitled to consideration. Compensation of masters this bill itself provides for ; compensation of the slaves has been suggested in another quarter ; and colonization of the manumitted slaves in another. I intend submitting an amendment which to some extent combines all these three different ideas and measures ; and I beg leave to state that this amendment did not originate with me—that is, the idea of it did not originate with me—but it was suggested to me by one of the most respectable and influential citizens of the District of Columbia, who has resided here, I believe, the whole of his life, and who is a slave-holder, a man of very great intelligence, who has thought much on this subject. He suggested to me the propriety of the amendment which I am about to submit for the consideration of the Senate. I do not know that it will meet with favor from anybody but myself. It does meet my own views of what would perhaps be a wise amendment to make to the amendment of the Senator from New Hampshire. . . ."

He offered an amendment looking to a provision for the freedmen.

" The compensation that is made under this amendment to the owners of the slaves, falls little below the compensation that would be made by the amendment of the Senator from New Hampshire, or the original bill. In addition to that, it offers an inducement to manumitted slaves to colonize themselves, to migrate to some country outside of the United States ; and, upon so doing, they are to receive some compensation—that would meet the views of the Senator from Kansas—for their past services. It combines these two objects. It certainly offers an inducement for voluntary emigration and colonization and will, perhaps, be more likely to result in the beginning of a system of that sort than any proposition that has yet been suggested. I may add, further, that the aggregate expense to the Government, I think, will not be at all increased by this proposition. The $1,000,000 appropriated by the bill, will, in my judgment, be entirely adequate to meet all the exigencies and all the demands that will arise under the bill if this amendment should be adopted ; for, if it should pass, some will die, some will not desire to emigrate, and so far as they do not emigrate there will be nothing to be paid ; so that there would be a diminution of the appropriation on the one hand, while there is no apparent increase of it upon the other. The measure gives to the owners of slaves at present very nearly as large a compensation as the original bill proposed. As I have already remarked, the amendment was suggested to me and urged upon my consideration by a most intelligent slaveholder of the District of Columbia, and it commended itself to my judgment and my approval upon his assurance that if this proposition were submitted to the people of the District of Columbia, he entertained no doubt that it would receive the endorsement of a very large majority of them."

Colonization was a favorite idea with the President as with Mr. Browning, although many of us apprehended that, if planted by themselves, in a sub-tropical region, the emancipated would sink into barbarism. There was also pending in both Houses a joint resolution, introduced under a special message of the President, to aid the people of the border States who might wish to free their slaves, with appropriations by Congress ; and the discussion of the emancipation bill of the district often enlarged itself and embraced both resolutions. Mr. Willey of West Virginia interrupted Mr. Fessenden in a speech on this broad subject.

MR. WILLEY.—"I will say to the Senator that I, with all my feeble powers, in the centre of secession, at the risk of my personal safety, have said that it was no part of the purpose of the Republican party to interfere with the institution of slavery in the southern States. It has been the labor of my life for eighteen months past to disabuse the public mind of the South on that point."

MR. FESSENDEN.—"Mr. President, that the Republican party would rejoice to see slavery abolished everywhere, that they would rejoice if it no longer existed, that they feel it to be a blot upon our fair institutions and a curse to the country, there is no doubt. I can answer, for one, that has been my opinion always, and I have expressed it here and elsewhere ; but, sir, I have held, and I hold to-day, and I say to-day what I have said in my place before, that the Congress of the United States, or the people of the United

States through Congress, under the Constitution as it exists now, have no right whatever to touch, by legislation, the institution of slavery in the States where it exists by law. I have said that, and I say it again, boldly ; for my position never has been misunderstood on this subject. But, sir, I say further, that so far as the people of this country have the power, under the Constitution, to weaken the institution of slavery ; to deprive it of its force ; to subject it, as an institution, to the laws of the land ; to take away the political influence which it has wielded in this country, and to render it, so far as they can, a nullity, they have the right to do so, and it is their solemn duty to exercise it. And I say, moreover, that honorable Senators make a mistake in endeavoring to excite the sensibilities of their people by complaining of any constitutional action of ours upon this subject, and in charging us with a breach of our plighted faith.

" Why, sir, do you suppose we came into power to sit still and be silent on this subject ; that we came into power to do nothing ; to think nothing ; to say nothing lest by some possibility a portion of the people of the country might be offended? That was the argument of the honorable Senator from Indiana [Mr. Wright] this morning, as I understand it. Sir, it is no more than ought reasonably to be expected—no matter whether in the progress of this war or not, no matter where it touches,—if the people of this country should see that the institution of slavery has been the prolific source of all that we now suffer, the ground upon which this rebellion originated and has been carried on, that they will strike at it, wherever they can constitutionally do so. All that anybody ought to ask is, ' Hands off wherever the Constitution prohibits you from touching it at all.'

" I do not grow restive, sir, because on this question I am no longer restive ; but I cannot help feeling a little wonder that Senators here or gentlemen out of this Hall should undertake to suppose that this cry, which we have heard so long and which has produced so much effect, that we must not touch the question at all, whatever may be its condition and whatever may be ours, is to be listened to. I will hold, as I have always said before, strictly and strongly to every pledge that I gave individually, or that my party gave and that I assented to ; but you must not expect me to take back all my opinions ; you must not expect me to hold back my hand where I can strike at the institution as an institution ; you must not expect me to restrain myself when I see an opportunity in any way to dissever this Government from the support of that institution directly or indirectly. I should be false to my own principles if I did so. I should be false to all the professions that I have made from my youth up. I should be false to all the instincts of my nature, and all the duty which I owe to my country, believing as I do that the institution is, has been, and ever will be, a curse.

" I did not intend even to be drawn to this length of discussing this question ; but I wish to say to the gentlemen frankly that they must not expect us to yield them too much. I will give them credit for believing, as undoubtedly they do believe, that all these things will be taken advantage of by the enemy ; and I will give them this credit, too, that the greater part of their anxiety arises from that source. I am certain it is so with my friend from Virginia [Mr. Willey]. I make all allowances for that. But, sir, reflect ; have we not duties to perform with our opinions? Can we defer the consideration of some of these subjects? Are they not before us every day? Do they not meet us at every turn? Why not, then, meet us upon proper grounds, and say, ' As long as you keep yourselves within the limits of the Constitution, do what seems to you best ; we acknowledge, with you, that this has been the moving cause of the rebellion and of the evils we now suffer ; be careful then to give no occasion for any man to say that you are forgetting your pledges to support the Constitution and the laws of the United States ; but within the limit we cannot expect you to do otherwise than to use all the power you have to strike at slavery as far as you may.' Why, sir, I should deem myself neglectful of all my duties if I should hesitate for one moment on a question like this."

There was alway a robust manhood in the Maine Senator. Few men were more alert and industrious in the Senate, in the first years of Republican ascendency, than John P. Hale of New Hampshire. I fear it may be said that he in a way survived his industry, if not his early promise and fame.

Mr. Hale said :

" Mr. President, I fear, from the long time that I have been entitled to the floor upon this subject, the expectation may have been indulged by some that I proposed to make some extended remarks on it: but I do not. I propose in a very brief manner to notice one of the objections raised by the honorable Senator from Kentucky [Mr. Davis] to this bill ; and that is in regard to the consequences that are to ensue upon the enactment of the bill now before the Senate. I may remark that of all the forms skepticism ever assumed, the most insidious, the most dangerous, and the most fatal is that which suggests that it is unsafe to perform plain and simple duty for fear that disastrous consequences may result therefrom.

" This question of emancipation, wherever it has been raised in this country, so far as I know, has rarely ever been argued upon the great and fundamental principles of right : the inquiry is never put, certainly in legislative circles, what is right, what is just, what is due to the individuals that are to be effected by the measure, but what are to be the consequences? Men entirely forget to look at the objects that are to be effected by the bill, in view of the inherent rights of their manhood, in view of the great ques-

tions of humanity, of christianity, and of duty ; but what are to be the consequences, what is to be its effect upon the price of sugar, tobacco, cotton,
and other necessaries and luxuries of life ? The honorable Senator from
Kentucky looks upon it in that point of view entirely. Let me here read
from his statement, for I shall not trust myself to state what a man said,
after the censure I had from the Senator from Illinois, without reading
from his own remarks. The Senator from Kentucky said, when this bill
was last under consideration :

" ' The negroes that are now liberated and that remain in the city, will
become a sore and a burden and a charge upon the white population. They
will be criminals ; they will become paupers. They will be engaged in
crimes and in petty misdemeanors. They will become a charge and a pest
upon this society, and the power which undertakes to liberate them ought
to relieve the white community in which they reside, and in which they will
become a pest, from their presence. This is a poor city at any rate. The
total amount of wealth here is very inconsiderable for the number of the
white population. The burdens and charges upon them are heavy, onerous,
oppressive, and this measure will make those burdens greatly more so.'

" I would thank the honorable Senator from Kentucky, if I misrepresent
him, to state so now. I do not misrepresent him. The honorable Senator
went further, and not only expressed this as his firm and undoubting conviction ; but he added, in his own emphatic manner, ' I know that it is so,'
Now, it does not become me to say that I know to the contrary ; it does not
become me to venture my opinions against the opinions of that Senator who
has lived among the population of which he speaks ; but it is as much my
prerogative as it is the honorable Senator's, to read a little of history, and
to know what is its teaching upon this question, and by that test to compare
the predictions of the honorable Senators with some other predictions of a
different character that have been made elsewhere on other occasions.

" With those who assume the ground that is taken by the honorable
Senator from Kentucky, the effects of emancipation in the British West
Indies and St. Domingo are pointed at continually, as if they furnished unerring proof of the accuracy with which they estimate the consequences that
are to follow emancipation. I ask the attention of the Senate for a few
moments to some facts in relation to that matter. I know very well that
upon the island of Jamaica, so far as that island is concerned, there has
been a constant deterioration and diminution of its productive industry in
regard to its great staples which formerly constituted its wealth ; and that
is pointed at triumphantly as proof that it is unsafe, unwise, and inexpedient
to adopt any such measure. But, sir, if gentlemen will look at the statistical history of the island of Jamaica, they will find indisputable figures taken
from the highest authority, to wit, the colonial reports made to the Imperial
Parliament of Great Britain, that the deterioration of Jamaica had commenced long and long before emancipation was even thought of, and that it
went down in a constantly decreasing ratio until emancipation, and subse-

quently. To prove what I say, I will give you a series of statistics, going back as far as the year 1801."

He followed this with a very full and satisfactory exposé of the British West India emancipation.

Nearly all the leading Senators took part in the discussion. Among them Saulsbury, and many Democrats ; Bayard closing the debate with an elaborate speech against the bill. The vote when taken on the Emancipation Bill was as follows:

YEAS.—Anthony, Browning, Chandler, Clark, Collamer, Dixon, Doolittle, Fessenden, Foot, Foster, Grimes, Hale, Harlan, Harris, Howard, Howe, King, Lane of Indiana, Lane of Kansas, Morrill, Pomeroy, Sherman, Sumner, Ten Eyck, Trumbull, Wade, Wilkinson, Wilmot, and Wilson of Massachusetts—29.

NAYS.—Bayard, Carlisle, Davis, Henderson, Kennedy, Latham, McDougall, Nesmith, Powell, Saulsbury, Stark, Willey, Wilson of Missouri, and Wright—14.

Thus the bill was passed.

CHAPTER XIX.

EMANCIPATION.

FEBRUARY, 1862.

The President's Plan—House Debate—The Bill was fully Debated in Committee of the Whole in the House—On its Passage Mr. Riddle Addressed the House.

The following is from the *Globe* on the passage of the bill by the House:

MR. RIDDLE.—"Mr. Chairman, a great truth is weakened by what men call elucidation. Illustration obscures it; logic and argument compromise it; and demonstration brings it to doubt. He who permits himself to be put on its defensive, is a weak man or a coward. A great truth is never so strong as when left to stand on its simple assertion.

"The thing which is right, forever remains right, under all possible circumstances and conditions; in all times, places, and seasons. Nor can it be changed at all. Not all power, nor the combination of power, no matter how employed or applied, can change it in the least. It matters not at all how men call it—though the unanimous world conspire to call it ill, and tag it out with vile epithets; though obscene mouths make it common, and lewd tongues toss it into sewers, and delicate and refined ears may not hear it—it is nowise changed. No matter what ill happens to it; though cast out, exiled, banished, and outlawed, marked and forever banned, made leprous with contumely and reproach; though prisoned, tried, condemned, and executed, and its body, like carrion, cast to vultures, it still lives, is still right; holds its old place and old sceptre. Nor can any man, by any power, under any circumstances, for anything, be absolved from the allegiance he owes it.

"So, too, its great opposite, wrong, must forever be wrong and not right. No matter, though taken from its native hell and enthroned a crowned

king ; though a universe bow to it and cry ' All hail ! ' though constitutions
be written to sustain it ; though laws be enacted in its name, and ermined
judges wrench the maxims of 'wisdom's gray fathers' for its support ;
though jurors be sworn by it, and all magistrates bound to enforce its de-
crees ; though its name be written in all holy places, and graved on all
shrines, and its maxims mingled in the rites of holy ministration, and its
sanctifying hand only can bless and curse, join and put asunder ; though it
reign till hoary prescription grows up and surrounds it with a wall of custom
and habit and use that existed 'time whereof the memory of man runneth
not to the contrary' ; still it is wrong, and not right. Its reign is an usurpation, its laws an outrage, against which rebellion is righteous ; and the immunities and privileges which it confers are the fruits of robbery, murder,
and ravishment.

" No man can rightfully do wrong ; nor can one man authorize another to
do wrong ; nor can ten, five hundred, nor five hundred thousand men. No
matter with what formality or solemnity the power is sought to be conferred,
whether by common consent or by the legislative forms of a State or nation,
the power of attorney is invalid, and the thing done pursuant to its scope is
a crime. A thousand years of growth cannot change wrong to right. . . .

" With me to argue, declaim, or inveigh against this measure is the idle
·waste of the most useless breath that indolent trifling can indulge in. I turn
to the great rules of right, and I see that you have razed out the decalogue of
Omnipotence, and have daubed and smeared over the eternal adamant with
the code of slavery ; and I know that it is all a huge lie, without semblance
or seeming of truth.

" It is idle to establish to me the inferiority of that sinless race. I see
that they are men ; useless, by curious physiological ethnological disqui-
sition, to affirm a difference between the African and Caucasian tribes—for I
know that God created both. It is, to me, blasphemy to attempt to show
that the Creator intended this race for slaves, for the very elements of our
common nature, which are the common basis upon which God planted
the races, gives that dogma the lie. If I were to base an estimate upon the
practical givings out of this House, on a recent memorable occasion, I
should suppose that these, my views, were not those of a majority of this
body. . . .

" So low in the ranks of humanity do these bondmen stand, that they were
deemed the proper subjects of taxation. The proprietary interest of the master in the slave predominates over the human interest of a man in himself ;
and had the selfishness of the masters and their allies permitted them to unite
with the large body of gentlemen who voted to tax slaves, the tax would
have been laid. Nay, so unhuman were they practically held, that they
could not be the subjects of a capitation tax even. For as a capitation tax
the scheme was conceded to be unconstitutional. I do not stop here to com-
bat that low dogma, that that is property which the law of the place makes
property. I only assert that property is the only universal basis of taxation ;

and where a given subject is assessed with a tax, that that is a practical recognition of such subject as property. It is idle to seek a confusion of ideas in a confusion of words, and so escape ; of what avail to call this a relation, and then say you license the relation. In that form the proposition is just as obnoxious to me ; I would for no millions permit such a relation, nor would I under any form derive money from it for any purpose. I would as soon think of filling the exchequer with the gains of prostitution.

" It need not be urged as a palliation or offset that the condition of the slave is more elevated than that of his ancestors or brethren in Africa. That, if true, was neither intended nor desired by the master. It is in opposition to his wish, and in spite of his most persistent efforts to the contrary. He has done all in his power to prevent it ; for just in proportion as the slave rises in the scale of manhood, he sinks in the scale of servitude. The master punishes with imprisonment a woman for teaching a slave to read, and the crude notions of Christianity that he permits them to imbibe are warped with a diabolism that makes them the more abased."

In regard to the efforts to reconstruct parties in the House Mr. Riddle said :

" And yet here and there are runnings to and fro, and a fearful putting together of soft addled heads, and terrible plottings and arrangings and re-arrangings of rickety, worn-out, useless, and obsolete party machinery. Oh, it is an absurdly idle and laughter-provoking farce, this reconstruction of the party. The great old leaders, where are they ? One prematurely slumbers where the translucent waters of his magnificent lake break in lisping wavelets at his feet ; and the rest, in grand proportions of patriots and heroes, march at the head of countless millions, whose armed tread tramples alike on the shackles of the slave and of the party.

" It is here alone that puny hands are raised, and piping, petulant voices cry out and exclaim against the progress of events, and propose to reconstruct the party. My colleague [Mr. Vallandigham] said well in the declaration that none of these men 'made his mark' ; and the aside, that 'none of them ever will,' was still better.

" With me this measure is one of power, and there can be no question of that. I read in the Constitution of our fathers that the Congress shall 'exercise exclusive legislation in all cases whatsoever' over this district. Not merely that Congress has legislative power, but 'exclusive' power ; not merely in a few specified cases, but in 'all cases whatsoever.' Where is the room for doubt, the ground for argument, or the excuse for cavil, in the presence of this explicit declaration? But we are told that the cession of this territory and people to the United States was accompanied by certain conditions that hedge in and fence around this slavery, and wall us away from all interference with it, except to aid it perhaps. Conditions ! What conditions ? Where are they set down, and in what terms?

"Ingenious and learned men have applied to this measure the little questions of technical legality, the subtile and artificial reasonings of the books
and courts, and find the law with us; while others have laboriously mined
back into the dark and crooked legislation of dark and crooked men for the
last hundred and fifty dark and crooked years, to establish, with such luck as
God permits, the rightfulness of slavery here, and an absence of power to
deal with it. I have no part in these labors, nor do I sympathize with
them nor their fruits; nor do I care a rag whether their results are for or
against me.

"I find here a clear God's truth that needs Congressional utterance. I
find a great right calling for legislative establishment. I find our weak and
faulty organs equal to the utterance of this truth, all unused to it as they are.
I find power ample to establish this right, and for these reasons, and for no
other, I propose to speak the truth and establish the right. I propose so to
do this right thing as neither to compromise it nor ourselves. . . .

"Those who would defer emancipation until a satisfactory plan for the
disposition of the slaves is devised, would do well to contemplate the ultimate catastrophe to both races if this scheme of slavery should go forward
unchanged fifty or a hundred years more, when our system could no longer
sustain its weight.

"What strange passages the sayings and doings of the American Congress
of this year of grace will furnish to the page of history—that now, when
this thing of slavery is tumbling to ruins about us, of self-begotten rotten-
ness, men can still be found so blind and stupid and fanatic as to seek to
stay and prop it up. There is not a man living that dares arise here and
say that he does not know that slavery is utterly all wrong. Nor can a man
here be found that will say that he does not believe that it is some time to
end; nor that when that end is reached, it will not be through convulsion,
anarchy, and blood. But yet, now, when that fearful end draws nigh,
through these fearful paroxysms, which can neither be mistaken nor denied,
men whose dearest interests are most involved, stand with their allies in
blind infatuation, and raise their paralytic hands to push the calamity by,
will not believe it is upon them, and hold those to be their bitterest foes
who implore and beseech them to care for and provide for their own and the
common welfare.

"Like a tigress that, stealing upon her prey, and falling into the hunter's
toils, in her great agony, whelps there her young, this slavery, overwhelmed
in its progress, spawned into the world this atrocious rebellion and war.
And these, her offspring, like Milton's hell-hounds, born of sin, turn ever to
tear and devour the hag that gave them birth.

"It is most fitting that, while the army marches to the restoration of the
national power, over the form of fallen slavery, and tramps its life out,
the solemn lustration of the nation's capital should be performed by our
hands; that these fetters should dissolve in our breath, so that when our
country again confronts her sister nations, though her feet would still be

ensanguined with the mingled blood of her filial and parricidal children, she may present her countenance in cloudless though saddened beauty, purged of its hideous deformity by her own unconstrained hand.

"There could be no moment so propitious for this great beneficence as this, preceded, as it is, by the prophetic voice of the Executive, whose calm and serene utterance has more startled the world than the great convulsion from whose bosom he spoke. Make haste to complete this great act, and it shall proclaim itself to the waiting and oppressed of the earth as the realized gospel of deliverance. The yellow waves of the Potomac, in their downward flow to the sea, shall whisper in liquid murmurs to the Great Sleeper on its banks, that the city that bears his name is now worthy of it." [1]

The vote on the passage was :

YEAS.—Aldrich, Alley, Arnold, Ashley, Babbitt, Baker, Baxter, Beaman, Bingham, Francis P. Blair, Samuel S. Blair, Blake, George H. Browne, Buffinton, Campbell, Chamberlin, Clark, Colfax, Frederick A. Conklin, Roscoe Conklin, Covode, Davis, Dawes, Delano, Diven, Duell, Dunn, Edgerton, Edwards, Eliot, English, Fenton, Fessenden, Fisher, Franchot, Frank, Gooch, Goodwin, Granger, Haight, Hale, Hanchett, Harrison, Hickman, Hooper, Hutchins, Julian, Kelley, Francis W. Kellogg, Killinger, Lansing, Loomis, Lovejoy, McKnight, McPherson, Mitchell, Moorhead, Anson P. Morrill, Justin S. Morrill, Nixon, Odell, Olin, Patton, Pike, Porter, Alexander H. Rice, John H. Rice, Riddle, Edward H. Rollins, Sargent, Sedgwick, Shanks, Sheffield, Shellabarger, Sloan, Spaulding, Stevens, Stratton, Benjamin F. Thomas, Train, Trowbridge, Van Horn, Van Valkenburgh, Verree, Wallace, E. P. Walton, Washburne, Wheeler, Albert S. White, Wilson, and Windom—91.

NAYS.—Allen, Joseph Bailey, Biddle, Jacob B. Blair, William G. Brown, Casey, Crittenden, Delaplaine, Dunlap, Girder, Hall, Harding, Holman, Johnson, Knapp, Law, Lazear, Mallory, Menzies, Morris, Noble, Norton, Nugen, Pendleton, Perry, Price, James S. Rollins, Shiel, John B. Steele, William G. Steele, Francis Thomas, Vallandigham,

---

[1] Mr. Greeley honored this speech with a letter in the *Ledger*.

Voorhees, Wadsworth, Ward, Chilton A. White, Wickliffe, and Wright—38.

Pending the bill to emancipate the slaves in the District of Columbia, the President sent us a message recommending appropriations by Congress for aid to such of the slave States as should manifest a desire to free their slaves. Mr. Conkling introduced a joint resolution, declaring it to be the duty of the General Government to aid any State which should make an effort to emancipate slaves. This passed the House as follows :

YEAS.—Aldrich, Arnold, Ashley, Babbitt, Baker, Baxter, Beaman, Bingham, Francis P. Blair, Jacob B. Blair, Samuel S. Blair, Blake, William G. Brown, Buffinton, Campbell, Chamberlin, Clements, Colfax, Frederick A. Conkling, Roscoe Conkling, Conway, Covode, Cutler, Davis, Delano, Diven, Duell, Dunn, Edgerton, Edwards, Eliot, Ely, Fessenden, Fisher, Franchot, Frank, Gooch, Goodwin, Granger, Haight, Hale, Harrison, Hickman, Hooper, Horton, Hutchins, Julian, Kelley, Francis W. Kellogg, William Kellogg, Killinger, Lansing, Loomis, Lovejoy, McKnight, McPherson, Mitchell, Moorhead, Anson P. Morrill, Justin S. Morrill, Nixon, Olin, Patton, Timothy G. Phelps, Pike, Pomeroy, Porter, Alexander H. Rice, John H. Rice, Riddle, Edward H. Rollins, Sargent, Shanks, Sheffield, Shellabarger, Sloan, Stratton, Train, Trowbridge, Van Valkenburgh, Verree, Wallace, Charles E. Walton, E. P. Walton, Whaley, White, Wilson, Windom, and Worcester—89.

NAYS.—Ancona, Joseph Baily, Biddle, Corning, Cox, Cravens, Crisfield, Crittenden, Dunlap, English, Harding, Johnson, Knapp, Law, Leary, Noble, Norton, Pendleton, Perry, Richardson, Robinson, Shiel, John B. Steele, Francis Thomas, Voorhees, Wadsworth, Ward, Clinton A. White, Wickliffe, Wood, and Woodruff—31.

It passed the Senate also:

YEAS.—Anthony, Browning, Chandler, Clark, Colla-

11

mer, Davis, Dixon, Doolittle, Fessenden, Foot, Foster, Grimes, Hale, Harlan, Henderson, Howard, Howe, King, Lane of Indiana, Lane of Kansas, Morrill, Pomeroy, Sherman, Sumner, Ten Eyck, Thompson, Trumbull, Wade, Wilkinson, Willey, Wilmot, and Wilson of Massachusetts—32.

NAYS.—Bayard, Carlisle, Kennedy, Latham, Nesmith, Powell, Saulsbury, Stark, Wilson of Missouri, and Wright—10.

A few days later the House passed a resolution covering the same proposition, which by its terms was referred to a select committee from the slave States, having representation in the House.. Of this committee Mr. Crisfield was chairman, and wrote the report, the sum of which was that these States would not entertain a proposition in any form for the abolition of slavery within their jurisdiction. The resolution itself passed by the following vote:

YEAS.—Alley, Arnold, Ashley, Babbitt, Baker, Baxter, Beaman, Bingham, Francis P. Blair, Blake, Buffinton, Campbell, Chamberlin, Clark, Colfax, Frederick A. Conkling, Davis, Dawes, Duell, Edgerton, Eliot, Fenton, Fessenden, Gurley, Hanchett, Hickman, Hutchins, Julian, Kelley, Francis W. Kellogg, Lansing, Loomis, Lovejoy, McKnight, McPherson, Moorhead, Anson P. Morrill, Justin S. Morrill, Nixon, Olin, Pike, Pomeroy, Potter, Alexander H. Rice, John H. Rice, Riddle, Edward H. Rollins, Sargent, Shanks, Sheffield, Shellabarger, Sherman, Sloan, Stevens, Stratton, Train, Van Horn, Van Valkenburgh, Verree, Wallace, Charles W. Walton, E. P. Walton, Washburne, Wheeler, Albert S. White, Wilson, and Windom—67.

NAYS.—Allen, Biddle, Jacob B. Blair, George H. Browne, William G. Brown, Calvert, Casey, Cobb, Corning, Cox, Cravens, Crittenden, Delano, Delaplaine, Diven, Dunlap, English, Fisher, Grider, Haight, Harding, Harrison, Horton, Kerrigan, Knapp, Law, Lazear, Leary, Lehman, Mallory, Menzies, Mitchell, Noble, Noell, Norton, Nugen, Pendleton, Perry, Timothy G. Phelps, Price, Richardson, Shiel, Smith, John B. Steele, William G. Steele, Vallandigham, Voorhees, Wadsworth, Ward, Webster, Chilton A. White, and Wickliffe—52.

It is an amazing thing that not a Democrat of either House voted for any measure looking, however remotely, to the abolition of slavery. Delaware, with Bayard and Saulsbury in the Senate, had in the House George Fisher, as staunch a Republican as we had on the floor. He made a very strong speech in favor of the joint resolution to aid the States in emancipation. He failed of re-election, and was placed by the President on the bench of the Supreme Court of the District of Columbia—a court of *our* creation, and for which we cleared the ground by sweeping the alleged disloyal circuit court from the board.

When Mr. Crisfield and his sub-committee were wrestling, heavy laden with Mr. White's (the last) resolution, he invited me to a conference with them. In the interview I urged every argument at my command, and with such force as I thought becoming, to give *some indication* that they would at *some time* seriously entertain a proposition, in some form, to emancipate their slaves. I said I would vote to tax the people of the free States to make compensation for their loss of property, this being their only chance to escape an inevitable loss; that in my deliberate judgment the war was the means in the hand of God to purge the land of slavery; that slavery would die in great convulsions, and was now in its *rigor mortis;* that they would have their States overrun with freedmen, who would know that they were set free by the hand of war against their masters' wills. I said much more, vain as I felt my labor to be.

CHAPTER XX.

DEMOCRACY IN THE HOUSE.

FEBRUARY, 1862.

Vallandigham's Scheme of Reconstruction—The Democracy Reorganized.

AN important movement among the Democrats of the House may be mentioned in connection with these votes. Whoever reflects for a moment, readily apprehends that when a nation is at war, and is confronted by an armed foe, whoever else attacks or opposes the Government of that nation, especially its measures for the prosecution of its war, thereby becomes an ally of that nation's enemy, whether the intention is to aid the belligerent enemy or not. Especially is this the position, and a trying one, of an opposition party. For the purposes of the war the Administration party for the time really becomes the nation. If the opposition supports the war it loses its identity, is merged with the Administration party, and is lost for the time; it can only preserve itself as a party by opposing the war. To oppose the war is to make itself the ally of the enemy—to become disloyal, in fact. We have seen that at the beginning of the war the Democrats in both Houses of Congress very cordially supported the national cause and effectively aided in perfecting many of the measures for that purpose.

On the 8th of July, 1861, Philip B. Fouke, a Democrat, of Illinois, introduced into the House a set of resolutions, the first of which was as follows :

" *Be it Resolved*, That we, the Representatives of the Thirty-seventh Congress, in view of the distracted state of our beloved country, and in order to secure harmonious action, and believing the Constitution and the Union to be considerations far above party ties and affiliations, solemnly ignore, during the impending war, all political differences heretofore existing between the people of the loyal states of this Union."

The rest, five in number, were equally patriotic. Mr. Lovejoy moved to lay the resolutions on the table, seemingly because they were proposed by an Illinois Democrat. Mr. Holman called for the yeas and nays on this motion. That gentleman had already secured the unanimous adoption of a resolution limiting the labors of the session to war legislation, under which the Speaker declared Mr. Fouke's resolutions out of order—this on the suggestion of John Hickman, of Pennsylvania, another radical Republican.

As we have seen, the Ohio Democrats united in recommending candidates to the President for brigadier generals.

At the present session it became apparent to Mr. Vallandigham, the political leader of the Democracy in Congress, that if this course of supporting the administration continued, the party would disappear. He was said to be of Southern origin and sympathies ; his political affiliations made him a political ally of that section. He unquestionably proposed the restoration of the States on the old basis.

During February, he introduced into the House his scheme of reconstruction, consisting of two amendments to the Constitution, prefaced with an elaborate preamble. The governing ideas were : A division of the States into four sections, naming the States to constitute each. This was to be worked out by the Senate. There the votes should be taken by sections, on a demand of one third of the Senators of each section, and a majority of the Senators of each section was necessary to pass a bill.   There was also a plan of secession in his scheme—a State, with the assent of its sections, could withdraw.   His scheme, as is seen, had for its object to strengthen the defences of slavery.

He saw that for effective action, as a party, the Democracy was fast losing its integrity ; he therefore secured a convention of his associates in the House, where a party reconstruction was made.   The scheme was reduced to writing and signed, the signers numbering thirty-one, the usual Democratic contingent in the House.   These constituted about one half of the usual opposition.   The rest were from the border States, Maryland, Virginia, Kentucky, and Missouri.   These were found against the war bills from that time on ; they had always been a unit upon all questions involving slavery.   From that unfortunate party compact the Democrats, whatever were the personal intentions and wishes of individual members, became, by the logic of their position, the allies in fact of the Confederate States, and were a serious obstacle to the progress of the Union cause.   This must be conceded. Upon a careful examination of the record it is found that the party, as such, not only opposed the Republican measures for the prosecution of the war, but they never brought forward any measures for its prosecution—not a single bill or resolution in either House.   The soul of the war, where its inner fires were most cherished and carefully sustained, was in the hall of the house of the people's representatives, where really dwells the government of the republic.   It is true that had every Democrat of that body absented himself, the integrity of the legislative body would have remained unimpaired ; yet a compact body of thirty-one trained men in the skilled hands of a bold and experienced leader like Vallandigham, always ready, was a serious obstacle in its influence upon the

Union cause—equal to twenty thousand trained soldiers added to the Confederate Army under Stonewall Jackson or J. E. B. Stuart.   In the field such a body might be killed and captured, but we had no such effective process.   Ex-, cept for the attitude of this able body in the House in opposition, *The Butternut Clubs, The Copperhead Bands, The Brotherhoods of Liberty,* and the formidable and dangerous order of *The Golden Circle,* that rendered volunteering impossible and conscription difficult, would never have been heard of.   Over and beyond all, in this indomitable band of ever-faithful allies in the citadel, the heart of the Union, dwelt one of the steadiest and strongest of the hopes of the Confederacy, and though soon to lose its intrepid leader, it may be questioned whether his loss was not more than compensated by a widespread sympathy and a deep-seated indignation " at the deep damnation of his taking off."

CHAPTER XXI.

INQUIRY CONCERNING BALL'S BLUFF.

DECEMBER, 1861—JANUARY, 1862.

Roscoe Conkling's Great Speech.

DECEMBER, 1861, Mr. Roscoe Conkling, by unanimous consent, introduced the following resolution ; which was read, considered, and agreed upon :

"*Resolved*, That the Secretary of War be requested, if not incompatible with the public service, to report to this House, whether any, and if any, what, measures have been taken to ascertain who is responsible for the disastrous movement of our troops at Ball's Bluff."

This the House sent to the war office, and had its day of anguish and tears over the fallen hero of the disastrous battle. The Secretary of War, Cameron, moved by our sorrow, solaced us with the following:

" WAR DEPARTMENT, December 12, 1861.
" SIR :
" I have the honor to acknowledge the receipt of a resolution of the House of Representatives, calling for certain information with regard to the disastrous movement of our troops at Ball's Bluff, and to transmit to you a report of the Adjutant-General of the United States Army, from which you will perceive that a compliance with the resolution, at this time, in the opinion of the General-in-Chief, would be injurious to the public service.
" Very respectfully,
" SIMON CAMERON,
" Secretary of War.
" Hon. G. A. GROW,
" Speaker of the House of Representatives."

168

" HEADQUARTERS OF THE ARMY,
" ADJUTANT-GENERAL'S OFFICE,
" WASHINGTON, December 11, 1861.
" SIR :
" In compliance with your instructions, I have the honor to report, in reference to the resolution of the honorable the House of Representatives, received
the 3d instant, ' that the Secretary of War be requested, if not incom-
patible with the public interest, to report to this House whether any, and if
any, what, measures have been taken to ascertain who is responsible for the
disastrous movement of our troops at Ball's Bluff ' ; that the General-in-
Chief of the army is of opinion that an inquiry on the subject of the resolution would, at this time, be injurious to the public service. The resolution
is herewith respectfully returned.
" Respectfully submitted,
" L. THOMAS,
" Adjutant-General.
" Hon. SECRETARY OF WAR, Washington."

During the half recess of the House for the holidays,
Mr. Conkling, the mover of the resolution, made a personal
examination of the ground and of the approaches to the
scene of conflict, and investigated all the attending circumstances, so far as information within his reach permitted ; and early in January he called the whole subject
up, and, by express permission of the House, was enabled
to state his conclusions on the floor.
Some passages of his remarkable speech will aid in
understanding certain features of the calamitous affair,
and also the spirit of the House.

" The resolution proposed no investigation whatever. It did not require
the disclosure of any fact or circumstance which had been ascertained by any
investigation already had. It simply requested the Secretary of War to
inform the House whether any, and if any, what measures had been taken to
ascertain who was responsible for a disastrous battle. It did not demand the
name of the person, nor even ask whether there was any such person.
" The resolution was referred by the Secretary of War to the Adjutant-
General, and was by him submitted to the General-in-Chief, as appears by
the report of the Adjutant-General laid upon our tables. The General-in-
Chief, I am willing to believe, did not read the resolution, because I would
not impute to any one concerned an intention to trifle with the House, or to
return an evasive answer. If he did read it, he entirely mistook its point

and purport. He seems to have received the impression that the resolution proposed a future investigation, and that of a very general character ; and laboring under this misapprehension, he expressed an opinion to the Adjutant-General, upon which that officer made to the Secretary of War a report in no sense responsive to the resolution, and the Secretary, in accordance no doubt with the practice of his office, simply transmitted that report to us and refers us to it. . . .

" This is no ordinary matter. The resolution relates to a great national concern ; it relates to an event which I believe to be the most atrocious military murder ever committed in our history as a people. It relates to a lost field ; to a disastrous and humiliating battle ; to a decisive triumph of rebellion. It relates to something more ; it relates to a blunder so gross that all men can see it—no man has ever dared deny or defend it—a blunder which, besides position, besides defeat, besides arms and munitions of war, cost us confessedly nine hundred and thirty men, many of them the very pride and flower of the States from which they came.

" The resolution proposed, in respect to the memory of the lost, in sympathy for the multitude of mourners who lament them, in deference to public propriety and self-respect, that the Nation should be assured that the military authorities had taken some notice of this prodigal and needless slaughter of the sons of New York, Massachusetts, and Pennsylvania ; it proposed that the Nation should know that some proceeding had taken place, something open or secret, formal or informal ; if not all that military usage requires, then something to excuse, or an apology for something. . . .

" The House is no doubt aware that the battle of Ball's Bluff, like many other things, has been made the subject of an issue between the regular army and the volunteers. Brigadier-General Stone, who was at the time commanding the division from which the detachment came which fought the battle, or attempted to fight it, is an officer of the regular army, and Colonel Baker, to whom, after a time, the command, or a part of the command, was assigned, was a volunteer. The friends of these two officers have indulged in much angry controversy as to which should bear the blame ; and on the one side the cause has been espoused as if its appropriate purpose were to fasten some stigma on the volunteer service, and to determine certain questions of precedence and merit between West Point and the volunteers of the Union. A writer in the *New York Times* stated, some time ago, that the friends of Colonel Baker would move an investigation, but that they had better not, for if they did, the friends of General Stone would retaliate, and make it recoil upon Baker and damage his memory. Mr. Speaker, I have no sympathy with this controversy to indulge in here. I have no patience with it as an obstacle to investigation. The effect of disclosing the truth on either of these officers or on both of them ought not in my judgment to weigh one feather against an investigation being had. Hit whom it may, I believe the truth should be known. Suppose its revelation shall shorten the plume of a dead Senator—what then ? Is that a reason, in a great public concern like this, why we should hush investigation, or falsify the truth of history? Suppose, on the other hand, it turns out that a brigadier-general, bred at West Point, an officer of the regular Army, holding the acting position of a major-general, commanding a division containing thousands of our countrymen, charged with their safety, their honor, and their lives; suppose, I say, it turns out that such a brigadier-general is a martinet and not a soldier; suppose he turns out to be half-way, either in his soldiership or his loyalty; is that a reason why investigation should be muzzled or throttled out of regard to his feelings or the feelings of his caste? Shall we proclaim indulgence for ignorance and incompetency, immunity for barbarous negligence, silence for military crimes?

" On the 21st of October, Leesburgh, in the State of Virginia, was occupied by insurgents. The force with which they held it amounted to not less than six thousand men. At the same time Poolsville, in the State of Maryland, was occupied by Union forces, and was the headquarters of a brigadier-general. Between these two positions, thus occupied, there rolled a swift and swollen river, with an island in the channel, nearest the Maryland side, three miles in length and two hundred yards across. On the same side of the river with Leesburgh, and within a day's march of that place, lay General McCall, commanding a division containing fifteen regiments, which mustered fully eleven thousand men. If Leesburgh were to be attacked, or if a reconnoissance in force were to be made in that direction, one of the first wonders in this case is, that the work should have been assigned to General Stone's division, divided as it was from the scene of action by a great river —indeed by two great rivers—when the division of General McCall was within a day's march of the spot, with neither river, mountain, nor barrier to be traversed. Those who, stimulated by curiosity not unnatural at a time like this, have refreshed their military history, or dipped into military books, or picked up the current smattering of military knowledge, have not failed to observe that a river unbridged and unfordable is a perilous obstacle to a military advance. Of all the barriers not absolutely impassable, nothing—if ordinary sources of information are to be relied upon—is to be so much dreaded by an attacking army, so much to be shunned at any cost, as a deep, rapid, stream, without wharfage or bridges; and this is true even when means of floating transportation are abundant and prepared. Common sense has so much to do with this, that any man who has ever seen artillery move, may, without presumption, assume to know and comprehend it."

An outline of the conditions may be stated. Stone, with headquarters at Poolsville, Maryland, supposed McCall with a considerable force to be at Darnsville. McClellan had ordered him to reconnoitre toward Leesburgh. He ordered Stone to demonstrate in force. Stone sent Colonel Devens over, with part of his regiment, also Colonel Lee, both of Massachusetts. Later, he ordered

Baker out, with his cavalry regiment, recruited in Philadelphia. In front of Ball's Bluff is Harrison's Island, which
had to be crossed, involving two shipments and landings.
The transit from Maryland was made in three scows, carrying in all one hundred and twenty-five men. Between the
island and the Virginia bank, a small metallic life-boat and
two skiffs were used, which altogether would hold thirty-
five. The bluff was some sixty feet high, and very steep,
up which a single path wound. There was a cleared field
at the top surrounded by woods. At Edwards' Ferry
Stone sent over some men, under. Gorman. McCall retired from Darnsville Monday A.M., of which Baker had
no notice. The battle was fought Monday P.M. When
Baker, who was left at discretion to go from Harrison's
Island to reinforce Devens and take command, decided to
do so, he had a right to expect aid if needed, both from
McCall and Gorman. There seems to have been no super-
vision by McClellan, the General-in-Chief, nor did Stone
direct Gorman to aid Baker, to whom orders were unnecessary, since the sound of battle would have been a
trumpet call to him. I quote further from Mr. Conkling,
who supposed there were four scows, two in each channel.
These four boats constituted the whole means of transportation upon which the expedition was based.

"These boats have been called scows, and I have taken some pains to
know what they were. They were flat-boats, made of hemlock, I think,
inch and a quarter or an inch and a half stuff. They were about twenty
feet in length and of corresponding width. They had no oars nor any other
means of motion. There was, as I said, no rope nor hawser to work them
by. They were navigated when loaded by being poled up-stream and out
into the current, and then allowed to drift or float down and across until
they struck the bank on the other side. Sometimes they would strike at the
landing-place, sometimes they would hit the shore far below, and be hauled
and poled back to the landing place.

"These boats were of sufficient capacity to carry about half a company,
some thirty-five men each, and the average time occupied in crossing from
Maryland to the island was about three quarters of an hour, leaving the
island and the remaining channel still to be traversed. The House will get

some idea of the rapidity with which this transportation could be carried on by the operations of the night previous to the day of which I am speaking. Before Colonel Baker is understood to have had command of the expedition, Colonel Devens was ordered to cross two companies of the Massachussets 15th. He did cross them. He commenced at two o'clock in the morning, and it was sunrise before he was ready to take up the line of march, showing that more than an hour was necessary for the purpose of throwing one company from the Maryland shore to Ball's Bluff.

"Colonel Baker's orders came to him about two o'clock in the morning, and found him sleeping in his tent. He commenced his crossing at sunrise. Without any wharf to lie to, without any hawser or rope to stretch across the river, the embarkation and transportation of troops, cannon, and munitions of war was, of course, a slow and tantalizing process. Eleven o'clock had come when only a commencement had been made. At this time a boat was found in the canal, and measures was taken to transfer it to the river. Whether this was observed on the other side I cannot say, but the time had come when it was too late to mend the matter or correct mistakes, for the rebel fire had opened upon the slender detachment which had crossed. From that time the boats began to pole back with the bleeding and the slain. The house on Harrison's Island had already become a hospital, and every room in it was occupied by wounded and dying men."

His description of the battle was striking. Baker had 1700 men, and was assaulted by the rebel General Evans, with 4000, who attacked under cover of the woods. Assailed thus, he must hold his position. He had no means of retreat. A smaller number might have escaped by the boats; but the 1700 had only to stand fast and perish.

Nobly did they fulfil their destiny. Desperate stubbornness and heroic courage served only to gild with glory that bloody picture of their fate.

"In an hour, in less than an hour, the field was a hell of fire, raging from every side. The battle was lost before it had begun. It was, from the outset, a mere sacrifice, a sheer immolation, without a promise of success or a hope of escape. It was worse than the charge of the Light Brigade, and as England's poet has said of the six hundred :

"'Cannon to right of them,
Cannon to left of them,
Cannon in front of them,
Volleyed and thundered.'

" Well might the historian here ejaculate with the poet there :

" ' Some one has blundered.'

" We all know the result. Those who did not die upon the field were forced down the steep bank behind them to the brink of the river. IIere, to save their arms from the enemy, they threw them into the stream, and many sought, and more found a watery grave. The last act of this terrible tragedy of blunders was the most sickening and appalling of all. The flat-boat, which by poling and drifting had been made to ply between the island and the bluff, now too heavily laden with the mangled, the weary, and the dying, went down, the quick and the dead together, in one struggling mass. Leesburgh was illuminated that night, illuminated by patricides and rebels, and another laurel was added to Big Bethel, Bull Run, the blockade of the Potomac, and the tame surrender of arms in the navy-yards and arsenals.

" Such, Mr. Speaker, was the battle of Ball's Bluff. Such it stands to-day upon the page of history. The mourners for that battle—those who suffered most severely in it—are the States of New York, Massachusetts, and Pennsylvania. To those States it was the battle of *Cannae*, for the very pride and flower of their young men were among its victims. No wonder that the army and the country burn with indignation at

" ' The deep damnation of their taking off.'

" I assume that an attack on Leesburgh, or a movement upon it, was justifiable at the time, and then I direct attention to the following propositions, in the light of the facts at which I have glanced.

" In the first place, the division of General McCall, numbering eleven thousand men, was on the same side of the river with Leesburgh, and within a few hours' march, uninterrupted by any formidable barrier, and yet these troops were not employed in the attack, nor made use of at all, but another division was selected lying on the *opposite* side of the Potomac.

" In the second place, the point of crossing selected was one of the worst and most dangerous to be found for many miles.

" In the third place, there was a want of transportation, insomuch that adequate means of crossing were wholly unprovided, although they might easily have been procured.

" In the fourth place, the number of men sent over to Ball's Bluff was wholly insufficient, and this though more than the needed number were close at hand.

" In the fifth place, no reinforcements came to the rescue, although, aside from the command of General McCall, there were troops and artillery on both sides of the river, *and within four miles of the field of battle*, while the engagement was progressing.

" All these grounds of censure may be answered. If they can be explained it is just to the living and the dead that an opportunity should be afforded. If they cannot be explained, then, for reasons higher still, inquiry ought not to slumber. We have had long chapters of accidents for which no one is blamed, though some one is to blame. Battles and positions given away, and no court-martial, no court of inquiry, no one shot, no one disgraced—nothing but promotions growing out of inglorious occurrences. My particular object to-day is to learn whether the military authorities have in any manner looked into the proceedings of the 21st of October, on the upper Potomac, and in order to obtain that information I offer the following resolution :

" ' *Resolved*, That the said answer [of the Secretary of War] is not responsive nor satisfactory to the House, and that the Secretary be directed to return a further answer.' " [1]

The debate became general and serious. Lovejoy put in the 7th chapter of Joshua.

Wickliffe offered his usual resolution that slavery had been many times settled.

The resolution of Mr. Conkling was adopted as follows : YEAS.—Aldrich, Alley, Arnold, Babbitt, Baker, Baxter, Beaman, Bingham, Samuel S. Blair, Blake, Buffinton, Campbell, Chamberlin, Clark, Colfax, Frederick A. Conkling, Roscoe Conkling, Conway, Covode, Davis, Dawes, Duell, Edwards, Eliot, Fenton, Fessenden, Franchot, Frank, Gooch, Goodwin, Gurley, Hale, Hickman, Hooper, Hutchins, Julian, Kelley, Francis W. Kellogg, William Kellogg, Lansing, Loomis, Lovejoy, McKean, McPherson, Mitchell, Anson P. Morrill, Justin S. Morrill, Olin, Patton, Timothy G. Phelps, Pike, Pomeroy, Potter, John H. Rice, Riddle, Edward H. Rollins, Sargent, Sedgwick, Shanks, Sherman, Sloan, Spaulding, Stevens, Benjamin F. Thomas, Trimble, Trowbridge, Vandever, Van Horn, Van Valkenburgh, Verree, Wall, Wallace, Charles W. Walton, E. P. Walton, Washburne, Wheeler, Albert S. White, Wilson, Windom, and Worcester—80.

---

[1] Roscoe Conkling always *acted*, as upon this occasion, even at his best. When he closed he sank into his seat exhausted. His brother, F. A. Conkling, brought his cloak and laid it over his shoulders. Then in a studied pose of his noble figure, his face to the crowded ladies' gallery, his golden curls clustering about his fine head, he affected to sleep. His speech was one of the most effective of the session. I was the only one who congratulated him upon it.

NAYS.—Joseph Baily, Biddle, Francis P. Blair, Jacob B. Blair, George H. Browne, Cobb, Corning, Cox, Cravens, Crisfield, Crittenden, Delano, Deven, Dunlap, Dunn, Fisher, Granger, Grider, Haight, Hanchett, Harrison, Holman, Horton, Law, Leary, Lehman, McKnight, Mallory, Maynard, Menzies, Morris, Nixon, Noble, Pendleton, Perry, Porter, Richardson, Robinson, James S. Rollins, Sheffield, Smith, John B. Steele, William G. Steele, Stratton, Francis Thomas, Upton, Vallandigham, Wadsworth, Ward, Chilton A. White, Wickliffe, Woodruff, and Wright —53.

The main burden of censure fell on Stone. He was accused of traitorous communication with the rebels. Stanton sent him to Fort Lafayette, and his papers were seized and withheld. Wade subpœnaed him before his committee—as he did McClellan and McCall. The result was that Stone was liberated in August following. No charges were ever preferred against him.

CHAPTER XXII.

THE COMMITTEE ON THE CONDUCT OF THE WAR.

NOVEMBER, 1861–FEBRUARY, 1862.

EARLY in this session, Mr. Chandler introduced in the Senate a resolution to inquire into the causes of the disaster of the 21st of July (Bull Run), supplemented by the sad affair of Ball's Bluff, and the fall of Colonel Baker, so forcibly brought to the notice of the House, as shown in the last chapter. The idea covered by it was most suggestive. That was the origin of the famous "Committee on the Conduct of the War," the most useful of the purely congressional agencies of the war. The ready House caught it up and passed a joint resolution, for a joint committee of seven—three of the Senate, four of the House.

Its efficiency, like that of all congressional committees, would depend entirely upon the qualities and conduct of its head. Nobody but Wade was thought of for chairman. Chandler and Andrew Johnson were with him, and Julian, Covode, Gooch, and Odell from the House.[1] The committee (omitting Mr. Johnson's name) made their first report by Mr. Wade, soon after the close of the 37th Congress, in April, 1863, which made three heavy vol-

---

[1] I think Johnson never acted on the committee. It was no place for him. Wade and Chandler were its two great men.

umes of over two thousand pages. Their second, made
on May 22, 1865, was a trifle more in bulk—six volumes
in all, of over four thousand pages. I may only mention
some of the leading subjects submitted to its care : "Bull
Run," "Ball's Bluff," "The Missouri Campaign," "Fremont," "The Hatteras Expedition," "Port Royal,"
"Burnside's Beaufort Exploits," "Fort Donelson," "The
Capture of New Orleans," "Invasion of Mexico," "Expedition to Accomac," "The Battle of Winchester," "The
Battle of the *Monitor* and the *Merrimac*," "The Army of
the Potomac," "Battle of Petersburg," Banks's famous
"Red River Cotton Raid," and Butler's equally famous
"Raid on Fort Fisher' (which Terry afterwards carried by
assault), "Treatment of Prisoners," "The Sherman-John-
son Capitulation," and many more events and incidents
of the war, important then, but long since forgotten. A
large edition, many thousands, was printed of these now
scarce volumes, where is recorded so much evidence of
value to the real historian, who will know the use of
original evidence, not referred to by the generals who are
now so busy picturing and patching their fames. It is
said that Wade seldom missed a session of the committee.
The most conscientious of men, he never neglected a duty
nor failed of an engagement.

CHAPTER XXIII.

SIMON CAMERON AS SECRETARY OF WAR.

DECEMBER, 1861–JANUARY, 1862.

Appointment of Thomas A. Scott—Appointment of Edwin M. Stanton.

IN my short, but to me memorable journey with Mr. and Mrs. Lincoln from Cleveland tó Painesville, Mr. Lincoln asked me what I thought of Simon Cameron. I answered that to me he was a mystery, that his influence in Pennsylvania seemed out of all proportion to his ability, but that he was a wonderful manager. Mr. Lincoln replied that he had the same impression of him. I was surprised that he was appointed to the Cabinet, for I did not then know so well that intellectual ability was a small factor in selecting a Cabinet Minister. I became much better acquainted with both Mr. Lincoln and Mr. Cameron —indeed I came to have very intimate professional relations with Mr. Cameron, appearing for him later in a *cause célèbre*. I saw much of him in the War Office. I soon became aware of the existence of a bitter feud between Mr. Stevens and Mr. Cameron, dating back to the time when Cameron was a Democrat, and perhaps to the famous " Buck Shot War " at the State Capitol of Pennsylvania, in which both had a hand. He professed to forgive Cameron, in consideration of the radical grounds taken against slavery by the Secretary in his annual report. I was present when some one announced to Stevens Cameron's appointment as Minister to Russia, "Ugh! Ugh! Send word to the Czar to bring in his things of nights," was his response.

His methods in the War Office seemed to me very peculiar. He was not at home there, and had none of the ordinary appliances for business at hand. In considering any official matter, instead of asking a secretary or clerk (I never found one in his room—and the Secretary himself appeared usually alone there), he would ask you to give its status, and what he had said last about it. Possessed of that he would look about, find a scrap of paper, borrow your pencil, make a note, put the paper in one pocket of his trousers and your pencil in the other. A gentleman of our House once replied to the question as to what the Secretary said or did last, by saying, "The last thing you did in this case, Mr. Secretary, was to put my pencil in your pocket."

Mr. Thomas A. Scott, the then rapidly rising young railroad monarch, was early appointed Assistant Secretary. Slight but symmetrical, with a face as sharply and beautifully cut as a cameo, he was the embodiment of energy, intellect, and wise unerring judgment. Whenever he was to be found in the office, what a relief to deal with him, with his electric brain and cool, quiet manner. The change occurred January 15, 1862, and Scott remained connected with the office, organizing transportation, throughout the war.

I then had no personal acquaintance with Edwin M. Stanton, but I was destined to know him well and serve him often. It is my intention to give him some space ere this memoir closes. In the *Life of Senator Wade* I find it written ;

" Largely we are indebted to Mr. Wade for the advancement of Mr. Stanton to the War Office. He strongly urged him upon Mr. Lincoln, who soon came to estimate Mr. Wade at his true value. Stanton had been the bitterest of Democrats. The Republicans then knew nothing certainly of his course in Buchanan's Cabinet. His appointment surprised the Senate. Wade knew and endorsed him there. That was sufficient.

" The army, the American world, thrilled under Stanton's first touch. At his word everybody moved, except McClellan."

He had succeeded Judge Black as Attorney-General, in Buchanan's Cabinet, and we know now that his stubborn resistance in Cabinet Council defeated Floyd's demand to withdraw the garrisons from the Charleston forts. In that contest Stanton declared that to give up Sumter would be a crime as infamous as that of Benedict Arnold. Floyd, defeated, retired disgusted, and resigned immediately.

Stanton's first labor was to prepare and to secure the President's assent to the famous order notifying the various commanders, by land and by sea, to prepare to make on the 22d of February ensuing, a movement upon the enemy in their front.

CHAPTER XXIV.

THE PRESIDENT'S GENERAL WAR ORDER.
FEBRUARY–APRIL, 1862.

A Solemn Ceremonial by the Two Houses—Campaign on the Cumberland—
Fort Henry Surrendered—Fort Donelson Captured—Battles of Shiloh
and Corinth—The Tide Turned.

WE of the House, desiring a solemn ceremonial on
Washington's birthday, invited the Senate, the Executive,
the Supreme Court, and the army and navy to unite
with us in our hall, in the ceremonies. The ladies and
diplomats were invited also, and we ordered a general
illumination for the evening.

Meantime, we knew that the President's second son, a
handsome, interesting boy of twelve, was lying dangerously
ill. Toward the close of the session of the 21st, Mr.
Knapp, of Illinois, arose and said : " Mr. Speaker, I desire
to offer the following resolution :

" ' Entertaining the deepest sentiments of sympathy and condolence with
the President of the United States and his family in their present affliction,
by the death of his son,
" ' *Resolved,* That this House do now adjourn.' "

To this was added the following :

" *Resolved further,* That in view of this afflicting event, the Commissioner
of Public Buildings be requested to omit the illumination of the public buildings to-morrow night."

The House agreed to these resolutions and adjourned.

In the Senate, Saturday, February 22d, the following proceedings took place :

The Vice-President laid before the Senate the following communication :

" *To the Senate and House of Representatives :*
" The President of the United States was last evening plunged into afflic-tion by the death of a beloved child.   The heads of the departments, in con-sideration of this distressing event, have thought it would be agreeable to Congress and to the American people that the official and private buildings occupied by them should not be illuminated in the evening of the 22d instant.

" WILLIAM H. SEWARD.
S. P. CHASE.
E. M. STANTON.
GIDEON WELLES.
EDWARD BATES.
M. BLAIR.

" WASHINGTON, February 21, 1862."

Mr. Hale submitted the following resolution, which was considered by unanimous consent, and agreed to :

" *Resolved*, That the Senate, entertaining the deepest sentiments of con-dolence with the President in his present affliction, in the death of his son, and in view of this afflicting event, the Commissioner of the Public Buildings be directed to omit the illumination of the public buildings to-night."

WASHINGTON'S BIRTHDAY.

A message from the House of Representatives, by Mr. Etheridge, its Clerk, announced to the Senate that " The House is now ready to receive the Senate, in order that the Farewell Address of George Washington to the people of the United States be read in the presence of the two Houses of Congress, assembled in pursuance of their joint resolution of the 14th instant."
    The Senate thereupon proceeded to the House of Representatives in accordance with the published order of the proceedings, as follows :

The Vice-President of the United States and the Secretary
of the Senate, preceded by the Sergeant-at-Arms.
Senators.
The President and Heads of the several Departments.
The Chief Justices and Associate Justices of the Supreme
Court of the United States.
Representatives from Foreign Governments, near this
Government.
Invited Officers of the Army and Navy.
Distinguished Citizens, and other Invited Guests.

In the House some preliminaries were adjusted, among
them the presentation of the rebel flags sent to the Capital
under a recent act of Congress as follows :

" That the Secretaries of the War and Navy Departments be, and they are
hereby directed to cause to be collected and transmitted to them, at the seat
of the Government of the United States, all such flags, standards, and colors
as shall have been, or may hereafter be taken by the Army and Navy of the
United States from their enemies.

" That all the flags, standards, and colors of the description aforesaid,
which are now in the possession of the Departments aforesaid, and such as
may be hereafter transmitted to them, be, with all convenient dispatch, delivered to the President of the United States, for the purpose of being, under
his direction, preserved and displayed in such public place as he shall deem
proper."

Then, having invited the ladies on to the floor, and
yielded them all possible space, we received the invited
guests ceremoniously.   Our record shows thus :

" Seats in the Hall had been prepared for a large number of invited
guests.

" The galleries, with the exception of that reserved for the families of the
Senators and Members, had been densely crowded from an early hour in
the morning.

" The Members of the House, by request of the Speaker, occupied the
rear seats in the hall on the left of the Speaker's chair.

" The doors of the main entrance to the hall were now thrown open, and
the Members of the House, rising, received the invited guests of the occasion in the following order :

" The Vice-President of the United States and the Secretary of the Senate, preceded by the Sergeant-at-Arms and the Chaplain.
" The Senate of the United States and its officers and official reporters.
" The Heads of the several Departments.
" The Judges of the Supreme Court of the United States.
" Distinguished citizens and other invited guests."

The entrance into the hall of the army and navy officers, in full uniform, headed by General McClellan, was greeted by a general manifestation of applause by the galleries.

The President of the United States, in consequence of the recent death of his son, was not present.

The Senators were assigned to seats on the left of the Speaker, in front of the members of the House. On the right, the seats nearest the main aisle were occupied in the following order, commencing at the area fronting the Clerk's desk:

1. The Heads of the Departments, of whom all were present.

2. The Judges of the Supreme Court, all being present except Chief-Justice Taney.

3. The officers of the army and navy, of whom about fifty were present, consisting of major-generals and brigadier-generals of the army, and officers of equal rank in the navy.

A large number of the representatives of foreign Governments were present, and occupied seats on the right of the officers of the army and navy, as the guests of the two Houses.

The other invited guests, to the number of about two hundred, including the heads of bureaus and many distinguished citizens, occupied seats on the extreme right.

The members of the House now resumed their seats, and the Speaker called the assembly to order.

John W. Forney, Secretary of the Senate, after invocation by our Chaplain, rendered *The Farewell Address* very effectively. Whereupon the Speaker announced that the proceedings directed by the two Houses of Congress having been concluded, the House would again resume its session.

The Senators and invited guests then retired from the hall.

As the General-in-chief of the Army rose to retire, some one in the gallery called for " three cheers for General George B. McClellan," which was most enthusiastically responded to, both in the gallery and on the floor of the House.

In pursuance of an order previously adopted, the Speaker declared the House adjourned until the Monday following, at twelve o'clock M.

The old residents, save a chosen few, had not then begun to look with favor upon us and our doings. They regarded the affliction of the President's family as a retributive warning from God, and were only too glad to be spared the humiliating glare of the intended illumination of the city.

The winter proved exceptionally mild, especially along the lines of the belligerent armies, and we of the House who urged vigor and real war, were restive under the frozen torpor of McClellan. True, at the close of our ceremonies of the 22d, the galleries cheered him valorously, but not a few mentally hissed him.

Spring would soon return, and we were hopeful. In the meantime things were silently preparing in the southwest for a surprise to both sides.

It will be remembered that 1861 had closed very gloomily ; and the opening of 1862 brought little to encourage the despondent. I was never for a moment discouraged or in doubt, though very impatient. Considering the immense territory and resources of the South and the warlike character of her people, and remembering, as I did, our defensive war of the Revolution, I never expected the war to end in Mr. Seward's sixty days, nor that it could be terminated on the first of July, 1862, as contended by Mr. Morrill in the House, in his very able speech on the Treasury Note bill. We made ample provision for gunboats on the southwestern rivers. We knew that Captain Foote was there with Porter and Phelps, and a formidable flotilla ; and we had an idea that a powerful fleet of them would sweep down the Mississippi. We knew no more of military strategy nor of the plans of the War and Navy Departments, than did any other two hundred men studying the conditions involved. Their secrets were not entrusted to us. We knew that we were blockading the rebel ports, and that we had a powerful inactive army along the two thousand miles of northern border, but to some of us this did not seem effective. We wanted to see heavy columns advancing upon Richmond, marching through their territory, seizing and holding their strong points, liberating their slaves, and cutting off their communication with each other. This surrounding and skirmishing along their interminable border seemed to many of us likely to be forever fruitless.

We waited impatiently for the execution of the order of the President referred to above.

The order ran as follows:

" EXECUTIVE MANSION, January 27, 1862.

" *President's General War Order No. 1.*

" *Ordered.*—That the 22d day of February, 1862, be the day for a general movement of the land and naval forces of the United States against the insurgent forces.

" That especially—

" The army at and about Fortress Monroe,
The Army of the Potomac,
The Army of Western Virginia,
The army near Mumfordsville, Kentucky,
The army and flotilla at Cairo,
And a naval force in the Gulf of Mexico,

be ready for a movement on that day.

"That all the forces, both land and naval, with their respective commanders, obey existing orders for the time, and be ready to obey additional
orders when duly given.

"That the Heads of Departments, and especially the Secretaries of War
and of the Navy, with all the subordinates, and the General-in-Chief, with all
other commanders and subordinates of land and naval forces, will severely
be held to their strict and full responsibilities for the prompt execution of
this order.

"ABRAHAM LINCOLN."

Of course McClellan waited till the rebels evacuated
Manassas, early in March, for purposes of their own, at
which time he was relieved of all command over the
armies of the other departments.

The army near Mumfordsville was Buell's command.
The army and flotilla at Cairo were Halleck's command,
and with him were Grant and Foote. Everything there
was already in motion; Grant and Foote needed no reminder from the Chief Executive. The squadron under
Foote captured Fort Henry on the Tennessee February
9th, the first news, probably, that we had definitely received of that rebel post. This placed our army nearly
in the rear of Columbus, and near the railroad connection
between that place and Bowling Green, the headquarters
of Joseph E. Johnston's right wing. Fort Donelson was
surrendered, after a series of bloody battles, on the 16th,
six days before the advance under the general order.

Then came a scampering from Paducah; Island No. 10
was reduced; Foote defeated the rebel flotilla at Mem-
phis, and the armies on both sides concentrated. The
rebels surprised our forces on Sunday morning, April 6th,
and brought on one of the great, though indecisive, battles of the world—Shiloh—or, as we called it, Pittsburg
Landing, the turning point of the year-old war. That
was followed by the successful battle of Corinth, fought
not twenty miles from the scene of Shiloh.

CHAPTER XXV.

THE BRILLIANT TENNESSEE CAMPAIGN.

JANUARY–FEBRUARY, 1862.

A Wonderful Stroke of Military Genius—Inquiry for its Author—Anna
Ella Carroll.

NONE of our later generations can ever understand the
wide and deep emotions of joy and gratitude with which
their fathers and mothers hailed the news of these late
victories, news dispelling the gloom that had shrouded
the entire North. We of the House shared this feeling
to the utmost, and we thanked everybody. Even Vallandigham, in a moment of utter forgetfulness, offered a
resolution of thanks to Halleck. Finally, we began to
surmise that there must have been a remarkable stroke of
genius in the conception of this short, decisive, and wonderful campaign, and on inquiry we were surprised that it
was not claimed for Halleck, Grant, or Buell, nor in fact
for anybody. There was a world of innocent wondering
over this, as the campaign certainly did not manage itself.
There was apparent in the record, even to us, the conception of a really wonderful brain. Whose was it?

We had heard Frank Blair, then a colonel or general,
assail Fremont, justifying his recall from Missouri, an
attack in which Frank showed much skill and some of the
Blair spirit, and to which Colfax replied, defending the
unlucky general. Fremont had already been criticised

by Adjutant-General Thomas, who with Cameron had
visited his headquarters, but even these astute masters of
war were mute on this question.   Stanton, and even Lincoln, were approached, but said "the public service required secrecy."   The world might never know, and
indeed it never has generally known.   Finally, it was
talked of a good deal in the House, and Olin and others
threatened to send a question to the War Office, but we
remembered the fate of our inquiry about Ball's Bluff,
and remained silent.   Much the same thing happened in
the Senate, though some, among them—Wade, knew the
truth.   All this time there sat daily in the galleries a
short, stout, middle-aged maiden lady, intently listening
through an ear trumpet to the ineffective talk which was
sure to break out over our resolutions of thanks.   This lady
knew all the time; she was Anna Ella Carroll, the eldest
daughter of Governor Thomas King Carroll, and grand-
daughter of Sir Thomas King, of Maryland.   She it was
who had stood so bravely by stout Governor Hicks in his
war to retain Maryland.   She pulverized Breckinridge's
great secession speech, and was thanked by members of
the Cabinet and by Senators.   She had made such valuable suggestions to the President, showing such aptitude
(genius we should call it in a man) for affairs, and for
schemes and plans of campaign, that at the suggestion of
Thomas Scott, Assistant Secretary of War, the President
sent her to St. Louis to advise as to an expedition down
the Mississippi.   She went, held counsel with the most
experienced river pilots, and advised against it, and her
reasons were so satisfactory that the scheme was abandoned.   She returned to Washington with the matured
plan of the Tennessee campaign, and when it was shown
to the President by Mr. Scott, the President ordered its
execution.   *She was a woman*, and that fact would discredit all the generals and professionals in the army, and
"*the good of the service*" required that she should be sup-

pressed, and suppressed she was. All this came out when want and illness drove her to Congress in 1871, and though committees of both Houses made the strongest reports in her favor, she has, like other great benefactors, sunk in neglect and out of public gaze until now. And now it is earnestly hoped that the services of this woman, whose unaided brain changed the fortunes of the war, and whose plans, if followed out, might have ended the rebellion in twelve months, may at least be acknowledged ere the earth close over her.[1]

Meantime we had the thrill-tragic, for the loss of our wooden frigates at Hampton Roads, and the thrill-triumphant at the dramatic appearance of the *Monitor*, and the defeat of the *Merrimac*. There was terror at the possibility (were it not for the *Monitor*) of a visit to the Capitol by the dreaded invulnerable ram, from the work of which the rebels expected to gain the independence of their Confederacy. When he recovered from the effects of the powder and cement blown into his eyes, we had Worden, the *Monitor's* commander, on the floor of the House. He was twice recommended for promotion, and early retired a rear-admiral.

---

[1] I became familiar with her case, and, aided by three or four of the " strong-minded," placed it again before the present Congress, and, though no journal would advocate her claim, with some prospect of success, April 9, 1892. She died in February, 1893. At this date, April 6, 1893, the case remains as above.

CHAPTER XXVI.

REVIEW OF LAWS ENACTED BY THE THIRTY-SEVENTH CONGRESS.

THE LONG SESSION.   DEC. 1861–JULY 1862.

Recapitulation of General Laws—Laws for the District of Columbia—The Division of Virginia.

I HAVE glanced at some of the scenes of the war to show their reflex action upon Congress.

We finally saw McClellan on his winding way to the rebel capital via the Peninsula, and then we saw him on his way back.   General Pope (who was a son-in-law of Representative Cutler of Ohio) was invited to the floor of the House during his brief campaign.

Every day, and often all the hours of the day, were given to work, and to work of the most exacting character, and I believe that the House perfected more than had ever before been accomplished in a single session. We matured and passed appropriation bills exclusively on account of the war, for the army and navy, aggregating more than $1,000,000,000.   Besides providing for all the civil wants of the Government, we perfected and passed during the session the following acts which went into the volume of general and permanent law: " The National Bank Act," already referred to ; " An Act to Establish a Department of Agriculture," an Act to

Secure Homesteads to Actual Settlers on the Public Do-
main," "An Act Authorizing Diplomatic Relations with
Hayti and Liberia," " An Act to Protect the Property of
Indians who have Adopted the Habits of Civilized Life,"
"An Act Chartering a Pacific Railroad Company," etc. ;
"An Act to Punish Polygamy in the Territories," etc. ;
"An Act to Donate Lands to Agricultural Colleges,"
"An Act in Reference to the Foreign Slave Trade."
For the District of Columbia many important laws were
passed : one " Establishing a General System of Common
Schools " ; one " Creating Schools for the Education of
Colored Children," the first in our history ; "An Act
Regulating Highways," " An Act to Incorporate the
Washington and Georgetown Railroad Company," " An
Act Reconstructing the Jury Laws of the District," " An
Act to Incorporate the Guardians Society for the Refor-
mation of Juvenile Offenders," " An Act for the Collec-
tion of Fines and Penalties," etc. ; " An Act Regulating
the Sale of Spirituous Liquors." These were among the
labors of that great session, which adjourned the 17th
of July 1862.

Mention has been made of a self-created and self-sus-
tained convention of Virginia, west of the mountains,
after the secession of that State. On the 31st of December, 1862, Congress passed the act dividing the State,
recognizing a " jacket-pocket " State government, with
Pierpont as Governor, and a small and select body of
Alexandrians as the Virginia Legislature. It seemed to
me then that the doctrine of legal fictions was being seriously strained, but I remembered Mount Vernon and
the recession of Alexandria County, and I voted for
the act.

Mr. Sumner had introduced into the Senate his favorite
scheme of declaring the seceded States so much vacant
territory, so far as civil government was concerned, and
dividing this territory into portions of convenient size,

13

which were severally to go through a needed pupilage, and were to be admitted again as States when duly prepared.   The old States and their names were to be

" Nameless here for evermore,"

save in history.

Much could be said in favor of this scheme, and he said the most for it, and the idea had some support in both Houses. In the debate on the Confiscation Bill, Mr. Riddle gave his views of the Sumner scheme. It was contended by Sumner that the act of rebellion had worked a legal dissolution of the States in the contemplation of the law.   Mr. Riddle contended that, as political entities, the States were indestructible. They were older than the Constitution, and in contemplation of the law they were all present at its formation. The States made the Constitution and General Government; the Constitution did not make the States, nor was it necessary to their perpetuity.   Government being not temporary but perpetual, they who consent to it cannot remain in its territory and withdraw their allegiance ; a State having come into the nation of States cannot withdraw. For national purposes, the Constitution by adoption had become the law of the land.   Destroy a State, and there on its soil you find the Constitution—ineradicably there, asserting itself and vindicating the right of the State to exist as a State with a Republican form of government. Conquest even does not, can not, eradicate it.

The whole ground was covered by him in an elementary way, as was the question of the punishment of the rebels. There were many great States full of them, the victims of a wide brain plague, rather than the doers of intentional crimes. They were American citizens of organized States. still in active existence, and it would be easier to subdue and win them back, than to attempt to efface their State lines and names or to force upon them new forms.   This people was not to be exterminated or extradited—they were to be the units, the integers, of the proposed new States. Mr. Riddle pronounced therefore against the whole scheme.

It seems to me impossible to reduce to a consistent and in any way a symmetrical narrative the varied and widely diffused labors of a session of the American Congress. The history of a single bill may be so treated, and something of the spirit of its discussions preserved, but there is and can be no continuous narration of all the events of a session, and no such complete history has been attempted. I note here two episodes of my own experience of that session, as showing something of the spirit of the congressional life of that strange time.

In the gloomy days of early February, Sam Cox came to me to arrange for himself and two of his friends a plan for obtaining the floor—though they must have known I was no favorite with the Speaker. Still, I had served some of them before. The trouble for them was, that in Committee of the Whole on the State of the Union, the Republican chairman, did not, as a rule, favor them. I asked him for the name of a Democrat whom he would prefer for the chair, and had no difficulty with the Speaker. The next day the House was not in working mood (as it sometimes was not), and I induced Mr. Stevens to go into Committee of the Whole. When the Speaker called to the chair the Democrat who had been suggested, it was understood that some old scores would be paid off. Cox took the floor. The House usually listened to him, though he was not popular on our side. His wit had a sting, as wit always has. He proceeded at once to a severe arraignment of the Republicans generally, and among the sins he chose to hold them responsible for was my little John Brown speech, once or twice mentioned before, which he sent to the Clerk's desk, where it was read. I confess I was surprised under the circumstances, for the thing was malicious on his part, but evidently it did not prove much of a card, some parts of the speech being received with decided marks of favor by the House. I quite appreciated his good intentions, and should have so expressed myself, but could not get the floor at the time, nor did I during that session of the committee, and the next day I did not care to reply. Grow, who knew how Cox secured the floor, thought the joke on me too good to keep, and the little speech lies, with many better, " in the bosom of the deep *Globe* buried," where it made about one column of the quarto. My reader will find this, a once much talked of effort, in the Appendix. It proved a sore matter for Cox. Cowles, of the Cleveland *Leader*, heard of it, and from that day, for twenty years, Cox was the pillow upon which he reposed all his animosities. He pursued him with rancorous venom, and when called to account for it, published the incident here mentioned.

I have spoken of Wadsworth of Kentucky. Few men have entered Congress with so high a reputation for public speaking. He early gave us an opportunity to estimate the justice of the popular judgment of him. The term *orator* hardly applies to any speaker of our time, for the art of oratory is lost. Wadsworth fully sustained his home reputation. He was strong, piquant, logical, and sarcastic, and he had a good manner. A Henry Clay Whig of the old school, he made a forcible arraignment of the Republicans. Few of us felt competent to reply without preparation, though several of us demanded the Speaker's recognition. He very properly gave the floor to Bingham, our readiest and one of our strongest men, practised and at home on the floor, who was then serving in his fourth Congress. Though unlike in mind and manner, the two were very fairly matched. Wadsworth, equal to giving many hard hits, had a flexile voice, facile and easy of modulation, never wearying. Bingham was too declamatory, and, like Kelley, his voice was monotonous. At fullest tide, it was like a steady, strong, onsweeping wind, roaring through and over a giant old forest, a powerful, steady, pealing blast. Wadsworth did not attempt to rejoin—did not care to. Some time afterward, in a speech of some length, he took occasion to refer to me (something in my utterance of January 27th may have offended Kentucky) in terms, as I was told, decidedly injurious. He was standing midway between me and the Speaker, and it was with difficulty I could hear him—in fact, I did not hear a word of his attack. I only knew he had made one when I found, after the House had adjourned, that there was disappointment at my not having claimed the floor. No one whom I met could or would tell me what he had said, but all concurred that I was obliged to notice it, and much curiosity was expressed as to what might come of it. It did not give me any uneasiness ; there might be occasion for a privileged question the next morning, and I was conscious of ability to take care of myself without troubling my friends. At that time the *Globe* issued a daily folio edition—a general newspaper, with the debates, a copy of which was laid on the desks of members. It could be had at the *Globe* building on the avenue, about 11 A.M.—earlier than members of Congress usually passed to the Capitol. I received a copy at that hour, and opened it out for examination as I walked along the empty sidewalk. I turned to Wadsworth's speech, and was intently scanning down the columns, when a hand (I had not heard a footstep) was lightly laid on my shoulder, and a pleasant voice said : "You wont find it there." Turning, I found that it was Wadsworth. "It is not there," he repeated. "I listened to an unworthy suggestion, and without time for thought, said what I did. When I reflected, I expunged it. I owe you an apology." He spoke earnestly. "Luckily I did not hear it," I replied. "I only heard *of* it, and between us it shall be as if unsaid. You have made the amplest apology." And we went on to the Capitol together.

We became at once and always remained warm friends. "As you will not rise to a question," he laughingly said, "there will be an unusual examination of the *Globe* this morning"—and there was.

I really never did know what the frank Kentuckian said, but no doubt it was something concerning John Brown or my speech referred to above.

CHAPTER XXVII.

CONGRESSIONAL ELECTION.

MAY–SEPTEMBER, 1862.

Congressional Election—19th District Changed—Interest in the 19th Ohio District—Greeley Advises to Run Independent—Would Aid—The Convention—Defeat—The Proclamation of September 22d—Antietam.

O HORACE! not him of Venusia, but of the *Tribune*, here is a bit of thy chirography, on paper darkened with the hue of time! I spread it out and try to follow its ever wavering flow which marks it as one of the score dear indeed to autograph hunter and collector of runic, cursive, and discursive cryptograph. I could once read even thee; now, with me, as I fancy with most living men, this has become a lost art, but I can make the date July something, 1862, and at the end, H. G. The letter has marks showing that it has been in the hands of Samuel Williamson, of Cleveland, Ohio, and a marginal note indicates that in it Horace Greeley expresses a decided opinion that I should claim re-election in the 19th Ohio District as an independent candidate, and in that event promises the aid of the *Tribune*. This chimed in with my own not timid spirit. Were the votes to be won for another—I never could bring myself to vote or ask others to vote for me, so I once lost the Speakership of the Ohio House through voting for the other

199

chap, who did not vote for me—all this showing how unfit I was for partisan politics as practised.

So, there now lie by me my daily letters written home
at that time, in which I find early references to this matter
of re-election, and where repugnance to life in Congress is
strongly expressed, and regret that in existing conditions
I was compelled to submit to it for another two years—if
the district should permit that.   One thing personally
pleasant I came to know, that many leading Republicans
of the House desired my re-election, had exerted themselves, as far as was decent, to secure it, and had managed
to learn something of the temper of my constituency.
Among these were E. B. Washburne, Olin, Frank Blair,
and Lovejoy.   Washburne was one of the strongest men
in Congress by reason of his intellectual ability, will
power, and character.   He had a little infirmity of
temper when he could not have his way, which sometimes
was uncomfortable to those of us who wished to stand by
him.   Olin of New York and Frank Blair (we had two or
three Blairs) became chums; they had a way of going out
after the morning hour and returning at three or four
o'clock, both none the better for it.   Frank sometimes
took a lounge in the cloak-room, and Olin took the floor—
if there was any opening—no matter what was up.   Olin
was one of the able men ; he had made much reputation
by writing *The Covode Report*, which the Pennsylvanian
had credit for throughout the country, a labor for which
Covode was as incapable as he was to write " the song
that was Solomon's "—another worthy who made a reputation in much the same way.   Olin was placed on our
District of Columbia bench later, where his weakness increased till, in Chief-Justice D. K. Cartter's words, "his
best opinions hardly amount to a er-er reasonable doubt."
Frank later overcame his unfortunate tendency and came
back from the wars robust and healthy.   Lovejoy was a
man of much more strength and ability than the House

gave him credit for. A weakness of temper and of judgment on the subject of slavery was his "easily besetting sin," and if a thought of that took him on the floor it took him off his intellectual feet. He at once went into an Achillian rage ; his face became inflamed, his speech vehement, and his invective something awful ; it seemed as if the flavor of his murdered brother's blood came freshly to him and drove him mad for the time. While it lasted the House remained silent, and no one took notice, in speech, of the ebullition. He was perhaps the worst dressed man on the floor. I early became interested in him and made a study of him ; the columns of the leading Ohio papers, as well as those of the *New York Tribune* and *Evening Post*, were open to me, and in one of them I devoted a column to an appreciative but discriminative analysis of the man. He had a really very superior working mind and was industrious, and would certainly, with continued life, have gone on to one of the high places ; this in effect being the conclusion of the paper ; mention also being made of his slovenly and mean dress as one of his defects. He was a graduated theologian, and was for many years an ordained Congregational minister, and something of his training and mode of thought was constantly, though never offensively, coming to the surface. A copy of the journal, with the paper marked, I had placed in his box at the House, and it reached him at his desk. I sat where I could observe him and notice its seeming effect ; apparently he was much pleased, and soon retired with it to the cloak-room and spent much time there.

It was noticed and spoken of the next day that he came in neatly dressed, securing the full benefit of his really good, rather stout figure, and I believe he afterward dealt with slavery in a more temperate spirit. The article itself was spoken of, but its authorship never came out. Lovejoy entered the 38th Congress and died in 1864, at the age of fifty-three.   He was capable of continuous growth, and might have reached eminence.

I recall that these gentlemen expressed a lively wish for my continuance in the House. Washburne told me that the thing had been talked over with Edgerton, who had been thrown into my district by the Ohio Legislature through efforts of the *Herald*, and that he had given assurance not only not to seek a third election, but to influence his friends in Summit County to aid me there; indeed something of this was mentioned to me by Mr. Edgerton himself. My friends in Washington had no conception of the feeling against me in my district, nor perhaps did they understand some of the defects of my make-up—better known in northern Ohio. When conscious of perfect integrity of act and word, no matter what misapprehension might exist as to my conduct, I could never bring myself to explain nor to attempt to do so.   Friends or opponents were left to correct their impressions as they might; when asked in regard to the Bull Run letter I could only repeat its statements, and though often on the platform, I never uttered five words on that theme.   People might live and die, as probably twenty thousand did, who believed that, to effect my own escape from the rebels, I had thrown a wounded soldier from my carriage into the highway to perish under the hoofs and wheels of the fleeing cowards and the pursuing rebels.   I had placed the means of correcting this impression within the reach of every man and woman in my district, and there I left the matter.

Ere Congress adjourned, Colonel Parsons returned from Brazil, and I got to understand the position of things in the Cleveland District.   It seems that Mr. Chase had managed to know very well about the matter, though I had never troubled him or any one else with it, and Parsons said that Chase had insisted that he should devote his best efforts to my re-election. I, however, exacted nothing from him, nor did I ever solicit the aid of anybody in the business.

During the vacation of Congress there was a notable excursion to Washington by three Cleveland gentlemen, Colonel Parsons, Dr. Everett, and Mr. Riddle. My object was to secure the appointment of Dr. Everett as Collector of Internal Revenue for the district. Colonel Parsons went as my friend, as I supposed, though not at my request. When we returned to Cleveland, Colonel Parsons had the collectorship, Mr. Chase saying to me that I was to be sustained. Perhaps I was.

The Congressional Convention was called at an unusually early day for that district, where I had not been for eight months, and I returned to find Judge R. P. Spalding, Mr. Parsons's law partner and Mr. Chase's leading friend in the State, actively in the field.

I had many personal friends in Summit, was well known at the Akron bar, and was very kindly received in the canvass, and I found, as I expected, that Edgerton had been announced as a candidate in the district to which he had been transferred.[1] I addressed a large mass-meeting in Summit (being Spalding's home), a meeting which had really been called in Spalding's interest, and I made such hasty arrangements as I might for the convention.

I had decided not to follow Mr. Greeley's advice. Who was I and my small affairs that I should make a bitter quarrel and war in the Republican camp, in the most important district of the State? Spalding was older and more widely known, and was doubtless esteemed the abler man. Let the district within the party settle it. Reuben Hitchcock, of the Peace Congress, residing at Painesville, a warm personal friend of mine, an eminent and popular man, was in the field in Lake County. I effected an arrangement with him, whereby that delega-

---

[1] This had been done before he or I knew it was intended. It was the work of Spalding's friends.

tion should be counted for him—to go for me as a possible
second choice. Seymour and other Lake friends repudiated that arrangement, put a ticket for me into every
township, and were beaten clean in the county, as I knew
they would be. I had a majority of the Cuyahoga delegates, city and county, Edgerton had half a dozen from
Summit, and Spalding had the rest. I had a plurality on
the first ballot in the convention, held my own in the
second, when my *friends* (?) made haste to withdraw me,
and Spalding was nominated.

There came finally the Emancipation Proclamation of
September 22d to salve and cheer. How utterly insignifi-
cant seemed my personal fortunes, disappearing from my
own mind in the radiance and glow of this, to me, the
greatest human utterance. The word was irrevocably
spoken ; it was like the speaking a new world into being
by Omnipotence.

We have seen the action of Congress on this chronic
national " grudge."

It will be remembered that Fremont, " The Path-
finder," on the 31st of August, 1861, had issued a proclamation, as commander of the department, freeing the
slaves in Missouri. The President revoked this proclamation. Later General Hunter (an always sadly under-
estimated man), in command of the Department of South
Carolina, Florida, and Georgia, on May 9, 1862, had
declared those States under martial law, and the slaves in
them free. The retraction of Fremont's proclamation
had produced a bitter feeling through the North, but,
notwithstanding, Mr. Lincoln also revoked Hunter's
order. He answered the delegations of northern clergy-
men who prayed him to declare slavery at an end in the
rebel States, by refusing their prayers. He answered in
the same way Horace Greeley's strong open letter, calling
for such action. Mr. Lincoln hoped something from his
scheme of " abolishment," recommended and sanctioned

by Congress, and therefore delayed. Then came a series of reverses in the field, the greatest of which was Pope's repulse in front of Washington. The President finally submitted to his Cabinet a draft of his proclamation, which Seward thought, if issued at that time, would be regarded as a despairing appeal, but McClellan's partial success at South Mountain, and the greater success at Antietam, September 17th, seemed to part the clouds, and the proclamation was issued.

In this year of 1862, the Ohio Democrats were early in the field with their State ticket. They put forth a string of resolutions asserting their loyalty, in proof of which they condemned the congressional legislation upon slavery, and all the war measures of the present Congress. The Republicans had what they called a union convention late in August, and also put a ticket in the field. A Supreme Court judge and one attorney-general were the only state officers to be elected, but the congressional and legislative elections gave importance and activity to the contest.

I was induced to undertake a two-weeks' canvass in southeastern Ohio. At an immense outdoor gathering at Salem, where I was the only speaker assigned, I heard of Bull Run. Among the sounds that greeted me upon being named on the stand to the crowd, were the bovine, heavy bass notes of the animal giving the name to that luckless run, after the manner of the popular Virginia nomenclature. The chairman, at my request, left the leader of the herd to me—with a speedy result, which made me the complete master of the multitude, and put it in possession of a more accurate idea of the battle. The press made such kindly mention of my disposition of the incident that no one cared to refer to Bull Run in my presence again.

This result of the Ohio election was something surprising. The Democrats elected fourteen of the twenty-one Representatives in Congress, against their eight in the 37th together with their State ticket and a majority in the Legislature.

The elections generally left the Republicans much weakened, and the 38th Congress might possibly find the House in doubt.

CHAPTER XXVIII.

THE THIRD SESSION OF THE THIRTY-SEV-ENTH CONGRESS.

DECEMBER, 1862–MARCH, 1863.

Mr. Lincoln's New Scheme for the "Abolishment of Slavery"—The Blockade Enforced—Conscription—Power Given the President to Suspend the Writ of *Habeas Corpus*.

OUR third and last session commenced December 1, 1862. What a bloody, weltering year had been this about to close! Fredericksburg, Chancellorsville, and Port Hudson had been succeeded by Donelson, Shiloh, and Corinth, and were soon to be followed by Vicksburg and Gettysburg, where fortune would be confirmed to the Union standards, and the President would proclaim a national Thanksgiving, while yet it was summer. If we only could have known!

We were all promptly back in our seats and committee rooms, and if not much wiser, we were even more determined; what we should do in Congress must be accomplished in ninety-three days.

Mr. Lincoln met us in his annual Message with a new proposition for the "*abolishment*" of slavery, which in part his proclamation had already abolished, and he now proposed three new articles to the Constitution. Every slave State that should abolish slavery before or at the *end of the century*, should be paid for the property, in

207

United States interest-bearing bonds ; all slaves who shall have *enjoyed actual* freedom by the war, any time before the end of the rebellion, to remain free ; Congress may make appropriations for the colonization of the freedmen *out of the United States.* The most of the message was devoted to a discussion of this scheme. It made no impression on the old abolitionists, for we had made up our minds to a speedier and cheaper end of the cause of war. It was the President's idea that, embodied in the Constitution, these articles would themselves end the war, or would greatly help to that end. To us that was visionary. We wanted to see the end of both the war and slavery, and we thought they should end together. While few of us expected to see January 1, 1900, without the help of the early abolitionists the President's plan could find very feeble support.

The Secretary of the Navy had told us that in the face of the declaration of Europe we could not make a real blockade of the insurgent ports ; but we had succeeded in doing it. We had extemporized four powerful fleets, and had so effectively walled up the rebel gateways to the sea that foreign states had felt obliged to respect the blockade. We gave him $71,000,000. The Secretary of War told us we had at that date 800,000 effective soldiers in the field, and that the process then in good working order would soon increase the number to a round million.

We appropriated for his expenses in the field a fraction less than $677,000,000, one item of $45,000 being for *artificial limbs !* Think of the ghastly significance of such an item ! Mr. Chase gave us a clear, strong *exposé* of his department and plans. He had organized the Internal Revenue Bureau. We gave him a comptroller of the currency and all the money he wanted to make. However, it is not my purpose to turn through the two volumes of the *Globe* of this session,

nor to make many clippings for the annoyance of my read-
ers. A rapid survey, with a pause at two or three points,
will close my labors with the 37th Congress.

To some of us it seemed as illogical to depend upon
volunteering for soldiers to wage the war, as it would be
to depend upon voluntary contributions to put and keep
them in the field, yet Congress, though sorely pressed,
was reluctant to adopt a scheme of conscription. It was
not till February 9, 1862, that Senator Wilson introduced
a bill for that purpose, which was reported back on the
16th, and the Senate did little but debate it for two days ;
of course it was there opposed by the seven or eight opposition Senators.

In the House, Vallandigham led the ineffective opposition. The bill passed the House, February 25th, one
hundred and fifteen for, to forty-nine against it, a few
Republicans voting with the Democrats. Conscription
was very unpopular throughout the North, producing
riots on attempts to enforce it, and in practice it proved
delusive and ineffective. In the next Congress, Garfield
showed that there were in practice at least twelve open-
ings by which men escaped the drafts. It *required soldiers
with nerve* to devise an effective law.

We passed through the House a bill to raise one hundred and fifty regiments of Africans, for five years—should
the war last—a scheme which was met at every point by
our enemies, my venerable Kentucky friend, Wickliffe,
being in sore dismay, and early reminding me of my
speech of the year before. The measure passed, in spite
of a day and a night or two of filibustering, February 3d,
by a vote of eighty-three to fifty-four, some Republicans
voting with the Democrats. When it reached the Senate,
that learned body declared that, under our *present* law,
persons of color could be enlisted. We supposed they
could, but not 150,000 in addition to those already authorized.

14

Under a former schedule, we had in the service thirty major-generals and seventy-five brigadiers, and at this time, by Act, we added forty to the first-class, and two hundred to the second. We authorized the President to dismiss any officer at discretion, and to suspend pay under certain contingencies, and we reconstructed the whole code of army regulations and ordinances.

One of the labors of the session was the Act known as the "Ways and Means," in which the difficult matter of the regulation of bonds and Treasury notes, the complex system of securities, credits, and loans, voluntary and forced, was revised if not improved.

It may be remembered that early in the called session, a bill was introduced and much debated, the purpose of which was to indemnify the President for doing such acts as under existing conditions the public good in his judgment required, and for which there was no other warrant. This bill was the subject of ardent debate through that and the ensuing long session, and was about the last work accomplished by the 37th Congress. It made the President practically a dictator, although he was then personally a subject of unworthy criticism among Republicans. It was called "An Act Regulating *Habeas Corpus* and Other Things." That ancient missive of freedom was made a thing of the President's will. His order when pleaded was constituted a legal justification in all the courts of the United States for the acts and things done pursuant to it. The measure was made retroactive and covered everything back to the fall of Sumter, and its passage in the House cost much filibustering.

This session also created the Freedman's Bureau; the District of Columbia Courts were reorganized, and many needed laws for the District were passed.

CHAPTER XXIX.

THE SHIP CANALS.

FEBRUARY, 1863.

Scheme to Secure Warships on the Lakes—The Defence of New York.

TOWARD the close of this last session, the New York and Illinois gentlemen of the House, with some prompt-ings from others of us, introduced a scheme for a ship canal to connect the Mississippi with Lake Michigan, and also for an enlargement of the New York and Erie Canal, so as to admit the passage of effective war vessels to the lakes, or from thence to the defence of New York, if need be. We had become accustomed to large schemes and to the use of huge sums, and this plan took hold of the imagination. Pennsylvania arrayed herself solid against it, as did Indiana, and, curiously enough, only a fringe of us along Lake Erie, with some few exceptions, favored it. The Ohio House of Representatives even instructed us of that State to oppose the plan, while New York, Massachusetts, and most of the East were for it.

There had been for some time along the northern border an ill-feeling against Pennsylvania for her course in the vexatious and very petty interruption of railroad transit across her " pan-handle," on the lake border at Erie. She persisted in maintaining a railroad across that neck of land of a gauge different from that of the through

line, thus requiring two transshipments of everything passing by the lake shore. This was for the benefit of her
local venders " of peanuts, small beer, and crackers," and
the controversy was known as the " Peanut War."

Some taunts of this had been thrown at the Pennsylvania gentlemen by some of us, and they had, or thought
they had, cause for quarrel with Mr. Riddle, who, as they
learned, had stimulated Worcester to go against Butler in
his noted contest. There was much difficulty in getting
the bill up for debate, in which Stevens led the opposition—Vallandigham and Cox both speaking against it,
with Olin, aided by Washburne and Arnold, to manage
the bill. Mr. Riddle's constituents decidedly favored it,
and failing to secure the floor, he secured leave (a bad
practice) to print his remarks. The speech, of course,
was watched for by the Pennsylvanians. It covered the
points sufficiently for the reader who may care for the
subject, and its length does not preclude its being
given.

MR. RIDDLE said :

" Mr. Speaker, I know the impotence of words, even when the bearers
of great arguments, to change the convictions of men whose conclusions
grow out of a settled purpose and are imbedded in an unhearing prejudice.
And I employ them now only to vindicate, to my own judgment, a great
measure that has not received the consideration from the House that it is entitled to.   I am amazed that it receives from gentlemen not manly opposition, not argument, not logic, not facts, but bold denunciation, measureless
misrepresentation, and slobbering balderdash.   Who authorized the gentleman from Indiana (Mr. Holman), to speak for Ohio who, with such a flourish,
flaunted a soiled rag of a newspaper in our faces, as if to remind my colleagues and myself that the Legislature of our State had spoken ?   Sir, Ohio
will select her own organs, and we will answer to her without the officious
aid of any meddler from outside.   I knew, sir, that the members of the Ohio
Legislature, for want of something else to do, had requested my colleagues
and myself on this floor, and had instructed our colleagues in the Senate, to
oppose this measure.   It is not the first time that respectable gentlemen
have gravely advised and instructed others about matters with which they
had as much to do as the signs of the Zodiac have with the weaning of
children.

" I ask the gentlemen of this House to turn their eyes for a moment to the northern boundary of this Republic. There they find, beginning within a few degrees of longitude of the ocean, and extending irregularly westward to near the meridian of the continent, a vast series of waters, almost equalling the width of the Atlantic. Let the eye run along the great extent of bays and capes and creeks and peninsulas that undulate their southern shore, and they find a coast line that nearly equals the whole Atlantic coast ; and, while the eye rests for a moment in its wearied survey, I pray these gentlemen to remember that this immense extent of coast is the northern frontier of the Republic. Turn the eye from the lake to the Atlantic coast, and mark, at the entrance of every bay and creek and harbor, and by every roadside, the formidable fortresses and fortifications that frown defiance along its whole extent, under the protection of which the hands of commerce and enterprise have built up the world's great marts. Mark, also, and wonder over the mighty naval armaments that oppress the Atlantic bosom, and all, all for the defence of the Atlantic coast, and mainly against one great rival. Turn again to the northern margin ; every league of the opposite coast that answers to this northern line is the soil of this same imperious rival. The whelps of its old lion project at us their muzzles from every promontory and headland of that opposite coast ; while throughout the whole extent of our line not a fort nor fortification worthy of the name exists ; and there floats on all those vast seas but a solitary vessel that carries a single gun under our flag. Nay, the National Government is under an enduring treaty stipulation never to construct vessels of war on these waters. Contemplate for a moment the vast spoils that there await the clutching hand of armed violence. Over those same waters float annually more than six hundred million dollars of commerce, all at the mercy of a single armed cruiser. On the southern shores of those lakes are clustered a group of great, populous, wealthy, but unarmed and utterly defenceless communities. My own State has a greater population and wealth, can raise a greater revenue, and has sent forth a larger army, than had the kingdom of Prussia when the second Frederick of Brandenburg ascended its throne. Yet her whole northern frontier is an open, unarmed coast, and she has not a fortification within her limits, and cannot arm a single gunboat.

" Look once again to those lakes, and mark the mighty river through which their vast waters flow to the sea ; and mark how entirely it is in the possession of our great rival, whose sea armaments equal the united navies of the rest of the world. Observe how wholly and completely the sole means of naval transit around the cataract of the Niagara are hers alone, and that, save this, there is no naval access to these waters. See ! how utterly and entirely we lie at the will and pleasure of this haughty and capricious power ; and how we must accept any humiliation at her hands, or leave to her bloody sickle the hoarded fields of our defenceless North. We know but too well what her present temper and disposition are. She may keep herself within the bare letter of international law ; but a man whose highest rule of conduct is the letter of the law, is neither a good citizen, a good neighbor, nor an honest man. We know that repeatedly during our present calamities she has violated the obligations of good neighborhood, and the amenities and equities that must regulate the intercourse of civilized races, and has persistently sought to force an open rupture with us. Sir, now, when our house is on fire, instead of aiding to extinguish the flames, she could not be content to remain an idle spectator, but she has fanned with her breath the fierce conflagration, and has done for the incendiaries what they could not do for themselves. When the emissaries of this treason could no more find means for a passage to Europe than they could fly to the sun, one of her own mail steamers was purposely placed at their disposal. And when with strong hand we took them thence, she made the act of carrying them her national act, and demanded them at the peril of war. She demanded them at the price of a humiliation that she then thought we would not submit to ; and the brow of the American youth will redden for ten generations that we accepted the humiliation. . . .

" The best military engineers declare that this scheme for a canal is entirely practicable, and give us the plans and estimates. The chairman of the Ways and Means, in his poverty-stricken speech of Saturday, declares that the thing itself cannot be done. And when the authorities are quoted in reply to him, he can only escape like that other venerable lady from a similar difficulty—' I and Paul differ.' ' In the event of a war with England,' says that gentleman, ' we will seize the Welland Canal,' Certainly, by all means ; I go in for that. Sir, one half of our own territory is now holden from us by an armed occupation that has thus far defied the power of the nation to repossess it. The broad tidal river that sweeps by this Capital has been blockaded for a year at a time, so that a herring could hardly navigate it. I think I see the Ways and Means invading the British Empire. We have had some useful experience in this war of invasion.

" But we are told that we can extemporize an armed fleet on these lakes ample in time and force for any emergency. Do gentlemen forget that our enemies possess just the same facilities for building ; as much means, men, money, and power, with as much practical skill and daring ; with ample naval transit from the ocean to the lakes? Sir, if a war were to break out to-morrow with England, no armed vessels of ours would ever float upon the lakes. They would be burned on the stocks by the enemy's gunboats from the ocean. Do gentlemen really desire a repetition of the fierce old battles for the empire of these very waters, even if we could enter upon the effort, as we cannot, on equal terms? Would it not cost us more than this canal ? Is the hazard nothing? Suppose we were to fail in the next great struggle ? What then ? My people demand that this risk shall not be run ; it can be avoided. There are three gentlemen now on this floor, Messrs. Crittenden, Wickliffe, and Grider, all of gallant Kentucky, who heard the roar of Perry's guns in that old-time sea fight. When Shelby and Clay and Johnson went plunging through the wilderness to the woody shores of the far-off Erie ;

among all that gallant host were none nobler, in the opening flush and rising glory of proud young manhood, than those who come from these distant bat-tle-fields, through all the wrecking vicissitudes of life and time here, to vote on this great measure, I hardly dare think how. I would remind them that the far-off frontier is as defenceless now as when they shielded it with their breasts.

" I know that the Rhode Island youth, who had with Preble and Deca-tur, chastised the Corsairs, came with his three or four dozen sailors, and, aided by the tanned hunters and frontiersmen of that hardy region, con-structed a fleet in less than ninety days, with which they went in quest of the foe. How eagerly the straggling dwellers in the wilderness hastened to the shore, if haply they might catch a sight of the sails that wafted their country-men to battle. And when that battle joined and its thunders rolled through the dim aisles of all the woods, what mortal of us can realize the terrible anxiety that questioned of the result ? No railroad brought it ; no telegraph flashed it. Long ago that fleet was dismantled, and the larger vessels sunk. And it is since my own manhood that the *Lawrence* was raised, and her tim-bers and spars carved into canes and picture frames and caskets and cabinets, and given and received as the most treasured mementos, souvenirs, and amulets. And the hero Perry passed—oh! long ago, to the memory and his-tory of his country ; and from the granite pedestal in the beautiful park of one of the loveliest cities of the globe, his form, in Parian marble, stands with his soul breaking from the lineaments of his face ; with his hand point-ing ever to the near sea, as a reminder that as that was the scene of a great achievement, so it is the source of a great danger. He stands there an ex-clamation point in marble, against the unmanly ribaldry with which the opponents of this measure seek to overwhelm it. Had Great Britain then possessed the Welland Canal, who is hardy enough to declare that Perry could have won the mastery of the lakes ? . . .

" My able colleague from the Dayton District (Mr. Vallandigham) opposes this measure, because he says that it is a direct war upon the interests of five or six States, and of as many great cities. This is a great declaration, indeed. It is kindred to the opposition of the two gentlemen from Indiana (Messrs. Holman and Voorhees), who with their tears swell the crystal waters of the Mississippi. They seem to regard this as a direct war upon that river, and to believe that if it succeeds, that rather respectable stream will incontinently ' dry up.' I cannot understand how this measure can affect the Mississippi. It makes it no longer ; it removes no town from its banks; it leaves everybody and everything that chooses to meander down its romantic and aromatic tide as ever, with no hindrance or additional burden. In what way could it result adversely to the States and cities of my colleague (Mr. Vallandigham) ? Why, a ship canal connecting the Mississippi and Lake Michigan would open up a finer and cheaper outlet so much nearer and more direct that the overburdened lands of the West and Northwest would be diverted from the older, more circuitous, and dearer routes, *and from the worse to a new and better market.* And the people of the States and cities referred to would thereby lose their profits made up wholly of these enormous charges for transportation and costs of marketing by these old and expensive routes. And to whom, pray, would the difference between the old and new transportation and cost of marketing fall by this change ? To the producer, to be sure, as it should. It increases to him, by just so much, the market value of every article he raises. It comes to the sweating worker of the million of fertile acres in the far-off West, whose products rot and moulder away on his hands or are burnt for fuel, offending heaven and the day with the smoke of blasphemous waste. It comes to him like a beneficence, for it brings an equivalent to the hungry remote thousands for whom God intended it. I was amazed at the logic of the gentleman from Ohio. That argument would have forever prevented the construction of a canal or railroad, that pack-horses and wagons might receive their accustomed patronage, and that wayside inns might still feed hungry men and horses. The wise legislator would, if he could, annihilate space between producer and consumer, and abolish the carrier who lives on both, producing nothing but devouring charges.

"And I beg my mourning Indiana friends, and in this I include the gentleman on my left (Mr. Porter) also, to remember that when we had this same Mississippi rolling its tide of fertilizing mud uninterruptedly to the sea, with the present means of transportation eastward all in working order, the poor workers still starved in Europe, and the poor workers still burnt corn in Illinois. All the nations of the earth rise up and condemn this state of things ; and when we propose to improve as we may this relation of the parties, the gentleman from Indiana (Mr. Voorhees) exclaims against it as a sin against nature. The old ways opened up by the Almighty are preferred by him, and these Indianians seem to think that their noble State was born of the Mississippi, as old Egypt was of Nilus slime. Sir, had the Mississippi been their only outlet, Indiana would have been a wilderness to-day, with not one hundred and fifty thousand inhabitants in her borders.

" This constellation of great Western States was born of the East, and, like the children of the Magians, their faces are ever toward the Orient.

" I can remember when there was not a harbor improvement from Buffalo to Milwaukee. I can remember, too, the sneers and jeers at this scheme of the ponderous-headed, deep-eyed Clinton, of connecting the waters of Erie with the Atlantic. And yet the prophetic voice that spoke it into existence invoked the mighty West into being. The dim recesses of interminable forests, the great empty prairies—empty since the dawn of time—heard that voice, and came forth with their teeming millions to realize the dreams of old imaginings.

" Sir, in my judgment, as a commercial and peace measure, there now exist the same reasons for the works proposed by this bill as existed for the great enterprise of Clinton. The same forces that produced that, still work with a tenfold energy ; and how any man can fail to see this, is to me incomprehensible ; and how any man of the West, or how one who sympathizes with it, or who loves to see his nation develop and swell to her grand and just proportions, can withhold his support from this measure—as I fear all my colleagues save two will—is still more incomprehensible.

"It was to be expected that Pennsylvania, although she rests upon the lakes, would oppose the plan solid, with the exception of a friend near me (McKnight from Alleghany). Nothing traverses her soil from which she does not exact tribute. And her citizens for a whole winter, with arms in their hands, recently forced the entire travelling North to patronize her peanut-venders at Erie, the place where Perry's fleet was built. The nation has cheerfully shaped its policy to develop her resources. Her coal and iron are exempt even from taxation ; and yet her Representatives stand here the 'goblins of the mines,' a stupid, inert mass of selfish obstinacy, to wall up the way of this great measure. We say to Pennsylvania too, we bide our time.[1]

"The unregenerated gentleman from Indiana (Mr. Voorhees) desires no artificial channels of intercourse and interest to bind together the remote parts of the Republic : the water-courses of nature are ample for him. Can that gentleman, in the blindness of prejudice, have forgotten that it is commerce born of thrift and gain, that has opened up all the beautiful ways of intercourse between the peoples of the earth, has been the bearer of civilization, preceded the missionary of Christianity, and trafficked in the arts and sciences themselves ? Under her genial care, the gentle and sweet amenities of domestic life—love, marriage, and family ties—have made alien tribes one people in blood and interest.

The bill was lost, sixty for, and seventy-two against it.[2]

---

[1] A day or two later, Mr. Moorhead, an ironmaker, who represented the Erie District, got leave to make a personal explanation. He was a man of wealth and consideration and a friend of Secretary Stanton's, and he was very angry. He had a pointed paragraph read from Riddle's speech ; somebody had prepared for him a condensed libel on its author and he read it effectively. The House was willing to hear Mr. Riddle's rejoinder, and, a very unusual thing then, applauded it. Moorhead asked for the floor again. McKnight arose and hoped that his colleague from "the peanut district" would be heard. Mr. Riddle asked a hearing for him, as did Cox, who liked the fun, but Stevens interposed, and the matter ended. Afterwards some of the House tendered Riddle a dinner.

[2] There was really no feeling on the part of any of the Pennsylvania gentlemen. Mr. Riddle was invited personally by Governor Curtin to Erie, to address a huge open-air convention, and was put forward to make the principal speech and warmly and profusely thanked by the Governor on the stand.

Later, with a really distinguished member, he was invited by the Loyal League to Philadelphia, and there addressed an immense open-air concourse.

CHAPTER XXX.

CRITICISM OF THE PRESIDENT.

FEBRUARY, 1863.

AMONG our later writers there can now scarcely be found any account of the constant and growing censoriousness towards the President on the part of a large number of the Republicans of both Houses of Congress. I borrow a page from the biography of Senator Wade, together with an extract from Mr. Riddle's speech, on the bill to indemnify the President, showing the painful and disrespectful stage which this criticism had reached at the end of the 37th Congress (2d edition, pp. 313–316).

"Very early there came to be a difference in the estimate of the President, his policy, capacity and intentions, between the distant northern public and the leading men of the two Houses, and he soon became the theme of criticism, reflection, reproach, and condemnation on the part of these gentlemen. The New York *Tribune* was largely the organ of these congressional critics, and, as was known, Mr. Greeley, with a lantern, was diligently searching all the summer, autumn, and winter of 1863 for a man to succeed him. To such extent did this condemnation reach, that, at the end of the Thirty-seventh Congress, there were in the House but two men, capable of being heard, who openly and everywhere defended him—Mr. Arnold of Illinois, and Mr. Riddle of Ohio. Corroborative of this, I quote from a speech of Mr. Riddle's on the ' Bill to Indemnify the President,' delivered in the House on the 28th of February. He dealt first, very directly, with the resounding clamor, denunciation, and vituperation of the President by the Democrats, and continued :

218

" ' But what can be said of a party in whose members it is thought to be a rare distinction that they are merely patriotic ; who to be true to the country must be better than their party, and who are loyal in spite of its teachings and of their political associations ? I am glad to say that on this floor there are many such brave and noble men, while the mass of their followers are true, as the people ever are. How easy it is to abuse, traduce, and denounce. That it requires neither wit, grace, nor truth, is illustrated by the assaults of those gentlemen on the President. I shall enter upon no laudation of the President, yet there are some words that I deem it fitting for me now to say in reference to him.

" ' Sir, the Executive is the arm of the people under our Constitution, and with it only can we deal a blow upon the rebellion. He who would strike that, save with his arm, strikes fully upon our own cause. Whoever strengthens this arm, strengthens the national cause ; whoever weakens it, strengthens the enemy. For the time being, the other branches of the Government might well be in abeyance, that all our energies might go to swell the mighty muscles of that arm. To save all, all must be risked. You cannot separate the Executive from the *personality* of the President ; and whatever detracts from him personally weakens the Executive force, as whatever elevates him gives to it added strength. So that whatever shakes the confidence of the people, or of any part of them, in the capacity or integrity of the President, by just so much aids the rebellion, as that which strengthens confidence in him gives vigor to the national cause.

" ' The President, without the people, and *all* of them, can no more conduct this war to a successful issue than can the people without him. Alone, no matter what are his personal qualities, he would be the feeblest driveller that ever perished under a great catastrophe, and the people must perish with him. With a united people, he is irresistible, in spite of mistakes and accidents. A united people with their President can control fate and compel success ; they must stand together, and woe unutterable to the wretches whose words or deeds shall separate them. From this it follows that if the President will not go with us we must go with him. The freedom of speech is the last franchise a free people will surrender, and our millions will exercise it in the midst of no matter what calamities. They will discuss the events and management of the war. It is *their* war, and the humblest of them has an interest in it equal to that of the first citizen, and they must and may discuss his acts with full freedom. But I submit whether the just limit of criticism and of manly debate has not been brutally outraged in the fierce denunciations of the President by gentlemen on this floor, denunciations which have been caught up and re-echoed by their partisan press? Sir, if these perverse revilers could gain credit with the masses, no power on earth could save us from destruction, for they would shiver the only arm that must bring us safety. I speak of the causeless tide of criticism—shall I call it?—that has been poured out upon all the military operations of the Administration. Was this world ever before enriched with such a quantity of valuable commentary on the art of war, and by such masters—generals by instinct and the grace of God? For a year and a half has this voluminous tide swept over us; and will some mortal tell of some good, the least, that has waited upon the labors of these critics? What mistake has been avoided, what error retrieved, or what blunder redeemed? And yet what jealousies they have engendered, what factions they have built up, and what feuds they have embittered!

" ' These outspoken comments of the other side here and elsewhere, have at least the merit of boldness; but what shall be said of this muttering, unmanly, increasing undercurrent of complaining criticism that reflects upon the President, upon his motives and capacity, so freely and so feebly indulged in by men having the public confidence? of these whisperings and ' complainings and doubtings and misgivings and exclamations and predictions? I have heard men complain that George Washington had died and others feebly sigh for a return of Andrew Jackson to life; what can be done with such puling drivellers,—men who have a morbid passion to exaggerate our misfortunes, and to multiply and riot in our calamities, and who are never so happy as when they can gloat over the sum of our disasters, which they charge to the personal account of the President? I am sick of this everlasting cowardice and pallor under reverses. Defeats must come, disasters must come, and still greater ones perhaps, and the end is not yet. These men would never have worked through the first Revolution; but that task was achieved in spite of them, as this will be.

" ' Sir, if we fail, it will be wholly because we are unworthy to succeed; because we will not, with our whole heart and energy, might, mind, and strength, give ourselves up entirely to this war, as do the rebels; study its portents and obey its demands alone. The task it imposes is for our human kind. Its work is the accumulated work of the dead centuries thrust upon our hands, and its hope is the hope of generations still to be born. If we doubt, assail, and cast down those who alone must lead us, we might as well now slough into any infamy that men will call peace, or skulk behind the mediating sceptre of no matter what despot, and hide forever our dishonored heads amid the ruins of our nationality. If any man here distrusts the President, let him speak forth here, as *these bad leaders do*, openly, and no longer offend the streets and nauseate places of common resort with their unworthy clamor. The President may not have in excess that ecstatic fire which makes poets and prophets and madmen; he may not possess much of what we call heroic blood, that drives men to stake priceless destinies on desperate ventures, and lose them; he may not in an eminent degree possess that indefinable something that schoolboys call genius, which enables its possessor, through new and unheard of combinations, to grasp at wonderful results, and which usually ends in ruin; or, if he possesses any or all of these qualities, they are abashed and subdued in the presence of a danger that dwarfs giants, and teaches prudence to temerity. He is an unimpassioned, cool, shrewd, sagacious, far-seeing man, with a capacity to form his own judgments, and a will to execute them ; and he possesses an integrity pure and simple as the white rays of light that play about the Throne.   It is these that have so tied the hearts and love of the people to him, and that will not unloose in the breath of all the demagogues in the land.   It is idle to compare him with Washington or Jackson.   Like all extraordinary men, he is an original, and must stand in his own niche.   He has assiduously studied the teachings of this war, has learned its great lesson, and in full time has uttered its great word.   He commits errors ; who would have committed fewer?   Think of the fierce and hungry demands that incessantly devour him.   Remember the repeated instances in our own times when the ablest of our statesmen in that chair, with Cabinets of their choice, and sustained by majorities in Congress, in times of profound peace, *have gone down*, and their administrations have perished under the bare weight of the government.

" ' And then contemplate, if you can, in addition to the burdens that have crushed so many strong men, the fearful responsibilities imposed upon this man.   Is it not a marvel, a most living wonder, that he sustains them so well ?   .   .   .

" ' But these gentlemen now denounce the President's policy of the war.   Sir, I remember that others, too, used to complain in the same way ; we have all added our mite, and just as if the President were responsible for it, and could furnish a policy for the war.   The war is greater than the President ; greater than the two Houses of Congress ; greater than the people, *with the reconstructed Democracy thrown in ;* greater than all together, and it controls them all, and dictates its own policy ; and woe to the man or party that will not heed its dictation ! ' " [1]

---

[1] The 37th Congress ceased at noon, March 4, 1863, and with it closed my brief Congressional career, never to be resumed.   Twice later, when the opportunity was proffered, I put it by.

CHAPTER XXXI.

METHODS OF THE HOUSE.

1861–62.

Difficulties of a New Member—Congressmen Bitten of Life at the Capital
—Joshua R. Giddings—Personal Experiences.

PERHAPS the first striking impression received by one
new to the House is the wonder as to how half the men
ever got there. One is next impressed by the audacity,
or serene stupidity, which enables so many men to be
willing to occupy these seats. Is there in the world so
melancholy a book as *The Political Register and Congressional Directory* of the United States of 1776–1878, by
Ben : Perley Poore ?

In it are recorded the names, with a brief mention of
their lives, of every man who sat in our Congress during
one hundred and two years,—years covering nearly our
whole national life. Whoever has patience to look the
book through, will find it a sadder burying-ground than
that on the Anacostia ; of the 5500 men who have held
seats in the American Congress, not more than fifty can
be described as really distinguished.

The conditions of the service are now very repressing.
Everything is in the hands of the party leaders. The
Speaker of the House is their property. He awards the
places on the committees, and everything now depends
on the committees. If a man has no place on an impor-

tant committee, he can secure no place on the floor, unless his constituency stand by him for a series of years, a thing which seldom occurs at the North. In the growth of the public business, there is a growing necessity to depend more and more upon the standing committees. They work into each other's hands, and the young stranger on the floor can neither find nor make his opportunity. He may have real ability, may have studied, may have aspirations, enthusiasms, high and pure ideals. He reaches a seat in the huge, crowded, noisy, seemingly unorganized House, to find himself smothered, lost, unrecognized by the Speaker, and unknown to the House.

The House is unquestionably the worst place in America for a man to speak in. The desirable opportunity never comes to the stranger. If he pushes himself into general speech-making " On the State of the Union," the members gather about him, take his measure, then saunter out, collect in groups standing between him and the Speaker, telling stories or loafing, and he who " has the floor " is obliged to raise his voice till the physical effort to pitch his words over their heads, to be caught at the reporters' desk, is so great as to preclude all free mental action. Many men of real oratorical ability never try the floor of the House but once or twice, and many with fine reputations at home are, much to the surprise of their friends, never heard of after reaching the Capital. If one is fortunate enough to throw light on subjects the House must act upon, helping it, however slightly, to right conclusions, he is appreciated, and then, if modest, is listened to.

The best debating in the American House is in Committee of the Whole, under the five minutes' rule. There a man has something to say, packs it into the smallest space, and often renders real service.[1]

---

[1] I had been accustomed to platform speaking since I was seventeen, and had no special anxiety about seeking the floor in the House. Such remarks of mine as are found in this volume are given as expressing my conclusions

I have always been unable to understand the attachment that men form for Congressional life. I can see how those fond of social life may appreciate the spirit that rules the Washington world; but how a man who avoids society, and whose wife and children are in a distant home, can become attached to Congressional life at the Capital, is amazing. Many men, honored Representatives on the floor, are often so bitten of it, that they come back and make lively campaigns to secure the position of Clerk, Sergeant-at-Arms, Postmaster, or Doorkeeper of the House where once they were masters.

Three of the most distinguished Members of the House from Ohio, may be cited as victims of this much sitting in the House. Elisha Whittlesey, after sitting from 1821 to 1838, thinking he had been there as long as he cared to be, resigned. Finding himself mistaken, he accepted the sixth auditorship of the Treasury, was finally promoted to be Comptroller, and died in 1863.

There was also Samuel F. Vinton who entered the 18th Congress with Whittlesey, and who, when his term of service expired, removed to the Capital. He was one of the commissioners to appraise the slaves under our Emancipation Act, and died at Washington in 1862. Joshua R. Giddings succeeded Whittlesey in the House, and served continuously to the end of the 35th Congress. He lived the life of a recluse, though constantly at war, and really became so attached to the Capital, that he was restless and unhappy elsewhere.

The 36th Congress established consular relations with Canada, with a consul-generalship at Quebec. Mr.

---

on the subjects discussed. My first remarks in the House were given under the short rule, on the River and Harbor Bill. Soon after, a reporter brought me the speech in manuscript. My colleague, Dr. Trimble, explained by saying that the reporters recognized me as one to be favored. Their reports were afterwards always given to me, nor did I ever have cause to complain of the inattention of the House.

Giddings wished for the appointment, and was entitled to anything in the President's gift. He had been a delegate to the Chicago Convention, and upon its refusing to accept his plank in the platform, he withdrew. Feeling himself in disfavor, he would not approach the President nor Mr. Seward. I could, and I asked Mr. Seward to appoint Mr. Giddings Consul-General to Quebec. Mr. Seward said he had earned a much more conspicuous place, and asked if he would accept that. I replied that I was authorized to speak for him, and that he would. " He shall have it. *He will do as little mischief there as anywhere,*" was his reply. Mr. Giddings was greatly pleased. He wished to know what the Secretary said, and laughed heartily when told. He died at Quebec, May 27, 1884, a man whose services in the war against slavery were second to none in our history. He did some most essential work, performed by no other hand, in finding the true ground where, under the Constitution, a party could stand and legally oppose slavery.[1]

I had at least escaped the personal injury of long service in the House. No man has ever served through three congresses and returned healthfully to take up his old life and pursuits. No matter how innocent and regular may be a man's life and habits in Washington, his mind does not escape the kind of dissipation that in a way unfits it for the ordinary pursuits of life. If his career has been passably successful, he has a scrap-book filled with newspaper laudations and criticisms, twenty or forty volumes of the *Globe*, innumerable public documents, and a general disgust and unfitness for ordinary useful avocation. His profession is gone, his wife is dwarfed by years of neglect, his children are strangers, and he comes to loathe the " Honorable " that men prefix

---

[1] Mr. Julian, in his, in many respects, valuable biography of Mr. Giddings (his father-in-law), is pleased to say that '' the President tendered him the post."

15

to his name,—the only emolument he has acquired, save personal and political animosities and alienated friends.

This second year of the war had fully awakened the inventive genius of the American people, and the Capital had a succession of eager visitors with models of plate armor and improvements in fire-arms, especially in projectiles for artillery. The War Office had several targets near the mouth of the Anacostia, and reserved two or three old worn guns for these amateur gunners, who kept up quite a constant cannonade. I remember a constituent who came on with a small cargo of shot and shell, which he would permit no other hand to touch, and which the yellow Potomac still keeps in its guardian depths.

One willing to be useful to his constituents soon finds that his duties in the House are the lightest and pleasantest of his services. He is expected not only to be a solicitor of places, but of patents and pensions. I was long haunted by a man who thought himself a born detective, and who said he had a clue to one of the awfulest conspiracies to plunder poor distressed Uncle Samuel, second only to the conspiracy to rend the Union. I went so far as to offer to introduce him to the Solicitor of the Treasury. "The Solicitor is a fool." Had he been to Colonel Baker? "Baker threatened to send him to the old Capitol." Had he seen the Secretary of the Treasury? "Chase was prejudiced." When I found how persistently he had waylaid and pursued that gentleman, I could understand that the Secretary probably was. I finally told him with the utmost plainness that I had become prejudiced also, and stubbornly refused to have my prejudices removed.

The service in the House became irksome to me. The building, its passage-ways and odors, grew offensive. Occasionally now, when there, the old dismaying flavor assails me, bringing momentary heart failure. Of the gentlemen on the floor, Dr. Trimble, Colfax, Morrill,

Fenton, Campbell, Conkling, and McKnight were my assured friends, as were Cox, Pendleton, and Vallandigham. Indeed, I have always found disinterested friends among the Democrats, and have observed among politicians that the warmest personal ties are usually across party lines. I always treated my constituency with frank confidence, and believe I received it in return. I never had anything to explain except my account of Bull Run, and I found in the Ohio House, as in the National House, that an independent course was always applauded. I was never questioned at home for retaining young Cox. The appointment of Henry Slade, a Democrat, was as well liked as the appointment of his brother William to a consulate. My course in the Lehman case was warmly approved. I never consulted the political weather-vane in my district. If I thought the people were in error there, I unhesitatingly told them so. No vote or speech of mine was ever censured, to my knowledge. At the time I decided never again to turn my attention to public life, I knew very well that with a little time, and perhaps less pride, nothing was easier or more certain in political fortune than my return to the House if I desired it.[1]

---

[1] Within three years my successor more than once offered to vacate the seat if I would return and stand for it.

CHAPTER XXXII.

EPISODES DURING ADJOURNMENT.

MARCH–AUGUST, 1863.

Riots and Victories—Vallandigham Arrested—Nominated for Governor of
Ohio—John Brough—On the Stump—Chandler, Anderson.

VALLANDIGHAM, a man of ardent temperament, bold,
daring, and ready to illustrate his utterances by acts,
had permitted his theories to carry him unconsciously
past the limits, his cooler reason would have recognized
eighteen months before, but who now stood on ground
logically based on the conclusions of leisure, reached
home at the close of the 37th Congress to be confronted
by the general order of Major-General Burnside, commanding the Department of the Ohio, with headquarters
at Cincinnati. This order defined as traitorous certain
acts—among them the habit of expressing sympathy with
the enemy, denouncing the government, etc., and declared
that such acts were to be tried and dealt with by courts of
military commission. At a Democratic meeting, held May
1st, at Mount Vernon, some forty miles north of Columbus, Vallandigham made this order the text of a fierce and
bitter philippic. Hundreds of men at this meeting wore
the Copperhead and Butternut badges. On Monday
evening, May 4th, a special train from Cincinnati, with
officers armed with an order for his arrest, proceeded to
Dayton, the city of his residence, arrested him in his own

house, and carried him to headquarters, where he was lodged in the military prison. Intense excitement was produced among his friends at Dayton by his arrest, and on the evening of the 5th, a mob of five or six hundred set fire to the office of the *Journal* (the Republican paper), which was burnt, with many other buildings on the same square.

From his prison Vallandigham issued a carefully considered proclamation to the Democracy of the United States. He was charged with the utterance of disloyal sentiments, sympathy with the enemy in arms, and denunciation of the government for the purpose of weakening it and rendering its efforts to put down the rebellion less effective. He was put on trial on the 6th, before a commission of military officers, and the proof amply sustained the specification. He was aided by George E. Pugh, but made no defense, contenting himself with a protest. He was found guilty and sentenced to be confined in Fort Warren, in Boston harbor, during the war. The United States Circuit Court refused a writ of *habeas corpus* in the case. The President changed the sentence to banishment beyond the rebel lines. The order was executed about daylight, the 25th of May, near Murfreesboro, Tennessee, where, on conference under a flag, Vallandigham was delivered over, saying to the private of an Alabama regiment, who received him, that he surrendered himself a prisoner of war.

The Administration press was not unanimous in the approval of the course pursued with Vallandingham. It seemed to me unnecessary and unwarranted. He had no hold on the thoughtful men of the Democratic party. The year before, the Democrats, with a clear majority in the Ohio Legislature, had re-elected Benjamin F. Wade to the Senate, an unique event in the history of American politics, and that too when Vallandigham had, in violation of all parliamentary rules, denounced him on the floor of the House as a liar and a coward. This was due to some forcible remarks made by Wade in a speech at the North, charging Vallandigham with treasonable utterances. Ohio and the Ohio Democracy were generally loyal to the Union. There was, however, a percentage of the younger men who would not volunteer, and who, fearing the conscription, put on the Butternut and Copperhead badges, and whooped, and yelled, and followed the demagogue whose ardent nature carried him out of the ranks of the loyal. Pugh (who had been succeeded in the Senate by John Sherman), and Cox, and Pendleton, who made a great noise in denunciation of the course pursued by the Executive, were careful to keep within the prudent lines of safety. There was an effort to canonize Vallandigham as a popular martyr, notwithstanding the hard lines of his nature and character, repellent of sympathy and tenderness; and a few did so regard him.

At the State Democratic Convention of June 11th, he was nominated for Governor by acclamation, with Pugh for Lieutenant-Governor.

The Republican Convention, on the 17th of June, nominated John Brough for Governor, and for Lieutenant-Governor Charles Anderson—a brother of the hero of Sumter.

The utmost concern was felt through the North for the result, largely shared by the timid in the State, on account of the absence of the heroes drawn off to the war. I had made myself familiar with the popular signs from very early manhood, and I felt there could be no grounds for apprehension. I wrote to the *Tribune* that Mr. Brough would be elected by thirty thousand on the home vote, which only provoked a sarcastic paragraph from Mr. Greeley. He would compromise on a third of that number.

My success in 1848 made me confident. Brough was the survivor of the Sam. Medary-McNulty-Byington Democracy, the only one fit to survive. As State Auditor he had devised the scheme of State taxation, which, though rejected by his party, Alfred Kelley, Seabury Ford, and other Whigs, had the grace and courage to adopt in 1845. Brough was not only one of the strongest men of the State, but was one of the best speakers in it, with the finest voice I ever heard for open-air speaking. He made a very powerful speech at Marietta, before his nomination, fully sustaining the Administration on all the points involved. To me he seemed the heaven-sent man. Correspondence with Cincinnati showed that the idea was common to a few of us. Governor Tod had been true and able, but had provoked criticism. It was no time to vindicate even good men. Consultation with R. F. Paine, Colonel Parsons, Cowles, Samuel Williamson, Dr. Everett, and others, settled Cleveland, and with the aid of Cincinnati, his nomination was effected.

The attempted conscription, July 9th, in the city of New York, precipitated (largely among the foreign-born) the bloodiest and longest continued riot that has thus far occurred in the history of the United States. The "populace" in a rage fell back at once to the lowest brutal elements and instincts of the undeveloped. All the criminal and base came forth, and for four or five days portions of the city were given over to blood, arson, and plunder. The rage was especially directed against persons of African descent. The police, though well handled, were unequal to the occasion, and it was two days before an effective force of the military and marines could be secured. These troops, directed by able officers, such as Canby and others, quelled the outbreak by well-directed discharges of fire-arms. It was estimated that at least a thousand of the mob were killed and wounded in the absolutely necessary assaults. Horatio Seymour was at the time Governor of the State. He had coquetted with the Vallandigham trouble in Ohio, to the literature of which he contributed a much-lauded letter.

On the night of the 15th of July a riot broke out in Boston, which for a time caused serious apprehension, and was occasioned by opposition to the drafting under the Act of Congress.

Ohio also had a conscription riot, an outbreak of the fierce Democracy of Holmes County, which grew to such proportions that six hundred of the State soldiery—infantry, artillery, and cavalry—were called out for its suppression. There were draft disturbances elsewhere; nor were they found alone in the Northern States. The South suffered the same experiences under the Confederacy.

That memorable summer was emphasized in Ohio by John Morgan's raid. The original project was the invasion of Kentucky and the capture of Louisville, and perhaps Cincinnati. Buckner was to command the army. Morgan, with a column of four thousand, was to make a hurried advance and cut and destroy all railroads and rolling stock. The advance of Rosecrans detained Buckner. Morgan met and overcame a small detached Union force in Kentucky, and crossed the Ohio into Indiana four miles below Louisville. The inevitable General Hobson, detailed to pursue and capture him, was delayed, and followed some days later. Morgan made wild work in Indiana. Meantime forces were gathering in southwestern Ohio. Hobson reached the Ohio as the last of Morgan's men crossed, and had to secure means of transit. He had pursued Morgan over seven hundred miles. The Indiana force paused at the State line. Of course Morgan's force was constantly diminishing. Hobson finally overhauled him and captured six or seven hundred, and Morgan and the residue surrendered, July 26th, at Salineville, three miles from Wellsville, on the Ohio, and near New Lisbon. A military court sentenced Morgan and his officers to the Ohio penitentiary, whence later he escaped.

In the early part of the season the great Ship Canal Convention, called by Mr. Arnold and Mr. Riddle, was

held at Chicago, attended by delegates from all the Northern States. There were large delegations from New England—that from Maine being headed by Vice-President
Hamlin. Many speeches were made and excellent resolutions passed, but the convention was out of time. We
had, however, apparently made such an impression by the
movement in the House, that it was deemed advisable to
deepen and embody it by a convention.

My successor in the House did not relieve me of the
minor duties of the place, and I made several journeys to
the Capital in the interests of the constituency, in connection with the war and public service. I passed through
Pennsylvania to Washington during the second day of the
battle of Gettysburg, and the atmosphere was in a tremor
with the rumors of a great and indecisive collision of the
armies. There was a half-scared air on the faces of men,
especially at Harrisburg, and so on to York, most marked
at the latter place, which had been visited and laid under
contribution.

While I was at Washington, came not only the news of
Meade's great victory, but also of the fall of Vicksburg.
These events were followed by another proclamation of
thanks from the grateful chief of the Republic.

The political campaign in Ohio, upon which so much
was supposed to depend, began early, and by the Republicans was pushed with the utmost vigor. It really was a
one-sided contest, the result of which was never for a
moment in doubt. I had a month's active duty, under the
direction of the State Executive Committee. They
printed a huge edition of my speech on the bill to indemnify the President, and I was assigned to the middle of
Ohio, having already spoken at several points in the northern part of the State. I met Senator Chandler at Painesville early in September, and he offered to accompany me.
He had a single well-worn and easy-going speech, not very
long, which always closed with a philippic against England.

I may note three or four incidents of our work. We were assigned to Millersburg, the seat of the Copperhead county of Holmes. It rained the night we reached the town, rained the next morning, rained after breakfast, rained hard till noon, and rained harder till night. The open-air meeting was abandoned early in the day. There we found Judge Luther Day, of Ravenna, a war Democrat, loved and confided in by all parties, a pale, nervous little man, of the finest, subtlest fibre all through, timid and shrinking as a woman. When I found him he was alone, ill, and utterly down-hearted. No one had received him, no one had recognized him, no one was there to do or say anything for him. I never yet saw a man whom I could not cheer up, by some means or other. Mrs. Seymour, at Painesville, had placed in my portmanteau two bottles of old wine and a pint flask of genuine brandy. Chandler had other resources. Judge Day was a Democrat, not averse to cheering fluids, but too dainty for the average Democratic drinks. I found him shivering in the cheerless reading-room in the morning, and took him to a bright little parlor, where we ordered breakfast—rather late, as Chandler's habit was.

It was astonishing what cheery words, bright comradeship, mellow wine, and a touch of *real* cognac did for a thin-skinned, nervous, and for the time doubting Democrat on a rainy morning in Millersburg. There really was a fine assembly, and about 11 A.M. we were in a spacious hall, filled to its entire capacity. I introduced Judge Day. We had decided he should make the speech, *and he did*, and one of the best and most effective of that stirring campaign. I had been with Ben Stanton and Columbus Delano, as strong men as the State had, and certainly as effective, and I remembered Day's effort as one of the very best. He spoke two hours; Chandler made an energetic little harangue, and we dismissed the crowd.

Somewhere west of Columbus, in a narrow valley of the

open country, was an immense Union gathering—thirty
thousand was the estimate—divided into three bodies,
with separate stands, so wide apart as to constitute three
immense mass-meetings. Charles Anderson, of Cincinnati,
candidate for Lieutenant-Governor, was present. I had
never met him before. He, Senator Chandler, and myself
were assigned to one stand. It was a sad trial to me.
Anderson, a native Kentuckian, a brother of the hero of
Sumter, had a great reputation as a speaker. He followed
Chandler. I was disappointed, surprised, and finally
angry. There seemed to be in his speech no doctrine, no
leading ideas, no idea of any sort. He was certainly a
fluent speaker, with a good voice and good delivery, and
he was a mimic. For nearly three hours he poured forth
an unceasing tide of rather coarse stories, but not a word
of the present condition of things, nothing of the war or
its cause, or of the duty of the citizen. The crowd was
made up of every-day folk—farmers, their wives, daughters,
and sons. I abandoned all expectation of speaking, and
soon all desire to. The crowd certainly seemed to enjoy
" *Charlie's* " oratory. I must stay till it was through, and
was then to be carried somewhere else. Chandler and I
were to part. I withdrew my attention from the speech
and employed myself in noting the people *prima facie*, a
different race from the descendants of New England on
the Reserve. Finally, Anderson did stop and I was
called. Half angry and wholly indifferent, I went forward to the edge of the platform. I knew by the sound
of my own voice that I was at par. I never told a story
in my life, and rarely made a quotation. The women,
though uneasy, turned to me as if hoping for something.
They always inspire men. A thing I had seen I could
describe effectively. I had aided in the landing of two
boatloads of wounded just from a red and rent field, the
most of whom had been in no surgeon's hands, and some
of whom ceased to breathe ere we could carry them to

the hospital. The scene was vivid and possessed me—I passed out of myself—I could hear my voice—seemed to see myself. The crowd surged forward eagerly, especially the women, and sobs and cries of anguish broke from hundreds of moved hearts. From the wounded it was a flash to the ghastly battle-field, strewn with the wreck of conflict—dead and mangled men and horses—with the heavy sulphurous clouds of smoke hanging over it; and the enemy—Americans like ourselves—mad because we preferred a man of our own for President, whom they refused to vote for—going to war with us for that—and because we would not permit them to bring their slaves upon our soil and reduce us—States full of workers—to the level of those scourged and servile, bought and sold laborers. And there were in our midst many, fierce and angry with us because we defended ourselves in this war —here in our own State, allies of the rebels, fighting us on our own soil. This was the issue: Should they or we prevail? If we could not enforce the national will, the Constitution, in Virginia, we could not in Ohio, and that was our hard necessity—to put down the rebellion or to see our State strewn with the wreck of a broken Union. I appealed to the women—the wives, mothers, sweet-hearts, and sisters of the men and boys in the fields and camps, on the march, in battle, in hospital, and in bloody graves, to see to it that those still spared to them voted right on this issue, and then I stopped. There was no applause—no one thought of that, nor had time for it if they did. There were single cries and exclamations, and men in knots came hurrying back out of the crowd, but no applause. As I ceased, calls came—"Go on! Go on! Go on!"

"No, I am going off, and it is time for you to go home," was my response.

My carriage with my traps had driven round to the

rear of the stand ; I ran down, to be temporarily detained by a small throng. My leave-taking was brief.

When I returned home I had Mr. Brough on my hands. Miss Ransome, the much-sought artist, had one or more orders for the portrait of the new popular idol. She found him as heavy and unmanageable as an old-fashioned Yankee " Indian pudding." He was heavy in person, and, when placed in a seat alone, became awfully solemn, not to say somnolent. I had to go in and stir him up mentally. He had a splendid head, and when awakened by sharp mental thrusts his heavy face lighted up and became very fine. I remember once, when he failed to keep the appointment at the studio, I sat for a right hand. The result was an admirable portrait of my thin, lean hand, as little like his small, plump, and pudgy one as my sharp aquiline face was like his, so round and ruddy.

At the election Brough had in round figures sixty-one thousand majority of the home vote, and forty thousand of the soldier vote, taken at the front,—one hundred and one thousand majority. It never occurred to me to say to Mr. Greeley : " What did I tell you ? " Indeed I had told him nothing so wild.

This Union victory in Ohio was as important to the national cause as the battle of Gettysburg, or the fall of Vicksburg.

CHAPTER XXXIII.

OFFICIAL VOYAGE TO CUBA.

JANUARY–FEBRUARY, 1863.

The U. S. *Vanderbilt*—The Consul at Nassau—Visit to the Blockade Runners.

I WENT as a consul to Matanzas, Cuba, via New Providence. I was expected to make the acquaintance of our consul there, and note anything I might discover of blockade running, the headquarters of which were at Nassau. I was to confer with the Consul-General at Havana and with Commodore Bailey of our squadron, then in those seas, to be of what service I might, and keep the State Department advised of all I noticed. I left New York January 4, 1863, with the mercury below zero, and my spirits much lower. My diary, written day by day on the steamer, is filled with bitter regrets for leaving the country. True the courts were nearly closed, but I might have been a Judge Advocate in the army, and worn the army livery, although this, for a non-combatant, would have seemed a mockery. Why did not I take a regiment at the beginning? Somebody had offered me a judgeship somewhere. But a judge is a second-rate functionary in presence of the leading advocates. I believe Mr. Chase thought I might be appointed to the Freedman's Bureau, but that would require solicitation, and my health was

238

broken. The Cleveland Bar gave me a dinner before
I left.

I sailed on the English steamer *Corsica*, Captain La
Missouria. He carried a large company of passengers,
most of whom proved to be blockade runners, Confederate
officers and agents, with a small knot of true-hearted
Americans, full of loyalty and courage.

Three or four incidents of my voyage and short residence in Cuba, connected with our great struggle, may
not be out of place in these recollections of the war.
I quote from my diary on shipboard four days out :

"While dressing this morning I was startled by the silence of the machinery and the general quietude on board. Looking out, I saw looming
up from the sleeping ocean about two miles away, a huge side-wheel steamer,
evidently a war-ship, and doubtless one of our own dear old Uncle Sam's.
Hurrying on deck, I found the *Corsica* lying to, flying the British flag, and
all hands mustered on the lower deck. On came the stranger, looming
higher and broader, on and on until the diminutive red flutter at her stern
expanded into our grand old flag. Lord, how the pulses throbbed when we
made that out ! flouting these pirate-haunted seas with scornful defiance.
On she came until within a quarter of a mile, when, pausing, a launch fell
from her davits, an officer and crew entered it with a flag, and she came
dancing over the wave crests, now sparkling in the risen sun and tossing
under a fanning breeze. Our ladder was lowered and Captain La Missouria stood forward with an anxious air, keeping a little space clear for his
guest, when a young lieutenant in full dress, with a fresh, eager face, and
flashing blue eyes, sprang lightly upon the English deck, saluting its commander with grace and receiving a courteous response.

"His ship was the U. S. man-of-war *Vanderbilt!* How the name ran
over our deck ! He was just from the Cape of Good Hope, whither they
had followed the *Florida*, and had merely called upon us for such newspapers
as were at hand. They had chased a light-footed blockade runner in these
waters the day before, which escaped after consigning her cotton to the sea.
The files of New York papers were brought, the officers saluted, and the
lieutenant turned to the head of the stairs, where I had a word with him,
making myself known, and giving him additional papers and the latest war
incidents. He was soon in the stern of his launch, and her sturdy, neatly
uniformed crew, bending to their oars, lifted the little craft almost out of
the water and sent her tripping over the sunlit sea to her huge parent. Immediately the *Vanderbilt* was in motion, came down and swept grandly in
a circle around the still motionless *Corsica*, so near that we could have recognized an acquaintance on her decks.

"We were a little knot of loyal Americans standing apart from our numerous, and now seemingly grim enemies ; and as our American war-ship, headed toward our home land, came nearest us, with her flag floating out as if to caress us, the impulse was irresistible, and glad words and cheers would escape from our throats, which, perhaps should have been repressed. Somehow it had come to be known that I was in the commission of the United States, and what was said of this ' breach of discipline,' as it was called, is charged to me.   Do I care ?   I had made the acquaintance of a bright, educated young Canadian of kindred Irish blood, who told me that some of the rebels on board made complaint to the Captain, but nothing but a day or two of black looks from that gentleman came of it.   It is some punishment for me to meet everywhere, on everything, especially the dinner service, the eternal and for ever rampant British lion, standing on one foot on nothing, and pawing with the other three at no particular thing in space. I wish Chandler of Michigan were here to twist his tail.

"We reached reluctant little Nassau in the night, and had to await dawn to pass into the channel.   What a day I made of it in that remote sub-tropical knob above the sea !

"At the Victoria, the only spacious building of that time, I found all our late voyagers, and each in his own proper character.   There was my room-mate, the gentle and cheery Johnson of Savannah, Georgia, who hid in the presence of the *Vanderbilt*, while my stolid Russian *vis-à-vis* in the dining-room was a young scion of a Moscow family, who had invested his patri-mony in two blockade runners—the blockhead !   He was here met with the exhilarating news that one had just been captured and the other had burst a boiler.   I remembered that I had declined to take wine with him at the *Corsica's* table.   Many others wholly unknown to me, developed into very well-known men here, and were received as if expected.   Among them a diminutive dark little man of Jewish aspect, named A. Wolf, who had made a fortune on a cargo of shoddy, landed in the dark of a conspiring moon and sold to the rebels.   I congratulated him.

"Our New York papers, which contained assurances that the whole rebel coast was unapproachable to blockade runners, were here read with shouts of derision.   The inside channel at Nassau held several deeply laden vessels from ' way down south in Dixey,' two of which arrived that morning, but two, long expected, were among the ' loved and early lost.'

"Later in the day I called upon the prim and rather stately American Consul—the first I had ever seen at his post,—who informed me that within the last three weeks more successful activity was apparent in that useful channel of the cotton trade, than during any other time for the last ten months.   He probably was impressed with the idea that I was a Northern Copperhead, as I came on the *Corsica*.   He was in evening costume and ex-cused himself on the plea of dining with a party of distinguished gentlemen.

"Meantime, my Canadian friend and I visited the blockade runners, and my companion surprised me on the first one, by announcing the presence on deck of an American Consul, and I don't care to mention what distinguishing additions were extemporized by him. So far from receiving me coolly, the officers felt called upon to show us special courtesy, and showed us their steamer. Indeed this distinction was accorded us on each one visited. The last one was the then famous *Alice*, which boasted the distinction of having already made three successful voyages, a very exceptional career, as was freely admitted. Indeed, so powerful and vigilant had our blockade become that few made more than one voyage. In a discussion with a very intelligent officer on the *Alice* he admitted that, taking the whole number of vessels engaged in this traffic of desperate gambling, and the whole capital and cost invested, it was doubtful whether the profit was greatly in excess of the loss.

" When I reached the *Corsica* at eleven at night, I found two *Conchs*[1] profoundly drunk and asleep on the floor of my state-room, retailing alcoholic drinks in vapor without a license.

" I took refuge on the cushions of a cabin. I had an interview next morning with Captain la Missouria, by his request, which led to a pleasanter and more spacious cabinet room, and to an agreeable acquaintance with the *Corsica's* chief, from whom I parted with regret. We made a bad exchange of passengers at Nassau. We lost two or three hundred gentlemen, and received in exchange a hundred or more scurvy, broken-down vagabonds.

" I see Sunday the 10th noted as marked by the duck trousers of the Captain and officers, the first flying fish, and an added depth to the deep and indescribable blue of the tropic sea, of which no conception can be formed till seen ; and the night succeeding as marked by a broad phosphorescent wake of white light, and my first sight of the Southern Cross low down in the southern horizon. I never met a Cuban who had seen that constellation. I left the island the 7th of April following, and may note an incident or two with which I was connected, as a part of my duties pertaining to the investigation into blockade running."

---

[1] A Conch was either a native or a long resident of New Providence and sister islands.

16

CHAPTER XXXIV.

BLOCKADE RUNNERS.

JANUARY–FEBRUARY 1863.

Built in Brooklyn—Sold and Transferred in Cuba.

ON my arrival at Matanzas, the Vice-Consul, Mr. H. C. Hall, one of our best consular officers, called my attention to a steamer in the bay, lying a half mile from the shore, and remote from other craft. He reported her as having arrived about the middle of December from the United States direct. She was a side-wheel steamer, light, and sharply built, painted white, with no standing rigging of any sort, and without accommodations for passengers, having nothing but two or three hundred tons of anthracite coal on board. She much resembled the Long Island Sound steamers.

Of American build and registry, she was consigned to Don Rafael Lucas Sanchez, whose first name (Rafile in Spanish) was placed on her wheel-houses. In her registry, Plutarcho Gonzales, of the firm of Martinez, Gonzales, & Co., of New York, appeared to be the sole owner. She was commanded by B. S. Briggs. Her papers were regular, except that her crew was shipped at *one dollar each* per month. This was to meet the requisitions of our law, requiring a month's wages to be paid each officer, seaman, or hand, on being discharged in a foreign port. A nominal sum would meet the statute, and show that all hands shipped with the expectation of being discharged in Cuba.

Another Briggs came out on her, armed with a bill of sale from Gonzales to Sanchez, to be executed before the American Consul. To overcome some of Mr. Hall's scruples and smooth the way for the transfer, Sanchez exhibited to him an affidavit made by Gonzales, the nominal owner, stating that the steamer was built in a shipyard in Brooklyn, on account of Sanchez, under the direction of the Briggses, who held a paper showing that Martinez, Gonzales, & Co., were his financial agents, that the name of Plutarcho Gonzales, a nominal American citizen, was used to effect a registry, so that the steamer could go abroad upon her proper business. She could be used alone for blockade running in the cotton trade. Don Rafael Sanchez was the gentleman to whom eight of the nine vessels escaping from the blockaded ports and reaching Matanzas were consigned. Briggs, his building agent in New York, brought the *Irene* from Charleston in 1862, which took the British flag at Matanzas, but she was afterwards, notwithstanding, captured at sea by Commodore Bailey's squadron. It came to be known to us also that Sanchez's contract with the Brooklyn ship-builders was for six steamers of the same pattern, of which the *Rafael* was the first, to be followed by the rest—one each month, until the sixth was delivered in Cuba.

Mr. Hall knew of my appointment, and waited in daily expectation of my arrival. My first labor in the office was a careful dispatch covering all we knew of the case, and the most probable of our suspicions. As the papers were all regular, Mr. Hall had no choice but to see the transfer properly made, and the discharged officers and crew paid, as set forth by the papers.

Mr. Hall, who had spent all his life from boyhood in Spanish-American countries and understood the Spanish and native character thoroughly, had gained the confidence of a Catalonian boatman[1] whom he had engaged, for me, to watch the movements on the *Rafael*. Not long after, he reported that the name on the wheel-house had been changed. *Rafael* had yielded place to the *Young Republic*, and other changes were made, rendering her identification more difficult. One night in the dark of the moon, our spy reported that the steamer would run out the next night. Our Consul-General at Havana had already been apprised of the situation. That evening my messenger with my dispatches left for Havana, express. At the same time I placed a duplicate in the Spanish post-office, addressed to Mr. Savage, American Consul-General, for the benefit of the Spaniards. This last was three days later delivered back to me by the Matanzas postmaster, in a slovenly condition, showing that it had been violated—as I had expected it would be. My private express, on whom I relied, delivered his missive punctually and a swift dispatch-boat reached the squadron in time. The *Young Republic* was sighted as she left the mouth of Matanzas Bay, was chased ashore where she could not be captured, and finally made her way by creeping along the coast, reached the Bay of Havana in a badly damaged condition, and was abandoned there.

I hardly expected to see more of Don Rafile's steamers.

With February 23d, however, came the *Conqueror*, spick and span in white trim, a twin of the *Rafael*, commanded by the same Briggs, owned by the same Plutarcho Gonzales, and consigned to the same Rafael Sanchez—officers and crew shipped at a dollar a head per month. Gonzales, the American owner, came out in person, all the papers were in due form, and Plutarcho

---

[1] No one can be a boatman or fisherman in a Spanish colony unless he has served in the Spanish navy—which no Cuban ever does. All Cubans hate Spain with a fury of hate real and unknown to us and are all our friends.

executed a bill of each to Sanchez. When he came to
pay off the crew, who were to be discharged in a foreign
port, the Consul presented him with a schedule of wages
at the established rates, and required the sum total to be
deposited with him as a condition precedent to the transfer. The Spaniard turned blue, and went away for
counsel. Whatever he may have learned, he came back
bland, suave, and tropical, and paid down the gold. Mr.
Hall proceeded to Havana with my dispatches, and so arranged with the officers of our squadron that the *Conqueror*
was captured when she put to sea. No more were sent
out. The unmistakable signs of yellow fever induced
the Consul's friends to hurry him away a week before the
time set by himself. He returned to New York on the
Eagle, Captain Adams.

Bluff, stout, coarse old Captain Adams and his fast
steamer, the *Eagle*, have long since passed from mention
among men. The *Eagle* was the fastest ocean-going commercial steamer of that day. She was in the passenger
trade between New York and Havana. I was to sail on
her on Saturday at noon. I reached Havana the Friday
before. At the American Consulate I met Captain Adams
and a dozen American gentlemen in a little flutter of
excitement.

The *Eagle* had, a few weeks before, given efficient aid
in the capture of a blockade runner, and with her heroic
old commander was specially set apart for vengeance. It
was rumored that the famous *Florida* had returned, and
one of her early enterprises was to be the destruction of
the *Eagle*. To the credit of the Americans in Cuba be it
said, that of all the many I met there, no matter of what
political association at home, I saw and heard of none but
men of the *most intense patriotism*. These men, who had
come to know, and many of whom had experienced, the
haughty arrogance and insolence of the Spaniard, shown
on all occasions toward the United States and the Union

cause, were at white heat in their fervor for the success of the national arms ; and I should add that to a man the Cubans were with us with all their tropical intensity.

At the Consulate I was shown two letters, one addressed to Captain Adams, advising him that a well planned attempt would be made on his second day out to capture his ship. The means to be used were not disclosed, but he was cautioned against his passengers. The other letter purported to be an intercepted communication forwarded to the Consul, advising him that a Confederate armed ship was hidden among the islands, and it was thought that she might have intentions on the *Eagle*. Both were unsigned. The quiver in the atmosphere of the time, the wild spirit of adventure and desperate enterprise born of the war, lent probability to these statements and gave piquancy to the impending voyage.

Early in the forenoon several of us, accompanied by Mr. Savage, went on board the *Eagle*, lying in the bay under the dazzling tropical sun. We scanned the appearance of every male and some female passengers, and the conclusion was that peril did not enter the steamer with any of them.

The last things to stand out individually on the receding Cuban coast are the royal palms of its highlands; the very last, the Pan of Matanzas.[1] They faded from vision, the phantoms of an exquisite dream in the presence of awakening consciousness.

As we anticipated, there were no persons on board who excited the slightest suspicion of sinister purpose toward the *Eagle*, her master, or passengers.

We were also on the look-out for a pursuing sail. What we looked for we saw. At about 11 A.M. Sunday, on the southern rim of the sea, there hung a craft that through

---

[1] Pan—loaf. There are two of them, near each other, seen from a vessel leaving or approaching Havana. They are in a line with the course, and seem one.

the glass had a suspicious look. She was many points to the westward, and on a course to intercept us leagues ahead. Within an hour she loomed to ominous proportions. An armed schooner, her two masts lifted to the loftiest height, carrying all canvas, and aided by a propeller. She had a good wind, and at her rate of speed would certainly intercept the *Eagle* if she kept on her course, as she was running eighteen or twenty miles an hour, and was capable in that water of doing even better. Whoever was in the secret of the warning to the *Eagle* could but feel a lively interest in the approach of the two ships to the point where their courses would intersect. When about a mile asunder, the chase signalled the *Eagle* to lie to. No heed was given to the signal. A minute later the ship's head turned to the wind, a white puff of smoke came from her side, and the boom of her gun reached us an instant later. The response to this was a burst of speed by the *Eagle*, and she darted ahead at a rate that seemed to defy pursuit. Immediately the chase rounded up her broadside to us, another white puff was seen, and a shot struck the sea a hundred yards from the *Eagle*, on a line with our wheel-house. Luckily it sank where it struck. With the last shot we were not displeased to see our own old flag, then for the first time, fluttering above her taffrail.

Instantly the machinery on the *Eagle* stopped and she put her head to the wind, awaiting the approach of her persistent pursuer. On she came, as beautiful a model of naval art as the sea floated. When within hail came a far-reaching voice, "What steamer is that?" "The *Eagle!*" in a hoarse voice in which years of tempest made themselves heard, responded angry old Adams. "*Can't you read?*" with the emphasis of a hand thrown upward to where the steamer's name floated in characters a fathom long. Turning its head to avoid us, the cruiser swept around in a narrow circle, the tops of the masts and upper yards bowing to us and seeming almost to dip, as beautiful and graceful a thing as the imagination could conceive. At the nearest point of her approach a voice went to her from one of the *Eagle's* passengers : " What ship is that ? " Immediately there was displayed above her bulwarks, " *Grand Gulf*," one of the newest additions to the permanent navy. She carried seven guns. Upon this response we gave her three hearty cheers, and she stood away as if to return to her former cruising ground. We were four days in the passage, and I was soon in my old Washington quarters. With nothing but the American papers of most uncertain arrival and disjointed dates, I had received but shreds and patches of the leading incidents of the war, in Congress, or at the front. My first work was to post myself up to date.

CHAPTER XXXV.

THE THIRTY-EIGHTH CONGRESS.

1863–1864.

A Glance at the War.

A GLANCE at the 38th Congress is necessary to this series of sketches of the war.

The House was elected in the dark days of 1862. Seldom has the personnel of a House been so completely changed without a change of parties. Indeed there were well grounded apprehensions that in the uncertainty of party lines in some States and districts the House might not be organized by an unquestioned Republican majority. Mr. Lincoln was really very uneasy. Three conspicuous generals had been elected to the House, while in the field, Garfield, Schenck, and Frank Blair, and he insisted that they should all be present at least at the organization of the House.

Of the new names in that body, several were destined to the front rank in the political history of the Republic, and three or four were to affect the course of the nation's history in a marked degree.

In the dark days of December, 1863, James A. Garfield, fresh from the field of war, met James Gillespie Blaine, recently from his editorial chair. Garfield was then thirty-one years old and Blaine thirty-three. Their entrance upon the stage was of as much latent significance to the

Republic as to themselves. Men with much in common that was brilliant and great, they yet presented great contrasts. They at once became fast friends, and from this friendship flowed influences and consequences largely shaping the destinies of the Republic, perhaps never to be fully understood outside of a small circle. Conkling was still in the House. He was ten years older than Blaine, and ripe in his Congressional career. How mysteriously the fortunes of these greatly gifted young men were made to mingle and become interdependent! From Ohio came also battle-scarred Schenck and Rufus P. Spalding; also Alexander Long of Cincinnati, who made the boldest treasonable speech ever heard in the House, and who underwent instant and total extermination at Garfield's hands, as may be told later. From Illinois came William R. Morrison, Eben C. Ingersoll, and John F. Farnsworth. Indiana contributed Orth. Iowa sent John A. Kasson and William B. Allison. Kentucky furnished Brutus J. Clay and Green Clay Smith. John A. J. Creswell entered the House from Maryland, to be transferred later to the Senate—a valuable acquisition and in good time. Henry Winter Davis returned to the scene of his earlier achievements. George S. Boutwell made his first appearance on the national stage in this House, as did Oakes Ames, of evil omen.

This Congress also saw the advent of Ignatius Donnelly in the House before he disposed of Mr. Shakespeare. Henry T. Blow from Missouri was there also. Additional men of importance came from New York—James Brooks, and Fernando Wood, with new names—Ganson, Griswold, Kernan, and others. Randall made his first appearance, as did Schofield from Pennsylvania. Thomas A. Jencks did honor to Rhode Island. Charles A. Eldridge came into the House from Wisconsin. A House with these accessions must be distinguished for ability; yet brains alone have not always made a useful and success-

ful House of Representatives, as our parliamentary history unfortunately shows.

The Senate also received some important accessions :
Buckalew from Pennsylvania, E. D. Morgan, Gratz Brown,
Reverdy Johnson, brave old Governor Hicks of Mary-
land, and Thomas A. Hendricks from Indiana.

The House lost none of its really leading spirits, nor
did the Senate.   Both were much strengthened, especially
the House, nor were the Republicans embarrassed by a
lack of numbers in that body.

Colfax was elected Speaker by one hundred and one
against eighty-two for all other candidates. S. S. Cox
received forty-two votes. The 37th Congress had taken
the true ground for dealing with the rebellion, and upon
the same principle the 38th broadly planted itself. Indeed there was no other, and with clear-sighted, brave,
tried leaders, steadily advancing on the old lines, the
tide of the war was to rise and sweep on till the Confederacy was overcome and swept away. The necessary assault on slavery culminated in this Congress in the logical
Thirteenth Amendment of the Constitution, abolishing
slavery in all the wide limits of the Republic. Still there
were armies and battles and bloodshed, and Grant's
bloody path through the Wilderness was yet to be
made.

On the great proposition of the abolition of slavery, the
Democracy remained true to its instincts and traditions,
and Hendricks in the Senate made a speech not to be
forgotten nor forgiven.

The October call for three hundred thousand men, notwithstanding the great bounties, produced but a fraction
of the required number. February 1; 1864, an order was
issued to draft five hundred thousand, to serve three years
from March 10th ensuing, minus those received prior to
March 1st. This was said to amount to a practical call for
two hundred thousand. The gains in number prior to

March 1st were quite cancelled in the disasters of the Red River cotton-plundering campaign under Banks.

Perhaps at no period of the war was Congress called upon for greater exertions than during the long session of the 38th Congress. All the available resources of the Republic were put in requisition. All the people of the hostile sections were at war. The powers of the executive and legislative departments were welded into one —a compound arm to place immense armies in the field. At the head of the legislative department stood the Military Committee of the House. More than one million two hundred thousand soldiers had been in the Union armies in 1863; of these, nearly three hundred thousand had left the ranks without leave during the last year of Halleck. It was the year of the ineffective draft and riot; of ruinous bounties so fatal to the army, of Vicksburg and Port Hudson, of Gettysburg, Stone River, and Chickamauga. The armies of the Tennessee, the Potomac, the Cumberland, and the Ohio were consolidated under Grant, and the year closed with not more than five hundred thousand effective soldiers in the field. Fifteen hundred thousand soldiers were required for the campaigns of 1864, so that, after all deductions and credits, about nine hundred thousand raw recruits were required.

The Secretary of War of the Confederacy in his report of December, 1863, was opposed to the employment of slaves as soldiers in its armies, so inferior were they in the requisite qualities. In our own army they were kept at a rate of lower bounties and pay than were the whites. This unjust distinction was determined upon in this year of 1864. General Grant was appointed General-in-chief of all our armies March 10, 1864. The first news of conflict in the field was of Banks's battle of Pleasant Hill, on the Red River. Sherman was still in the southwest. The Army of the Potomac, nearest us, was being reorganized preparatory to its plunge into the wilderness on its final advance upon Richmond.

Very soon came the offers of the four States of Ohio, Indiana, Illinois, and Iowa, of the hundred-day men for home duty, guards, and garrisons. There was a feeling of determination, strength, and courage. The war had educated our people and had toned them up to its needs.

The conscription laws needed to be revised and reformed. This was mainly the duty of the Military Committee of the House. It must devise a more efficient means of placing in the hands of the drill-masters and company officers the needed supply of the raw material of which soldiers are formed.

Experience at the front was quite as necessary to fit a man for a post on this important committee as for the command of a regiment in the field. As may be remembered, crippled, grim old General Schenck was at the head of it, with Garfield, Frank Blair, and others to second him.

I found Schenck—an old friend—and Garfield[1] in the old John Quincy Adams house on C Street near 4½ Street, an historic neighborhood. On one side was the house

---

[1] Garfield had been my law student, and, as may be supposed, I had free access to his quarters. My observation at their breakfast table one morning showed me some of the ways of the place. The hour was early for the Capital. I understood the reason. Though early and prompt, I found the hosts waiting and Schenck a little grim. The door already had a crowd of common folk impatiently waiting its opening. Among the guests I found the elder of Senator Wade's sons, a captain of cavalry, and Judge Newton, a distinguished man, and the meal proceeded at once, and rapidly. The half mob inside the house had crowded the stairs and were soon in close siege of the breakfast-room door. The clamor and noise disturbed the senior general. Garfield had a second guard placed at the door. The noise increased. The brow of the crippled general darkened. He beckoned his valet and ordered him in the voice of the battle-field to " Tell them by G—d that the animals are feeding, and dangerous" ;—with the emphasis of his fist on the table, which caused every article on it to leap an inch from its surface. It was not necessary to repeat the order.

that long sheltered Professor Morse; on the other the former residence of Dr. Bailey of *The National Era*. Opposite were the old-time residences of Daniel Webster and of Lewis Cass. Schenck's and Garfield's house was then a second army headquarters, where might at one time and another be met numbers of the distinguished generals of the army; also the inventors of new arms and projectiles, the devisers of schemes to end the war, and similar unappreciated geniuses.

The defects of the first draft law have been mentioned: under it the draft of three hundred thousand yielded to the service but twelve thousand. A new bill, prepared by our generals, was reported, and was debated six weeks; then came a motion to strike out the first section. In a shot-and-shell five-minutes' speech, Garfield declared that the man who voted for the proposition did not want the rebellion to be subdued. The motion nevertheless prevailed by one hundred to fifty.

The next day, the President went to the committee-room and had an interview with the Republican members. With a sad, mysterious light in his melancholy eyes, as if they were familiar with things hidden from mortals, and the grand pathos of his voice and manner, he stated the position of things at that time, the last of June. Three hundred and eighty thousand Union soldiers then in the field would return home by the ensuing October. Under the existing law, a draft of one million of men would be required to give fifty thousand to the army. If the departing soldiers could not be replaced, Grant could not maintain himself before Richmond, and Sherman must retire from before Atlanta. He was answered: "It is on the eve of the election. Our places in the House depend on that. The President's own election is involved; all depends on these two." Drawing himself up in his seat, he answered: "I have thought that all over; my election is not necessary; I must put down the rebellion; I must have five hundred thousand more men."

A substitute for the decapitated bill was at once introduced, and the war over it flashed up anew. On the 25th of June, General Garfield delivered a masterly and exhaustive speech in its favor. The bill was passed. The President issued his proclamation for three hundred thousand men, and the people responded:

> " We are coming, Father Abraham,
> Three hundred thousand more."

A new inspiration and fresh life restored the strength and courage of the North.

CHAPTER XXXVI.

DISLOYALTY IN THE HOUSE.

APRIL, 1863.

Garfield's Answer—Colfax Moves Long's Expulsion—Democrats Sustain
Long—He is Censured by the House—A Reminiscence of Long (note).

A GENERAL theme of conversation among men interested in Congressional debates and business, was as I
found on my return to the Capital, a treasonable speech
recently delivered by Alexander Long,[1] of Ohio, and Garfield's instant reply.   In February, Long brought forward
a joint resolution in the House for the appointment of
Franklin Pierce, Millard Fillmore, Thomas Ewing, and
others, as commissioners, to meet a commission of the
rebels, to patch up a peace and to patch a piece upon the
Constitution.   The proposition was rejected, without debate, by a vote of twenty-two to ninety-six.   On the 8th
of April, in Committee of the Whole on the President's
Message, Long made   the most studied   and elaborate

---

[1] Long was in the Ohio Legislature of 1848–49, when his party attempted
to steal the House, by breaking into the old State House before daylight,
and trying to organize.   The Whigs went in later, and organized on their
side of the hall.   The constant Democratic session of the next three weeks
created a perfect pandemonium.   When Long, from Mill Creek, brought
forward his great sanitary plan, the hall had to be kept in order by the
members, two to be detailed each morning.   Ball, of Muskingum, dedicated Long and his scheme to ridicule.   Long was youthful, had a girlish
face, and wore a profusion of ringlets ; of course he became " Miss Lucy
Long."

treasonable speech of the war. He was no longer " Miss Lucy Long." The speech will always remain a curiosity, if not a monument. He had a singular misunderstanding of the attempt which had been made in April, 1861, to aid Fort Sumter. According to him, the pretended succor was dispatched by a conspiracy of certain governors of the North, who had rightly forecasted that the result of such a measure would be the bombardment of Sumter. When the dispatch announcing that result to Mr. Lincoln was read to him, he exclaimed: " I knew they would do it !" which, to the orator's mind, was conclusive that this was the purpose of the expedition. He followed this by a carefully prepared *résumé* of the disasters to the Union cause of the three years of war. Here is a passage:

" If Mr. Lincoln had made a gift of millions of greenbacks to Jefferson Davis, to be used as bounty money in recruiting the Confederate Army, he could not have done better service to the cause of the South than he has done by his silly, absurd, and insulting amnesty proclamation,[1] and his equally absurd attempt to create State governments by dictatorial power."

The leading measures of the war were enumerated, and each stigmatized as foolish, absurd, fraudulent, criminal, flagitious, and all as unwise, giving, he asserted, the right to the States to secede, and, of course, it was criminal to attempt by war to compel their return.

" The Union is lost, never to be restored. . . . I see, neither North nor South, any sentiment on which it is possible to build a Union. . . . In attempting to preserve our jurisdiction over the Southern States, we have lost our constitutional form of government over the Northern. . . . In striving to retain the casket of liberty in which our jewels were confined, we have lost those precious muniments of freedom. . . . There is not a vestige of the Constitution remaining. . . . No peace is attainable upon the basis of union and reconstruction."

He had no interest in the question as to how the war should be conducted. He did not want the Democracy to be in any way responsible for the war.

---

[1] Of December 8, 1863, United States Statutes at Large, pp. 737-9.

17

"I say further, Mr. Chairman, that if this war is to be still further prosecuted, I, for one, prefer that it shall be done under the auspices of those now conducting its management, as I do not want the party with which I am connected to be in any degree responsible for its result, which cannot be otherwise than disastrous and suicidal; let the responsibility remain where it is, until we can have a change of policy instead of men, if such a thing is possible. Nothing could be more fatal for the Democratic party than to seek to come into power pledged to a continuance of the war policy. Such a policy would be a libel upon its creed in the past and the ideas that lay at the basis of all free government, and would lead to its complete demoralization and ruin. I believe the masses of the Democratic party are for peace, that they would be placed in a false position if they should nominate a war candidate for the Presidency and seek to make the issue upon the narrow basis of how the war should be prosecuted.

"For my own part, as I have already indicated, I fear that our old government cannot be preserved, even under the best auspices and with any policy that may be now adopted, yet I desire to see the Democratic party, with which I have always been connected, preserve its consistency and republican character unshaken."

Mr. Garfield replied :

"Mr. Chairman, I should be obliged to you if you would direct the Sergeant-at-Arms to bring a white flag and plant it in the aisle between myself and my colleague who has just addressed you.

"I recollect on one occasion when two great armies stood face to face, that under a white flag just planted I approached a company of men dressed in the uniform of the Confederacy, and reached out my hand to one of the number and told him I respected him as a brave man. Though he wore the emblems of disloyalty and treason, still underneath his vestments I beheld a brave and honest soul.

"I would reproduce that scene here this afternoon. I say, *were* there such a flag of truce—but God forgive me if I should do it under any other circumstances !—I would reach out this right hand and ask that gentleman to take it ; because I honor his bravery and his honesty. I believe what has just fallen from his lips is the honest sentiment of his heart, and in uttering it he has made a new epoch in the history of this war ; he has done a new thing under the sun ; he has done a brave thing. It is braver than to face cannon and musketry, and I honor him for his candor and frankness.

"But now I ask you to take away the flag of truce ; and I will go back inside the Union lines, and speak of what he has done. I am reminded by it of a distinguished character in *Paradise Lost.* When he had rebelled against the glory of God and 'led away a third part of heaven's sons, conjured against the Highest,' when after terrible battles in which mountains and hills were hurled by each contending host 'with 'jaculations dire' ;

when at last the leader and his hosts were hurled down 'nine times the space that measures day and night,' and after that terrible fall lay stretched prone on the burning lake, Satan lifted up his shattered bulk, crossed the abyss, looked down into Paradise, and, soliloquizing, said :

> " 'Which way I fly is hell ; myself am hell.'

" It seems to me in that utterance he expressed the very sentiment to which you have just listened ; uttered by one no less brave, malign, and fallen. This man gathers up the meaning of this great contest, the philosophy of the moment, the prophecies of the hour, and, in sight of the paradise of victory and peace, utters them all in this wail of terrible despair, 'Which way I fly is hell.' He ought to add, 'Myself am hell.'

" Mr. Chairman, I am reminded of two characters in the war of the Revolution as compared with two others in the war of to-day.

" The first was Lord Fairfax, who dwelt near the Potomac, a few miles from us. When the great contest was opened between the mother country and the colonies, Lord Fairfax, after a protracted struggle with his own heart, decided that he must go with the mother country. He gathered his mantle about him and went over grandly, solemnly, and impressively, and joined the fortunes of Great Britain against the home of his adoption.

" But there was another man who cast in his lot with the struggling colonies, and continued in their behalf till the war was wellnigh ended. But in a day of darkness, which just preceded the glory of the morning, that other man, deep down in the damned pits of his black heart, hatched the treason to surrender forever all that had been gained, to the enemies of his country. *Benedict Arnold* was that man.

" Fairfax and Arnold find their parallel in the struggle of to-day.

" When this war began, many good men stood hesitating and doubting what they ought to do. Their doctrine of State rights, their sympathies, all they had ever loved and longed for, were in the South, and after long and painful hesitation some of them at last went with the enemies of the nation.

" At that time Robert E. Lee sat in his home across the river here, doubting and delaying, and went off at last almost tearfully to join the enemies of his country. He reminds me in some respects of Lord Fairfax, the stately royalist of the Revolution.

" But now, when hundreds of thousands of brave souls have gone up to God under the shadow of the flag, and when thousands more, maimed and shattered in the contest, are sadly awaiting the deliverance of death ; now, when three years of terrific warfare have raged over us, when our armies have pushed the rebellion back over mountains and rivers and crowded it into narrow limits, until a wall of fire girds it ; now, when the uplifted hand of a majestic people is about to let fall the lightning of its conquering power upon the rebellion ; now, in the quiet of this hall, hatched in the lowest depths of a dark treason, there rises a Benedict Arnold and proposes to surrender us all up, body and spirit, the nation and the flag, its genius and its honor, now and forever, to the accursed traitors to our country. And that proposition comes—God forgive and pity my beloved State !—it comes from a citizen of the honored and loyal Commonwealth of Ohio.

"I implore you, brethren in this House, not to believe that many such births ever gave pangs to my mother State such as she suffered when that traitor was born. [*Suppressed applause and sensation.*] I beg you not to believe that on the soil of that State another such growth has ever deformed the face of nature and darkened the light of God's day. [An audible whisper, "*Vallandigham.*"] But ah ! I am reminded that there are other such. My zeal and love for Ohio have carried me too far. I retract. I remember that only a few days since a political convention met at the capital of my State, and *almost* decided to select from just such material a Representative for the Democratic party in the coming contest ; and to-day, what claim to be a majority of the Democracy of that State say that they have been cheated or they would have made that choice. I therefore sadly take back the boast I first uttered in behalf of my native State.

"But, sir, I will forget states. We have something greater than states and state pride to talk of here to-day. All personal or state feeling aside, I ask you what is the proposition which the enemy of his country has just made ? What is it ?

"For the first time in the history of this contest it is proposed in this hall to give up the struggle, to abandon the war, and let treason run riot through the land ! I will, if I can, dismiss feeling from my heart, and try to consider only what bears upon the logic of the speech to which we have just listened. . . .

"Suppose the policy of the gentleman were adopted to-day. Let the order go forth ; sound the 'recall' on your bugles, and let it ring from Texas to the far Atlantic, and tell the armies to come back. Call the victorious legions back over the battle-fields forever now disgraced. Call them back over the territory which they have conquered. Call them back and let the minions of secession chase them with derision and jeers as they come. And then tell them that that man across the aisle, from the free State of Ohio, gave birth to the monstrous proposition.

"Mr. Chairman, if such a word should be sent forth through the armies of the Union, the wave of terrible vengeance that would sweep back over this land could never find a parallel in the records of history. Almost in the moment of final victory the recall is sounded by a craven people not deserving freedom ! We ought every man to be made a slave should we sanction such a sentiment. . . .

"I remember to have stood in a line of nineteen men from Ohio on that carpet yonder on the first day of the session, and I remember that with up-lifted hands before Almighty God those nineteen took an oath to support and maintain the Constitution of the United States. And I remember that another oath was passed around, and each member signed it as provided by law, utterly repudiating the rebellion and its pretenses. Does the gentleman not blush to speak of Galileo's oath ? Was not his own its counterpart ?

" He says the Union can never be restored because of the terrible hatred engendered by the war. To prove it he quotes what some southern man said a few years ago, that he knew no hatred between peoples in the world like that between the North and the South. And yet that North and South have been one nation for eighty-eight years ! . . . .

" I said a little while ago that I accepted the proposition of the gentleman that the rebels had the right of revolution ; and the decisive issue between us and the rebellion is, whether they shall revolutionize and destroy or we shall subdue and preserve. We take the latter ground. We take the common weapons of war to meet them ; and if these be not sufficient, I would take any element which will overwhelm and destroy ; I would sacrifice the dearest and best beloved ; I would take all the old sanctions of law and the Constitution and fling them to the winds, if necessary, rather than let the nation be broken in pieces and its people destroyed with endless ruin.

" What is the Constitution that these gentlemen are perpetually flinging in our faces whenever we desire to strike hard blows against the rebellion ? It is the production of the American people. They made it, and the creator is mightier than the creature. The power which made the Constitution can also make other instruments to do its great work in the day of its dire necessity. . . .

" I am reminded here of a fact which I had wellnigh forgotten. Last summer, I remember, a Union spy came to our camp bringing two letters addressed to ' Major-General John C. Breckinridge, C. S. A.' They were letters of introduction stating that the bearer desired to obtain a commission in the rebel army, and commending him as a gallant and reliable man whom Breckinridge could trust. One of these letters was signed by a man who lately held a seat in this House !" [*Cries of* " *Name him !* " *from the Democratic side of the House.*]

Mr. GARFIELD.—" I will produce the letter in due time. It is not here with me. The other letter was from an associate of his, prominent in the local Democratic politics of the State of Indiana. I am responsible for producing those letters." [*Cries of* " *Name !* "]

Mr. HOLMAN.—" I hope the gentleman will give the names now."

Mr. GARFIELD.—" When I produce the letters any further testimony that may be called for can be had at my hands.

" Mr. Chairman, let me mention another class of facts in this same connection. We were compelled last year to send our secret-service men to ferret out the insidious work of that organization known as the ' Knights of the Golden Circle,' which was attempting to corrupt the army and destroy its efficiency ; and it was found that by the most subtle and secret means the signs and passwords of that order were being made known to such men in the army as were disaffected or could be corrupted. Witness also the riots and murders which their agents are committing throughout the loyal North, under the lead and guidance of the party whose Representatives sit yonder across the aisle; and now, just as the time is coming on when we are to select a President for the next four years, it throws up the blue light which will be seen and rejoiced over at the rebel capital in Richmond as the signal that the traitors in our camp are organized and ready for their hellish work. I believe the utterance of to-day is the uplifted banner of revolt. I ask you to mark the signal that blazes here, and see if there will not soon appear the answering signals of traitors all over the land. If I am wrong in this prediction I shall be thankful, but I am only too fearful of its truth.

"Let me say in conclusion, if these men do mean to light the torch of war in all our homes; if they have resolved to begin the fearful work which will redden our streets and this Capitol with blood, the American people should know it at once and prepare to meet it."

Mr. Long rejoined. On the next day Speaker Colfax offered the following, with a preamble:

"*Resolved*, That Alexander Long, a Representative from the Second District of Ohio, having on the 8th of April, 1864, declared himself in favor of recognizing the independence and nationality of the so-called Confederacy now in arms against the Union, and thereby ' given aid, countenance, and encouragement to persons engaged in armed hostility to the United States,' is hereby expelled."

After a long and very able debate—Mr. Colfax having accepted an amendment changing "expulsion" to "censure," because, as he said, no Democrat would vote for expulsion,—a vote was reached on the 14th, on the resolution as amended. A division being demanded, the first proposition was, as follows,

"*Resolved*, That said Alexander Long, a Representative from the Second District of Ohio, be, and he is hereby, declared to be an unworthy member of the House of Representatives,"

was adopted by a party vote, eighty for, sixty-nine against it.

The second resolution was as follows:

"*Resolved*, That the Speaker shall read the resolutions to the said Alexander Long during the session of the House."

Mr. Colfax offered to withdraw it. The Democrats objected, and Mr. Holman moved to lay it on the table, which motion prevailed by a vote of seventy-one to sixty-nine.

It is thus seen that the Democrats, to a man, sustained Long, nor did any in debate condemn his utterances. How will they appear on the final page of history ?

And here I take leave of the *Congressional Globe*, with a moderately firm purpose of not serving even the daintiest slip of it to a reader again. *I* am not without cause of fear that the inflated *I*, from which *I* have already liberally drawn, will be hardly more to his taste, yet from that stand I shall hereafter address him, dealing with some of the more conspicuous civilians of the Cabinet and Capital, with whom my profession brought me often into personal and sometimes confidential relations.

CHAPTER XXXVII.

FRANK BLAIR'S LAST SPEECH.

FEBRUARY, 1864.

The Blairs—Commercial Intercourse with the Seceded States Authorized by Congress—Regulations of—Frank Blair Charges the Secretary of the Treasury with Corrupt Acts under These Regulations—Chase Told that the President was a Party to the Attack—Achillian Rage of the Secretary—Mr. Riddle's Interview with Mr. Chase—An Interview with the President Arranged.

IT will be remembered that on the floor of the House I had criticised the policy of the President in my remarks of January 27, 1862, but that in my last utterance of February 28, 1863, I did him ample justice. Something of my relations with Mr. Chase have already found mention. It was my fortune to be of service to both these great men at a sharp crisis in their relations, a crisis which involved in a very grave manner the welfare of the Republic.

It is to be remembered that by the 5th Section of the Act of July 13, 1860, the President was authorized to license commercial intercourse with any section of the insurrectionary States at his discretion, the rules and regulations for which were to be prescribed by the Secretary of the Treasury. Mr. Chase, with great care, prepared a draft of regulations, and submitted it to the President and a full Cabinet, where it was discussed, amended, and

264

finally adopted, in fact, the regulations thus became the act of the President and Cabinet.

Doubtless the President's license was sometimes used as a pretence, and covered some mischief.

Very early, the relations between Montgomery Blair, Postmaster-General, and Mr. Chase, Secretary of the Treasury, became strained, and there was little intercourse between them outside of the President's counsel chamber. Blair was also on bad terms with Secretary Stanton. Frank Blair shared his elder brother's sentiments regarding the Secretary of the Treasury. He was at the front in command of a division in the southwest, and saw and heard something of the workings of the scheme of intercourse with the enemy, which appeared to him as if devised for corrupt purposes. In the campaign of 1862, in which he was a candidate for the House, he brought this matter prominently before the public, and made statements reflecting unfavorably upon Mr. Chase, personally and officially. It will be remembered that on his arrival at the capital, the President made an arrangement by which, when he could be spared from the House, he might resume his resigned commission, and that his service in Congress should be no detriment to his position in the Army.

In February, 1864, certain friends of the Secretary of the Treasury and other Republicans—critics of Mr. Lincoln,—almost without the Secretary's knowledge, and certainly without his suggestion, placed him before the country as a candidate for the presidency. On the 22d day of February, Mr. Chase wrote a frank, manly letter to the President, and sent with it his resignation. On the 29th Mr. Lincoln wrote a characteristic reply. He saw nothing in their attitudes to each other nor to the pending Republican convention, that need in the least embarrass either in the full discharge of official duty to the country, and expressed a frank wish that he should remain. I do not know that this matter rendered their relations in the least unpleasant. Mr. Chase was really never for a day in the canvass as a candidate, and did not so consider himself. He knew that Mr. Lincoln well understood Frank Blair's course towards him, and had, with this knowledge, made the stipulation for return to the army above referred to, without attempting to clear the atmosphere of the cloud caused by his attacks if such existed.

I remained in Washington, at Mr. Seward's request, to perform some work in the State Department, an item of which was to write a reply to a request from Congress, for an opinion and information upon a section in the Consular Bill, then pending, as to the necessity or expediency of creating a sub-class of consular employees, to be known as consular clerks. My draft of a letter was adopted without change, and transmitted with no addition but the signature of the Secretary of State. I had determined to leave Saturday morning, the 28th of April, for Cleveland. The evening before I was invited by Mr. Chase to go with him and the immediate members of his family to the opening of the Sanitary Fair in Baltimore on Saturday and remain until the ensuing Tuesday. I accepted, with the understanding that I must return to Washington on Sunday, in time to leave for Cleveland that Sunday night. Mr. Chase, Mrs. Sprague and her sister, were to go to the station in a carriage. General Sprague and myself were to walk from the Chase mansion on the corner of E and 6th Streets. I went that morning to take leave of the President. I had seen him but once before. I was pained, almost shocked, by the change in his looks and manner wrought during the intervening five months. He looked like a man worn and harassed with petty faultfinding and criticism, until he had turned at bay, like an old stag pursued and hunted by a cowardly rabble of men and dogs. He received me as if he hardly knew whether he had not to ward off a baiting. I came to understand something of this on that Saturday forenoon at the White House. There were a number of people in the President's ante-room, and I very soon found that the President himself was undergoing a rude roasting at the hands of those who were waiting for admission to his presence. Even my amiable and excellent friend Worcester, spoke ironically of him as " that great and good man." The one most loud and bitter was Henry Wilson, of Massachusetts. His open assaults were amazing. I withdrew to the President's desk to escape, but was annoyed by it even there, and I turned upon the Senator in indignant surprise, asking why he did not assault him in the Senate,—get a seat in the June convention, instead of opening on him in the streets and in the lobbies and offices of the Executive mansion itself. He conceded what I asserted—that the entire North stood with the President and would renominate him, and said that, " bad as that would be, the best must be made of it." " Yes, and this is the way you are doing your share of that best work," was my rejoinder.

I was a little late in reaching the Chase residence in the afternoon. The Secretary and his daughters had left for the station, and Sprague and I followed them.[1]

I was shown to Mr. Chase's presence in the car set apart for his use. He was alone, and in a frightful rage, and controlled himself with difficulty while he explained the cause. The recital in a hoarse, constrained voice, seemed to rekindle his anger and aggravate its intensity. The spacious car fairly trembled under his feet.

Frank Blair had taken the floor in the house late this same afternoon against Mr. Chase, with added incidents and Blairian fervor and intensity, had then gone to the

---

[1] I never could get on with the Ex-Governor of Rhode Island ; perhaps I did not care to. We walked the half-mile to the station side by side, bent upon the same purpose—a pleasure excursion together—but were not for an instant in company. We reached the train with still many minutes to spare. On our approach Mrs. Sprague left the group about the sisters, met and told me that her father was in the President's car, alone, and wished to see me.

Executive Mansion, held a brief interview with the President and received from his hands his old commission, with an order from the Secretary of War, countersigned by Mr. Lincoln, assigning him to the command of a corps, and then had left Washington for the front.

All this was told to the Secretary after he reached the station, and with added circumstances that left no shade of doubt in his mind but that all this, including the speech, had been done with the cordial approval of the President, a view fully shared by some of his immediate friends. Mr. Chase thought of remaining in the city, and at once tendering his resignation to the President. I implored him not to act hastily, and said that next week—after a better ascertainment of the facts—he would be able to act in accordance with a dignified consideration of all the conditions, as was his usual rule.

I was much relieved to find the train in motion, and mentally made up my course of action. I said to him that it was impossible that the President could have been a party to Blair's assault upon him, either before or after the act, and that I would return to Washington that evening, seek an interview with the President, and secure his personal assurance that he had no knowledge of this last attack, and that it had his distinct condemnation ; I argued that even if the President had acquiesced silently, it was purely a matter between him (Mr. Chase,) and Mr. Blair, and his friends could hardly justify his resignation to the country simply because of Mr. Blair's attack ; that to permit himself to be driven from a post more important than the command of the armies in the field, by a speech on the floor of the House, would fill the world with amazement.

At Baltimore, I saw Mr. Chase and the rest of his party, with the Committee of Reception, enter their carriages ; and returned to Washington by the first train.

I knew Mr. Lincoln was hard pressed by the many clamorous demands of the last importance, but Mr.

Nicolay, to whom I at once applied, after much exertion arranged an interview for Monday evening, the earliest hour the President could name. I had to be content. Sunday and Monday the city was full of rumors of a quarrel between the President and the Secretary, with all manner of censure assigned and all sorts of consequences predicted. There really was a very unpleasant state of feeling among thoughtful men of both parties, the old abolitionists generally were in a rage.

CHAPTER XXXVIII.

THE DANGER OF THE SITUATION.

FEBRUARY, 1864.

Mr. Lincoln's Speech—Mr. Chase's Candidacy—The Blairs Labor to Form
an Anti-Slavery Party in Missouri.

MY successor in the House, R. P. Spalding, the personal
and confidential friend nearest the Secretary, was absent
in Ohio, but was expected back on Sunday night. He
came on Monday. I had an interview with him, and heard
that he had met Mr. Chase at Baltimore and had found
him in a very unpleasant state of mind.

I was alarmed by the fear of a threatened defection of
the Chase men at the coming convention, and more particularly in the campaign and at the polls. It was of the
utmost importance that every possible vote should be
secured for Mr. Lincoln. To me, it seemed possible that
the resignation of Mr. Chase for reasons reflecting on Mr.
Lincoln, might defeat him. Mr. Chase's resignation would
be made to appear to them as solely due to the President.
Spalding fully adopted my views, and at my request accompanied me to meet the President, toward whom he had
never been cordial, though he was never among his
detractors.

Mr. Lincoln received us politely but with no pretence
of cordiality. After brief salutations he passed around to

the other side of the long wide table and sat down by a
bundle of papers, grimly awaiting my assault.[1]

"Mr. President," I said, "I am one of the personal and political friends
of Mr. Chase, who believes that the safety of the Union cause requires that
you should be unanimously nominated at the June Convention, and should
receive in November the eagerly cast ballot of every man devoted to our
country. It is this conviction which brings me here to remove, if I can, a
most seriously disturbing cause which threatens to render this consummation
impossible.

"As you are aware, on last Saturday, General Frank Blair, a Republican representative from Missouri, repeated on the floor of the House his attack of the early part of the session upon the Secretary of the Treasury, and
this with added acrimony. You are aware of the unfortunate occurrence between General Blair and the Executive, in reference to the resumption by Mr.
Blair of this Government's commission and his assignment to one of the
highest commands in the army, and you are also aware of his departure, following immediately upon the close of the speech. These events, coinci-
dent with his attack, seemed as if planned for dramatic effect, as parts of a
conspiracy against a most important member of the Cabinet and Administration. The always alert, jealous, and somewhat exacting abolitionists, forgetting how impossible it is that you can be guilty of an attack upon your
Secretary—upon your own administration, believe that Blair must have had
at least your countenance in this wretched business, and they demand the
instant resignation of Mr. Chase. It is only by the strenuous exertions of
one or two persons that this has been delayed.

"Mr. President, Mr. Chase's abrupt resignation now would be equal in
its effects to a severe set-back of the army under Grant. It would foretell
the defection of his friends at Baltimore, equal in effect to the defeat of that

---

[1] Two or three weeks later, I received a letter from Mr. Chase, requesting
me to write out and forward to him a verbatim report of the interview. He
said Spalding told him I had trained myself to try long cases, and carry all
the evidence without a note. Spalding had not told him that upon the completion of the trial, every shred of the evidence and generally the case, had a
way of vanishing from my memory. This interview was unusual and its
details were remembered. I made the attempt very unsatisfactorily to myself.
My rough draft is before me, and helps me to reproduce the substance of what
was said. I should add that on the receipt of Mr. Chase's request, I wrote
Mr. Nicolay, saying I would comply with it by the consent of the President,
who might regard the interview as confidential, but in any event I would
transmit it for his examination and revision. His reply was that the President
would feel obliged if I would meet Mr. Chase's wish, and that he would trust
to my accuracy in the report.

army in a pitched battle. Their defection in November might be the destruction of our cause.

"I pray you remember who these abolitionists are. They are the first, the oldest anti-slavery men—the abolitionists who conquered, foot by foot, the pro-slavery North, and who, with later allies, have conducted this great struggle to the issue of war—who made your accession to power possible. I know they have at times been over-hasty. Have I not personally heard their demands upon you and your answers? They were, however, the first to leap to your side, and who have pressed most closely after you, nay, would push you forward.

"Mr. President, I am not the emissary of these men, come to demand terms ; I am not the agent of Mr. Chase. I have said to them, that I would return to them your word that you were in no way a party to or responsible for a word uttered by Mr. Blair. He was an independent representative of his constituency and spoke for them and himself, and could no more be dictated to by the President than you could think of dictating to him ; and, having spoken, he was not responsible to you for his utterances.

"I invited Judge Spalding to be present, to hear your assurances, and with me bear them to our waiting friends."

Spalding, a handsome "personable" man, of fine manner, added a few words to the effect that he coincided with me in position and sentiment.

I had addressed the President standing, as had Spalding. The effect was marked ; he arose, came round, and with great cordiality took each of us by the hand and evinced the greatest satisfaction at our presence and the sentiments we had expressed. Mr. Lincoln then returned, took up his papers and standing, addressed us for nearly half an hour. He spoke in his best manner, as if before a very select audience. He said—

"Gentlemen, I am glad to meet you, glad for your mission, and especially for your way of executing it. It makes my statement easier than I expected. I nevertheless will say about what I intended. Your frankness and cordiality shall be fully responded to."

Taking up some papers—"Have you seen my letter to Mr. Chase of Feb. 29th, in reply to his of the 22d, concerning his candidacy, and offering his resignation?"

MR. SPALDING—"I have."

MR. RIDDLE—"I have not."

Mr. Lincoln read it :

" WASHINGTON, D. C., February 29, 1864.

" . . .

" I should have taken time to answer sooner yours of the 22d, but that I did not suppose any evil could result from the delay, especially as, by a note, I promptly acknowledged the receipt of yours, and promised a fuller answer. Now, on consideration, I find there is really very little to say. My knowledge of Mr. Pomeroy's letter [1] having been made *public* came to me only the day you wrote ; but I had in spite of myself known of its *existence* several days before. I have not yet read it, and I think I shall not. I was not shocked or surprised by the appearance of the letter, because I had had knowledge for several weeks of Mr. Pomeroy's committee, of the secret issue which I supposed came from it, and of secret agents who I supposed were sent out by it. I have known just as little of these things as my friends have allowed me to know. They bring the documents to me, but I do not read them ; they tell me what they think fit to tell me, but I do not inquire for more.

" I fully concur with you that neither of us can be justly held responsible for what our respective friends may do without our instigation or countenance, *and I assure you, as you have assured me, that no assault has been made upon you by my instigation, or with my countenance.*

" Whether you shall remain at the head of the Treasury Department is a question which I do not allow myself to consider from any standpoint other than my judgment of the public service, and in that view I do not perceive occasion for change. " ABRAHAM LINCOLN."

MR. LINCOLN.—" The Blairs are, as you know, strong, tenacious men, having some peculiarities, among them the energy with which their feuds are carried on."

MR. RIDDLE.—" Yes, Montgomery says that when the Blairs go in for a fight they go in for a funeral."

MR. LINCOLN.—" Exactly. As you know, they labored for ten years to build up an anti-slavery party in Missouri, and in an action of ejectment to recover that party in the State, they could prove title in any common law court. Frank has in some way permitted himself to be put in a false position. He is in danger of being kicked out of the house built by himself, and by a set of men rather new to it. You know that they contributed more than any twenty men to bring forward Fremont in 1855. I know that they mainly induced me to make him a Major-General and send him to Missouri."

He spoke of the quarrel between Fremont and Frank Blair, and said he did not know the actual facts of that matter.

---

[1] Mr. Pomeroy was the chairman of a committee of Mr. Chase's friends, and the letter referred to was an official circular of his.

Mr. Lincoln added that before the meeting of Congress General Schenck had an interview with the President and Stanton (Secretary of War), and he gave the substance of his reply to the House on the subject. After stating the arrangement with Frank Blair as to future service, and reading his letter to Montgomery Blair, he said that the arrangement had been made without reference to any possible question of law, and if he had had no power to make it, Frank Blair was in fact no Major-General. Just before Congress assembled General Grant had assigned Frank to the command of a corps, not knowing that the Secretary of War had assigned General Logan to the same command. Logan found the army engaged in the brilliant movements which resulted in the defeat of the enemy at Chattanooga, and he generously waived his claims to command till the campaign was over, and being thus engaged, Frank Blair was absent from the organization of the House. When he left the army he made his St. Louis speech attacking Mr. Chase, of which the President spoke disapprovingly.

Mr. Lincoln said that, on Frank's arrival in Washington, he called on him on some business, and that as he was leaving, he, Frank, said that he wanted to make a speech in the House on the Mississippi Trade Regulations, to which he, Mr. Lincoln, replied:

" If you will do the subject justice, showing fairly the workings of the regulations, and will collect and present all the information on the subject, you will doubtless render a service to the country and do yourself much credit ; but if you intend to make it the occasion of pursuing a personal warfare, you had better remain silent."

The President used stronger expressions than I can recall. He was annoyed and mortified by the speech. The trade regulations themselves were revised and arranged in Cabinet council, and he and each member of the Cabinet was as much responsible as was the Secretary of the Treasury. The speech was an assault on the

Government, and when it assailed Mr. Chase for the working of the machinery it undoubtedly did him injustice.
He had never been called upon in the premises, and did
not know that he could interfere.

Shortly before Frank left for the army, he called and
asked that the arrangement with him should be carried out,
and Mr. Lincoln sent an order to the War Office to have
the order of his restoration made, and supposed it had been
done.   He heard no more of it till about noon of the day
on which Frank made the last of that series of speeches,
when he called on him and said he must leave that evening, and that the all-important order had not been made.
The President then sent a messenger to the Adjutant-
General, who replied that Mr. Blair was not known in the
Department as an officer ; whereupon the President ordered his resignation to be cancelled, which was done.

" Within three hours," said Mr. Lincoln, " I heard that this speech had
been made, when I knew *that another beehive was kicked over*.   My first
thought was to have cancelled the orders restoring him to the army and
assigning him to command.   Perhaps this would have been best.   On such
reflection as I was able to give to the matter, however, I concluded to let them
stand.   If I was wrong in this, the injury to the service can be set right.

" And thus you see how far I am responsible for Frank Blair's assaults on
Mr. Chase."

Mr. Lincoln appealed several times to proofs of his
statements, and concluded with re-assertions of their
accuracy.

MR. SPALDING.—" Mr. President, spare us all other evidence.   We only
ask your word."

MR. RIDDLE.—"Your word, Mr. President, is the highest human
evidence."

Mr. Lincoln also spoke of Maryland politics, in so far
as this was essential to a full understanding of the present
position of men and things.   He said that in the formation of his Cabinet, he was for some days balancing between Montgomery Blair and Henry Winter Davis, and

finally settled on Mr. Blair. He added that in the disposition of the Maryland patronage, he had, as far as possible, met the wishes of Mr. Davis. Subsequently he regarded Mr. Davis as holding ground not the most favorable to the best interests of the country. Still later, that gentleman made a speech in the House which wholly disabused his mind, and he was greatly rejoiced to find his first opinion of him correct. In Mr. Davis's contest for Congress, he had rendered him all the aid he consistently could. He also understood that Mr. Chase favored Mr. Davis's Union opponent. Since that election, Mr. Davis had desired some aid in the Maryland Constitutional election, which he could not see his way to afford him, and Mr. Davis had become very cool towards him. In fact, the President believed he was now an active friend of the Secretary of the Treasury.

At the close of his statement Mr. Spalding said :

" Mr. President, I desire to know whether your letter to Mr. Chase, just read by you, expresses your present views and wishes in reference to the continuance of Mr. Chase in your Cabinet ? "

MR. LINCOLN.—" It does most fully. I cannot see now, as I could not then, how the public service could be advanced by his retirement."

Mr. Lincoln was fully an hour in making his statement —his explanation, as he called it. He was plain, sincere, and most impressive.

Mr. Spalding expressed himself as perfectly satisfied, and was sure Mr. Chase and his friends would be also. I certainly was.

Mr. Lincoln expressed great satisfaction, and with many cordial expressions we withdrew. The interview occupied nearly two hours.

The presence of Mr. Spalding was fortunate. Widely known, and trusted by Mr. Chase and his friends, his word and influence were useful in smoothing the way to a cordial unanimity of sentiment in support of Mr. Lincoln in the approaching presidential contest, upon which so much depended.

The two days of enforced stay at the Capital were not without use in another respect. It seemed to me that the selection of a prominent friend of Mr. Chase to preside at the coming Baltimore Convention would be a graceful appreciation of their final attitude towards Mr. Lincoln. Ex-Governor Denison, so unceremoniously turned down by us in Ohio, was mentioned as suitable. I found that the leading men of the President's managers then in Washington cordially accepted the first proposition, and would leave the selection to us. A little correspondence placed Denison in an eligible position. He was then not very widely known out of Ohio, and I was urged to be present at the opening of the Convention.

Among the remarkable men about the capital after the second year of the war, was Judge Jeremiah S. Black, of York, Pa., formerly Chief Justice of that State, and later Mr. Buchanan's Attorney-General. On Mr. Cass's retirement he became Secretary of State. It was by his influence that Mr. Stanton succeeded him as Attorney-General.

Judge Black was in many ways the intellectual superior of most of the leading men of his party, though lacking the qualities that make a successful leader. There is a tradition that when his father was about to make a very rare visit to Philadelphia, and had charged himself with the individual desires of each of the older members of the family, he came to the youngest—a dark, slender boy of nine. " Jerry, what shall I bring you ? " said he. " Please bring me Shakespeare's Plays." " And what else, my son ? " " Nothing—only Shakespeare's Plays." I came to know him well. A man of wider reading and study in unusual and recondite fields, I never knew.

He was at home upon subjects in law, art, and literature, that were but meaningless names to many well-informed men. When his counsel was sought, his opinions and advice were full of courage and audacity, to be acted upon by the most courageous only. He was the only man I ever heard before the Supreme Court of the United States, who felt free to say what was in his mind. Passing around in front of the tables and bending his tall form nearly to the Clerk's desk, with his splendid head, glowing eyes, commanding voice, free elocution and action, he was in many ways the best advocate of my time at that bar, recalling the traditions of Webster, Pinckney, and Wert. I may add that good speaking is rare at that bar, and for this the Court is largely responsible. That Court with its gowns and glamor, its history and the traditional awe that surrounds it, oppresses the average man, who needs to have all his trained resources well in hand, and to know what he is to say and how he will say it. We rarely hear any really good speaking there ; all our courts repress fine or effective speech. Dry, humdrum, commonplace talk is now in vogue there, as everywhere.

My introduction to Judge Black was unique. During my second winter at Mrs. Irving's, he with Mrs. Black, his daughter Mrs. Shunck and her husband, were there for a week and were placed opposite me at the table. On taking my place on our first day, I was much impressed with the head, face, and broad shoulders of a man who was proceeding with a monologue begun before my entrance. He was dealing with the still famous Oberlin slave rescue case, tried in the Circuit Court at Cleveland in the summer of 1859. I had been the leading counsel for the defence and was at once interested, and soon was advised of the narrator's identity.

He rapidly sketched the case. A slave had been captured at his refuge in Oberlin, and a mob of the leading men, professors of the college, students, black and white, pursued the fleeing officers ten or twelve miles, overtook them and rescued the slave, whom they sent to a freedman's colony in Canada. When prosecuted, the twenty-three men refused to give bail, and were placed in the Cleveland jail pending trial. Two were convicted. Their counsel had then taken the record with the order of commitment on the sentence to prison—had secured a writ of *habeas corpus*, returnable before the full Supreme Court of the State of Ohio, and demanded their discharge, on the ground of the unconstitutionality of the Fugitive Slave Law. It was supposed that a majority of the Court would hold that the Act was unconstitutional and void, and would order the convicted to be set at large, which would liberate all the rest. The situation was one of serious and most critical danger. Chase, the Governor of Ohio, was a most determined man, who would sustain the decision of the Ohio Court with the strength of his militia, while he, the Attroney-General, was determined to enforce the judgment of the Circuit Court of the United States, at all hazards, and had made the necessary preparations. The Judge's loud and rapid narrative had arrested much attention.

"Fortunately," he went on, "the Ohio Court held the law constitutional by three to two."

"What became of the rest of the causes?" was asked.

"There came in the master stroke of the defence of the rescued," said Judge Black, "Their counsel procured an indictment of the Kentuckians, the Deputy Marshal, and every man concerned in the capture of the slave in the county in which Oberlin is situated, for kidnapping, under a severe law of that State, and as there was then no possible way for the indicted parties to prove that the man they had seized was really a slave, they were certain of being convicted before an abolition jury, and sent to the penitentiary. The defendants could not testify for themselves nor for each other. Then the counsel of the Oberlin rescuers proposed if the United States would discontinue—*nolle* all the rest of its cases against the rescuers, they would *nolle* the cases against the kidnappers, and really we had to accede to that, so the prosecution came to an inglorious end."

"By the way," resumed the Judge, after the little buzz caused by his story had subsided, "I would like to know what became of the young lawyer that managed that defence. Some one sent me an argument of his in a famous poisoning case in Ohio, as well as his speech in the rescue case, and I expected to hear more from him."

" I am happy to gratify you, Judge Black," spoke up Dr. Welling (editor of the *National Intelligencer*) from the lower end of the table, " he is now sitting exactly opposite you. Judge Black, Mr. Riddle, of the Cleveland district, Ohio. I am glad to name you to each other."

There ensued a rather sharp discussion of the political aspects of that famous case tried in 1859. After the very handsome things he had permitted himself to say, I was easily won to regard him most favorably, and we became pleasant and appreciative acquaintances, in fact friends.

While in Cuba I received a long letter from him, a fool's-cap sheet full (now yellow with time), inviting me to return and form a partnership with himself and his son Chauncey, at Washington, for the practice of law. Of course this with the proposed terms was flattering. I was not averse to leaving Cleveland.

Early in June I received a note from Mr. Fred Seward, saying (Mr. Giddings having died) that the Counsel-Generalship of Canada was to be disposed of, and that if I felt interested in it, they would like to see me at the Department. I made ready for a visit to the Capital. I was also due at the Baltimore Convention. Somehow I had a premonition that I was leaving Ohio, and had a day of inexpressible sadness as I mentally bade the dear old State, its old homes, kindred, and their burial places, adieu.

On presenting myself at the State Department, I found among the many names suggested for the Quebec position that of John F. Potter. " If I do not desire the post will it be given to Mr. Potter?" I asked. " It probably will," was the reply. " Give it to Mr. Potter," said I ; and it was given to him.

I sought Judge Black, who was then in the city, and met also Mr. Chauncey Black, whom his father destined to become a great advocate. He certainly did not lack ability. Meantime, Mr. H. L. Stevens, a distinguished lawyer, had died, leaving two or three juniors and a large business, and the survivors applied to me to take his place.   Judge Black did not at that time intend to change his domicile to the city, and we concurred that, for the present, I had better accept the offer of the Stevens firm. I did, and found myself occupying the whole of the third floor of the Colonization Building on the avenue, with a fine library and offices well furnished.   My friend, Chief Justice Carter, and my Congressional associates, Olin and Fisher, with Wylie, made up the Supreme Court of the District, then in session.   I appeared there, was admitted, and the thing was done.

CHAPTER XXXIX.

SUMMER AT THE CAPITAL.

MAY–JUNE, 1864.

The National Convention—Mr. Chase Retires—The War—The People.

THE Republican National Convention, which was held at Baltimore on the 7th of June, comprised a numerous, united, and enthusiastic body of men. On the evening of the 6th we extemporized a reception for ex-Governor Denison, on which occasion I officiated as usher. My principal was in good form and made a good impression. On the following day he was made president of the convention, and in due time Postmaster-General. The only thing beyond the platform was the Vice-Presidency. The convention was enthusiastically unanimous for Mr. Lincoln, nor was there finally any opposition to Mr. Johnson. It was understood that the President favored Johnson, though certain I am that he made no open declaration of his wishes, nor could there have been any one authorized to speak for him. Lincoln would never permit himself to attempt to influence the convention. The truth is, we were accustomed during the war to turning down our own men for democrats who were not so good, but who were better than the majority of their party. I had become somewhat an admirer of Mr. Johnson. He was the one Southern senator true to his oath of allegiance. I saw him daily on his way to the capitol. He was usually alone, always well-dressed, his smooth face, crowned with iron-gray hair, turned toward the ground as if in sombre thought. Silence fell on groups of men as he approached, and as he moved rapidly past, there was a turning of heads to follow his receding figure—a notable and striking form in those days of darkness that brooded over the city. I came to know him well in the after anxious months and years.

Mr. Chase retired from the Treasury Department in that June ; Mr. Cisco, Assistant Treasurer at New York, resigned. Mr. Chase nominated Mr. Field, Assistant Secretary of the Treasury, but Senator Morgan of New York objected. He insisted that the office in New York, as managed, was politically a nuisance. Mr. Chase resented this interference and words passed between him and Morgan. Mr. Lincoln was inclined to favor Senator Morgan. Mr. Chase wrote one of the best of his manly, dignified, and independent letters to the President, and resigned. The Baltimore convention had done its perfect work, there was then no special thing in the way, and the President gratified Mr. Chase and accepted the resignation. The two great men parted in amity and each retained the confidence of the other.

Congress adjourned on the 4th of July, the members of the House hurried away to look after their own re-election, and Washington became deserted. I found I was the one Republican lawyer of the District. I had made offensively radical speeches which did not immediately commend me to a Washington clientage. We were accustomed to the war, and in our neighborhood had heard the smothered thunder of more than one conflict. We heard of the great southwestern struggles, we had Mr. Stanton's bulletins of blood and battle daily, and Grant's chronic " battle in the wilderness." We were accustomed to defeat and disaster on the Virginia fields, though none of us for an instant felt doubtful of the end. I had observed the growing warlike feeling of our masses, among whom I had never detected a shiver, not a premonitory symptom of discouragement. On the contrary they developed a steadier and stronger determination to put down the rebellion. Popular songs, pictorial magazines, and periodicals, the mass of army correspondence, picturesque and attractive; the constant visits of fathers, mothers, wives, sisters, and sweethearts to the front, to hospitals, and to battle-fields, kept alive the patriotic ardor of our people, aroused the widely diffused heroic elements of their composite nature, and generated and matured a spirit for war, almost for the sake of war, in men and women to whom national wars had been but traditions. The character of our people was undergoing a radical change. War will never again inspire them with terror—much as they will deplore its recurrence. They have become accustomed to war and victory on the largest scale, have tested their strength and capacity, and, should the occasion arise, they would not shrink from a contest with Europe itself.

CHAPTER XL.

THE LAST INVASION.

JULY, 1864.

Wallace Defeated at Monocacy—The Capital Alarmed—Rumors—Fugitives Come in—Rebels within Five Miles—The Sixth Corps to the Rescue—Battle—The Rebels Retreat—Early at Silver Springs.

THE Capitol, deserted by Congress, was to be rudely awakened, and was to hear the tramp of the rebel war horses if not to see them. Jubal Early came in the beginning of July and rather abruptly shook us up. Grant and all his armies were waiting near Petersburg. We were still receiving shiploads of the wounded from City Point. Sigel had failed to make an impression on Lynchburg, which seemed almost as impregnable as Richmond. Hunter, who succeeded Sigel, finally felt obliged to retire over the mountains into West Virginia for rest and re-organization, as was said, but really for safety.

This opened Maryland to invasion. Sigel had a small force at Martinsburg, a few miles above Harper's Ferry, on the Baltimore and Ohio Railroad. Lee at Petersburg had unemployed troops available for the opening, and he detailed a force, large enough to take care of itself, for the third invasion under Early. That might compel Grant to detach soldiers to meet them. Sigel retired to Maryland heights. The President issued a call for 12,000 militia from Pennsylvania, 12,000 from New York, and 5000 from Massachusetts, to repel the invaders. Governor Curtin and General Couch were stirred up in Pennsylvania to put their border on the defensive. The valley of the Cumberland was over-run and Hagerstown and Frederick laid under contribution. The slender forces of the United States moved toward Chambersburg. General Lew Wallace had a small force on the Monocacy and was repulsed on the 9th of July, near Monocacy Junction. The enemy soon after attacked him in force, and a battle of considerable severity ensued, lasting some hours. Wallace was largely out-numbered, his right out-flanked by the enemy, who opened an enfilading fire and swept off 500 or 600 men, with General Tyler and his staff. After many days the captured General reappeared sound and ready for another fight. General Ricketts, with a small force sent up by Grant, formed Wallace's left in the battle, in which we lost about 1200 men, including a number of officers.

The defeat of Wallace disturbed us at the Capital a good deal, though we were hardened beyond a panic. I heard of some secreting of valuables, of many people leaving the city, and of others arranging to go.

Some notes under dates may be sketched in here. We heard of the advance down the valley on the 2d of July. There was great alarm at Baltimore on the 4th, and also at Hagerstown and Frederick. On the 5th, we heard of the battle between the *Kearsarge* and *Alabama*, and the details of the affair reached us the next day. We also learned on the 5th of the partial uprising of the " Secesh " at Baltimore, and of the burning of Governor Hicks's country residence, four miles from that city.

On the 6th came news of more rebels crossing the Potomac, and of a panic at Hagerstown. Great excitement prevailed also in our neighboring Georgetown. Boats arriving on the canal brought wild rumors. Forty thousand of the enemy were said to have crossed the Potomac, 7000 crossing at Muddy Run.

On July 7th there were 30,000 rebels in Maryland, Hagerstown was plundered, Union men and secessionists were robbed, without distinction.

On July 8th Hagerstown was laid under contribution, and we heard that the enemy had shown themselves at Laurel, a station twelve miles from us, on the Baltimore and Ohio Railroad.

On the 9th there were 12,000 rebels at Frederick, as we were assured. On Sunday fugitives arrived in the city, exciting it with wild rumors. On the 12th we were made to believe that Washington was really the object of the invasion. The rebels were at Rockville. Their whole force was estimated at not less than 40,000 men. We heard of the battle of Monocacy, where, as was said, the enemy had 20,000 men engaged. Fighting on the Seventh Street turnpike was also reported. On the same July 12th the railroad and wires were cut off between Washington and Baltimore. In the early morning of that day a part of Wright's soldiers, of the Sixth Army Corps, landed and marched through the city. A rumor of this flashed over the excited town, but was contradicted. Some of us, being early abroad, had ocular proof of their presence, hurrying to the scene of invasion and battle. Some overwrought souls lapsed to serene but elevated joy at the sight.

The Nineteenth Corps, on its way from New Orleans to General Grant, commanded by General Emory, had entered Chesapeake Bay, and was dispatched to the aid of the threatened Capital. When Grant became aware of the possible object of Early's expedition, a body of 4000 or 5000 men from the Sixth Corps was detached from the Petersburg lines and hurried to our assistance. A column of rebel cavalry threatened Baltimore, while Early, with the main force, headed toward Washington, effected a junction with a considerable advanced body. Augur was in command of the troops at the Capital.

Meantime two or three courts-martial were suspended, and the generals and colonels were sent to the earthworks, which were manned by the Ohio hundred-day men. General Paine of Port Hudson renown, the president of one of the courts-martial, had already requested active service in defence of the city, and was assigned to the command of the District of Columbia force ordered to the field to meet Early. On his first appearance at the front he was chagrined to find no show of soldiers for his command. Early the next morning his brow cleared, and he was gladdened by the approach of Colonel Alexander and his regiment, a numerous, well-armed, and fine-appearing, resolute body of men. The Colonel, not a trained officer, but a gallant man of some experience, and having the confidence of his soldiers, was there for immediate service. General Paine had carefully inspected the ground along the line of the expected approach of the enemy, and at once placed his force in a well-chosen position. As previous indications of the rebel advance were confirmed by their appearance in force, Paine was relieved by the approach of the men of the Sixth Corps. He opened his line for their passage, holding himself as a reserve under orders. The advance brigade of Wright was just in time. The opposing forces of veterans met and fought a sharp pitched battle, under the eyes of the reserves of General Paine and Colonel Alexander. The parties engaged were about equal in numbers and were well handled, and Paine still speaks of the affair as one of the completest things of the war. It lasted some hours, when the enemy drew off and abandoned the field, leaving over 100 killed or too badly wounded to be taken off in haste. Eleven officers and 90 men were placed on the premises of the senior Blair.

Our casualties were quite 200, counting the slightly wounded. Just why the rebels should, under the circumstances, have fought this little battle is not apparent. They must have recognized Wright's men (old opponents of theirs), and have realized that the idea of capturing Washington, if ever entertained, must be abandoned. It may have been their object to enable the rest of their force to withdraw, as most of them recrossed the Potomac late that day. The next day the whole force approached the river, and the invasion was at an end. Wright with his division and with two divisions of the Nineteenth followed. He crossed below Edward's Ferry, and pursued Early towards Leesburg. Crook, with his cavalry, captured part of one of the enemy's trains, and drove his rearguard through Snicker's Gap. This virtually ended the raid, and the respective forces were re-absorbed in the main armies, or remained to renew the contests and races in the Shenandoah Valley, the most hunted over ground of the war.

The last affair was fought within the limits of the District, about five miles north of Pennsylvania Avenue, just beyond Brightwood, which was then a hamlet. Fort Stevens was on the west side of the turnpike. A little farther north, on the east side, is the neatly kept cemetery in which sleep all the victims of the battle, while some 1200 lie with their head-stones at and near the Old Soldiers' Home, who had been slain in battle, or who had died in the hospitals in the neighborhood of Washington. Soldiers desperately wounded, and the bodies of some who died in the shelter of woods and thickets near by, were found near the scene of this sharp affair some days after the battle and the retreat of the enemy.[1]

---

[1] To us in the city there seemed an unaccountable delay in the advance upon the Capital (if that was an objective point) by the invasion. As is known, Early and his officers, though they burnt the residence of the younger Blair, the Postmaster-General, made themselves the guests of the

19

PERSONAL EXPERIENCES.

My part in this campaign was very inconspicuous. I was engaged with Mr. Walter S. Cox, now a Justice of our District Supreme Court, in the defense of two sutlers before Doubleday's court, when the members were all ordered to the defence of the city. On returning to my office at evening I found a notice that I was enrolled in Captain ——'s company of militia, and ordered to appear for duty at eight o'clock the next morning at a point named now forgotten, as is the captain's name. In my congressional days Henry Slade had presented me with a rifle of the Kansas war pattern, of the first edition of breech-loaders, the weapon he bore in the conquest of Alexandria (not on the Nile, but the Potomac), under the gallant Carrington. That gun had had a checkered history, and a varying place of deposit. Slade soon bore it away, and declared it to be a trophy of disaster and flight brought back by myself from fateful Bull Run. Still later he presented it to me again as a rebel gun of Mosby's troop, but my search for it on this eve of battle was unavailing. I anticipated the hour the next morning and armed myself with an umbrella, after the manner of the Pope's soldiers of Voltaire's time. I found no one there—I never did find the captain, whose name I had lost, nor did I find any of his heroes. My notice was issued by Colonel Wisewell, Military Governor, under whom the city then groaned, as the secessionists said; a gallant man, " but of limitations in other directions," as General Browne described him. I went to his headquarters, but found small signs of a movement toward the

---

senior Blair at Silver Springs, for the sake of the memory of General Jackson. In the freedom of uninvited guests they early discovered two casks of Bourbon, then late from a two years' ocean voyage, an unsuspected Union ally. Their allegiance to Bourbon was said to have absorbed them for twenty-four hours. Montgomery Blair the younger assures me that this is true.

enemy ; and joining with two strangers, we started in a carriage a little after twelve o'clock. The city that morning was all of a quiver with excitement. We pushed on out. I had my faithful little Remingtons, carried more from habit than thought of their possible usefulness. I hoped to reach Fort Stevens, where Paine commanded.

I saw a part of Wright's men that morning, as they passed up from the river and up Seventh Street, which relieved me of all anxiety as to the fate of the city.

We made our way with little difficulty, going out Fourteenth Street and on the Piney Branch Road, till we reached the Blagden place. From there the way was much obstructed. We soon heard the sound of the ordnance, shelling the rebels, as I learned later, and our driver refused to go farther. I finally lost my companions, and made my way to Brightwood, where I saw the smoke of the fight, and had some glimpses of the combatants.

Of course the large secession element of Washington had never before been so moved as on Early's approach at the head of a numerous, well-appointed, and presumably conquering army. For a year Grant had been in command. Hope of direct liberation by a conquest of the Capital had grown faint, but now at last, by this sudden, unexpected advance and successful invasion, the aspect had totally changed; hope had overcome uncertainty and doubt in a measure, and all contributed to create a crisis of confused emotions in their circles. A secessionist was now known by the radiance of his face— "At last, at last, thank God!" was quoted, as exclamatory bursts from them. Many, as was said, had already sought the enemy's camps and forces, to aid as they best could in the reduction of the Capital. The accounts from Baltimore, mentioned above, showed almost an outbreak of the powerful rebel element there upon the approach of the invading army. It was the long-sighed-for, unattainable liberation, now about to be consummated. These things in the atmosphere of the cities made the last two or three days of the invasion, days of great anxiety.

Happily, the arrival of Wright's and Emory's veterans cleared the atmosphere, and restored to the Union Heart a sense of security not again to be shaken.

CHAPTER XLI.

THE PRESIDENTIAL ELECTION.

JUNE–NOVEMBER, 1864.

The Convention—General Fremont—The Campaign—At the Capital.

THE renomination of Mr. Lincoln at the Baltimore convention of June 7th, and the nomination of Mr. Johnson for Vice-President, have been briefly mentioned above.

The platform of the convention was quite up to the expectations of the radical Republicans. Indeed there were now no others.

The leading features of the admirably framed declaration of the convention were expressed as follows:

It pledged the nation to put down the rebellion by force of arms.

Declared the determination to accept no terms of peace except the unconditional surrender of the enemy.

Slavery was the cause and strength of the rebellion and should be extirpated from the soil of the Republic.

It thanked, sustained, and applauded the President, the Army, and the Navy, and had confidence only in those in the public counsels (Congress) who approved and sustained these principles.

The Democrats did not call their convention together till the 29th of August. It was held at Chicago and was presided over by Governor Horatio Seymour.

As was predestined, General McClellan was nominated for the Presidency, receiving 202½ votes to 23½ for Governor Thomas H. Seymour, of Connecticut. Mr. George H. Pendleton was nominated for the Vice-Presidency.

The convention declared itself unswervingly devoted to the Union.

It declared *the war a failure,* and demanded a cessation of hostilities, and an ultimate convention of the States, to the end that peace might be attained.

The object of the Democratic party was stated to be to preserve the Union and the rights of the States unimpaired. The usurpations of the Administration were vigorously denounced.

The convention also denounced the arbitrary imprisonment of citizens, and extended the sympathy of the Democratic party to the soldiers and sailors.

The candidates accepted in due form their nominations.

On May 6th an address by the so-called "radical" Republicans was issued in favor of General John C. Fremont, calling on his friends to assemble at Cleveland, in mass convention, and to take steps to place him before the people as a presidential candidate. This was followed by another, from some of the State officers of New York, for the same purpose. A third call, signed by a number of the well known abolitionists, also appeared to the same effect.

Some five hundred citizens assembled under these calls and placed the General in nomination, with John Cochrane, Attorney-General of New York, for Vice-President. The platform of this body was sufficiently incisive and covered some important propositions not connected with the war.

General Fremont accepted on June 14th. He withdrew on the 2d of September, supplementing his withdrawal with a letter the next day, and later presided at a Lincoln and Johnson meeting.

The Democracy had troubles of its own. Vallandigham had returned and was at Chicago. He and a band of war-like peace Democrats, repudiated McClellan, and resolved upon an independent nomination. The Woods, Fernando and Ben, were active in the conspiracy, and Alexander Long also took a prominent part. They resolved to hold a convention in Cincinnati, but the convention did not *convene.* Pendleton was charged with the scheme, and had to write a letter to Honorable John B. Haskin of New York. He was totally opposed to having two governments in the once United States, and was in favor of all constitutional means (not naming them) for the restoration of the Union. The threatened bolt never reached an outbreak, however, but died a natural death.

The fact that at no time in the history of the District of Columbia could its people vote for a President, however indirectly, would seem to insure them against any intensity of feeling, as well as to spare them from the strife and expense of a campaign. But in fact there are no people in the United States more immediately interested in a presidential or a congressional election than the residents of Washington, and few enter upon a campaign with more eagerness and zeal. True, they cannot in any direct way influence the result, but they dwell constantly in the eye of the nation, and what is said and done at the seat of the national government is seen, heard, and talked about all over the country.

The political campaign opened late, due to the delay of the always tardy McClellanites in getting into the field. No efforts were needed to get out votes, nor was there any labor for election day, for there was no voting to be done in the city.

The Democrats had a huge ratification meeting in front of the City Hall, with an immense procession, and three stands occupied by many able speakers.

The Republicans formed a Lincoln-Johnson Club, with

branches in some of the wards. They serenaded the President, who made a speech, a kind of trumpet call to the Union forces ; they serenaded Mr. Seward, who repeated his very effective New York speech ; they serenaded Mr. Chase, who responded in his usual thoughtful manner. [1]

The Republicans at the Capital held one notable outdoor meeting, at the northeast corner of Seventh Street and Pennsylvania Avenue, on an exquisite late October afternoon. Ex-Secretary Chase, Governor Andrew of Massachusetts, and A. G. Riddle were announced as the speakers. There was an immense throng of men, and a sprinkling of ladies. The meeting was notable for the comparative failure of the two distinguished gentlemen to fill the parts assigned them.

By request, Governor Andrew spoke first. He stated that he had been detained a day or two in Washington from important official duties at his own capital, then delivered a brief but effective exhortation and went away.

Mr. Chase made a few general remarks—spoke in terms very like irony of the party who would follow him, and took his departure. Neither had occupied more than thirty

---

[1] I was with Mr. Chase in his last Ohio gubernatorial canvass, and learned something of his methods. He wrote out a general address, covering all the principal points, and from this he seldom departed. He wrought it out on the stand, improving, curtailing, enlarging, as he became familiar with it, the speech constantly gaining in effectiveness. He was not a quick, spontaneous speaker ; he needed preparation, and trusted to the weight of thought rather than to the graces of oratory. His voice lacked a little in clear, resonant quality ; he was a speaker of the Thomas Ewing order, strong, massive, satisfying, rather than of the class of Thomas Corwin and John Brough. The latter had the finest voice for the field that I ever heard. He had a trick, when interrupted by applause, of resuming in the same tone and volume as when broken in upon, producing the impression that he had spoken steadily on through the storm ; he was the only man I ever knew who had that art. Corwin had a marvellous voice, capable of every inflection, intoned to every emotion. To this were joined a face and eyes the most flexible and expressive, which could carry on the discourse when the tongue became mute. I have witnessed the marvellous effect wrought by them unaided by the voice.

minutes.[1]   The crowd was good-natured, responsive, and docile, when it discovered that a man was not speaking for applause.

What an autumn that was !   Messrs. Jay Cooke & Company reported each day for the city press the rates of the public securities.   It is curious now to turn over the time-stained files and mark the fluctuations of gold in the market.   Soon after the Chicago convention, gold reached 254½, under the influence of the presidential struggle.   The fall of Atlanta, the capture of Fort Morgan, the defeats of Early by Sheridan in the Valley, reduced gold to 191.

November 8th was the day of election for President, in which twenty-five States participated.   The whole number of votes cast was 3,964,298 ; of these Mr. Lincoln received 2,203,831, and McClellan 1,760,467, giving Mr. Lincoln 443,364 majority of the popular vote.

In the Electoral College Mr. Lincoln received two hundred and twelve votes and General McClellan received twenty-one, and this was the nation's response to the Chicago platform and to George B. McClellan.

---

[1] It is a satisfaction to a man similarly situated to feel absolute master of himself, and to know that the whole field lies well digested in his grasp, and whom experience has assured that within two minutes he would be master of the multitude. The crowd stood solid around the third speaker till darkness melted it into an indistinguishable mass, and then insisted that he should " go on."

CHAPTER XLII.

RECONSTRUCTION.

JULY, 1864.

Radical Difference between Congress and the President—The President's Scheme—Congress Passed a Bill not Signed—Mr. Wade—Mr. Davis.

WHILE Mr. Lincoln, with skilful and unsparing policy had dealt the most vigorous and conclusive blows upon the rebels, he had at the same time employed the arts of persuasion and solicitation to an extent not in accord with the views of the leaders of the national cause in the two Houses.

His famous *Amnesty Proclamation* of December 8, 1863, was at once so sweeping and liberal, that its universal rejection should have satisfied him that the war could never be ended by offer and acceptance of pardon, and yet this was two or three times amended and made easier for the offenders, who remained obstinate. The discussion in Congress incidentally disclosed that the views of the two departments were widely divergent on this grave problem.

On the 15th of February, 1864, Henry Winter Davis, from the Committee on the Belligerent States, reported a bill in the House to guarantee a republican form of government to the States at war with the republic. His bill received an exhaustive discussion in both Houses and passed the House by a vote of seventy-three for to fifty-nine against it. In the Senate, Sumner moved an amendment to ratify the President's Proclamation of Emancipation of January 1, 1863. It was lost by eleven for to twenty-one against—and seventeen absent. The bill then passed the Senate—twenty-six to twenty. It required the President to appoint a provisional governor for each of the rebel States (of course only when the rebellion was ended), who were to enrol each white male citizen of their States respectively and to request each to take an oath of fidelity to the Constitution. The names of those refusing the oath were to be marked and returned to the several governors, and if the rolls showed that a majority had taken the oath, the loyal citizens were, on a certain day, to elect delegates to a State convention, to declare the will of the people relative to the re-establishment of a State government under the Constitution of the United States. The delegates were to be elected by the whites, on a day to be named, at an election held by appointed commissioners, and to take an oath of allegiance to be prescribed by the governor, who should make due returns of the election to the government. The governor was by proclamation to convene the delegates—the convention to be presided over by the governor, who should administer the prescribed oath to each delegate. The convention was to declare on behalf of the people of the State their submission to the Constitution and laws of the United States, and was to adopt the following: " No person below the rank of colonel in the Confederacy, shall vote for, or be eligible to the office of, Governor, or as a member of the Legislature. Slavery shall be forever abolished. No Confederate public debt shall be recognized or paid by the State."

The Constitution was to be submitted to a vote of the people. If the convention refused the conditions imposed, the governor was to call another, which was to be dissolved or a State government certified. In the meantime, the governor was to enforce laws and preserve order, and to assess and collect taxes, which were to be applied to public expenses and accounted for. Section twelve abolished slavery. Persons holding Confederate offices, after the passage of the Act (except ministerial), below the grade of colonel, should be citizens of the United States. The bill passed on the last day of the session and reached the President an hour before final adjournment.

It was not signed. On the 8th of July, the President replied to it by solemn proclamation, to which the bill was appended. One provision contained a scheme of reconstruction to which the President was unwilling to bind himself, and hence could not approve. He was unwilling to set aside the recently formed free State governments of Louisiana and Arkansas, and thus discourage the loyal people of the revolted States; and he was unwilling to admit that Congress could abolish slavery in the States. He trusted to an amendment of the Constitution for that purpose. Yet he was fully satisfied with the scheme proposed as proper for the loyal people who might accept it, and he would aid the people of any State in so doing, in which case military governors would be appointed, with directions to proceed under the provisions of the bill.

The proclamation of December 8th, may be glanced at for a clear understanding of Mr. Lincoln's views on this vastly important subject. That offered pardon and amnesty to those taking the special oath of allegiance prescribed by it, and provided that whenever the thus qualified citizens, in any of the Confederate States, except Virginia, equalled in number one tenth of the whole number of the votes cast in a given State at the presidential election of 1860, they should establish a State government, which should be republican, and which was to be recognized as the true State government. It also enjoined care of the freedmen, and recognized a condition of temporary servitude. The oath enjoined obedience to all the laws of Congress in reference to slaves.

It is thus evident that the President assumed that the reconstruction of the States was the labor of the Executive exclusively, and he would not perfect the bill of Congress to an Act by appending his official signature to it, nor did he recommend the scheme that an Act should be passed by Congress. This body in return stigmatized his December proclamation as the "ten per cent plan."

Congress had adjourned, and nearly all the members of the House had left the Capital before this extraordinary disposition of their carefully framed plan was made by the proclamation of July 8th.—(13 *United States Statutes at Large*, pp. 744–747.)

This remarkable proclamation, however, did not escape a crushing reply and criticism from Messrs. Wade and Davis, the chairmen of the respective committees of the Senate and House to which the President's declaration would have been referred. It came from the pen of Mr. Davis, and is one of the strong papers of the war.

I epitomize this protest, which can, in fact, not be condensed with justice.

The authors admit the indignation with which they read the proclamation. They assert the right and duty of the legislative branch to hold in check the aggressive tendencies of the executive. To pass that missive in silence would be a failure of that duty. The President had not signed the bill passed by Congress after the most mature deliberation. The bill, in consequence, came to nothing. The proclamation, which was neither an approval nor a veto, is a paper unknown to the Constitution. As an excuse for withholding the executive signature, it is a declaration against the friends of the government. To execute a bill not a law, is usurpation.

The paper then summarizes the proclamation, and replies to its positions. The bill was presented with others which were signed, although at the last hour of Congress. The President, when asked if he had further communication to make, had none, saying he had resolved not to sign the bill. Time had nothing to do with it. The President was fully informed of the provisions of the bill. A draft of it had been furnished him beforehand. He was not taken by surprise. He was so well informed of the bill, that he had resolved to defeat it without the responsibility of a veto. It was known to General Banks and to his staff in New Orleans, that the bill would be delayed in the Senate to permit this method of defeating it. The experience of Senator Wade, who had charge of the bill, fully accords with this.

Had the proclamation stopped there, it would have been but another defeat of the will of the people by the Executive perversions of the Constitution.

They then quote the President's proclamation, where it professes to lay the congressional plan of reconstruction before the people, for *their* consideration. Shall it become a law by such approval, at the President's will? Will he then deem it to be a law? Or is this a mere device to defeat the bill?

They then reply to the reasons for withholding the President's signature. He was unprepared to commit himself to a fixed plan. His wisdom was to guide alone in this most important matter. He was not prepared to set aside the new governments of Louisiana and Arkansas, declared by the protest to be but shadows, and repudiated by Congress. The condition of these States is set forth, showing that their territory was almost wholly in the hands of the rebels.

By the schemes of State government, as designed by the President, the electoral vote at the ensuing election would be wholly in his hands, subject to the vicissitudes of the war. This feature of the Executive scheme is severely condemned. The bill declared that there were no State governments in the seceded States which could take part in the national election, and it devises a scheme for the creation of such governments. The proclamation holds this action of the law making power for naught, and plunges headlong into the anarchy of the 8th of December proclamation. If presidential electors are created by this means, a sinister light will be cast upon the President's motives in the creation of these State governments. The power to declare or recognize State governments rests wholly with Congress. They cite the decisions of the Supreme Court to sustain this position. The President admits that it rests with the two Houses to decide whether, under his scheme, Senators and Representatives can sit from the States. This is utterly inconsistent with his scheme of forming State governments.

The right to have Senators and Representatives is an absolute right of a State government. Without State governments there can be no Senators nor Representatives. The two Houses can alone, without aid or hindrance of the President, decide who shall be the members of their body severally. When they are thus admitted, that act declares that their State government exists. When they are rejected, such State government does not exist.

To this decision the President must submit. The President denies that Congress has the power to abolish slavery. Cannot a State government abolish slavery? Surely Congress can create a State government with the assent of the Executive. He has already signed three bills freeing, under authority of Congress, certain classes of slaves of the rebel States. Why he should scruple at our doing what he does by our authority, is not clear. The bill contains no provision inconsistent with these views. Can the President claim to be sincere in his proclaimed wish to abolish slavery when he refuses to sign this bill, which, as a law, would then require each new State constitution, in terms, to abolish slavery within the State limits?

Yet the President, though refusing to sign the bill, declares his purpose to execute it as a dictator. The protest recites the President's language, and declares it is a studied outrage upon the legislative authority of the people. Congress passes a bill; the President refuses to sign it, yet proclaims his purpose to enforce so much of it as suits his purpose, by officers unknown to the Constitution and laws.

The bill proposed provisional governors, to be appointed as the Constitution directs. The President defeats the bill, and proposes to appoint them without law and without the consent of the Senate, and this dictatorial power he has already exercised in Louisiana, and the protest gives the form of the appointment of governor Michael Hahn, and contends that he remains a private citizen so far as law and the Constitution are concerned, maugre the President's appointment.

The President, after nullifying the bill itself, proposes to instruct his governors to proceed according to the bill. Whatever is done will be at his will and pleasure, not because it is the will of the people, declared in constitutional forms and binding upon him, but because it is his will. Should the rebel States adopt the provisions, well and good. If not, it would be just as well. It is all left to the rebels to choose between the stringent bill or the lax proclamation. The protest contrasts the provisions of the two schemes, not to the advantage of the President's plan, and with great skill shows their working in the practical matter of government.

The paper throughout shows great analytical power, logical force, and clearness of statement.

Outside of Washington, the people took sides with the President and against Messrs. Wade and Davis. Mr. Wade was with his own people for many months under a very dark cloud. Young Garfield, who was at once called to other States, found on his return to Ohio that his people were unanimously against him, and on the assembling of the nominating convention of his district he was sent for and put on his defense before that determined body. They accused him of writing the paper. He made his reply short, emphatic, and decisive, to the effect that he fully approved of the paper, and strode haughtily out of the hall. The effect was such that he was nominated by acclamation, and heard the cheers given for him as he was moving away from the hall where the convention was assembled, supposing they were for his defeat.

Everywhere, north, east, south, and west, the masses were with Mr. Lincoln. No President was ever more cordially sustained by the people.

At the Capital, thinking Union men were quite unanimous in sustaining Mr. Wade and Mr. Davis, as was the majority of both Houses of Congress. It is difficult to sustain the position of the President in this most unfortunate difference. The whole scheme of the erection and acceptance of States into the Union, as well as deciding who shall represent them and their people in the two Houses, is broadly within the jurisdiction of Congress. It was a curious statement in the proclamation of July 8th that if the loyal people and States should adopt and act upon the congressional bill, the Executive would give them all the aid in his power, when the bill provided that the President must take the initiative by the appointment of a provisional government, and that until this was done action on the part of the loyal people was impossible. This was the beginning of the divergence of the two divisions of the government, a divergence to be exaggerated and emphasized when Mr. Lincoln was succeeded by Mr. Johnson. It is difficult to see how some of the troubles of the next years could have been avoided, had Mr. Lincoln remained to enforce his plan and policy.

20

CHAPTER XLIII.

MILITARY COMMISSIONS.

1862–1864.

The City in a State of Siege—General L. C. Baker—Provost-Marshal Office
Secrets—The Milligan Case—Other Cases.

As before stated, the city of Washington was, at the beginning of the war, wholly in sympathy with the South. Something of this I came to know while in the House. Much of the time it might have been regarded as a city in a state of siege. It had a military governor, and the Provost-Marshal was General L. C. Baker, the detective, whose position and services made him, in the eyes of all Southerners and their friends, the most odious of men. Nominally he was the Colonel of the District of Columbia Regiment of Cavalry, usually under the command of his brother, as Lieutenant-Colonel. Lieutenant-Colonel O. E. Conger served in this regiment, which was one of the most effective of the volunteer regiments of cavalry of the war. Colonel Baker, though occasionally in the field, was, unless on detective duty, confined to the city, having his office on Eighteenth Street, near F, Northwest. He was a man of little culture, dark, taciturn, square-shouldered, and of powerful frame, who had seen service under the Vigilance Committee of San Francisco.

At the seat of government and around about it having

almost irresponsible power, the limit of which was his relentless will ; compelled to act promptly on such information as he could gather, there were undoubtedly, with the
writ of *habeas corpus* in chronic suspension, many acts of
oppression, and much individual wrong suffered at his
hands. Yet, with all the complaint of his despotic and
unwarranted conduct, it is a curious and significant commentary upon him, that he was never prosecuted in the
District but once, nor was there ever a suit instituted
against him to recover for unlawful arrest, or maltreatment
of the person, save the instance referred to. He had a
large number of assistants and constantly kept horses
enough to mount a troop of cavalry. He was born a detective, and made some of the most surprising hits in the
field of detective service, often rendering invaluable aid to
the government. I came to know him well personally,
and shall have occasion to mention him later.

It will be remembered that in the War of 1812 the
British, under General Ross, had captured the city and
burnt the Capitol, and that Congress erected a large
wooden building at the corner of Second Street East
and North A, which was used as the Capitol till the central part of the present building was in condition for the
use of Congress. This building was, early in 1861, devoted to the purposes of a prison, and was called the old
" Capitol prison." A long row of buildings fronting the
Capitol grounds, running from East Capitol Street to
South A, known as " Duff Green's Row," and also as the
Carroll prison—was in fact an annex to the first named.[1]

---

[1] It was said that, as a rule, counsel were obliged to see their clients in
these prisons in the presence of an officer on duty.

The rule was never enforced against me, and I doubt whether there ever
was such a rule in existence.

My first visit was attended with an unusual incident. I was called to see
a young man, John Devlin, from New York City, who was charged with
sundry acts committed in New York detrimental to the United States, and
who, although not in the military service, was to be tried before a military

W. P. Wood was the Governor of the old Capitol, a rough, uncultured man, despotic, but kindly natured, and not intentionally harsh ; yet how could he be otherwise to men imprisoned for no defined offence, whose friends often could not, for months, ascertain the cause of their detention, and who, when discharged, were dismissed without explanation or compensation.

The celebrated case of *Milligan and Others* belongs to this period. It will be brought fully under notice for another purpose. In the order of time, and as illustrative of character, it must receive mention here.

The secret history of the Provost Marshal General's office at Washington, and its connection with the War Office, of which it was an agency, never can be written, perhaps never should be. It is known, however, that the old Capitol and Carroll prisons were thronged with men against whom no charges were ever preferred, who were never tried, and yet who were arbitrarily detained against remonstrance and without a shadow of constitutional authority. The writ of *habeas corpus* was suspended, and there were no legal means of relief. In this condition of affairs a statement concerning the prisons, with many details, was sent to the Military Committee, which so startled the generals at its head, that they went to the prisons and made a personal inquiry. They saw several of the prisoners and heard their stories, which excited their surprise and indignation. On the next day Garfield offered a resolution demanding an inquiry. The House adopted the resolution, and directed the Military Committee to make the inquiry. On the day following

---

commission in the District of Columbia. On being conducted to his room, his first act was, in silence, to remove a small steel plate, by the use of a screw-driver, from the bottom of the heel of his left boot, and take from a box secreted in the heel a $1000 Treasury note, which he handed to me as a retainer.

Thousand-dollar retainers had before been known to me, but had never before been drawn from such a bank of deposit.

General Garfield was detained from the House at its
opening. When he entered he found it listening to
Thaddeus Stevens on his motion to rescind Garfield's
resolution of the day before, which the old man denounced as needless and mischievous intermeddling on
the part of a young man with the management of the
War Office. Garfield replied with great spirit, stating the
origin of the resolution, his personal inquiry and what he
had found ; related in indignant terms the outrages upon
Union men ; told the story of a Union colonel who was
wounded at the second battle of Bull Run ; then denounced the great Secretary of War as worthy of im-
peachment, and told the House to rescind the resolution
if it would. The House declined so to act, and there was
an immediate emptying of the prisons, which rendered
the inquiry useless. The daring of the young tribune in
thus bearding the terrible Secretary won the admiration
of all men, and especially of Mr. Stanton himself, which
was manifested in a striking way. Meantime, Milligan
and his co-conspirators were in prison awaiting execution,
and the kind Lincoln was sorely perplexed.

In this exigency Judge Black and one or two leading
Democrats approached Garfield, laid the case before him,
and asked him to appear in it before the Supreme Court
of the United States. The defendants were poor, abject,
and odious, but their case involved the same great questions of right, constitutional law, and civil liberty, so
promptly and effectively vindicated in the case of the
Capitol and Carroll prisons. Garfield did not hesitate.
His sense of duty in the defense of the principles involved
compelled him, at any personal sacrifice and peril, to undertake the case. He prepared his great argument,
printed his brief, presented the case, convinced the court,
saved the wretched men, and restored to menaced rights
the support of the law of the land.[1]

[1] See Chapter I., Part V., *Life of Garfield.*

The instances of arresting citizens in States where the administration of the laws was in healthy and vigorous enforcement by the legal tribunals, transporting them across States where no hostile foot had intruded, and putting them upon trial before a military commission, were of alarming frequency. I may mention some instances in which I appeared for the defense.

It was of course the case with the condition of things existing all along the disordered borders of the States at war, favorable to the grossest abuses on the part of unworthy men, who, as spies or messengers, couriers, or licensed agents, under the Act of Congress referred to, often brought about the arrest, imprisonment, prosecution, and so-called punishment of perfectly innocent men, citizens, and residents of the loyal States.

Of all the employees who became personally known to me, Pardon Worsley was the most unscrupulous, the most criminal, and the most mischievous. He was nominally a Union spy, and to enable him the better to execute his missions, he was a licensed dealer within the enemies' lines, *and of course*, to secure the confidence of his customers, he *occasionally* furnished information to the rebel generals. This was his pretense; known as a blockade runner, he was furnished with special permits from General Augur to purchase goods with which to ply his pretended vocation of Union spy. These permits he exhibited to his intended victims, and by their aid made large purchases of dealers in Washington, and much larger of two wholesale dealers in Baltimore. All of these dealers were arrested and tried before military commissions in the city of Washington, and several were convicted before General Doubleday's court. The case against the Easters, of Baltimore, was tried at great length by young General Fessenden's court, consuming weeks of time.[1]

[1] In this trial, Archibald Stirling and C. J. M. Gwynn, son-in-law of Reverdy Johnson, and later Attorney-General of Maryland, of Baltimore,

The case of the Easters followed that of the Washington parties, Johnson and Sutton, and was succeeded by that of the clothing-house parties of Baltimore, and others.

I had more than one interview with Secretary Stanton and the President, in which I urged every argument that seemed worthy of consideration, to induce the abandonment of this mode of dealing with offenders not connected with the military service. Mr. Lincoln had become shaky on the subject. Stanton, though a thoroughly educated lawyer, who must have acquired a lawyer's instinct for adherence to the constituted judicial forms, remained inflexible.[1]

At length the Milligan case, in the Supreme Court of the United States, put an end to this in every way illegal and discreditable practice.

Landin P. Milligan, a citizen of Indiana, was arrested October 5, 1864, by order of General Hovey, Commandant of the District of Indiana, and on the 21st was put on trial before a military commission at Indianapolis, on charges preferred by Judge-Advocate Major Burnett, first, for conspiracy against the government; second, for giving aid to the rebels; third, for inciting insurrection, etc.

Milligan, who belonged to the Order of American Knights, was found guilty, and sentenced to death by hanging, on the 19th of May, 1865. The President approved of the record, but ordered that execution should be delayed. Milligan applied to the Circuit Court of the United States, setting up the record, praying to be dis-

and Governor Tom Ford, were with me, examining the witnesses. The labor of making and reading the defense was performed by me. But one was convicted—Weedon A. Clark.

[1] He ironically said that an abandonment of the military courts for the trial of civilians would diminish my revenues, and that I ought not to complain. He was restive under my appearance for the defendants, but I was under no general retainer by the United States, and my sympathies were with those thus needlessly prosecuted.

charged on *habeas corpus*. In that court there was a dis-
agreement on three material points : Ought a writ of
habeas corpus to be issued? Ought said Milligan to be
discharged on the showing? Had the military commission jurisdiction to try said Milligan?

In the Supreme Court, McDonald, Judge Black, James
A. Garfield, and David Dudley Field, appeared for Milligan, and Attorney-General Speed, Henry Stanbery, and
B. F. Butler for the United States. Garfield won his spurs
in this great cause. Speed and Butler argued the case for
the United States.

At the end of the term the Chief-Justice announced the
points decided; Milligan was discharged, as were the
parties in two other cases. The opinion was delivered
by Justice David Davis, the great personal friend of Mr.
Lincoln.

On the main point the Court declared that in a State
not invaded and not engaged in the rebellion, in which
the federal courts were in the unobstructed exercise of
their powers, military courts had no jurisdiction to try,
convict, and sentence a citizen who was not a resident of
a rebellious State, not a prisoner of war, nor in the military or naval service, and that Congress could not invest
them with any such power.[1]

This was the end of these abnormal courts, and all the
victims of the great mistakes, who were still in custody,
were at once set at large.[2]

The Chief-Justice was Salmon P. Chase, appointed
during October, 1864.[3]

---

[1] 4 Wallace, *United States Reports*, p. 2.

[2] Major Burnett, who prosecuted the case, was a rapidly rising young lawyer of Ohio, well known to me. Mr. Stanton, on Burnett's application,
desired that I should aid him before the Commission. Fortunately my en-
gagements rendered that impossible.

[3] The request for his appointment came from all parts of the Union
States. The old anti-slavery men were very urgent, nor was there any other
name prominently before the President. But Mr. Lincoln was slow to act,

and Mr. Chase desired that I should interview the President on this grave matter. I undertook it reluctantly, but his wish was law.

Mr. LINCOLN.—" Do you expect that Chase will relinquish his desire to become President ?"

Mr. RIDDLE.—" Mr. Chase's ambition springs from a consciousness of great ability to serve. It is said that a man once bitten of the Presidency dies of it."

Mr. LINCOLN.—" I should deplore seeing a man trying to swap the Chief-Justiceship for the Presidency."

Mr. RIDDLE.—" Mr. President, you are fully aware that Mr. Chase is a man of the most elevated character, and that personal dignity in him rises to grandeur. A traffic such as you suggest would be impossible.

" There is a consideration which I beg to suggest. The weighty matters involved in this war have been thoroughly discussed by Congress and the President. They are undergoing the arbitrament of battle. They will next inevitably be submitted to the Supreme Court for the last and final human decision. Do you know a man in the world to whom you would sooner submit them ?"

Mr. LINCOLN.—" Would you have me pack the Supreme Court, Mr. Riddle ?"

Mr. RIDDLE.—" Would you appoint a man with no preconceived notions of law ? There is not a man at our bar whom you or I would call a lawyer, who has not convictions on these questions."

Mr. LINCOLN.—" This is matter for reflection." And I took leave.

CHAPTER XLIV.

1862–1864.

STANTON AS SECRETARY OF WAR.

The Time : Its Needs and Labor—The Man—Reminiscences—A Case—
The Raw Conditions at the Great Genesis.

CONGRESS became an agency for the evolution of a great purpose which no one had yet formulated.

No one unaided by memory can have a just apprehension of the chaotic condition of things in the minds of the men then found in Congress, the cause of which rested in each man's individuality, his intelligence, and reach of thought.

The crisis was caused by a race movement, as in primitive time, blindly in the right direction. For the time government was a powerless form. No excesses were committed, for observance of order had become the law of the born American's nature ; when he is lawless it is that law may be better enforced. Emperors and kings look upon the American as a paradox—the freest but most conservative of mortals. In any other nation, the primal bond of association would for the time have disappeared ; in ours, the Peace Convention sat and survived its own work. Leaders, armies, new projectiles were in demand ; the conflict must be purely material. The first armed collisions settled nothing, but that war was to be. No American general on either side had then seen 20,000 of his countrymen in a body under arms; Santa Anna's Mexicans at Buena Vista were the largest army that any of them had ever beheld; no one of them had a conception of a great continental war, its course, nor strategy; Cæsar, Napoleon, the latest writers, could only furnish them hints. These human atoms, highly charged, were to be wrought into effective armed bodies, and generals to command them were to be discovered and trained. The 660,000 were units, not soldiers, in fragmentary regiments scattered through the North—ineffective, useless, awaiting the man to bring about cohesion and organization. Who he would be, when he would come, were sore problems. We were familiarized with carnage; war was yet to be organized and men drawn into it of volition; there was no compulsory process. The later conscription, with its twelve exceptions, was a sieve that let everybody through; 300,000 were called for under it; the conscription produced 50,000 only. For a long time Congress refused to amend the system. A man who could grasp these conditions, take the raw units, transmute them into soldiers, sustain them, hurl them against the enemy,—a man inflexible to cruelty, firm to obstinacy, wilful to despotism, was needed,—a warrior born, one who loved relentless fight as the dearest of things (no other can make successful war),—a man inhuman if need be, not seeing nor feeling small scruples nor obstacles but to overcome them, and knowing what there is in men and the ways to make them most available.

It matters little how such men as Stanton are trained, they get growth by any regimen. He was forty-seven years old, with perfected frame and health, when called to the position of Secretary of War. We were all surprised by the name; few of us knew anything of him save as Mr. Buchanan's Attorney-General, and what he had really done in his Cabinet had not transpired—Judge Black had resigned that post upon becoming Mr. Buchanan's Secretary of State, and had him appointed to it.

In the early night of a wintry day Senator Pearce, of Maryland, told some of us that Stanton was Secretary of War; "Wade answered for him to the Republicans," he said. Wade's word satisfied us; we cared nothing for republicanism, as such, then; that he was a Democrat enhanced his value. I had known of him as a lawyer in his native Steubenville, and called early to pay my respects. He was alone, received me courteously, speaking in a low musical voice, which, as I was to observe, could be lower, softer, even sweet, under the excitement of anger; a round, compactly built, personable man, with short limbs, small hands and feet, thick neck, large round head, with black brows, and long, curling black hair, the lower face lost in a grizzly beard. His eyes were very striking—large and liquid like some women's, they were mysterious, to me seeming to have a message, and looking reproach that I did not understand it. We had much to do with the War Office—all had good men for the army and wanted orders for new regiments, batteries, etc. Orders for two or three of mine had been made by Mr. Cameron; something from the new Secretary (as of course I thought) was wanted to give them effect; I sought this early; he refused flatly, and ungraciously cancelled his predecessor's action. I lingered an instant to recover myself, and said very quietly, that "They were the only things I had asked."

The Secretary (in the sweetest, most exasperating voice) replied: "I permit no man to address me in such language." "Mr. Secretary," I said, with a profound bow, "permit me to retire, and with *final leave.*" That was not the end but a beginning. It was the time of McClellan's advance, when no man of the army could get leave. Three days later a surgeon came to me from a hospital with the case of an officer dying of camp diarrhœa and homesickness; the only hope was leave to return home; the President would not interfere, and there was nothing but to appeal to the black-browed, inflexible, soft-voiced Secretary

of War. I went to him direct—he might have the qualities that would make him gracious to me,—I made him no
bow, stated the case in the fewest words, and laid the papers on his desk, before which he stood, on a raised step, his
invariable working position ; glancing at me, his first words,
with his eyes on the paper, were, " Twenty days is too
short." He made it thirty, and added his all-powerful
initials. Pushing the papers to me, he said in a cheery
voice : " Something happened here the other day which I
would have prevented,—what did you then wish ? " " Mr.
Secretary, my present wish is to get these papers back.
When you are at leisure I will call," I replied. " I am sure
you wish nothing but the best service and can help me,"
he added.

Mr. Stanton in the War Office was at once everywhere
felt—through the camps, hospitals, recruiting stations, and
notably in Congress and the Cabinet. The grasp of his
nervous hand on the limitless power of his department,
which was then not well defined, sent a thrill through the
land. With most men not specially trained, the first idea
of war then was collision at once with the enemy, and
there was a forward movement immediately. That may
not have been McClellan's idea ; all but he advanced. If
not actual war, it led to war, organized and aggressive,
without compromise or treaty—Stanton would never hear
of that,—a war for the extinction of the enemy as such.
The continent was the arena, the resources of the American
people the means, the existence of the Republic the issue.

A vast amount of preliminary work was performed, the
skeleton regiments were consolidated and sent to the front,
every department and branch reorganized and made effective. In the rush of all sorts of persons into the service
as officers, a mob of incompetent, inefficient men had become a serious evil. Congress promptly passed, at the
Secretary's wish, a law authorizing the summary dismissal
of officers by the President at discretion—the discretion

of the Secretary of War. "Move or be removed" was
his rule; the incompetent were thinned out. Undoubtedly
there were individual instances of hardship. How could
that be avoided? The Nation was in its death-struggle;
a pause of the great leader, a relaxation in the awful tension of the spring of the War Office, which pushed the
army upon the foe, would have been fatal; a man in that
place who would be turned aside to search out nice details
could never have decided the issue in our favor.

Mr. Stanton was capable of arduous and long-continued
work beyond most men with whom history is familiar, and
his days and nights were given to it. He lived in the War
Office, literally; his bed was there; his food was there;
his presence in his own household was a rare event. He
bravely assumed responsibility, leaving the President the
full measure of praise, the fame of benefactions and favors,
and shouldered the odium that followed many needed acts.

It has been said that the war fought itself; that by a
process of selection it supplied itself with soldiers, generals, legislation; its mishaps were due to those thrust upon
it in spite of itself. In part this is true, and though it may
be doubted whether the Secretary of War ever directly
changed his mind on cumulative evidence, he was under
the influence of this force, as were the President, Congress, the generals, and the people who furnished them all.
Commanders could only be selected tentatively; no one
could tell *a priori* who would prove himself a general any
more than who will be the great man of forty years hence.
They appeared, as will the future great, from unexpected
quarters. That McClellan failed in the field as the commander of a great army scarcely admits of argument. He
retired to become the candidate of the Democratic party.
Individually the Democrats hated the Secretary of War;
they soon hated him with added party intensity; it was
an article of faith, and none the less because he was a
Democrat.

Sherman has told the tale of his personal wrongs.¹ Can
any man read that and acquit the great leader of grave
faults? He calls it "*my folly*" in his account of it. In
the pardonable exuberance of feeling at the great success
to which he had so largely contributed, he permitted the
rebels to dictate the terms of their submission to him, by
which they alone were to lose nothing by the war. No
matter what Stanton may have said to him at Savannah,
he knew the Secretary had no power to determine the
status of the rebel States as political bodies. On the grand
stand, with his army passing in review, in the presence
of the President, Cabinet, and representatives of foreign
nations, the Secretary of War arose, met and proffered
him his hand, in token of mutual amnesty and oblivion—
asking and giving; Sherman not only refused his own,
but ten years later boasted of it—one of the pitiable tales
of the war.

There were but a few of the more conspicuous men
made enemies, to be supplemented by the convicts of
all the military commissions, the cry against which—as
against him and against Mr. Lincoln upon his account—
was a war-cry in the presidential contest of 1864. The
sum of these odiums was greater than ever before charged
against any man in our history, and, as may be seen, possibly not even the smallest part of it was his due. To determine this would require a careful examination of every
case; to claim that in no instance was he in fault, would
be to proclaim him superhuman, and he was greatly
human. Whoever declares, in any important case, that he
acted consciously from motives other than for the public
good, makes an averment that will forever remain
unproved.

One purpose only controlled the action of Mr. Stanton
—the utter overthrow of the rebellion—to war against and
pursue it to extinction, root and seed. It was for this

¹ *Sherman's Memoirs*, vol. ii., beginning at p. 346.

he accepted a place in the evil days—*the last of days* they were near being—in Mr. Buchanan's Cabinet, where, in a fierce philippic, he assumed his true position as exterminator of the rebellion. For this purpose he coveted the War Office later ; whatever best tended to that object he would undertake ; for no other purpose would he work. No scruples of the Constitution disturbed him ; when it was urged that a proposed measure had no warrant in that instrument, " Was the country made for the Constitution ? " he asked in his sweetest voice. On another occasion, with soft tones, " When the country is gone it will be a comfort to know that *the Constitution is saved.*" A raid was to be organized upon remote Andersonville ; he would not hear of it. Men had suffered and died ; more must do the same. He would deal concentrated blows with the last fibre of power upon the armed foe.

Stanton never could have said to Sherman at Savannah the things attributed to him. Less effusive than his chief, his vision at times seemed clearer, further-reaching. He was more thoughtful, if less magnanimous in victory, but no man was ever more easily moved by native tenderness to mercy when approached on the sweeter side of his sympathies.[1]

---

[1] An educated young Irishman, a gentleman, was induced by my nominal partner to enter the army. Influence secured him the post of captain's clerk in a company stationed near Washington. In midwinter of '64–5 a letter from his young wife informed him that she would sail from Liverpool for New York on a day named, expecting confinement in childbirth, about the time of arrival there. Neither had friends nor acquaintances in America. The young soldier applied for leave to meet her and was refused—this occurred at about the time of the fall of Richmond. In despair, he resumed his civilian's garb, escaped, and made his way to New York. His girl-wife had been confined on shipboard and lost her baby ; they made their way to Washington to find him posted as a deserter. An attempt was made to reach the inexorable Secretary through Mrs. Stanton and others, but shut away in his office he was too well guarded. The case was desperate ; my English clerk finally brought them to me. I asked him to write a condensed statement in his best hand —which was wonderful penmanship. When finished the words were the fewest, the chirography the most striking and beautiful,—it made the pathos and appeal a vision. I went with it to the Secretary. He had an unusual

In 1862 the Legislature of Indiana adjourned without appropriations to carry on the State Government. Governor Morton went to Stanton for advice, and the Secretary at once drew a warrant on the Treasury for a quarter of a million, payable to Morton's order. "If the Cause fails," said the Governor, "you and I will be covered with prosecutions, imprisoned, driven from the country" —a curious speech for Morton. "If the Cause fails " (in his softest voice), "I do not care to live," was Stanton's response. He was the man around whom the great war governors—Andrew, Curtin, Brough, Morton, and Oglesby—gathered directly.

There were some sharp differences between the Secretary and his chief, in which the Secretary had his way, as was best undoubtedly. General Weitzel did have permission from the President to convene the rebel legislature at Richmond, after its fall. It was recalled at the urgent request of Stanton. The order to Grant to limit terms with Lee to purely military affairs was his work.[1]

----

surrounding of distinguished visitors, and was in his own anteroom, sitting opposite the door. He saw me and beckoned me forward ; I held the manuscript open to his eyes. " What is it ? Tell me," he said ; but that was not my purpose. The text caught his eye, the tale caught his attention ; as he read he arose and moved, reading, toward the desk across the room. " I'll do it ; I'll do it," he said to himself. "I would have done that myself. The man who would not, is not fit for a soldier." He opened and glanced at the inside of a small file, and indorsed on the back : " This soldier's absence is justified. He will report for duty. His captain will see this order executed. Stanton, Secretary." Pushing the papers to me, he told the story, in tremulous voice, to the attentive senators, generals, governors, and others present, repeating : "I would have done it myself. The man who would not, is not fit for a soldier." With the papers I hurried to the sad, brown-eyed girl, leaving the Secretary's visitors wondering at the revelation of his unsuspected nature. This was not a solitary instance, no one felt an inclination to relate similar cases, and never in any instance did he say a word or cause the contradiction of the injurious stories told against him. He was like Seward in this respect.

[1] See Supplement B, Mr. Riddle's address to the meeting of the Washington Bar on the demise of the ex-Secretary.

21

During my service in the House, I made very few acquaintances with the resident people of the District, and seldom met any of them. My residence brought me more directly in contact, and I found among them many brave and ardent patriots. Conspicuously so were Mr. Lewis Clephane and Mr. Sayles J. Bowen, both in the public service. These gentlemen and their associates had formed a patriotic club to aid the Union cause by all means in their power, and especially to aid the heads of the departments in the necessary labor of clarifying the civil service of the large disloyal element found in every branch of it. Washington was, from the first, open to entrance and exit, and practically remained so till Lee's surrender. Alexandria was held in enforced loyalty, and communication both by river and railroad maintained between the two cities; no one was obliged to secure a permit, unless to enter the rebel lines. Much of the contraband communication between the enemy and their numerous and active friends in Washington was kept up by women messengers and carriers; their garments became literally a mantle of charity. With a corps of trained detectives, Baker's headquarters were constantly enlivened by tales of the adventures of these fair " Secesh " blockade-runners.[1]

The first jury case in which I was engaged before the District Supreme Court was a suit for libel against Mr. Clephane. As chairman of his committee he had reported to Mr. Stanton that a clerk in the War Office was disloyal, and gave particulars. The Secretary promptly removed the clerk. A friend sent a copy of Mr. Clephane's communication to the party accused, who promptly commenced an action for libel. On the trial to a *subpœna duces tecum* the Secretary personally appeared, and made

---

[1] *The Secret Service*, by General Baker, has many varying accounts of their adventures, and there has sprung up quite a literature, the heroines of which are from the ranks of this useful service.

return with an affidavit that the communication was privileged.   On argument, Justice Olin so ruled, and then absurdly held that an action could be maintained upon it, and the plaintiff could prove the writing by a copy.   The jury returned a heavy verdict, and we took the case to the General Term, which reversed it, Olin giving the opinion of the court.[1]

---

[1] This case brought me professionally under Mr. Stanton's notice.   The answer to the *subpœna* was made and prepared under my advice, and led to my employment by him in many cases.   Colonel Wm. A. Cook appeared with me in the case.

I may here add that many of the Northern States had agents stationed at the Capital to look after their soldiers and military interests generally ; Mr. Cook was the resident agent of Pennsylvania, and hence his title.   I was employed in the case at his instance.

CHAPTER XLV.

CONGRESS—SECOND SESSION.

DECEMBER, 1864—APRIL, 1865.

The Thirteenth Amendment—Rebel Prisoners of War—Rebel Prisons—
The Evacuation of Richmond.

THE 38th Congress convened for its second session on
the 5th of December, 1864. Those familiar with the 13th,
and greatest, of the amendments to the Constitution, will
remember that it passed the Senate March 28th, of the
first session, by 38 to 6. The members of the House, as
will be remembered, had been elected in the dark days of
1862 ; the amendment was brought to vote there on the
14th of June ; the vote showed 93 for to 65 against it, and
23 not voting ; among these last were Henry Winter
Davis, Theodore M. Pomeroy, and several other Republicans. Mr. Lincoln had this measure greatly at heart.
Early in this second session, after long and earnest consultation, the task of securing the requisite two thirds of the
House for a final struggle was committed to the hands of
Mr. Ashley of Ohio. The trouble now would not be with
any of the Republicans, but two or three Democrats were
absolutely necessary. Finally we were told, in confidence
of course, that Mr. Ashley could report the acquisition.
A New Yorker greatly desired a federal place in New
York ; he had a brother, a Democrat, in the House, who

was assured that his vote for the abolishing amendment would largely augment his brother's chances.   There was also a contest for a seat in the next House—a Democrat in the present House was a party to that contest; he came to see that the result would depend entirely upon his vote on the impending 13th amendment.   It was found necessary to secure the absence of one Democrat from the House on the day of the vote.   A railroad in Pennsylvania was threatened with the passage of a bill by Congress greatly adverse to its interests—the bill was in Mr. Sumner's hands, ready to be reported; the road had struggled to have action on the bill *deferred till the next Congress*—thus far without avail.   The lawyer for the railroad was a Democratic member of the present House.

The vote was taken in that body on the 14th of January, 1865, and resulted in there being 119 for and 56 against, 8 not voting.   The amendment was carried; upon the announcement of the result the Republicans breaking into the wildest demonstrations of joy and excitement.   When that subsided, they adjourned the House, and the demonstrations were renewed.

As I was informed, the two Democrats voted for the amendment, and the railroad's lawyer *was taken so ill* that he could not be carried to the House; the New Yorker had the coveted post; the Democrat secured his seat in the 39th Congress, and the august Sumner *did not* report the bill during that session.[1]

Late in December, 1864, the earnest attention of both Houses was turned to the condition of our soldiers held in rebel prisons.   It was said that the enemy held about 45,000 of ours, and that we had 80,000 or 90,000 of theirs. Just why there was not an exchange was a sore prob-

---

[1] I do not vouch for the means employed to secure the Democrats. Everything else is a matter of record, and warrants the belief of its truth.

lem to Congress.   Mr. Cox offered a resolution of inquiry as to why an exchange was not made; Mr. Stevens thought it a reflection on the War Office, but after some debate the resolution was adopted.

In January, 1865, Mr. Wade introduced a joint resolution in the Senate, prescribing the same treatment for the rebel soldiers in our hands as that given to ours held by them.   The resolution provoked much discussion, and the whole ground was gone over with great feeling and much earnestness.   Mr. Sumner proposed and procured the adoption of an amendment modifying the character of the resolution to one condemnatory of the practice of the enemy, and enjoining a humane and Christian treatment of the prisoners in our hands—which was adopted.

On the 18th of January, Mr. Ganson of New York offered a resolution in the House for thorough inquiry as to the number and cause of arrest of persons confined in the old Capitol and Carroll prisons, to be made by the Military Committee ; it was adopted, and Mr. Stevens of Pennsylvania moved a reconsideration, which was debated at length.   Mr. Garfield, who had been to the prisons in execution of a resolution, came into the House while the debate was in progress, and made a sharp speech against the motion to reconsider, and this motion was defeated by the decisive vote of 136 yeas to 5 nays.   This led to a general liberation of the unfortunate prisoners.

January 20th, the House called upon the President, Secretary of State, and Secretary of War to report the names of all persons arrested and held for any offense against the United States and still held in custody.   This action, both as to prisoners of war and prisoners arrested without due process of law, showed a healthy sentiment in the two Houses for the rights of individuals as to their liberty of person and humane treatment.

Innumerable resolutions and bills were introduced, debated, and disposed of, bearing directly upon the war ;

upon each and all of these, Senators and Representatives invariably divided on party lines.

One among them was a gratuitous resolution declaring that rebel States were not entitled to representation in the Electoral College for the choice of President and Vice-President for the term of office commencing March 4, 1865.

Through the winter the Capital was free in its immediate vicinity from the alarms of war.

Something we heard of that curious episode—the conference of the President and Secretary of State with Alexander H. Stephens, R. M. T. Hunter, and John A. Campbell, held at Fortress Monroe, on the 3d of February, 1865; it was initiated by the elder Francis P. Blair, who visited Richmond in January, and the whole is set forth in Mr. Seward's letter to Mr. Adams, at the Court of St. James, under date of January 9th, and sent to the Senate on its request.

The conference lasted four hours, without the presence of secretaries or reporters, and was wholly oral.   Mr. Davis's envoys really wanted an armistice; Mr. Lincoln wanted a disbanding of the rebel army.   Of course nothing came of it, for which the Union men of the Capital were thankful.   It was a pure pretence on the part of the South to gain time.   This plan failing, the rebel Congress passed an act to arm their slaves.

We were sensitive over the planting of Maximilian in Mexico, and some of us would have been glad to see 50,000 soldiers, with Sheridan at their head, drive the Austrians off the continent.   Yet we were willing to see this postponed until we were in possession of Richmond, and for that end things were ripening faster than we realized.

We knew that Sherman had reached Savannah—knew of Hood's defeat at the decisive battle of Franklin; but Grant's inaction at City Point we did not understand; it seemed to us like torpor, which we did not at all approve of. We had watched the filling of the quotas of the new levy by the States, and had noted that the conscription was peacefully carried out. We supposed the interview at Fortress Monroe was sought by the rebels in the hope of a respite in which to recruit. We were confirmed in this when we heard of efforts by the Richmond Government to strengthen its armies, and the enactment of laws for arming the blacks. We felt, rather than knew, that the Confederacy was exhausted, while we were never so strong, never in such high spirits, so determined and so confident ; surely the end was near.

We had in the field on the 1st of March, of all arms, 965,000 men, of whom over 600,000 were effective for duty. The army of the Confederacy had been on the decline steadily during 1864 and the early part of 1865.

Marching orders were issued on the 31st of January to the Second, Fifth, Sixth, and Ninth Corps of the Army of the Potomac. The rapid progress of Sherman warranted this movement. The indications of Lee's weakness rapidly multiplied, and toward the end of March it was apparent that the collapse of the armed rebellion was a thing of days, and the President went to the front to be on the ground when the crisis culminated.

On April 2d, the Secretary of War gave out two telegraphic dispatches from the President of the closing scenes. On the 5th his bulletin to General Dix announced the evacuation of Richmond on Sunday, the dissolution of the Confederate Government,—its Executive and Cabinet having fled,—and of the occupation by General Weitzel.[1]

---

[1] I remember well a little scene on Monday A.M., when we heard of the fall of Richmond. I was at the War Office on some business matter, when a telegram to Mr. Stanton, just received, was read aloud. In a minute the whole department was in an uproar ; men rushed into each other's arms with cries and tears like long separated brothers or lovers ; an hour was required

On the 9th the terms of the surrender of Lee at Appomattox were signed.

At ten o'clock that night Secretary Stanton ordered a salute of two hundred guns to be fired at the Capital, at the headquarters of every Army Department of the United States, and at every post and arsenal. On the evening of the 11th, the White House, public buildings, and Union residences were illuminated. This was the real end of the war in the field, though some soldiers were still to be slain, and one or two armies remained to be surrendered.

I remember the day of President Lincoln's second inauguration. We had access to the roof of the Colonization Building on Pennsylvania Avenue, which gave a commanding view of the pageant. It was a warm, smoky day, with dun-colored, cumulus clouds floating up from the southern horizon, with fitful yellow sunshine and no rain. A curious celestial phenomenon, generally observed in the city, appeared at about 11 A.M. Almost directly at the zenith, like a small, sharply pointed diamond, shining by its own light, strong eyes could see a star. It was mentioned in some of the public prints of the day, but seems to have passed from the popular memory.[1]

---

to reduce even the clerks to order, and many did not return to their desks the next day. And this after *four years !* Joy over great events affects men peculiarly. There was in one of the corridors a small group of five or six distinguished gentlemen, when one of them proposed to "all go and get drunk." They immediately left the building, and twenty minutes later I met one of the party quite overcome with joy and whiskey. The proposition struck me then, and now, as unique, and where they secured fluid of such dynamite power I cannot imagine. The loyal part of the city was quite given up to exuberant rejoicing. We heard something of the mourning and grief of the Southern sympathizers ; many families had husbands, sons, or brothers in the Southern army, or employed as clerks in the departments at Richmond. We had no notice of their going, we knew nothing of their return, and no one was ever questioned for joining the rebels.

[1] Unpleasantly impressionable, though free from superstition, the sharp vision of that star seemed to give me a mental stab which is always repro-

Lincoln's inaugural address of the occasion was most masterly, and regarded by some as the best of his many remarkable utterances, the last, and in some respects the most memorable, was in response to a serenade at the White House, on the evening of April 11th, after his return from the last Virginia campaign, in which he discussed the statue of the Confederate States, and redeveloped something of his plan for restoring them to their places in the Republic, which he illustrated in the case of Louisiana.

How events of the gravest magnitude grouped and pressed each other in these last days! and the sad, weary look of the President's face seemed about to give place to serene satisfaction—when for him the end came.

His eyes—surely the saddest and most solemn that ever looked on the wars of a sorrowing world—had seen the surrender of Lee, his feet had pressed the recovered soil of Virginia, had trodden the streets of the enemies' capital, and he now saw himself ruler of the whole recovered country, with no slaves upon its soil and with no armed foe within its borders.

It is not necessary for me to linger over the incidents of those last days which are still fresh in the memory of the survivors.

---

duced upon the mention of that weird day. I remember that the music of the bands was to me like a funeral march.

It recalls the incident in the inaugural procession of President Garfield, in which a hearse became involved and moved a block in front of the President's carriage.

CHAPTER XLVI.

THE DEATH OF THE PRESIDENT.

APRIL, 1865.

L. C. Baker's Wonderful Detective Feat—Death of Booth.

THE events of the night of April 14, 1865, are ever at my recall. Mrs. Riddle, a friend or two, the younger of our household, and myself, were spending the evening quietly together in our family-room, when a little past 9 o'clock I heard the quick step of our eldest daughter hurrying up the stairs followed by the rapid tread of her escort— they had been at Ford's Theatre to see Laura Keene in *Our American Cousin.* Throwing open the door, and with pale, frightened face and wild eyes, she managed to gasp out : " O Father ! Wilkes Booth has shot the President. He leaped down upon the stage and rushed back, and im- mediately a tall man [1] from the crowd rushed after him." This was confirmed by the pale-faced young gentleman who stood in the doorway.

The savage old spirit to kill came upon me again ; seiz- ing my Remingtons and the gift of my Cuban friend, I was soon in the street. Already there was a murmur of excited voices, and a shiver of fright all through the city. It was a square and a half to Stanton's on K Street,

[1] Colonel J. B. Stewart would certainly have captured Booth had not the stage carpenter closed a door in his face. He was then a partner of the author.

where a few were hastily gathering ; the thousand-tongued rumor repeated the assassination of the President and added the names of Vice-President Johnson, Seward, and others of the Cabinet. I rushed on to Seward's—I knew Mr. Johnson was out of the city, and came to realize something of the nature and extent of the conspiracy, which that night and for several days was supposed to include a large band of active conspirators in the city, leagued to take the lives of the President, Cabinet officers, and other leading men. For a time the structure of the government seemed shattered, days passed and its machinery moved by the law of inertia.

There was a moon in the half-clouded sky that night, lending a weird effect as the shadows and lights moved over the scene. Several of us, after hasty consultation, dispersed each to visit designated points of the city and look for suspected persons or signs of their presence. The river was patrolled—the exits by the eastern branch (Anacostia) and Georgetown. I patrolled the boundary from 14th to 7th streets ; luckily no suspicious-looking person met my eyes, and the revolvers were not taken out of their places. Much later, in the trial of John H. Suratt, in which I represented the State Department, it was shown that he had made his way out of the city on the north side towards Baltimore.

I saw nothing of Major Webb or his police that night, though there was no complaint of them. The Major was at his post.

For the time, save in the person of Secretary Stanton, the general government was in abeyance. The Chief-Justice, as well as the other judges, for the time, resolved themselves into commissioners to receive testimony, and devoted many days to taking the statements of every person who had, or who pretended to have, information tending to throw light on any part of the transactions of that night.

The Secretary of War offered a large reward for the persons suspected. The city of Washington offered $20,000 for the apprehension of the assassins, and detectives from all of the great cities hurried to the Capital and set themselves to work in the case.

The President ceased to breathe during the ensuing night, and was laid in state at the Capitol, and finally the funeral cortège, with the Nation's dead, took its way to distant Springfield (Illinois), and still there was no glimmer of light upon the hiding-place or course of flight of Wilkes Booth. A week elapsed and the indignant and impotent grief of the Nation was augmented by a conviction sunk into the souls of men, that the murderers had escaped, that the police of the loyal Republic, notwithstanding the magnitude of the crime and the fame and money awaiting the capture of the assassins, were unequal to their task.

L. C. Baker, Chief of the Military Bureau, was absent from the Capital on duty. He returned to Washington, in response to a summons, on the 16th day of April, to find the whole field in the possession of his rivals and enemies, who refused to share with him their information or theories, or to furnish the least aid, if any were in their power. He was obliged to take the case up as wholly new, with many of the first clues and indications practically effaced by the lapse of days.

He came to the conclusion that Booth and Harrold had or would escape into Virginia by the way of lower Maryland and the Potomac, and that they would seek refuge in the land of the rebels. On the 24th, he sent one of his men into lower Maryland with a telegraph expert, and placed an attachment on a wire connecting with his headquarters. Two days later that man brought an old negro to him from whom Baker claimed to learn that, on Saturday night, the 22d, two men had crossed the Potomac into Virginia, near Matthews Point, in a boat, and that one of them was lame. These, he decided, must have been the fugitives; from the description, the lame man was doubtless Booth, who in his flight had received an injury.

An order from Secretary Stanton placed under Baker's orders Lieutenant Dougherty, of the 16th New York Cavalry, and twenty-five soldiers. Baker put the troop under the command of Lieutenant-Colonel O. E. Conger, formerly of his regiment, aided by Lieutenant Baker, of the same, a nephew of L. C. Baker, recently mustered out but then in Baker's service.

Before the starting of the party, the Chief spread out a map of Virginia and designated the crossing-place of the fugitives and the place where they had probably landed ; then, taking a compass, he placed one point at Port Conway, where a road crossed the Rappahannock, and drew a circle, which he said included a space of ten miles around that point, and within that territory they would find the fugitives. The party got off at once, crossed safely, and moved on all night. At the ferry named, late the next day, they received certain information of the fugitives, who were captured after midnight of the second night within Baker's circle.[1]

The conception and successful execution of Baker's scheme, of the arrest of Booth and Harrold, must certainly rank with the most famous exploits in the wide field of detection.

One incident of it deserves further mention. The old negro informant is to be relegated to the realm of myth ; all the means taken to reproduce him were futile ; *he was*

---

[1] *History of the Secret Service*, L. C. Baker, Philadelphia, p. 552. The sworn statement of Colonel Conger and Lieutenant Baker at length, written by the author at their dictation. Later, I brought a suit for these parties against the city of Washington, to recover the reward. Lieutenant Dougherty and Boston Corbett were concerned, and all their depositions were taken in full. Later, when the case was ended, the Court issued an order permitting me to withdraw all the papers, which are now in my possession— a complete and verified narration of this episode in our history, and of the parts performed by the deponents severally.

never again heard of or found, and became the theme of the unsparing gibes and sarcasms of Baker's rivals and enemies.

He was a pure creation of the genius of L. C. Baker. His intuitive grasp of the conditions of the case made it certain that the assassins would seek cover in Virginia. His study of the map and the formation of the two sides of the river demonstrated the crossing-place, time, and course of flight inland. For the execution of his conception he could trust to the fertile resources of Colonel Conger. He was himself too well known, and by too many persons, to conduct the expedition personally.

The old negro was a necessary creation, to *give color* as a real informant, and to make seeming ground on which the expedition could rest ; and those who derided the invention unconsciously did homage to the genius of the inventor.

On the return of Baker's party, the Secretary of War doubted, as did many, the accuracy of his statements, that Booth was slain and Harrold captured, which yielded only to the identification of the dead Booth and living prisoner.

CHAPTER XLVII.

LAST WORDS.

MAY–JULY, 1865.

The War over—The Grand Review—Some Final Words of Abraham
Lincoln—Mr. Stanton's Exit.

THE war was over. The two great armies of Grant and
Sherman were assembled and encamped near Washington
for the final grand review, previous to their disbanding
and the return of the soldiers to their distant homes. On
the 22d of May the army of Grant, moving from the west
by companies, solemnly and silently marched past the re-
viewing-stand of the President in front of the White
House, 170,000 strong. All day long, from curb to curb,
with their battle-torn banners, wheeling now to the right
at Fifteenth Street, and New York Avenue, and then
to the left, on Pennsylvania Avenue, were they marching
on to the East front of the Capital not breaking until
night for their camps.

On the day following, with the same impressive silence
and strength, marched Sherman's scarcely less numerous
brigades. For hours I stood just below the President's
stand, my eyes filled with unconscious tears, as rank after
rank of these solemn faced war-scarred veterans smote the
earth with their simultaneous tread: the infantry, with
their rifled muskets and bayonets; the artillery, which performed the service of its arm; the cavalry, which had

steadily advanced in merit and achieved as high a prestige as ever reached by cavalry; it was these men, *these who had fought out the war.* Thus the war ended.

What strange visions of war vicissitudes flashed on the imagination as Custer's horsemen passed, each man with a pink ribbon at his throat for identity; and how we recall the dramatic incident of their chief holding the head of his column for space, which, when gained, his horse, breaking from the restraint of the hand, dashed over it at full speed, to be turned back that his rider might again "witch the world with noble horsemanship."

Two things were observed of the Sherman army: the marked superiority in height and personal bearing of the Western men over the men of the Army of the Potomac; and the obvious fact that they were in large part of the same rank and class in civil life with their officers.

Some final words of Mr. Lincoln, of the man as he appeared to me, and I speak from my personal impressions wholly. He was not a leader, a commander of men, nor yet one born to rule, as men understand that term. In the great war he could not pose as a royal Bourbon with golden crest and *fleurs de lis;* nor as a belted Bearnese prince, the royal Knight of Navarre; nor yet as a Murat at the head of his charging column; or a Pickett storming the iron- and steel-clad heights.

He was in no common usage of the term a leader. He was a Manager of men, of the rarest aptitude; a Persuader of wonderful endowments; a Conductor of nations, peoples,—and he was of special gifts.

To him the war was an embodied force, endowed, shapeless, and vast, with power to impress him who in a reverent spirit and an all-trusting heart should docilly seek and await its communing.

Coming not from the *scum* but from the *dregs* of the people, inheriting its folk-lore, its traditions, its superstitions, its faith in signs, and in the deliverings of its half-witch

22

crones, who deal in charms and foretell fates, and of whom
people of ordinary culture have not the slightest knowledge; this strangely gifted man with this origin, placed at
the nation's head in this crisis of its career, was to conduct it through to the firm ground of peace and safety.
I see him bending patiently at the feet of the great war,
seeking its teaching, questioning of any who had a word
to say—not alone of the world's wise, but of the lowly,
the far down—if haply some one would utter the word
which should bring the charm of deliverance. God only
knows of all with whom he took counsel; listening, bowed
in the depths of his soul for the inner voice to the inner
ear, felt rather than heard, and making those great utterances of what was thus given him, to the common folk
about him.   All his givings forth were to these—whether
messages, State papers, proclamations, or from the ros-
trum.

None of the great, the chosen ones, claim to have
shaped the policy of the war. Nor was it the result of
their many counsels. It was conceived in, or imparted
to, the solitary soul of that rare man. The human soul is
ever solitary. Its organs and faculties lie rudimentary
and voiceless in the prison-house of earth, and when the
man is set apart by his fellows and is dedicated to the
awful responsibility of the safety of a great people, of
many peoples, struggling in the grasp of the world's
crisis, the soul is thrice set apart and doomed to awful
solitude. None but God can commune with it.

The awakening, uprising, and arming of the peoples of
the North was as the great movements of the primitive
tribes and races in the older times. They were to traverse
unknown land—land newly formed, which no human foot
had ever trod. Abraham Lincoln was their conductor,
their chosen of God and of man. One so unique, before,
never appeared on this earth. A conductor, not a leader
with pomp and trumpets and banners, but on foot, walk-

ing as one of the common mass which his height commanded, where his heart and sympathies ever were, where
next to God his trust and hope and confidence rested.
With what care and solicitude he inspected every rood to
be traversed of the unknown land covered by brooding
twilight.   There might lie hidden in its depths a bottom-
less quicksand—

> " A gulf profound as that Serbonian bog
> Betwixt Damiata and Mount Casius old,
> Where armies whole had sunk."

With the advanced and leading was his place.   Many
were prospecting and skirmishing ahead of him, ever turning and looking to him for indications of the course.
Eager men, delegations of the clergy, importuned him to
turn this way, turn that way, or all would be lost.   He
put them by with apt stories in· the structure and language of the common people, extemporized, but full of
pith and local color.   To the eager and impatient he
seemed to loiter, stand still; men upbraided, denounced,
frantically urged and implored him to move forward, to
strike here, there, anywhere, and rush on; they scoffed
and derided him.   His faith was in the people, the average common folk, who to a man, to a woman, to a child,
loved and trusted him.   He knew and he moved only as
they moved with him in their might and multitude, sub-
jugating the new, strange land as they went, so that a
second crusade would be impossible.   As he and they
moved their pace was accelerated, their enthusiasm
kindled, and their final impact swept the unformed Confederacy from the earth.

   To me his greatness consists in the docility with which
he apprehended the lessons of the war, in the singleness
of purpose and certainty with which he obeyed them.

   During the conflict the energies of those remaining
loyal to the Republic were intently given to its restora-

tion under the command of the President, who had developed to be the true head of the Nation. In a way, he was regarded by the masses as the Nation, the State, as were despotic rulers, and our experience made us acquainted with the forces and ways which, in a people less developed politically, would transform a constitutional ruler into an irresponsible dictator. The blow which struck him down appeared for an hour to dissolve the State. Chaotic visions of blood seemed palpable for a night.[1]

The close of the great career was as dramatic as a conception of old Greek tragedy. Mr. Lincoln was present at the great surrender, his feet trod the streets of the hostile capital, and then he passed away. His assassin had not the manliness to stand in arms with the enemy, nor the patriotism to be on the side of the Republic. Consumed by the ambition to be ranked with the assassins of Henry IV. and William the Silent, he in turn fell by the hands of a crazed religionist, and his grave was long unknown.[2]

Andrew Johnson succeeded to Abraham Lincoln's theories and plans. In his temporary eclipse in a private

---

[1] So entirely had Mr. Lincoln won the heart and soul of the masses, that the common mind accepted his decision as right in all cases, beyond criticism or cavil. One of the gravest of all the problems springing from secession was the reconstruction of the Republic. Unquestionably the President was wrong both as to the depository of the power and the best method of reconstruction. Yet we have seen that the people stood as one with him, and denounced the before-ever-trusted Wade ; Ohio repudiated him, and the brilliant Winter Davis had to leave Congress. What would have been the result had Lincoln lived?

[2] I was asked to aid in the defence of Mrs. Suratt. On the trial of her son, extradited and returned by the efforts of the Secretary of State, Mr. Seward asked me to appear and aid in his prosecution. On the trial it came out that, after the conviction of his mother by the military commission which tried the conspirators, the Government offered that if John H. would surrender himself to the United States, his mother should be unconditionally pardoned. He was then secreted in Baltimore, and we were morally certain, from the proof, that this was conveyed to the wretched son, whose only response was flight to Rome, where he took service with the Pope's Zouaves.

hospital, with Mr. Seward hovering between life and death from the hands of one of the assassins, and the Chief Justice remaining Chief Justice, the Secretary of War was the only man of the government who was equal to the occasion. For two or three days he was the government—the sole recognized source of authority and power ; and both by official position and a born nature to rule he was one in whose hands a nation, a people, can find safety in emergencies. The picturesque and trying days of President Johnson (a modified prolongation of the war, in Washington) are beyond my present field of labor. They will prove the most difficult for the real historian when he comes, as they were certainly the most trying for Secretary Stanton, with whom I am for a moment to linger.

On the surrender of Lee, Mr. Stanton tendered his resignation to Mr. Lincoln, who induced him to remain, Mr. Johnson being at this time in the care of the Blairs, who were not friends of the Secretary. In the first days of the new President's rule, Montgomery Blair concurring, he placed himself in the hands of Senator Wade as his leading adviser, and this association put him at one with the radicals for a brief space. These were the days of breathing vengeance and punishment for treason, and even Wade could not induce him to forego wide punishment.[1]

Mr. Seward recovered and resumed his old place at the head of the board, when a change marked the course of the President. The Republican Congress that had adjourned with a sense of security, convened in the 39th Congress to be confronted by the President and his reconstructed States ; and then came a contest almost as deadly as that of the rebellion.

The majority of the two Houses humiliated the President—bound him hand and foot, by the " Tenure of

---

[1] I was present at one of his early interviews with Mr. Wade, and do not speak from hearsay. That was the occasion when, at the President's request, the Senator selected the dozen upon whom justice might be expended.

Office " Act passed over his solemn veto. Finally the President suspended the Secretary of War, and General Grant became Secretary, *ad interim.*

The President was suspected of conspiracy to overthrow Republican rule, by the withdrawal of the Northern Democrats from the House and Senate, and the recognition of the Southern Representatives and Senators, thus forming another Congress, to be sustained as such by the President, with the army, if necessary. I always doubted his connection with any such scheme, though I do not doubt its being proposed to him, and the first attempt to impeach him failed. Congress sat on its own adjournments pursuant to its own acts, passed over the Executive veto. Finally, the President removed, or undertook to remove, the Secretary of War in violation of the Tenure of Office Act, and the House impeached him—a grave mistake.'

The President had been a warm admirer and friend of the Secretary of War, and had retained him against the advice of his nearest personal friends, and had tried in vain to win him to his sudden and complete change of policy in reference to the Confederate States and their leaders. This, of course, before Mr. Stanton's suspension.

Under the existing conditions, painful and repulsive to every impulse of his nature, Mr. Stanton felt constrained to remain in the War Office, though long absent from the councils of his nominal chief.

The services of a general at the head of an army are capable of estimation, as are those of a leading legislator. There are no means of rewarding the labors of a Cabinet Minister in this country, nor can the responsibilities of Mr. Stanton be easily compared with those of Mr. Chase or Mr. Seward. His labors were very great, and probably no other man of his time could have performed them so well.

---

[1] I was asked to aid the managers in preparing the evidence, and declined. By my advice, L. C. Baker declined to aid in this also.

Stanton's services were too great for any formal recognition or reward by Congress or by his countrymen ; and wisely neither made the attempt. General Grant appointed him Associate Justice of the Supreme Court, and he was pleased with the post. He was a very able lawyer, a really great advocate, and, like advocates in general, he may have seen one side of the case too intensely to be able at once to take a judicial balance. Great advocates do not always make great judges, though Mr. Stanton was more than an advocate—he was a man great in action, and could not have failed.

However, death intervened before he assumed the robes, and before the earth closed over him there were men who said that the end was by his own hand, and from remorse! Remorse for what, in the name of things holy ? From time to time this groundless tale against the memory of the great Secretary takes its ghastly flight through the land, and perhaps will continue to, however persistently slain.[1]

---

[1] For a final analysis and summing up of Mr. Stanton, see Appendix II.

APPENDIX I.

ADDRESS DELIVERED AT CLEVELAND ON THE EVENING OF THE
EXECUTION OF JOHN BROWN ; READ IN THE HOUSE
BY REQUEST OF HON. S. S. COX.

LADIES AND GENTLEMEN : These are strange, eventful days
and times, full not only of portents and omens, but incidents of
great moment, filled with the startling conclusions of old logic,
and the fulfilment of old prophecy. .

Never in the world's history were old dogmas and formulas
so rudely catechised, and old shams and seemings so irrever-
ently pulverized ; never before did men cast themselves so
boldly upon their convictions ; never before were the dreams
of old speculation so realized ; never before did opinion so
congeal into conduct, and thought become embodied action.
And never before did events by such sharp, crisp turns bring
men face to face with unexpected conclusions—as if by a flash
of revelation.

This is a day, not a fraction of a week or month, but a full,
complete day. This is an event—not an item—a mere incident. It may be an era, opening up a new way ; it is at least
a most portentous way-mark. These unwonted manifestations are not the mutterings and incantations of party con-
jurers ; they are the voices of the gathering storm. This glare
is real, red, live lightning, leaping fresh from the embodied
tempest. This tremor is not the weakness of coward knees,
but the shudder of the solid earth in its recoil from the deed
of to-day.

Wherein is the significance of this act, that has caused unseen hands to drape these walls in funereal weeds, and the bells throughout the land instinctively to toll out their knell ? Is it because John Brown is dead ? John Browns have died before. Has a man been strangled ? The gallows-tree has stood darkly against the background of human history, affrighting heaven and appalling earth with its hideous, ghastly fruit, since the dawn of civilization ! Men do not revere murder and venerate treason. It is not because Virginia has executed a culprit. Virginia did not do it. Embodied and in the presence of the two hemispheres of the Republic, slavery seized its eternal contrary in the person of John Brown, and with the gleam and pomp of military display, at mid-day, ostentatiously put him to death ! It is that which sends this mortal shiver through the land.

It matters nothing that this has been done under the form of law ; that the facts written by history upon the forms of eternity were sworn to by so-called witnesses ; nothing, that men, as jurors, hissed a verdict through teeth with which they would have torn their unshrinking victim ; and still less that an atrocious burlesque upon the Judiciary was executed by the thing upon the bench. The condemnation and death of John Brown are to be estimated by equites, in which the Throne of Eternal Justice alone has its foundation.' In these scales legal formulas are dead and weightless. Doctors of the Hebrew Law, by its letter, make a conclusive case against Jesus Christ, and show that His condemnation and execution, by the Roman " Governor Wise " of their " Virginia," were according to the forms of law ! And yet the faith and hope of Christendom rest on the basis that that judgment and death were the sacrificial and sacramental seals of the Messiahship which stamped the peasant-born, the Saviour of the world. In measuring this case by these eternal principles, do not quote "unions " and " compacts " and " constitutions " to me ! I deny their validity ! I pronounce them temporary and trashy when they attempt to contravene the Immutable !

A great while ago a gang of Portuguese pirates stole a cargo of Africans, and other pirates, French and English, stole other cargoes, and they were deposited in chains among the nebu-

lous forces out of which was to be formed a new State, mingled
with its elements while in the milk, and it grew up and became
organic, with slavery a part of its every fibre. And other
States sprang up around it with this thing growing also from
their seminal principles. And still other States, not having the
body of slavery in them, but poisoned with its malaria, came
and grouped themselves around this State. And all these
States formed a solemn league, an indissoluble compact and
law ; these slave States were treated as higher and better by
reason of slavery. They were expressly granted powers and
privileges solely and exclusively because they had it. And no
provision looking to its abrogation, nor a cessation of those
powers and privileges, was made. Not only so, but every State,
and all the free States and every man in them, were solemnly
pledged and enjoined to seize and return every fugitive from
slavery.

And so the States became a nation, and their peoples one
people ; and slavery became " king " ·and ruled, as it would,
royally—making and moulding parties, policies, and presidents,
stealing territory from one nation to extend itself in, and people from another to enslave upon it. Breaking down, at last,
the old Northern barrier, it thrust its fettered victims into our
faces and upon our soil. Our people were aroused ; they said
they would war against it, but they were powerless ; the Union
and Constitution walled them out ; the hand that would strike
was self-manacled ; the very breath with which they would exclaim against it was beaten out of their bodies. They were
estopped by their bond, and could feed a fleeing slave only by
stealth. Then arose John Brown, soldier and prophet ; do
not say he was crazy, do not think it, do not so cloud his
glory,—and scanning this slavery, said : " It was wrong, all
wrong, allied to nothing good or even indifferent, but wholly
wrong, no matter how old it is nor how deeply imbedded in
institutions ; no matter how guarded by State constitutions
and laws, nor how esteemed and revered as good. No matter,
though hedged in by the Union and walled round by the triple
bars of the national compact, though thirty-three crowned
sovereigns with arms in their hands stand around it, it is wrong,

and shall be dealt with as wrong. I cannot approach it
through the law,—that forbids me. I cannot strike it through
the Constitution,—that protects it. I cannot move the power
of the Union to crush it,—that shields it. Yet all revelation
commands me, all the instincts of humanity impel me, all the
voices of the free creation call me, and I fall back on the
eternal reservation of rights and obey." So said John Brown ;
and, seizing that old battle blade, with which the second
Frederick of Brandenburg clove down and hewed asunder the
holy alliances and slavery propaganda of the old world ; and
the same with which George Washington sundered the old
fetters of the new ; with this sword, coming thus lineally to
his hand, he struck one full blow, not at the Commonwealth of
Virginia (God bless her if He will !)—not at the Union
(Heaven help it if It can !)—not at any man nor thing, but
fully upon the iron fetters of Slavery, rusted with sweat and
crusted with gore, until their canker teeth had gnawed away
the muscles and had eaten out the hearts and lives of whole
generations of that unsinning race ! And it was for this that
Slavery seized him and choked his soul out of his body, and
thrust him back, cold, into the arms of the wife God had given
him.

And shall Slavery for all this repose in safety this one
night ? Shall it not imagine the soul of John Brown, in the
form of the red-visaged Angel of Retributive Wrath, hovering
on the pinions of fright and terror over all her doomed domain, distilling ghastly images of blood upon the starting eye-
balls of her cowering votaries ! And that blow, what a wonder
and what a revelation ! That little metallic clink, not so loud
as that which the sullen anvil gives back to the hammer, shook
a continent ; and its echoes and re-echoes as they repeat
grow louder and louder and shall never die away ! It shattered
the fetters of every slave in the land ; and could the Moses
have gone on, another Exodus would have been possible. It
revealed the utter, deathly weakness of slavery. At once and
forever it dissipated the cloud, the mystery, and darkness that
enshrouded it ; and an awakened world beheld it—empty and
hollow and naked and helpless and hopeless, languishing

and dying in its deformity, and there were no reverent sons walking backward with its garment to cover its unsightly hideousness from a mocking universe.

It revealed, too, the innate cowardice with which Slavery endows its worshippers ; making palpable the shapeless forms of dread that throng their paths by day and brood and cower around their hearths by night. All the manifestations, all the quaking images of white-faced fear driven mad, which the world has ever jeered at, have been outrun and forgotten in the shiverings of the " chivalry." It also revealed the radical cruelty which the " institution " plants in otherwise brave and noble natures ; demonstrating the anachronism of slavery itself ; which has brought out, amid the refinements of the nineteenth century, the qualities and characteristics of the rudest savage. I care not with what exterior grace the slave-holders discharge the outer amenities of ordinary life, nor with what solemnities they assume the name and fellowship of Christianity, they oblige us to pronounce ·them unreclaimed and unregenerated barbarians.

And what a revelation, too, this act has made of the character and conduct of John Brown himself, showing us that men of the grand old type, souls of the great heroic mould, are still possible, still have their birth in our land ; men who realize the images that have haunted our memories since the tales of our childhood.

The earth has never seen the paragon of that incident in the last struggle ; when everything had failed but the sacrifice, and as if "without the shedding of blood there could be no remission," and that the offering might be perfect, while one son lay dead before him, with the lapsing pulse of the other boy ebbing from under the fingers of one hand, with the other still grasping his rifle, the voice of the old soldier-prophet was still heard ringing out over the din of battle, calling the last of his band to death !

To-day the earth mourned in storm and darkness the departure of its truest child. To-day the " Pearly Gates " opened with light and gladness to the grandest soul that has passed their portals for the last thousand years !

APPENDIX II.

AT THE MEETING OF THE WASHINGTON BAR, COMMEMORATIVE
OF THE DEATH OF THE LATE HONORABLE EDWIN M.
STANTON, JANUARY 3, 1870.

Mr. Riddle spoke as follows :

Some things I want to say and probably the most inappro-
priate possible. The small conventionalities that determine
the fitness of little things I have never learned and I never
ask pardon for their violation.

There is a new-made grave in our midst, so large as to fill
all the land, and the earth that rounds it up is streaked with
the red of the great battle-fields of the continent, and I have
some words to say of him whose remains rest under it. Not
eulogy ! God forgive the man who attempts that. Anything
—words of earnest hate are more fitting than eulogy. Some
strong, forceful, earnest words, with meaning—or silence for
me. The sun, storm, and clouds may eulogize the rugged
mountain,—not I.

This was no ordinary man, and he lived in no ordinary time ;
and our common standard of weights and measures will not
apply to him. If I cannot comprehend him as he was I will
not attempt to dwarf him to my apprehension. There has
been and will be enough of lawyer talk over him. I will
speak of him as one of a primitive formation may speak of the
primal man.

I very well remember the close of that short, dark, rainy
day, eight years ago, when Senator Pearce told me that the

Senate had confirmed EDWIN M. STANTON as Secretary of
War. He said that Wade had endorsed him to the Republicans; and I remember my first impression when I met him the
next morning : the compact head, the pale, sad face, and the
deep light of his melancholy eyes that always conveyed to me
some mysterious message that I could never quite understand.

I attempt no analysis of the man. I speak of him from the
outside, and as he appeared as Secretary of War.

Those days were the beginning of the Exodus, when we
were gathering—a doubting, unknowing multitude—on the
shore of the Red Sea, the bosom of which was covered with
darkness ; how we shuddered and shrank from its icy
waters !

The great blow which had fallen, shattered the government
and sent us staggering back towards elementary conditions,
and our people stood forth not in the compacted strength and
unity of political organization, but reduced to simples, to individuals whose unity was the unity of blind, instinctive,
common impulse, and of vague, half-formed, and wholly
unexpressed purpose.

It was a blow that stripped high office of sanctity and
power to command, and men were heard and heeded only as
they were pointed out by natural fitness to command and
lead ; and such men had not appeared, and whether they
would come in the persons of those elected and summoned to
high places was then the sorest of problems.

Lincoln had not learned the rudiments of the terrible lesson
set for him, and his two leading secretaries seemed without
plans and almost without convictions.

Hundreds of thousands of men were arming and drilling,
marching and camping, fighting and buffeting, with some
blind, unformed, and hardly-felt purpose—an object yet to be
condensed and indurated from nebulous revolutionary elements hardly to be perceived ; and this man, unknown and
untried, not knowing himself, was launched into space and
bidden to become a new centre, to grasp out and to clutch to
himself this nebula and help to mould a fixed purpose, and to
shape and fashion raw material into organized and perfected

bodies, of a number and magnitude never dreamed of on this continent, and never surpassed by any nation in modern times ; and when so organized and perfected he was to supply the intelligence to direct, and impart the force that should propel these mighty agencies to the accomplishment of that purpose.

The twin Genii of Treason and Rebellion were tearing asunder the Republic, and the widening fissure threatened to swallow up, not merely *habeas corpus* and trial by jury, but the foundations and possibilities of civil government.

The ordinary machinery of laws and courts, such as we employ here, were but shreds of mockery, the instincts of men turned at once to the exhaustless source of reserved power that lies below and outside of conventional government.

The two houses of Congress, in the glare of volcanic fire, found new readings of the Constitution ; they became great executive councils, huge committees of ways and means. The ordinary functions of the government were in abeyance and all the primal energies of an aroused people went to inspire the brain and strengthen the arm of the Executive. The Executive was the government. Lincoln was the prominent figure before men's eyes, towering and growing colossal ; back of him was *Stanton ;* back of *Stanton,*—nothing.

There, upstairs in that ·dingy office on 17th Street, throbbed and worked the heart and brain and arm of the war, never ceasing, never fainting, never running low. There lay coiled, in awful tension, the mighty mainspring that drove with such terrible energy the gigantic machinery of the war.

"I used to think," said his associate at the bar (Mr. Phillips), "that his energy made him dangerous as a *nisi prius* lawyer." I think it might. What a luxury to him it must have been when he could liberate his boundless force and leave it to work at will in his limitless field ! And there never was a time, under the severest pressure, that there did not still lie unemployed in the man energy and power enough to propel the governmental machinery of the civilized world. Men say that he was rough. Of course he was. He was a primal force of nature, used to break up the old crust of the

23

earth, throw up new mountains, and change the configuration of a continent. I fancy him in twilight solitude, by some sounding sea, quarrying a mountain and throwing up a giant's causeway in a single night.

He at once grasped the sole purpose of our side—the extinction of rebellion by force. That was his task, and no fateful destiny ever moved more inexorably than he to its performance. He would see and hear and know nothing else ; whatever would help he used, whatever would hinder was ruthlessly thrust by, nothing could deter nor divert. To the world he was dark, cold, inscrutable, inexorable. Union soldiers were perishing or becoming idiots in Andersonville—he would rescue them by crushing Richmond, and would deal the blow when he got ready

How men hated him ! Did he know it ? Did he care ? Did men love him ? He never asked ; love was not necessary to him then. How he was lied about ! Did he hear it ? Whether he did or 'not, no word of his was ever uttered to contradict, deny, explain, or expose. Lies and liars were to him as if non-existent.

Though the earth wavered like a storm-tossed sea, he stood firm ; though it was covered from sight by dead men, he saw them not ; though the bosom of the storm discharged fire and blood and gobbets of mangled human flesh, he seemed unconscious of it.

Incorruptible ! With him was that a virtue ? The wavering, vacillating, changeable are bought, but when was *Stanton* ever known to change ? And of all the inducements to change, money would on him have been the least force. So inflexible were his resolves, I sometimes thought that human testimony had not the power to enlighten him.

How inscrutable that the stanch ship that had so defied and outrode the storm should go so suddenly down, under a sunny sky, in its harbor. After all, what was left for him ? The one place proper for him might never come to him. What other was there that he would not have to step down to ?

I confess, I think it best for him as it is—that now his nobler part should follow up that golden strand that connects this with the better life. I know how he is wanted by that mourning group, whose great bereavement veils them from our observation, and I know how intensely and tenderly he loved them ; as I know untold incidents that marked his heart as a fountain of the quickest, tenderest, and most exalted of human sensibilities.

After all, to me it seems well that the great seal of death should certify him and his case up to the high tribunal of impartial history. His services were too great for reward, or acknowledgment even, and his countrymen attempted neither.

I will not pretend to anticipate the place he will occupy in history ; nor will this nor the next generation of men know his position. We were all too near, too interested, and too prejudiced, too familiar with his features and career, and they do not strike us as they will strike strangers, looking at them through a purer atmosphere. We can form no conception of how even our rebellion and war will be estimated by the historian who shall finally analyze the events and place them where they belong in the world's annals.

Long hence, when this atmosphere is cleared and the light becomes white, when the sources of events are laid bare and the springs of action are disclosed, when all the hiding-places of information are revealed, some broad-browed, deep-eyed, thoughtful student of history, with infinite care, will construct the story of our struggle, and Lincoln and his Secretaries will take their rightful places. Long ere then we shall have passed away ; the pressing footsteps of thronging generations will have beaten the green roofs of our resting-places back to the level plain, and our names and memories will have perished from the earth.

Judge Cartter said :

" Let the resolutions be entered upon the records of the court."

APPENDIX III.

THE THIRTY-SEVENTH CONGRESS—STATES REPRESENTED.

CALIFORNIA.

SENATORS.

Milton S. Latham.   James A. McDougall.

REPRESENTATIVES.

Frederick F. Low.   (Took his seat June 3, 1862.)
Timothy G. Phelps.   Aaron A. Sargent.

CONNECTICUT.

SENATORS.

James Dixon.   Lafayette S. Foster.

REPRESENTATIVES.

Alfred A. Burnham.   James E. English.   Dwight Loomis.   George
C. Woodruff.

DELAWARE.

SENATORS.

James A. Bayard.   Willard Saulsbury.

REPRESENTATIVE.

George P. Fisher.

ILLINOIS.

SENATORS.

Stephen A. Douglas.   (Died June 3, 1861.)
Orville H. Browning.   (Appointed in place of Stephen A. Douglas,
deceased ; took his seat July 4, 1861.)
William A. Richardson.   (Elected senator in place of Stephen A.
Douglas, deceased, Orville H. Browning having been appointed
pro tem. ; took his seat January 30, 1863.)
Lyman Trumbull.

REPRESENTATIVES.

William J. Allen. (Elected in place of John A. Logan, resigned; took his seat June 2, 1862.)

Isaac N. Arnold. Philip B. Fouke.

Anthony L. Knapp. (Elected in place of John A. McClernand, resigned; took his seat December 12, 1861.)

William Kellogg.

John A. Logan. (Resigned in 1861.)

Owen Lovejoy.

John A. McClernand. (Resigned in 1861.)

William A. Richardson. (Elected senator in place of Stephen A. Douglas, deceased.)

James C. Robinson. Elihu B. Washburne.

INDIANA.

SENATORS.

Jesse D. Bright. (Expelled February 5, 1862.)

Henry S. Lane.

David Turpie. (Elected in place of Jesse D. Bright, expelled, Joseph A. Wright having been appointed *pro tem.* ; took his seat January 22, 1863.)

Joseph A. Wright. (Appointed in place of Jesse D. Bright, expelled; took his seat March 3, 1862.)

REPRESENTATIVES.

Schuyler Colfax. James A. Cravens. W. McKee Dunn. William S. Holman. George W. Julian. John Law. William Mitchell. Albert G. Porter. John P. C. Shanks. Daniel W. Voorhees. Albert S. White.

IOWA.

SENATORS.

James W. Grimes. James Harlan.

REPRESENTATIVES.

Samuel R. Curtis. (Resigned August 4, 1861.)

William Vandever. (Election unsuccessfully contested by Le Grand Byington.)

James F. Wilson. (Elected in place of Samuel R. Curtis, resigned; took his seat December 2, 1861.)

KANSAS.

SENATORS.

James H. Lane. (Election unsuccessfully contested by Frederick P. Stanton.)

Samuel C. Pomeroy.

REPRESENTATIVE.

Martin F. Conway.

KENTUCKY.

SENATORS.

John C. Breckinridge. (Expelled December 4, 1861.)
Garrett Davis. (Elected in place of John C. Breckinridge, expelled; took his seat December 23, 1861.)
Lazarus W. Powell.

REPRESENTATIVES.

Henry C. Burnett. (Expelled December 3, 1861.)
Samuel L. Casey. (Elected in place of Henry C. Burnett, expelled; took his seat March 10, 1862.)
John J. Crittenden. George W. Dunlap. Henry Grider. Aaron Harding. James S. Jackson (died in 1862). Robert Mallory. John W. Menzies. William H. Wadsworth. Charles A. Wickliffe.
Geo. H. Yeaman. (Elected in place of James S. Jackson, deceased; took his seat December 1, 1862.)

LOUISIANA.

REPRESENTATIVES.

Benjamin F. Flanders. (Took his seat February 23, 1863.)
Michael Hahn. (Took his seat February 17, 1863.)

MAINE.

SENATORS.

William Pitt Fessenden. Lot M. Morrill.

REPRESENTATIVES.

Samuel C. Fessenden.
Thomas A. D. Fessenden. (Elected in place of Charles W. Walton, resigned; took his seat December 1, 1862.)
John N. Goodwin. Anson P. Morrill. Frederick A. Pike. John H. Rice.
Charles W. Walton. (Resigned May 26, 1862.)

MARYLAND.

SENATORS.

Thomas H. Hicks. (Appointed in place of James A. Pearce, deceased; took his seat January 14, 1863.)
Anthony Kennedy.
James A. Pearce. (Died December 20, 1862.)

REPRESENTATIVES.

Charles B. Calvert. John W. Crisfield. Cornelius L. L. Leary. Henry May. Francis Thomas. Edwin H. Webster.

MASSACHUSETTS.

SENATORS.

Charles Sumner.   Henry Wilson.

REPRESENTATIVES.

John B. Alley.
William Appleton.   (Resigned in 1861.)
Goldsmith F. Bailey.   (Died May 8, 1862.)
James Buffinton.   Henry L. Dawes.   Charles Delano.   Thomas D.
  Eliot.   Daniel W. Gooch.
Samuel Hooper.   (Elected in place of William Appleton, resigned;
  took his seat December 2, 1861.)
Alexander H. Rice.   Benjamin F. Thomas.   Charles R. Train.
Amasa Walker.   (Elected in place of Goldsmith F. Bailey, deceased;
  took his seat December 1, 1862.)

MICHIGAN.

SENATORS.

Kinsley S. Bingham.   (Died October 5, 1861.)
Zachariah Chandler.
Jacob M. Howard.   (Elected in place of Kinsley S. Bingham,
  deceased; took his seat January 17, 1862.)

REPRESENTATIVES.

Fernando C. Beaman.   Bradley F. Granger.   Francis W. Kellogg.
Rowland E. Trowbridge.

MINNESOTA.

SENATORS.

Henry M. Rice.   Morton S. Wilkinson.

REPRESENTATIVES.

Cyrus Aldrich.   William Windom.

MISSOURI.

SENATORS.

John B. Henderson.   (Appointed in place of Trusten Polk, expelled;
  took his seat January 29, 1862.)
Waldo Porter Johnson.   (Expelled January 10, 1862.)
Trusten Polk.   (Expelled January 10, 1862.)
Robert Wilson.   (Appointed in place of Waldo Porter Johnson,
  expelled; took his seat January 24, 1862.)

REPRESENTATIVES.

Francis P. Blair, Jr.   (Resigned in 1862.)
William A. Hall.   (Elected in place of John B. Clark, expelled
  July 13, 1861; took his seat January 20, 1862.)

REPRESENTATIVES *(Continued).*
John W. Noell. Elijah H. Norton. John S. Phelps.
Thomas L. Price. (Elected in place of John W. Reid, expelled ;
took his seat January 21, 1862.)
John W. Reid. (Expelled December 2, 1861.)
James S. Rollins.

NEW HAMPSHIRE.

SENATORS.
Daniel Clark. John P. Hale.

REPRESENTATIVES.
Thomas M. Edwards. Gilman Marston. Edward H. Rollins.

NEW JERSEY.

SENATORS.
John C. Ten Eyck.
Richard S. Field. (Appointed in place of John R. Thompson,
deceased ; took his seat December 1, 1862.)
·John R. Thompson. (Died September 12, 1862.)
Jas. W. Wall. (Elected in place of John R. Thompson, deceased,
Richard S. Field having been appointed *pro tem.* ; took his seat
January 21, 1863.

REPRESENTATIVES.
George T. Cobb. John T. Nixon. Nehemiah Perry. William G.
Steele. John L. N. Stratton.

NEW YORK.

SENATORS.
Ira Harris. Preston King.

REPRESENTATIVES.
Stephen Baker. J. P. Chamberlain. Ambrose W. Clark. Frederick
A. Conkling. Roscoe Conkling. Erastus Corning. Isaac C.
Delapaine. Alexander S. Diven. R. Holland Duell. Alfred
Ely. Reuben E. Fenton. Richard Franchot. Augustus Frank.
Edward Haight. James E. Kerrigan. William E. Lansing.
Jas. B. McKean. Moses F. Odell. Abraham B. Olin. Theodore
M. Pomeroy. Charles B. Sedgwick. Socrates N. Sherman.
Edward H. Smith. Elbridge G. Spaulding. John B. Steele.
Burt Van Horn. Robt. B. Van Valkenburgh. Chas. H. Van
Wyck. Chauncey Vibbard. William Wall. Elijah Ward.
William A. Wheeler. Benjamin Wood.

OHIO.

SENATORS.

Salmon P. Chase. (Resigned March 6, 1861.)
John Sherman. (Elected in place of Salmon P. Chase, resigned; took his seat March 23, 1861.)
Benjamin F. Wade.

REPRESENTATIVES.

William Allen. James M. Ashley. John A. Bingham. Harrison G. Blake. Samuel S. Cox. William P. Cutler. Sidney Edgerton. John A. Gurley. Richard A. Harrison. Valentine H. Horton. John Hutchins. James R. Morris. Warren P. Noble. Robt. H. Nugen. George H. Pendleton. Albert G. Riddle. Samuel Shellabarger. Carey A. Trimble. Clement L. Vallandigham. Chilton A. White. Samuel T. Worcester.

OREGON.

SENATORS.

Edward D. Baker. (Died October 21, 1861.)
Benjamin F. Harding. (Elected in place of Edward D. Baker, deceased, Benjamin Stark having been appointed *pro tem. ;* took his seat December 1, 1862.)
James W. Nesmith.'
Benjamin Stark. (Appointed in place of Edward D. Baker, deceased ; took his seat February 27, 1862.)

REPRESENTATIVE.

George K. Shiel.

PENNSYLVANIA.

SENATORS.

Simon Cameron. (Resigned March, 1861.)
Edgar Cowan.
David Wilmot. (Elected in place of Simon Cameron, resigned ; took his seat March 18, 1861.)

REPRESENTATIVES.

Sydenham E. Ancona. Elijah Babbitt. Joseph Baily.
Charles J. Biddle. (Elected in place of E. Joy Morris, resigned.)
Samuel S. Blair. James H. Campbell.
Thomas B. Cooper. (Died April 4, 1862.)
John Covode. William Morris Davis.
Galusha A. Grow. (Elected Speaker July 4, 1861.)
James T. Hale. John Hickman. Philip Johnson. William D. Kelley. John W. Killinger. Jesse Lazear.
Wm. E. Lehman. (Election unsuccessfully contested by John M. Butler.)

REPRESENTATIVES *(Continued).*
Robert McKnight.   Edward Mcpherson.   James K. Moorhead.
John Patton.   Thaddeus Stevens.
John D. Stiles.   (Elected in place of Thomas B. Cooper, deceased ;
took his seat June 3, 1862.)
John P. Verree.   (Election unsuccessfully contested by John Kline.)
John W. Wallace.   Hendrick B. Wright.

RHODE ISLAND.
SENATORS.
Henry B. Anthony.
Samuel G. Arnold.   (Elected in place of James F. Simmons, re-
signed ; took his seat December 1, 1862.)
James F. Simmons.   (Resigned in 1862.)
REPRESENTATIVES.
George H. Browne.   William P. Sheffield.

TENNESSEE.
SENATOR.
Andrew Johnson.
REPRESENTATIVES.
George W. Bridges.   (Took his seat ·February 25, 1863.)
Andrew J. Clements.   (Took his seat January 13, 1862.)
Horace Maynard.

VERMONT.
SENATORS.
Jacob Collamer.
Solomon Foot.   (Elected president *pro tem.* July 18, 1861.)
REPRESENTATIVES.
Portus Baxter.   Justin S. Morrill.   Ezekiel P. Walton.

VIRGINIA.
SENATORS.
John S. Carlile.   (Elected senator in place of R. M. T. Hunter,
withdrawn ; took his seat July 13, 1861.)
Waiteman T. Willey.   (Elected in place of J. M. Mason, with-
drawn ; took his seat July 13, 1861.)
REPRESENTATIVES.
Jacob B. Blair.   (Elected in place of John S. Carlile, resigned ; took
his seat December 2, 1861.)
William G. Brown.
John S. Carlile.   (Resigned.)
Joseph E. Segar.   (Took his seat May 6, 1862.)
Charles H. Upton.   (Election unsuccessfully contested by S. F. Beach.)
Killian V. Whaley.

WISCONSIN.

SENATORS.

James R. Doolittle. Timothy O. Howe.

REPRESENTATIVES.

Luther Hanchett. (Died November 24, 1862.)

Walter D. McIndoe. (Elected in place of Luther Hanchett, deceased; took his seat January 26, 1863.)

John F. Potter. A. Scott Sloan.

COLORADO TERRITORY.

DELEGATE.

Hiram P. Bennett.

DAKOTA TERRITORY.

DELEGATE.

John B. S. Todd.

NEBRASKA TERRITORY.

DELEGATE.

Samuel G. Daily. · (Election unsuccessfully contested by J. Sterling Morton.)

NEVADA TERRITORY.

DELEGATE.

John Cradlebaugh.

TERRITORY OF NEW MEXICO.

DELEGATE.

John S. Watts.

UTAH TERRITORY.

DELEGATE.

John M. Bernhisel.

WASHINGTON TERRITORY.

DELEGATE.

William H. Wallace.

INDEX.

A

Act, of July 22, calling for 500,000 volunteers, 36; of July 29, increasing army, 36
Adams, C. F., referred to, 327
Adams, Captain, aids in capturing blockade runners, 245
Adams, J. Q., views on Oregon controversy, 73 ; house, 253
Alabama-Kearsarge, battle, 286
Alexander, Col. B. S., assists in defending Washington, 288
Alexandria re-ceded to Virginia, 16 ; war episode, 28
Alley, J. B. (app. iii., 358) ; favors 1862 Bond bill, 116
Allison, W. B., elected 38th Congress, 250
Amnesty proclamation of Lincoln, 298
Ames, Oakes, elected 38th Congress, 250
Anderson, C., nominated Lieut.-Gov. Ohio, 230 ; in Ohio campaign, 235
Andrew, Judge J. A., speaks in Lincoln campaign, 296 ; relations with Stanton, 321
Appleton, Wm., resignation, 101
Arkansas free State government, 300, 302
Arlington estate, 127
Army, efficiency in 1861, 33 ; increased, 36 ; position and size in 1861, 69-71 ; recruits at Washington, 77 ; daily expenses, 100; criticism on inactivity of, 186, 187; responds to Lincoln's war order

No. I., 188 ; negro soldiers added to, 209 ; regulations revised, 210 ; officers increased, 210 ; condition and needs of, in 1863, 252 ; reinforcements called for, 251 ; increased, 255 ; in 1865, 328
Army (Confederate), position and size in 1861, 70, 71 ; declines, 328
Army of the Potomac, size in 1861, 70 ; reorganized, 252 ; orders issued to, in 1865, 328
Arnold, I. N. (app. iii., 356) ; influence of, 33 ; favors ship canals, 212 ; and Mr. Riddle call Ship Canal Convention, 232, 233
Ashby's Black Horse cavalry, 50
Ashley, J. M. (app. iii., 360), member 37th Congress, 5 ; favors Thirteenth Amendment, 324
Atlanta, fall of, 297
Augur, Gen. C. C., commands troops defending Washington, 288; relations with Pardon Worsley, 310
Austria, sustains Maximilian in Mexico, 327

B

Backus, F. T., contests Mr. Riddle's candidacy, 4 ; Peace Commissioner, 6
Bailey, Commodore Theodorus, referred to, 238
Bailey, Dr. Gamaliel, editor *National Era*, 254
Baker, E. D. (app. iii., 360), senator 37th Congress, 6 ; speeches, 5, 6 ; referred to, 15, 177 ; war-

INDEX. 367

convened Dec. 2, 1861, 69; in session during holidays, 81; confronted by financial problem of 1862, 100; work of, 128; total appropriations of, 192; review of laws enacted by, 192–198; career of, 249–255

Congress (rebel) passes act arming slaves, 327

Congressional cemetery, 17

Congressional life and its influences, 225, 226

Conkling, F. A., speaks on Bond bill, 113, 114

Conkling, Roscoe (app. iii., 359), mem. 37th Cong., 30; opposes Crittenden compromise, 40; calls for information concerning Ball's Bluff disaster, 73; speech on Bond bill, 113; resolution aiding States voluntarily freeing slaves, 161; resolution concerning Ball's Bluff disaster, 168; speech on Ball's Bluff disaster, 169–175; personality of, 175; referred to, 227

Conqueror, blockade runner, 244, 245

Conscription laws, revised, 253; defects of old, 254

Conscription, resort to, 209; riots, 231, 232

Conway, M. F. (app. iii., 356), mem. 37th Cong., 30

Cooke, Jay, & Co., report gold fluctuations, 297

Cook, W. A., defends Lewis Clephane in libel suit, 323

Copperhead bands disloyal, 167

Corbett, Boston, referred to, 334

Corcoran, Michael, taken prisoner at Bull Run, 73

Corinth, referred to, battle of, 188

Corning, Erastus (app. iii., 359), mem. 37th Cong., 30; complimentary vote for Speaker, 31; mem. House com. on Banks and Currency, 101; mem. House Ways and Means Com., 101; opposes bond issue, 101

Corwin, Thomas, mem. 36th Cong., 6; opposes Crittenden compromise, 40; as orator, 296

Couch, Gen. D. N., defends Penn, against Early's raid, 286

Court of Claims, Lincoln's views concerning, 71

Covode, John (app. iii., 360), mem. 37th Cong., 30; on Com. on Conduct of War, 177; report of, 200

Cowan, Edgar (app. iii., 360), votes against Confiscation act, 34; at Bull Run battle, 54; presents sword to Penn. reg., 76; votes against expulsion J. D. Bright, 84

Cowles, Edwin, appointed postmaster of Cleveland, 24; animosity to S. S. Cox, 196; supports Brough for Gov., 231

Cox, J. D., enters on military career, 26

Cox, S. S. (app. iii., 360), Mr. Riddle's first relations with, 19; origin of name "Sunset," 19; mem. 37th Cong., 30; complimentary vote for Speaker, 31; *Three Decades of Federal Legislation*, by, 45; acknowledgment to, 45; quotes Mr. Riddle's Bull Run letter, 50, 51; and others name candidates for Brigadier-Gens., 65; opposed to Lovejoy's slavery bill, 129; speech arraigning Republicans, 195, 196; opposes ship canals, 212; referred to, 227; denounces Vallandigham's arrest, 230; defeated for Speaker 38th Cong. 251; resolution concerning exchange of prisoners, 326; requests reading Mr. Riddle's John Brown speech, 345

Cox, W. S., referred to, 290

Crane, C. H., at Bull Run battle, 53

Crisfield, J. W. (app. iii., 357), mem. 37th Cong., 30; speaks against Bond bill, 115, 116; attitude towards fugitive slaves, 139, 140; adverse report on bill aiding States freeing slaves, 162; conference with Mr. Riddle, 163

Creswell, J. A. J., elected 38th Cong., 250

Crittenden compromise, 40

Crittenden, J. J. (app. iii., 357), speeches in 1861, 5; mem. 37th Cong., 30; votes to expel J. B. Clark, 35; resolution on supremacy of Union, 41; suggested as Peace Comr., 73

Crook, Gen. George, captures Early's wagon trains, 289

Currency, fractional, 125

\

INDEX.   373

Bond bill, 123 ; bill denationalizing slavery, 129 ; Fouke's resolution tabled, 165 ; personal characteristics, 200, 202 ; death, 201
Lyon, Gen. Nathaniel, thanked by
Cong., 128

M

McCall, Gen. G. A., at Ball's Bluff
battle, 169, 175 ; subpœnaed by
Wade, 176
McClellan, Gen. G. B., number of
forces commanded by, 26, 69 ;
effect on military, 63 ; delay before Manassas, 64 ; made Com.-
in-Chief, 68; estimates Confederate forces, 71 ; dilatoriness of, 76;
thanked by Cong., 128 ; orders
given at Ball's Bluff, 171, 172 ;
subpœnaed by Wade, 176; cheered
at Capitol, 186 ; criticised for
tardiness, 186, 188 ; Peninsula
campaign, 192 ; South Mountain
and Antietam, 205 ; Democratic
nominee for President, 294 ; votes
cast for, 297 ; as Commander, 316,
318
McClernand, J. A. (app. iii., 356),
mem. 37th Cong., 30
McCook, Gen. A. McD., referred
to, 28 ; commands 1st Ohio, 66 ;
made Brigadier-Gen., 65
McCook, David, killed at Bull Run,
50
McDonald, J. E., defends Milligan
and others, 312
McDougal, J. A. (app. iii., 355),
anecdote of Brigadier-General,
77 ; Sen. Ways and Means Com.,
101 ; speech on abolishing slavery
in Dist. Columbia, 143, 144
McDowell, Gen. Irvin, leads grand
army into Virginia, 44 ; at Bull
Run, 46
McKean, J. B. (app. iii., 359), mem.
Elections Com. in Lehman-Butler
case, 85, 89
McKnight, Robert (app. iii., 361,
mem. 37th Cong., 30 ; referred
to, 227
McPherson, Edward (app. iii., 361),
mem. 37th Cong., 30
Madison, James, referred to, 37
Magruder, Gen. G. B., forces commanded at Manassas by, 64

Manassas, troops in battle of, 44 ;
evacuated, 188
Marshal, Gen. Humphrey, defeated
by Garfield, 75
Marshall, Chief-Justice John, cited
by E. G. Spaulding, 105
Maryland, attempts to secede, 61, 62;
slavery in, 139 ; members support
Vallandigham's reconstruction
scheme, 166 ; politics, Lincoln's
reference to, 275, 276; and Early's
raid, 285-287
Mason, J. M., debates on Peace
Cong. propositions, 6 ; expelled
from Senate, 35 ; captured, 72 ;
House resolution concerning in-
carceration of, 73
Mason, Col. Rodney, reference to,
28
Massachusetts, Lincoln calls for
5,000 troops from, 286
Maximilian, supported by Austria,
327
Maynard, Horace (app. iii., 361),
mem. 37th Cong., 30
Meade, Gen. G. G., victory of, 232
Medary, Samuel, on Ohio politics,19
Menzies, J. W. (app. iii., 357), in
Lehman-Butler case, 85, 89
Merricks of Wales, 1
Merrimac, defeat of, 191
Mexico, Maximilian, 327
Miles, Gen. D. S., at Bull Run
battle, 46
Military Com. of House, importance
of, 252, 253
Miller, Judge S. F., decision on
Treasury notes, 126
Milligan and others, case of, 308,
312 ; defended by J. A. Garfield,
309
Mulligan, L. P., charges against,
311 ; acquitted of, 312
Mill Spring, Union victory at, 75
Mississippi trade regulations, 284
Missouri members support Vallan-
digham's reconstruction scheme,
166 ; attitude on war measures,
166
Mitchell, C. B., expelled from Sen-
ate, 35
Monitor, victory of, 191
Moorhead, J. K. (app. iii., 361), on
ship canals, 217
Morgan, E. D., elected 38th Cong.,
251

Ibervoes of the Iftations.

EDITED BY

EVELYN ABBOTT, M.A., Fellow of Balliol College, Oxford.

A SERIES of biographical studies of the lives and work of a number of representative historical characters about whom have gathered the great traditions of the Nations to which they belonged, and who have been accepted, in many instances, as types of the several National ideals. With the life of each typical character will be presented a picture of the National conditions surrounding him during his career.

The narratives are the work of writers who are recognized authorities on their several subjects, and, while thoroughly trustworthy as history, will present picturesque and dramatic "stories" of the Men and of the events connected with them.

To the Life of each "Hero" will be given one duodecimo volume, handsomely printed in large type, provided with maps and adequately illustrated according to the special requirements of the several subjects. The volumes will be sold separately as follows:

Cloth extra $1 50
Half morocco, uncut edges, gilt top . . . 1 75

The first group of the Series comprises the following
volumes:

Nelson, and the Naval Supremacy of England. By W. CLARK
RUSSELL, author of "The Wreck of the Grosvenor," etc.

**Gustavus Adolphus, and the Struggle of Protestantism for Exist-
ence.** By C. R. L. FLETCHER, M. A., late Fellow of All Souls College,
Oxford.

Pericles, and the Golden Age of Athens. By Evelyn Abbott, M.A.,
Fellow of Balliol College. Oxford.

Theodoric the Goth, the Barbarian Champion of Civilisation. By
THOMAS HODGKIN, author of "Italy and Her Invaders," etc.

Sir Philip Sidney, and the Chivalry of England. By H. R. FOX-
BOURNE, author of "The Life of John Locke," etc.

Julius Cæsar, and the Organisation of the Roman Empire. By
W. WARDE FOWLER, M.A., Fellow of Lincoln College, Oxford.

**John Wyclif, Last of the Schoolmen and First of the English Re-
formers.** By LEWIS SERGEANT, author of "New Greece," etc.

**Napoleon, Warrior and Ruler, and the Military Supremacy of
Revolutionary France.** By W. O'CONNOR MORRIS, sometime
Scholar of Oriel College, Oxford.

Henry of Navarre, and the Huguenots in France. By P. F. WILLERT,
M.A., Fellow of Exeter College, Oxford.

Cicero, and the Fall of the Roman Republic. By J. L. STRACHAN
DAVIDSON, M.A., Fellow of Balliol College, Oxford.

Abraham Lincoln, and the Downfall of American Slavery. By
NOAH BROOKS.

**Prince Henry (of Portugal) the Navigator, and the Age of Dis-
covery.** By C. R. BEAZLEY, Fellow of Merton College, Oxford.

**Julian the Philosopher, and the Last Struggle of Paganism against
Christianity.** By ALICE GARDNER, Lecturer on Ancient History in
Newnham College.

Louis XIV., and the Zenith of the French Monarchy. By ARTHUR
HASSALL, M.A., Senior Student of Christ Church College, Oxford.

To be followed by:

Saladin, the Crescent and the Cross. By STANLEY LANE-POOLE.

Joan of Arc. By Mrs. OLIPHANT.

The Cid Campeador, and the Waning of the Crescent in the West.
By H. BUTLER CLARKE, Wadham College, Oxford.

Charlemagne, the Reorganiser of Europe. By Prof. GEORGE L.
BURR, Cornell University.

Moltke, and the Founding of the German Empire. By SPENSER
WILKINSON.

Oliver Cromwell, and the Rule of the Puritans in England. By
CHARLES FIRTH, Balliol College, Oxford.

Alfred the Great, and the First Kingdom in England. By F. YORK
POWELL, M.A., Senior Student of Christ Church College, Oxford.

Marlborough, and England as a Military Power. By C. W. C.
OMAN, A.M., Fellow of All Souls College, Oxford.

Frederic the Second, the Wonder of the World. By A. L. SMITH, of
Balliol College, Oxford.

Charles the Bold, and the Attempt to Found a Middle Kingdom.
By R. LODGE, M.A., Fellow of Brasenose College, Oxford.

**Alexander the Great, and the Extension of Greek Rule and of
Greek Ideas.** By Prof. BENJAMIN I. WHEELER, Cornell University.

G. P. PUTNAM'S SONS

NEW YORK   LONDON
27 WEST TWENTY-THIRD ST.   24 BEDFORD ST., STRAND

The Story of the Nations.

MESSRS. G. P. PUTNAM'S SONS take pleasure in announcing that they have in course of publication, in co-operation with Mr. T. Fisher Unwin, of London, a series of historical studies, intended to present in a graphic manner the stories of the different nations that have attained prominence in history.

In the story form the current of each national life is distinctly indicated, and its picturesque and noteworthy periods and episodes are presented for the reader in their philosophical relation to each other as well as to universal history.

It is the plan of the writers of the different volumes to enter into the real life of the peoples, and to bring them before the reader as they actually lived, labored, and struggled—as they studied and wrote, and as they amused themselves. In carrying out this plan, the myths, with which the history of all lands begins, will not be over-looked, though these will be carefully distinguished from the actual history, so far as the labors of the accepted historical authorities have resulted in definite conclusions.

The subjects of the different volumes have been planned to cover connecting and, as far as possible, consecutive epochs or periods, so that the set when completed will present in a comprehensive narrative the chief events m the great STORY OF THE NATIONS; but it is, of course, not always practicable to issue the several volumes in their chronological order.

The "Stories" are printed in good readable type, and in handsome 12mo form. They are adequately illustrated and furnished with maps and indexes. Price, per vol., cloth, $1.50. Half morocco, gilt top, $1.75.

The following volumes are now ready (March, 1895):

THE STORY OF GREECE. Prof. JAS. A. HARRISON.
" " " ROME. ARTHUR GILMAN.
" " " THE JEWS. Prof. JAMES K. HOSMER.
" " " CHALDEA. Z. A. RAGOZIN.
" " " GERMANY. S. BARING-GOULD.
" " " NORWAY. HJALMAR H. BOYESEN.
" " " SPAIN. Rev. E. E. and SUSAN HALE.
" " " HUNGARY. Prof. A. VÁMBÉRY.
" " " CARTHAGE. Prof. ALFRED J. CHURCH.
" " " THE SARACENS. ARTHUR GILMAN.
" " " THE MOORS IN SPAIN. STANLEY LANE-POOLE.
" " " THE NORMANS. SARAH ORNE JEWETT.
" " " PERSIA. S. G. W. BENJAMIN.
" " " ANCIENT EGYPT. Prof. GEO. RAWLINSON.
" " " ALEXANDER'S EMPIRE. Prof. J. P. MAHAFFY.
" " " ASSYRIA. Z. A. RAGOZIN.
" " " THE GOTHS. HENRY BRADLEY.
" " " IRELAND. Hon. EMILY LAWLESS.
" " " TURKEY. STANLEY LANE-POOLE.
" " " MEDIA, BABYLON, AND PERSIA. Z. A. RAGOZIN.
" " " MEDIÆVAL FRANCE. Prof. GUSTAVE MASSON.
" " " HOLLAND. Prof. J. THOROLD ROGERS.
" " " MEXICO. SUSAN HALE.
" " " PHŒNICIA. Prof. GEO. RAWLINSON.
" " " THE HANSA TOWNS. HELEN ZIMMERN.
" " " EARLY BRITAIN. Prof. ALFRED J. CHURCH.
" " " THE BARBARY CORSAIRS. STANLEY LANE-POOLE.
" " " RUSSIA. W. R. MORFILL.
" " " THE JEWS UNDER ROME. W. D. MORRISON.
" " " SCOTLAND. JOHN MACKINTOSH.
" " " SWITZERLAND. R. STEAD and Mrs. A. HUG.
" " " PORTUGAL. H. MORSE STEPHENS.
" " " THE BYZANTINE EMPIRE. C. W. C. OMAN.
" " " SICILY. E. A. FREEMAN.
" " " THE TUSCAN REPUBLICS. BELLA DUFFY.
" " " POLAND. W. R. MORFILL.
" " " PARTHIA. Prof. GEORGE RAWLINSON.
" " " JAPAN. DAVID MURRAY.
" " " THE CHRISTIAN RECOVERY OF SPAIN. H.
         E. WATTS.
" " " AUSTRALASIA. GREVILLE TREGARTHEN.
" " " SOUTHERN AFRICA. GEO. M. THEAL.
" " " VENICE. ALETHEA WIEL.
" " " THE CRUSADES. T. S. ARCHER and C. L. KINGS-
         FORD.
" " " VEDIC INDIA. By Z. A. RAGOZIN.